EGYPT, TRUNK OF THE TREE

EGYPT, TRUNK OF THE TREE

Vol. I : The Contexts

Simson Najovits

Algora Publishing
New York

ISBN: 0-87586-221-7 (softcover)
ISBN: 0-87586-222-5 (hardcover)

Library of Congress Cataloging-in-Publication Data

Najovits, Simson R.
  Egypt, trunk of the tree : a modern survey of an ancient land / by Simson R. Najovits.
    p. cm.
Includes bibliographical references and index.
  ISBN 0-87586-222-5 (alk. paper) — ISBN 0-87586-221-7 (pbk. : alk. paper)
1. Egypt—Religion—History. 2. Egypt—Civilization. I. Title.
BL2441.N23 2003
932—dc21
                        2003002755

Printed in the United States

TABLE OF CONTENTS

TIMELINE

c. 4000–3100 BC: Predynastic Naqada Civilization

Totemism, animism, nature religion, female fertility and male ithyphallic figurines, divinized and demonized animals and plants, amulets, fetishes and magical beliefs and techniques.

c. 4000–3500 BC: An agro-sedentary society and corresponding religious values emerge.

c. 3500 BC: The fusion of indigenous Nile Valley, African, North African and West Asian ethnic types into the Egyptian Mediterranean type is probably almost completed.

c. 3300 BC: Harnessing of the Nile: irrigation canals and ditches. Probable Sumerian influence in technology, crafts, art and religion.

c. 3100: The invention of hieroglyphic writing, "the words of the gods."

Divine kingship among henotheistic gods probably exists in many towns and regions.

c. 3100- 2686 BC: Early Dynastic Period

c. 3100 BC: Legendary date for the unification of Upper (the south) and Lower Egypt (the north) into Ta-Wy, "The Two Lands" by a legendary (?) Upper Egyptian King – Menes, Narmer, or Aha — who defeats Lower Egypt and is the god Horus on earth.

A surplus agricultural economy, specialization in crafts, division of both parts of Egypt into sepat, regions, and major urban centers. A distinctive Egyptian culture emerges.

By at least 2950 BC: The invention of papyrus.

c. 2700: First elaborate mummification.

c. 2686–2181 BC: Old Kingdom

Early in this period, the Goddess Maat represents the divine order and harmony of the world, "truth," as it was instituted with creation, "the first time," *zep tepey*.

Memphis gradually becomes Egypt's capital and major city, taking-over from Abydos and Thinis.

c. 2660: Egypt invents cut stone. The building of the pyramids begins with Djoser's "Step Pyramid" and the three great and "true" pyramids in Giza are built within the next 150 years. These tomb-pyramids are a major aspect of Egypt's solar religion. Ninety-seven major pyramids going up to c. 1550 have been found.

From at least the 4th Dynasty (c. 2613–2494 BC): An elaborate polytheistic system is established with pantheons, enneads (nine gods and goddesses in animal-headed-human, human and animal forms) and chief gods and a theological system based on the immanence and diversity of the divinities in Nature and the divinity of the pharaoh who rules on earth and maintains prosperity. The maintenance of magic, including the widespread use of amulets and spells.

Several rival, and sometimes contradictory, creation myths are elaborated in Heliopolis, Hermopolis, Memphis and elsewhere. They all basically postulate that the universe emerged from a watery chaos with a primeval mound, the *benben*, and then either Atum, Re, Ptah or Amun-Re created the gods and mankind, with the goddess Maat maintaining divine order, truth and justice.

Re is firmly established as chief god in the solar religion and has amalgamated several gods into a single chief and sun god, Re-Horakthy, with the amalgamated gods, including Horus, becoming aspects of Re, but also with these amalgamated gods continuing to have independent existences.

c. 2550: The conventional date for the first "wisdom texts" (*sebayt*), but they seem to have been written at later dates. These texts, notably that of Ptahhotep (c. 2414–2375 BC) are already an indication of the flirt that Egypt carried-on with ethics, with the notion of "doing the maat," doing the correct thing, but what is usually stressed in the wisdom texts is correct and expedient behavior in society rather than the "spiritual" ethics that we generally associate with the much later Hebrew and Christian Bible.

c. 2494–2345: 5th Dynasty. An exceptional period of artistic creation and somewhat atypical to Egyptian art's fundamental trend of depicting people and things not as they are, but how they should ideally be. Egypt has surpassed Sumer in architecture and art, but not in technology.

c. 2375–2125: The Pyramid Texts, the world's oldest body of elaborate religious and magical doctrines designed to ensure an afterlife for the pharaoh. Only the pharaoh has a soul (or rather souls) and a right to an afterlife.

The rise of Osirisian resurrection and afterlife beliefs, merging chthonian and solar values, and the Osiris/Seth/Isis/Horus myth as the founding myth of the nation. The reigning pharaoh, already Horus when alive, becomes Osiris in the afterlife.

c. 2181–2055 BC: First Intermediate Period

A troubled period of disunity, decline in royal power and perhaps some religious pessimism.

c. 2055–1650 BC: Middle Kingdom

A time of renewal and expansion after the collapse of the Old Kingdom and the troubled First Intermediate Period, with many texts, like *The Protests of The Eloquent Peasant*, indicating a thirst for justice and other texts, like *The Admonitions of Ipuwur* and the *Dialogue of a Man with his Ba*, constituting warnings against a return to the calamity and spiritual crisis of the First Intermediate Period.

The Coffin Texts, now in generalized usage, indicate that the right of the individual to five souls and an afterlife have now been extended to everybody, but in practice the high cost of tomb construction and furnishing and mummification limit these rights to the notables and the rich. Osiris is now not only the pharaoh's savior god, but history's first savior god for everybody, offering resurrection and an afterlife to all — or, rather, all those who can afford it.

c. 1650–1550 BC: Second Intermediate Period

The West Asian Hyskos establish themselves in Egypt by immigration or war and establish the 15th and 16th Hyksos Dynasties.

c. 1550–1069 BC: New Kingdom

c. 1550 BC: The Hyksos are defeated and expelled by Ahmose, ruling from Thebes.

The New Kingdom is the apex of Egyptian political, imperial, economic, religious and artistic power carried-out under the aegis of the Theban god Amun who amalgamates all the gods as his aspects.

Thebes becomes Egypt's greatest city and its Karnak Temple becomes the biggest space ever built in the world for a religious purpose.

The Book of the Dead codifies all the existing beliefs in the afterlife and how to magically, technically (and more infrequently, ethically, and by fraud, if necessary) earn an afterlife, the right to "*wehem ankh*," repeating life, in the Duat.

c. 1504–1492 BC: Thutmose I, the first pharaoh to be buried in a rock-cut tomb of the Valley of Kings on the Theban West Bank, which will become an immense artistic and engineering achievement.

c. 1473–1458: Hatshepsut usurps the throne and is perhaps the first woman to become a powerful pharaoh rather than the supposed female pharaohs before her, who might have been regents rather than pharaohs.

c. 1458–1425: Thutmose III extends Egypt's control to the Euphrates River and deep into Nubia. Egypt is more and more a part of an Egyptian-West Asian Continuum.

c. 1352–1336 BC: Akhenaten (Amenhotep IV) invents the first monotheism with Aten (the sun-disc) solar monotheism.

A revolutionary period in art, known as Amarna Art, with a combination of naturalistic, realistic painting and sculpture and a perhaps a new — and to some, a grotesque — aesthetic system to indicate the divinity of the pharaoh, his family and associates.

c. 1323–1295 BC: Horemheb completes the elimination of solar monotheism and restores the strongest Amun-Re chief god polytheistic system, but Amunism includes a strong monotheising tendency.

c. 1279–1213 BC: Rameses II, one of Egypt's greatest builders and the longest reigning pharaoh.

Rameses II builds the Abu Simbel Temple in Nubia formally dedicated to Amun, Re and Ptah, but in fact largely dedicated to himself as a god.

c. 1274 BC: The Battle of Kadesh (on the Orontes River) results in a stalemate between Rameses II and the Hittites and consequential power sharing in the Levant.

During Rameses II's reign, The Hymn to Amun presents the triad of Amun, Re and Ptah, as an organic unity of all the gods with Re and Ptah as aspects of the supreme, creator, concealed Amun. This may have been a prefiguration of Christian multiform monotheism.

c. 1250 BC: The most probable time for the legendary (?) exodus of the Hebrews from Egypt.

c. 1209 BC: The first mention of Israel in history on Pharaoh Merenptah's stele, found in 1886 by William Matthew Flinders Petrie, the founder of modern scientific archaeology.

c. 1099–1069 BC: Rameses XI's reign culminates the general decline in royal and Egyptian power, which had been ongoing since the previous mid-century.

c. 1069–747 BC: Third Intermediate Period

This period is marked by rival pharaohs, some of them Libyan, ruling from different cities, frequently in competition with fundamentalist Amun-Re High Priests in Thebes.

c. 747–332 BC: Late Period

Political, religious and artistic decline and the rise of extreme zoolatry mark this period. It is opened with the Nubian (Kushite) conquest and then rule of Egypt until c. 656.

c. 716–702: Shabako claims that an Old Kingdom papyrus from the Ptah Temple in Memphis has been found and recopied. This papyrus, "copied" on the Shabako Stone declares that Ptah created the world with his heart (the mind for the Egyptians) and the tongue (the word). This doctrine may have influenced both the Hebrews and the Christians.

c. 669–660 BC: The Assyrians conquer and vassal Egypt and sack the Karnak Temple in 663 BC.

c. 605: The Battle of Carchemish, on the Euphrates River, the Babylonian King Nebuchadnezzar II defeats Egypt and Babylonia emerges as the new super-power.

c. 525–404 BC: First Persian Period

The Persian Cambyses conquers and occupies Egypt. The core of "Egyptian" Egypt in religion, politics, art and social values is mocked by the Persians and undergoes a generalized decline.

c. 440 BC: Herodotus visits Egypt and triggers an early phase of "Egyptomania" by describing Egypt's magnificent monuments, attributing to her a vast influence on the Greek religion and frequently misinterpreting Egyptian beliefs and customs.

From 5th Century BC: Plato and other Greek philosophers admire Egypt's achievements in many domains, but generally do not attribute any Egyptian influence on Greek philosophy.

c. 404–343 BC: Brief period of restored Egyptian independence.

c. 360–343 BC: Nectanebo II is the last indigenous pharaoh of Egypt.

c. 343-332 BC: Second Persian Period

c. 332–32 BC: Ptolemaic Period

c. 332 BC: The Macedonian Greeks, led by Alexander, conquer Egypt and gradually but deeply modify Egyptian beliefs. Alexandria is founded and gradually becomes the world's greatest center of science and philosophy. Greek rationalism and Egyptian magical thinking clash, but the Greek religion is frequently identified with the Egyptian religion. Greek becomes the official language of Egypt.

c. 305–285 BC: An Egypto-Greek god, Serapis, is invented, merging Osiris, Apis the bull aspect of Ptah and several Greek gods including Zeus and Dionysos.

Early 3rd Century BC: Manetho, an Egyptian priest, writing in Greek, establishes a Kings' List spanning 30 Dynasties.

c. 30 BC– AD 395: The Roman Period

c. 32–30 BC Octavian (Augustus) attacks Egypt and becomes pharaoh.

The Romans continue the transformation of Egypt begun by the Greeks.

First Century AD: The cult of the Egyptian mother goddess Isis is popular throughout the Greco-Roman Mediterranean world.

The Instruction of the Papyrus Insinger (a wisdom text, perhaps written at the end of the Ptolemaic Period) mixes traditional Egyptian advice on expediency and correct behavior in society with austere, pessimistic Greek religious ideas on fate, fortune and destiny being decided by the gods rather than on the traditional Egyptian ideas of maat order and harmony.

From the Second Century: The rise of Christianity in Egypt.

From the Third Century: Christian Alexandria is a key player in the frequent Christological quarrels concerning the nature of Jesus.

394: The last inscription written in hieroglyphics.

395: The conventional date for the end of "Egyptian" Egypt with Egypt becoming a part of the East Roman Empire as a Christian nation.

Fifth Century: Egypt elaborates Monophysite Christianity — in which Jesus has only one nature, divine — and comes into conflict with most of the rest of Christianity.

The Christian Period

535: The last Egyptian polytheistic temple (the Isis Temple in Philae) is closed down by the East Roman Emperor, Justinian I.

642: The Moslems conquer Egypt and gradually convert it into a Moslem country, with a Christian (Coptic) minority remaining.

From the 15th Century: A largely "imaginary" Egypt arises in Europe among philosophers, theologians, esoterics and scientists and attributes vast religious, esoteric and scientific knowledge to the ancient Egyptians, including the existence of an original or concealed monotheism. Many of these views, including some very loony ones, persist in modern "Egyptomania."

1798–1801: Napoleon conquers and occupies Egypt. He is accompanied by a scientific and artistic team who catalogue, describe and sketch Egypt's monuments and discover the Rosetta Stone, written in hieroglyphics, demotic Egyptian, and Greek.

1822–1832: Jean François Champollion, using the Rosetta Stone, deciphers hieroglyphics, and opens the road to the rediscovery of a "realer" Egypt.

19th and 20th centuries: Western museums and the Cairo Museum constitute and catalogue vast collections of Egyptian art.

1885: The German Egyptologist Adolf Erman, in *Life In Ancient Egypt* and other books, makes the first scientific and realistic attempt to understand ancient Egypt and concludes that it was truly magnificent, but also that its religion was confused, contradictory and incoherent right from the start and became more so as its history unfolded.

1919: Heinrich Schäfer, in *Principles of Egyptian Art*, deciphers the codes of Egyptian art.

1912: The American Egyptologist James Henry Breasted, in the Development of Religion and Thought in Ancient Egypt and other books, concludes that Egypt represented the earliest chapter in the moral development of man, followed by an analogous development later among the Hebrews.

1939: Sigmund Freud, in Moses and Monotheism, declares that Moses' Hebrew monotheism was a version of Akhenaten's Atenism.

1939 to the present: Egyptologists and historians increasingly debate to what extent Hebrew monotheism used Egyptian Atenism and Amunism as counter models, models, or both, or was an independent invention.

1948: The Dutch Egyptologist Henri Frankfort, in Ancient Egyptian Religion: An Interpretation, concludes that the Egyptian religion was always thoroughly polytheistic, was concerned with divine order and maintenance of harmony rather than evil or ethics in the Biblical sense, and that its religion was a coherent system based on a multiplicity of approaches, multiple answers and meaningful inconsistency.

1955: The Senegalese scholar Cheikh Anta Diop, in Nations Nègres et Culture, declares that Egypt was a black African civilization.

1950 to present: Most major Egyptian religious, political and societal texts are reliably translated (notably by R.O. Faulkner and Miriam Lichtheim); Egyptian history is dealt with scientifically by many historians (including Alan Gardiner and Nicolas Grimal); Egyptian art is decorticated by many art historians (including H.A. Groenewegen-Frankfort and W. Stevenson Smith); and together with the easy availability of ancient Egyptian sites, makes it increasingly possible and valid to carry out independent speculation on what Egypt was and wasn't.

INTRODUCTION

The ancient Egyptians may have surpassed every other civilization in history in their ability to change the substance of their society and religion, while simultaneously pretending that no changes had really been made.

To them, change was impossible. Truth had been established for all time, from creation, from "the first time" or the "first occasion." But in practice, the Egyptians were constantly making fundamental changes and creating new, more complex and logically incomprehensible molds by heaping layer after layer of beliefs, meanings and names together without eliminating any contradictions.

The first goal of this book is to cut a navigable path through this vast and confused tangle of concepts, changes, subtleties, syncretisms, amalgamations, contradictions and enigmas.

Part I of *Egypt, the Trunk of the Tree* situates the Egyptian religion, political system and society within the contexts — some of them stretching back as far as before c. 4000 BC — of the early history of religion, mythology, technology, art, psychology, sociology, migratory movements and geography. The anchoring of religious belief in divine immanence and diversity, but a frenzy for religious change without change, the omnipresence of magic, the immense powers of the pharaoh-god and the turning point for man that ancient Egypt represented in many key theological, political, artistic and technological domains from very early dates are examined. Part II examines how these early contexts led to specific consequences and to original Egyptian solutions to political, societal, religious, existential and metaphysical problems. The establishment of a system in which eventually everybody had five souls, the optimistic solution to the problem of death and the setting up of an ambiguous ethical code are especially

1

examined. These Egyptian solutions and rationalizations paradoxically consecrated both a real and an imaginary trunk of the tree role for Egypt in the history of mankind and these roles continue to flourish in our time. The Egyptian view is compared with those of the other great ancient religious societies and especially with the Sumerian, the Hebrew, the Hindu, the Zoroastrian, the Greek and the early Christian views. Egypt's place in the history of religion is evaluated along with the plausibility of a considerable (although unprovable) influence in the evolution towards monotheism and ritual and mythological influences on Judaism, Christianity and the Greek and Roman religions (and *a contrario* on atheism).

One of the most intensive periods of religious, political, technological cultural and economic change that ever occurred took place in Egypt starting in about 3100 BC, and continued for 2000 years. Together with Sumer, Egypt became an advanced Early Bronze Age sedentary, literate society which had incorporated and gone beyond Neolithic values. The era of surplus economies and organized societies and religions adapted to the values of a high yield agro/irrigation society was opened. Egypt then became the main zone of development, the vanguard, the motor and the soul of humanity from the firm establishment of its system about 2700 BC until the beginning of its decline in the 12th century BC.

Religion was the central framework of all societies during these times, but never before had religion been so successfully used as the central reality and justification of human life. Never before had a system of religious magic and mythology, grounded in an animistic perception of the immanence of the divine in nature, been so perfected and made so credible. Never before had such an elaborate religion and such an all-inclusive mythology been invented. Never before had the multiple realities of the universe and existence been so astutely bonded together in a sacred system of diversity, dualism and primeval order and harmony re-created on a daily basis.

The pragmatic Egyptians fervently believed that magic was truth, and not a miracle. They believed that magic was a part of the divine laws and that it was expressed in their mythology (which was of course not mythological as we understand the term, but a true description of the universe and its origins and man and the correct behavior to be adopted. As false and illusionary as it was, the complex Egyptian system of magic, and the animistic belief in the divine aliveness of nature and mythology gave them efficient tools for building the most modern and vital religion and state of the time.

2

Never before had such an immense pantheon of animal, human and animal-headed human gods and goddesses been assembled in such a new, complex and emerging revolutionary system — authentic, or true, polytheism based on the needs of an agro-sedentary society.

Sumer and then Egypt radically changed the course of history with the invention of writing and then Egypt, with the hieroglyphs, invented what is surely the most aesthetic form of writing in the history of mankind. Writing for the Egyptians was the magical language of the gods.

Never before had art, and especially architecture, been used in such a revolutionary, monumental and widespread way for the purposes of magic and indoctrination, as a tool of religion and especially for tombs (seen as an entry point into the afterlife). The most extravagant and intimate link between art and magical religion since Magdalenian times 12,000 years earlier was achieved in Egypt. New canons of aesthetics and artistic-religious meanings were established to artificially portray the essence of an idealized world and idealized peoples. From the building of the first pyramid around 2660 BC, the revolution of cut stone architecture was achieved, enabling Egyptian architecture to tower over humanity for thousands of years and also to build temples which until today remain the biggest ever built by any people.

The world's the first nation and its basic pivot of divine kingship were established by c. 3100 BC. By about 2600 BC, the first central national administrative system and civil service in history was set up in the capital, Memphis. Pragmatic efficiency, intelligent organization and the all-pervading system of magic geared together in a credible whole. Theocracy, a strict hierarchically structured society and the conviction of being the only people of the gods were woven into an intricate system which was rarely challenged. By about 1458 BC, Egypt became the world's greatest imperial power, remained so for more than 200 years until the 1274 BC Battle of Kadesh, shakily persisted for another 150 years as a super power and continued to sporadically fight for an imperial role in Asia until its forces were crushed by the Babylonian Nebuchadnezzar II at Carchemish on the Euphrates River in c. 605 BC.

For the first time in the history of man, a seemingly credible, efficient solution, or illusion, to the problem of death was proposed. The Egyptians invented "repeating life," eternally reliving one's happy life in an afterlife. This solution constituted the most optimistic approach to the *scandal* of death ever invented until their time. It resulted in the greatest material and magical religious effort ever deployed by man to assure an afterlife. The revolution in afterlife concepts began around 3100 BC, with the building of massive tombs and was followed by the inventions of the preservation of the body — mummification — pyramid tombs and a complex system of several companion souls. The Egyptians invented the startling belief that the body could be preserved and stay alive after death. Over the next few hundred years, a savior god, Osiris, offering resurrection and a positive afterlife was invented and this afterlife was gradually extended from the pharaoh to everybody who was "equipped," who could afford to pay for the required architectural, artistic, ritualistic and magical preparations.

From at least 2300 BC, numerous attempts to link ethics and religion were made. The Egyptians flirted with the caveat that if one did not behave decently in this life, there would be no afterlife. Nevertheless, they never really accepted a strict ethical basis for this life or the next life and clung to a reliance on magic, so-called correct societal behavior . . . and fraud. Although its main thrust was magical rather than ethical, as early as about 2180 BC, the first known court of justice (which ruled on eligibility for an afterlife) was set up.

By about 1550 BC, Amunism and its concept of simultaneous diversity and unity — of amalgamating all the gods as aspects of a single god while maintaining the individual existences of all the gods — had been carried to unprecedented levels. Despite its ambiguity between unity and diversity — its absolute refusal to reject the fundamental Egyptian vision of the universe as diversity — it nevertheless represented a monotheizing tendency and then led to the invention of monotheism, with the brief period of solar proto-monotheism in the mid 14th century BC. Although it lasted only about 15 years, Atenist proto-monotheism constituted one of the most consequential changes ever operated by man and one of the key periods in the history of mankind.

An interminable debate linked to Amun-Re solar theology, Atenism and notions of an original, early, hidden or virtual monotheism in ancient Egypt, has been going on since the 17th century regarding Egypto-Hebrew relations and the central issue of the origins of monotheism. The notions of an original, early, hidden or virtual monotheism in Egypt are basically loony, but Atenism was indeed the first monotheism, even if it was not full-blown, authentic monotheism.

After about 1099 BC, Amunism skidded into religious totalitarianism, fundamentalism and fanaticism. After 747 BC, and especially after the Persian conquest of Egypt in 525 BC, animal worship reached an apex and produced one of the most excessive forms of religion ever invented.

There is great debate concerning the date for the end of a characteristically Egyptian Egypt. Was it in 525 BC, with the deeply humiliating first Persian conquest? In 332 BC, with the Greek conquest and the ensuing influence of Greek philosophy? Was it the conventional date of AD 395, when Egypt as a Christian nation became part of the East Roman Empire? What is certain is that the authentic heart of Egyptian religion and society had been dead long before 395.

What is certain is that at least by the sixth century BC, Egypt had entirely lost its vanguard role and was in deep religious and political decline. Other peoples advanced in their quest for better, clearer and subtler religious, and political and secular answers and rationalizations; Egypt clung to magical religion, and lagged behind. The Hebrews, with ethereal spirituality and authentic monotheism; the Persians, with a final eschatological destiny for man; the Christians, with the ideal of love and forgiveness and more moral and egalitarian morality; and the Greeks with non-mythological rational philosophical inquiry and scientific clarity, all soared ahead. None of these leaps seem to have been within the traditional Egyptian animistic mental and emotional reach.

The usual view is that very little evidence exists that would show an Egyptian influence behind these leaps. On the other hand, the Greek historian Herodotus in the fifth century BC, was the first to postulate enormous Egyptian influence, especially in religion. Over the centuries and into our time, this school of thought has blown into an excessive Egyptomania proffering preposterous theories ranging from an identification of Egypt with the so-called lost continent of Atlantis, to vast esoteric meaning in the pyramids, to the affirmation that Akhenaten, the Egyptian founder of the first proto-monotheism, was in fact Moses, to the notion that Egyptian wisdom was at the origin of Greek philosophy and science, etc.

All these views will be examined, but the thesis that there is a credible middle view will be adopted — that is, the self-evident nature of the role of independent development in the leaps forward which many peoples made after the Egyptians, but also, as formally unprovable as it is, that some of these leaps could have been made both using and rejecting the Egyptian heritage. However it may have occurred — in reality, or through a mangled reconstruction of what ancient Egypt was — man's overall evolution was deeply affected and deeply influenced. The results both propelled man powerfully forward and mired him in immense poetic illusion.

Over 3000 years — from c. 3100 BC to AD 395 — Egypt was presided over by more than 200 pharaohs, including several pharaohs of Libyan origin, interspersed with several periods of foreign domination or occupation, including six Asian Hyksos pharaohs, five Nubian (Kushite) pharaohs, two Assyrian kings and/or their Egyptian puppet rulers, nine Persian emperors, three Greek kings, 17 Greek ptolemies and 52 Roman emperors.

A remarkable mixture of the new, the useful and the beautiful and the persistence of primitive magic, obscurantism, and the infantile but extraordinarily poetic, characterized Egyptian society, its religion, politics, agriculture, technology, the crafts, writing, architecture and the arts. Egypt was both a vanguard, innovative society and a rear guard, conservative society; but it was also unquestionably one of the most optimistic nations in the history of mankind. The Egyptians invented optimistic answers to many of man's fundamental questions and these answers remained "true" for longer than any other society's in history.

Unceasing admiration for what Egypt accomplished using magical religion persists until today, alongside the massive rejection of what it represented religiously.

The vastness of Egyptian history, coupled with its claim of theological and political permanency (while in fact Egypt's permanent characteristic was change without acknowledging change) cannot be emphasized enough. Theology and domestic political policy and foreign policy underwent constant change.

The result of this attitude was a vast maze of concepts and contradictions. Despite the extraordinary abundance of societal documents, literature and artistic and architectural relics, the barriers to a minimally clear understanding of ancient Egypt not only remain immense, but frequently insurmountable. The emergence in Europe of an imaginary Egypt in the 15th century and the frequently curious influences this exercised, and continues to exercise (notably on modern esoteric groups, alternative religions and on the Afrocentrist movement), have further complicated matters.

The rediscovery of the real, or a realer, Egypt starting in the early 19th century is gradually eliminating the imaginary and loony visions of ancient Egypt. Nevertheless, this process of rediscovery and reinterpretation poses the same central question as the earlier extravagant interpretations — was Egypt the trunk of the tree of mankind?

All these views, including the frequently contradictory opinions of the major Egyptologists and historians (and the major loonies) will be examined in an attempt to come closer to Egypt's core meaning and influence. Hopefully, this attempt at clarity will illuminate, and not tarnish, the marvelous, enchanting, imaginative beauty of the Egyptian saga. Hopefully, something will be added, too, to the seemingly inexhaustible pleasure of exploring the Egyptian patrimony and capturing the glow of ancient Egyptian society.

Realistically, all this is accompanied by the admission that nobody, including the most distinguished Egyptologists and historians, has ever fully grasped the core substance and meaning of ancient Egypt and nobody seems likely ever to satisfactorily achieve this. Egyptologists have been rejecting each other's theories since the mid-19th century and even ever since the 5th century BC, if we include the virulent criticism that hit Herodotus.

Certainly, we are not likely ever to have as clear a picture of Egypt as we have of ancient Greece, but it is obvious that we have a clearer factual picture of Egypt than we have of ancient Israel — even if we have a better understanding of how the Hebrews thought and felt. Neither are we likely ever to discover a coherent framework of meaning for Egypt, for the simple reason that there may not have been such a coherent framework, or that, like our own modern framework, it was too complex and varied to grasp.

Egyptologists and archaeologists have achieved truly marvelous results, but ultimately their search to construct meaning has been disappointing. Only a few Egyptologists provide anything like a clear overall view of Egypt. Some modern Egyptologists have opened new ground by attempting to demonstrate that all the enormous number of layers of meanings, contexts, amalgamated gods and apparent and confusing contradictions in Egyptian religion constituted the particularly Egyptian multiple but coherent way of grasping reality. However, this view remains insufficient for solving the problem of a core meaning for the Egyptian religion; and the opposite view, that one of the main characteristics of the Egyptian religion — as for all religions — was confusion and contradiction, has to be given as much consideration.

During at least the past 30 years a new phase in Egyptology has been opened. A huge amount of art and architecture *in situ* and in museums has become accessible to a wide public, as is also the case for well-translated primary texts and inscriptions in all domains. Of course, marvelous discoveries are still likely, but it is now possible for competent scholars, writers and journalists, and not only professional Egyptologists, to navigate through the extraordinary Egyptian maze and struggle to find some kind of coherent meaning — or its absence. Despite the door that this has opened to amateurs taking an irrational approach and to superficial, sensationalist media reports, eventually this is likely to have positive results. Perhaps, it will also eventually take us a few steps beyond the frequent academic bickering and artificial search for the *great find* and the *great explanation* of many Egyptologists, which sometimes seems to be more related to glory seeking than to the search for knowledge.

I am not a professional Egyptologist, although I have struggled to find my way in the Egyptian maze for many long years; I'm a journalist, a writer and a specialist in systems of religious beliefs and I quite simply share the passion of many people to understand and appreciate Egypt. I have attempted to do this using the vast means now available to the general public.

Such an undertaking involves both impartial descriptions of Egyptian religion, magic, art, literature, society and history and a considerable — and I hope, creative –analysis and interpretation. The method employed is to use the best available scholarship without dismissing outright dissenting and maverick views, and to be as realistic, exact and intelligible as possible. This method necessarily implies using the same criteria as would be used to describe and analyze any historical civilization or any series of events in the history of mankind. This notably implies accepting that religion was the central factor in ancient Egypt, as in all ancient societies, and rejecting the concept that subjects of a religious nature are "sacred cows" or taboos requiring more than a normal degree of respect.

A few final, practical considerations:

It has become conventional to refer to the gods and goddesses and cities of ancient Egypt as the Greeks renamed them after Alexander conquered Egypt in 332 BC. Egypt's ancient cities were also renamed in Arabic after the Moslem conquest in AD 642. The use of Greek names has resulted in a loss of the feeling of what ancient Egypt was, but solely using the ancient Egyptian names (with which few people are familiar) also results in confusion. There is no easy way of dealing with this; perhaps the least confusing or awkward system, and the one which preserves some of the feel of ancient Egypt, at least in first mentions, is to use the best-known name of a god or a goddess, adding his or her Egyptian name when this differs considerably, and to use the Egyptian and Greek names for sites in the same manner.

There is also great confusion in the dates attributed to most events in ancient Egypt; and the variations may be considerable, depending on the source.

It must be emphasized that there is no such thing as an exact date in ancient Egyptian history, especially concerning the earliest dates from -3000 BC to well after 1500 BC. The dates used in this book have been selected from the analysis of many sources — the calculations of modern Egyptologists, works of arts, ancient Egyptian and other authors of antiquity, cross-checked with historical events in neighboring countries. In most cases, this has led to the adoption of the dates generally used by the British Museum and the Oriental Institute of the University of Chicago.

Until the Greek-influenced Egyptian priest/historian Manetho (fl. c. 300 BC) divided Egyptian royalty into 30 dynasties, the Egyptians themselves, in their Kings' Lists, calculated solely by the number of years of reign of successive pharaohs, beginning with the gods who ruled Egypt and the earth before the pharaoh/gods. In addition to Manetho's 30 more or less verifiable dynasties, Egyptologists have somewhat arbitrarily divided Egyptian history into at least eight clearly-defined periods and three so-called intermediate periods and there is now no more coherent, or at least no less confusing, framework available.

There is also no such thing as a sole or perfect rendering of the meaning of many Egyptian religious and everyday terms. The lack of vowels in the Egyptian written language means that we can not reproduce a sole or perfect vocalization or pronunciation for many Egyptian names and terms, especially the earliest ones. Nevertheless, an extensive use of vocalizations is necessary to catch at least something of what might have been the sound and the linguistic character of ancient Egyptian.

Finally, the footnotes have been simplified in those cases where a full citation is given in the Bibliography.

CHAPTER 1.
THE EARLY RELIGIOUS AND SOCIETAL CONTEXT

ROOTS: TOTEMISTIC, NATURE RELIGION, ANIMISTIC, HENOTHEISTIC AND MAGIC RELIGION

A new type of society emerged in Egypt sometime around 4000 BC. In primitive versions its roots, its oldest concepts and divinities, probably reached back to the opening of the Neolithic Age in about 5800 BC and the introduction of farming and animal raising in many locations — Fayum, Merimda and Omari in middle and northern Egypt, and Hammamia, Badari and Tasa in the Nile Valley, in Upper Egypt.

Agriculture in this period probably was enormously facilitated by the existence of a natural siliceous clay silt fertilizer in the waters of the Nile, which had appeared just before the opening of the Neolithic Age. Rainfall was minimal and so, even in this early period, agriculture depended on the waters of the lake oases and the Nile.

Relics from the Neolithic Badarian A and B Periods (c. 5500–4000 BC) indicate the existence of two fairly distinct early agricultural societies. Towards c. -4200 BC, Badari in the south and Omari in the north were prosperous farming communities.

The Naqada I culture (or Amratian, named after the sites of Amra and Naqada) arose in southern Upper Egypt between 4000 and 3500 BC and spread throughout most of this zone, including northern Nubia. Nekhen (Hierakonpolis in Greek) emerged as a major site and its huge necropolis has yielded some of the earliest Egyptian art. Traces of a fishing village in Nekhen can be dated to between 7000 and 5000 BC.

In all likelihood, the Naqada Civilization saw a general confrontation between nomadic hunting and fishing and sedentary farming values, and a confrontation between farmers and semi-nomadic shepherds. However, as immense a revolution as agriculture and animal raising represented, Egypt seems to have succeeded in maintaining much of the content of hunting magic religion, totemism and prehistoric mythology in the new agro/polytheistic synthesis that it was gradually establishing. This maintenance of pre-Neolithic, pre-agricultural, values common to peoples of various origins may have attenuated confrontations among the mixture of populations which was clearly taking place at this time.

As in all Neolithic societies, women were linked to fertility — human fertility, surely, as had been the case in Paleolithic times, but perhaps also that fertility which spontaneously came from the earth, and the new artificial agricultural fertility.

A considerable number of Naqada I clay figurines, vases, cosmetic palettes and other pottery objects have been found in Per-Hathor (archaeologically known as Gebelein, "The Two Hills," and as Aphroditopolis in Greek) and elsewhere in Upper Egypt.* They depict abstract motifs, animals, fertility figurines with exaggerated feminine characteristics and frequently without hands, and ithyphallic masculine figurines with pointed beards and handless and legless bodies. There are several figurines with big eyes who could be "eye" gods and goddesses who protected against evil spirits.

[*They are now in the Lyons Musée Guimet, the Louvre, the Brussels Musée du Cinquantenaire, the Baltimore Walters Art Gallery and other museums.]

The female figurines seem to be a continuation of the Badarian Fifth Millennium Egyptian female figurines like the one with big lapis lazuli eyes, big breasts and a heavily accentuated and pit-marked groin, and like the roughly sculpted one with a big head, big eyes and nose, big breasts and a heavily accentuated pubic triangle (both are in the British Museum). Some of the female statuettes are depicted with cow's horns or a cow's head, indicating a prefiguration of the great mother cow goddesses, Bat, Hesat and Hathor (Het-Heru), and the later Egyptian system of animal-headed gods and goddesses. This prefiguration of animal-headed divinities can perhaps also be seen in the splendid Naqada I (c. 4000–3500 BC) painted clay figurine of a dancing woman with a bird's head and uplifted arms found near Hierakonpolis (and now in the Brooklyn Museum).

The evolution towards an advanced agro-sedentary society seems to have begun during the Naqada III Period (from about 3300 BC). A system of canals and ditches brought the rich waters of the Nile beyond its banks several miles inland, irrigating a vast expanse of previously arid land. This development (with its corresponding agro-polytheistic religion, which will be examined in Chapter 2) rendered Egyptian society capable of providing the resources for a rapid increase in population and for the emergence of thriving urban centers with production rather than subsistence economies. Among the most important of these new urban centers were Nubt (in Greek, Ombos; but best known as Naqada, the archaeological designation for the nearby ancient town and necropolis), Nekhen (Hierakonpolis) and Tieny (Thinis)/Abdu (Abydos). The Naqada III culture gradually spread northwards into the Fayum region (where traces of settlement going back to 5800 BC have been found) and into the Nile Delta.

The Egyptian religion of the Naqada III Period featured significant magical, totemistic, nature, animist, agricultural and henotheistic aspects. More than 2000 Naqada tombs containing human remains, pottery fragments, seals, sculptures and carvings were excavated in 1895 by the great English archaeologist and Egyptologist William Matthew Flinders Petrie (1853–1942) and his then assistant J.E. Quibell (1867–1935). The objects depict humans and animals and female figurines with accentuated sexual characteristics; they probably illustrated and conjured agricultural and reproductive fertility, reflecting the mother goddess and totemistic beliefs and rituals of a preliterate society. Motifs on ceramics, notably depicting boats with animal emblematic banners, probably illustrated clannish totemistic beliefs which were prefigurations of regional (nome) emblems of identity.

These objects were so radically different from anything ever found before in Egypt that Petrie first misunderstood their origin and labeled them the work of a "New Race," a foreign group which he thought had settled in Egypt during the First Intermediate Period (c. 2181–2055 BC). Jacques de Morgan (1857–1924) proved in 1897 that Petrie had in fact discovered remains of the Naqada I and II Periods (c. 4000–3300 BC).

All these predynastic objects point to the probability that animist concepts and family cults were deeply rooted. In Egypt as elsewhere, these included the belief that there were guiding spirits in the forces of nature, that the spirits of ancestors and heroes and demons hovered about in the world, that these spirits had to be fed, contented, worshipped and quasi-divinized; that protection was needed against the demons; and that various aspects of the soul survived after death, namely the *ka* — the double, the other, the companion soul.

Linked to these beliefs was magic religion, expressed in the wide use of personal animal fetishes and amulets, some of which date as far back as the Badarian Period (c. 5500–4000 BC). A wide variety of animal amulets have been found in graves and tombs — falcons, jackals, scarabs, lions, cats, dogs, bulls, and others. Amulets of dangerous animals like hippopotami — or animals believed to be malevolent, like gazelles — were often depicted in disabled form so that their powers could be annulled. Amulets, and parts of animals like the tail or a paw, or representations thereof, were believed to understand what occurred in their environment, to be able to transfer their powers to the wearer, and to be capable of magically manipulating events for protection and healing. Priests and leaders wore ceremonial animal skins and parts of animals, not essentially as clothing but as fetishes; they clearly felt more powerful this way. And some of Egypt's first Predynastic (c. -3100 BC) and Early Dynastic (c. 3100–2686 BC) kings had animal names and emblems, like the two "Scorpion" kings, "Catfish" Narmer and "Serpent" Djet.

Scenes of harvests and animal husbandry were painted on the earliest elaborate tombs. Known as mastaba (from the Arabic word for "bench"), these tombs first appeared in the Early Dynastic Period (beginning from about c. 3100 BC).

At the Hierakonpolis site between 1897 and 1899, James Quibell and F.W. Green (1869–1949) unearthed decorated palettes, ritual objects, weapons, utensils and figurines dating to c. 3000 BC in the Early Dynastic Period as well as the remains of what may have been one of the earliest Old Kingdom temples (after c. 2686 BC).

In the Abydos Umm el-Qa'ab Necropolis, the "Mother of pots," the tombs of several Early Dynastic Kings and a huge amount of pottery, ebony and ivory labels and various objects were found between 1894 and 1898 by the French Egyptologist Emile Amélineau (1850–1915). Petrie, in 1900 and 1901, found more revealing objects and correctly interpreted their immense significance for understanding early Egyptian history. In 1988, Tomb U-J, in the U predynastic (before c. 3100 BC) section of the Umm el-Qa'ab, was excavated and yielded an immense number of Naqada III objects, many of them decorated with scorpion hieroglyphs and probably linked to one of the two predynastic kings called "Scorpion."

Animistic nature religion — the personification and divinization of natural sites like mountains, rivers and trees, natural forces like the sky, winds, water, tides, and fire and so-called "stars" like the sun, the moon, Venus, Sirius, Orion — and the divinization of animals were probably key foundations upon which much of this emerging religion was based. Plants and natural elements upon which human existence was dependent were seen to have personality, power and will.

The great Dutch historian, archaeologist and Egyptologist Henri Frankfort (1879-1954), a disciple of Petrie, and his wife H.A. Groenewegen-Frankfort (1896-1982), in *The Intellectual Adventure of Ancient Man*, defined "the phenomenal world" as being "primarily "a 'Thou' for ancient — and also for primitive — man," while it is an 'It' for modern scientific man." They summed up this attitude as even going beyond "the usual 'animistic' or 'personalistic' interpretations." The Frankforts saw "a relation between 'I' and 'Thou' [which was] absolutely *sui generis*."[1] Indeed, it is this unique, peculiar relationship which goes a long way towards explaining not only the essence of animism, in Egypt and elsewhere, but also why man sought to magically manipulate the elements in nature, why he revered them and how natural elements eventually became gods and goddesses.

Such a process was probably in the making ever since the Egyptian Naqada II Period (c. 3500–3300 BC). It involved the gradual animistic and totemistic transposition of the functions of nature and plants and animals and their behavior into full-fledged gods and goddesses, demons, religious myths of a primordial watery chaos and of creation and order and rules of standard human behavior. The first Egyptian gods and goddesses seem to have been emblematic totemistic animals and plants transformed into tutelary, protective clan and territorial gods and divinized natural elements like the sun, the moon and the air, including the winds. It is extremely important to emphasize that the divinized animals were not just emblematic or symbolic; they were indeed believed to be divine.

If this bedrock of animism and nature religion can hardly be doubted, it seems that there was no integral totemism in Egypt in the sense that some of its major aspects such as exogamy and the totemistic meal were missing. However,

---

1. Frankfort, Henri and Groenewegen-Frankfort, H.A. in *The Intellectual Adventure of Ancient Man*, p.4.

there is hardly any doubt that prehistoric and proto-historic Egypt was one of the ancient societies which was most deeply impregnated by many key aspects of totemism and a linked animal worship. This is evident in the fact that the power of the vast majority of Egyptian divinities did not extend beyond local areas either as emblem/totems or then as gods and goddesses. The overall influence of animal and plant worship and aspects of totemism seems to have been far greater in ancient Egypt than in ancient Sumer and its West Asian zone of influence, where, while emblem/totems together with deified ancestors seem to have played key roles in the establishment of tutelary city gods, animistic nature religion without animal worship emerged as the more important and general tendency.

In everyday life, fascination, fear, reverence, connection and identification with animals must have been strong. Animals, like plants, were of course above all connected to man for their usefulness for food, clothing and tools. However, the central concern with animals in pre-Neolithic hunting times (before c. 8000 BC), before the domestication of animals, was not only linked to food needs but probably also to religious beliefs. Perhaps the fact that animals constituted an essential food resource led to the consequential belief that animals were the repositories of the divine, that animals, like humans, have souls. While it was necessary to hunt animals for food, the hunter had to make allowances for their divinity; they had to pacify their souls.

There can hardly be any doubt that the Aurignacian (Chauvet, c. 32,000–23,000 BP) and Magdalenian (Lascaux, c. 17,000 BP) cultures and religions were centered on animals, even if it cannot be definitively proven that their art also indicates a hunting magic religion. The belief in continuity between animals, man and the divine seems likely in those times. Perhaps, even the totemistic notion that animals are aspects of the gods and provide divine protection already existed. In any case, cults of animals and bones existed and fear and veneration of animals can be assumed.

All these beliefs emerged independently or seeped into Egyptian religion, as they did in one form or another into all early post-Neolithic religions; but in Egypt these beliefs remained particularly strong throughout its history. The French ethnologist and paleontologist André Leroi-Gourhan (1911–1986) in *Les Religions de la Préhistoire* saw the use of animals like "the eagle, the lion and the bull...in the mythologies [of] Mesopotamia, Scythia, Egypt, China, India" as a direct result of the past, beginning with the Aurignacian Period, 32,000 years before.[2] The vestiges of similar beliefs among the Shamanists of Siberia give us an idea of what the Egyptian believed about animals. However, it must be noted that Egyptian beliefs about animals, and religion in general, differed from shamanistic beliefs in that magic concerning the hunt, or anything else, was performed on the earth and not by an intercessory trip by a shaman to the gods in the beyond.

The Egyptians loved to eat meat, loved hunting, and practiced an enormous amount of animal sacrifice; but mistreating animals was clearly *bewete*, an abomination, taboo, and some animals were either too impure or too sacred to be eaten or sacrificed. While it was in the order of things that animals represented necessary food, the right to use them as food had to be accompanied with prudent consideration for their souls. Animals, like the gods and humans, had both good qualities and bad sides and could foster well-being and exercise vengeance.

In short, the ancient Egyptians were a few steps ahead of Descartes (1596–1650), and other philosophers in the Renaissance, who held that animals were machines and adamantly rejected that they could have souls. The Egyptians were closer to what has become a modern scientific fact — that animals and humans are in the same large family. Despite widespread hunting and sacrifice of animals, the ancient Egyptians were also close to many of our modern animal rights movements. Needless to say, the cloning of animals would have horrified the Egyptians. That said, the Egyptian treatment of animals paradoxically degenerated during the Late Period (c. 747–332 BC) when animals were so revered for their divine attributes that they were specially bred, killed, mummified and sold as fetishes.

In Naqada Egypt, many animals came to be seen as emblematic, as being protective or demonic. The behavior of animals and their relations with nature were seen as role models for the functioning of the universe and analogies for acceptable human behavior. Animals were divine representatives of physical characteristics which were often more powerful than those of man. Moreover, animals are neither moral nor immoral; they do what they must do and do it in a self-confident and imperious way.

Animals were perceived as naturally epitomizing the entire range of powers, qualities, skills and emotions: strength and virility, like the bull and the ram; motherhood, like the cow; sovereignty, power and aggressiveness, like the

---

2. Leroy-Gourham, André, *Les Religions de la Préhistoire*, Quadridge/PUF, Paris, 1964, p. 155.

17

lion, savageness like the crocodile, magnificent majesty and total free-flying freedom like the falcon, regular, predictable behavior like the scarab; speed, like the hare; beauty, like the wildcat; protection for herds and man, like the dog, etc., etc. The magnificent free-flying ways of the falcon, the power of the lion, or the virility of the bull did indeed supremely symbolize kinds of freedom and power which only divine forces or the gods could possess.

A wide range of animals was demonized. These included the pig, the scorpion, the snake, the hippopotamus, the crocodile, the turtle, the goat, the antelope, the donkey, many types of fish and birds, and reddish animals in general. Some of these became linked to the evil Seth (Setekh), which explains their demonization; while others, like some fish, were considered to be impure. For some dangerous animals, notably the snake, fear and sacred reverence were inextricably mixed and accentuated by the cyclic shedding and regeneration of its skin, seen as a sign of perpetual rebirth and immortality. But as we shall soon see in the section on taboos, several dangerous animals were both revered and detested.

Placed within such a totemistically influenced culture and context, the deification and demonization of animals were therefore logical developments. The belief that animals were the repository of the divine almost necessarily led to the practice of divinizing animals, but it also led to the demonization of dangerous animals. The creation of gods and demons who were composites of animals or who combined animal and human characteristics was also logical. This process rendered these gods and demons more divine, more powerful, more protective or more dreaded. Certainly the Egyptians rank among the most prolific and creative god- and demon-makers of this type.

Hundreds, if not thousands, of animals and plants in Egypt were involved in a transposition which made them the emblematic divinities of tribes. Sacred plants and animals emblematically marked the identity and protective forces of individuals, families, clans and tribes. Tribal totemistic animal and plant gods were usually linked to specific sites and then became the sacred animals of regions and cities. Regions became sites ruled by tutelary, protective emblem/totem gods and goddesses, each with its banner inscribed with the animal or plant image of its totem. Cults to these divinities were invented. The emblematic standards of identity played key rallying and protective roles in warfare.

Somewhere, probably between about 3300 and 3100 BC, figurines of animals and plants hoisted on poles (perhaps first used as military standards) and then pictograms inscribed on banners probably eventually led to both the falcon and the banner becoming the first hieroglyphs which designated a deified force, a god, a *netjer*. The term "god," or at least the idea of a divine force, had now passed from the world of images into the world of written language.

These first hieroglyphs for gods consisted of a falcon or of banners which were not inscribed — blank banners — followed by the hieroglyph designating the name of a god. More than 20 glyphs to designate the terms god, goddess and their plurals were eventually invented by the Egyptians. The emblematically inscribed banners of the gods, *netjeru*, continued their career in religious rituals and processions and on the first regional (nome, *sepat*) shrines of the gods. Eventually, these banners were widely used inserted into specially built openings on the monumental *bekhenet* (pylon) gateways of the temples where the gods to which the temple was dedicated were named.

Emblem totemistic banners were the forerunners of flags, military standards and badges. Although the divine aspects of most modern flags, emblems and badges have become obscure, the same schema of identity and pride is obviously still in play.

The emblem/totem divinities became tutelary, henotheistic gods; they protected their villages, towns or zones and were appeased and influenced through offerings and sacrifices in exchange for protection and prosperity. They were usually revered to the exclusion of the henotheistic gods of the neighboring zones with the same functions, but these other gods were usually feared and respected. In Egypt, as in other societies influenced by totemism, it can be assumed that all cities and regions had animal and/or plant emblem/totems; many of them remained identified with their geographical places of origin and many others became part of the general system of divinities, demons, religion and mythology.

There was a deep, virtually inseparable link between all these elements — the clan, the village or town and its surrounding land, the animals in this zone and particularly the animal totem which emblematically embodied the protection and prideful identity of the clan and had become a divinity. Above all, the inseparable link, the centrality, in Egyptian nature religion, animism, emblematic totemism and henotheism was magic, *heka*. The Egyptian magical system and its consequences will be examined in greater detail in Chapter 4 and elsewhere.

During the Early Dynastic Period (c. 3100–2686 BC), Egypt was gradually divided into regions, or *sepat* — villages or towns of clans and their surrounding land. The totemistic system of animal and plant emblem/totems transformed into divine forces and divinities was superimposed on this new structure. Throughout Egyptian history, most of the emblems of these *sepat* remained linked to plants or animals. (The *sepat* have come to be known as nomes, from the Greek *nomos*. Just as the Greeks renamed Egypt's cities and these names have become the standard reference for Egyptian cities, the term *sepat* was virtually eliminated in favor of the Greek term of *nomos*, or nome in Western languages.)

The magical and totemistic framework in ancient Egypt is a perfect fit for the analysis by the father of sociology, Emile Durkheim (1858–1917). He saw magic as "a primitive form of religion...made (like it) of beliefs and rites...myths and dogmas, but only more rudimentary (than religion)." For Durkheim, the most elementary form of religion in history was totemism and it was "the beneficial guardian of the physical and moral order, dispenser of life, health, of all the qualities men esteem..." and "the totemistic principle scattered throughout the species includes the mythic ancestor, the animal-protector, civilizing heroes, tutelary gods of all kinds and degrees."[3]

THE FALCON GOD HORUS — THE OLDEST EXAMPLE OF THE CONSTANT TRANSFORMATION AND AMALGAMATION OF GODS

King of the sky, the falcon (*bik*) is perhaps the oldest and most spectacular Egyptian example of the transfer from nature and animals to divinity and henotheisitic status in specific sites. In hieroglyphic representation the falcon was a *netjer*, a divine force, a god, and on a totemistic perch or standard it became the falcon sky god and incarnation of divine kingship, Horus (Heru). The wings of the Horus falcon were the celestial reaches; its eyes were the sun and the moon; and the speckles on its underside were the stars in the sky. Just as spectacularly, and in typical Egyptian fashion, Horus was simultaneously one god and many gods with various forms or aspects who underwent numerous transformations and was amalgamated to other gods.

There is no easy way to separate all the Horuses, their various animistic, totemistic, henotheistic, royal divine kingship, national and local functions and their merger or amalgamation with other gods. And so, what here should be strictly a description of the transfer from nature and animals to divinity and henotheisitic status must, in Horus' case, also become a brief, first outline of this

---

3. Durkheim, Emile, *Les formes élémentaires de la vie religieuse*, Quadridge/PUF, Paris, 1960, p. 584.

god. It must also become the first reference to one of the key questions in the ancient Egyptian religion and one of the central problems in trying to understand that religion: the confusing amalgamation of many gods into single gods, while the amalgamated gods continued to have independent existences. Was this a result of confused, haphazard development, or, as shall be examined in Chapter 4, was it the illustration of a sophisticated, holistic system based on what some Egyptologists have called "multiple approaches and answers,"[4] "complementary concepts," "the one and the many"[5] or "the one in the many"[6]?

Broadly speaking, there were two series of Horuses and several Horuses in each series. The first gravitated around the falcon-headed Haroeris, "Horus the Elder," of the Predynastic and First Dynastic Periods (from before c. 3100 BC to c. 2890 BC). The second series, perhaps from about 2375 BC at the end of the Fifth Dynasty, gravitated around Horus, in falcon, human, or combined falcon/human forms, as the son of Osiris (Asar) and Isis (Aset), Harsiesis, "Horus the Younger." By at least the end of the Old Kingdom (c. 2181 BC), the two series of Horuses were increasingly subjected to a confused merger.

Heru, "the distant one," the Egyptian name of Horus, is linked to *hert*, distant, far away and above, and by extension, the sky. One of Horus' divine titles was "the distant one." The falcon Horus was the essence of higher beings, an aspect and an incarnation of divinity. In falcon forms, he represented divine kingship, leadership, strength and the fabulous free-flying liberty of birds. He was also the sky, and then the sun and the moon. Originally, Horus as Haroeris was closely linked to the mother/cow goddess Hathor, who was his mother and his wife. Horus as a sun god rose and set inside Hathor, who as a sky goddess was Het-Hert or Heru, the house of Horus, above. Ihy, the player of the sacred sistrum rattle, was their son. However, Haroeris' four more famous sons — the *mesu* Heru: Hapy, Imsety, Duamutef and Qebehsenuef, who represented the four cardinal points — were said to be the children of Isis, the mother of Harsiesis, "Horus the Younger." The *mesu* Heru were inserted into the Osirisian cycle and came to be seen as children of "Horus the Younger," with their main role being the protection of the canopic jars stuffed with mummified innards.

Perhaps one of the oldest and most clearly traceable tutelary falcon emblem/totems in an identifiable site can be situated among the clans or tribes of

---

4. Henri Frankfort in *Ancient Egyptian Religion*.

5. Erik Hornung in *Conceptions of God in Ancient Egypt*.

6. Jan Assmann in *Moses the Egyptian*. The terms in notes 4, 5 and 6 are discussed in Chapter Four.

the powerful city of Nekhen (named Hierakonpolis, "the city of the falcon" by the Greeks), in Upper (southern) Egypt. This falcon with two feathers on its head, the Nekheny, was absorbed at a very early date by the falcon Horus. The henotheistic Horus of Hierakonpolis may have virtually replaced the Nekheny falcon, even before the First Dynasty and then advanced to chief status in several parts of Upper and Lower Egypt. This Horus might be the oldest Egyptian god to have clearly evolved from emblematic totemistic terms of reference.

The Golden Falcon Head, found in the Hierakonpolis "Main Deposit" cache by J.E. Quibell in 1897 (and now in the Cairo Museum), perhaps dating from only the Sixth Dynasty, but perhaps much earlier, clearly illustrates the role of the falcon Horus as the god of Hierakonpolis. It seems to have been this falcon god Horus who was depicted on early works of art such as Narmer's Palette (c. 3100 BC). The *Shemsu-Hor* (the followers of Horus)[7] may have been Predynastic kings of Hierakonpolis in Upper Egypt and of Buto in Lower Egypt. The early twin falcon gods Anty and Nemty can also be traced to Upper Egypt and Anty as a falcon war god maintained a position of great reverence in several Upper Egyptian nomes until at least the mid-Sixth Dynasty (c. 2345–2181 BC).

The Haroeris/Horus had several aspects or forms in various cities. Behdety, the falcon-winged sun disk became a popular a Haroeris/Horus form in Behdet (Tell-el Balamun) on the northern Delta coast, in Djeba or Mesen (Edfu) in southern Upper Egypt and in Timenhor (Damanhur) in the western Delta. This Behdety form of Horus, as the son of Re, the god/King of the earth, fought a battle against his brother Seth, although this myth seems to have arisen after the second Horus, Harsiesis, became the son of Osiris and the nephew of Seth and fought another battle against Seth. The falcon-headed "Souls of Pe" (Pe-Dep, Buto) in Lower Egypt may have been early gods or demigod-kings incarnated as Horus-type falcons.

The apex of the falcon Haroeris/Horus emblem/totem came with the unification of Upper and Lower Egypt around c. 3100 BC. As the original totemistic Predynastic sky, kingly falcon emblem and then henotheistic and chief god of Hierakonpolis, which apparently won the war against Lower Egypt, the falcon Horus was logically incarnated in the ruling pharaoh-god of united Egypt, as Egypt's first chief and royal god. In this role, Horus was the incarnation of divine kingship. Almost all of the Early Dynasty (c. 3100–2686 BC) pharaohs were identified with Horus. Many objects have been found in several sites in

---

7. See Alan Gardiner in *Egypt of the Pharaohs*, pp. 414 and 421-422.

both Upper and Lower Egypt, dating from about 3100 and the succeeding centuries, depicting the first royal emblems of identity, preceding the cartouche, the *serekh* (a palace facade, topped by the falcon Horus as the royal god of the first dynasties of united Egypt). The royal residence of the pharaoh, the *khenu*, also came be known as *bikt*, the falcon city.

Haroeris, "Horus the Elder," and especially his Horemakhet, "Horus in the Horizon" form, was merged, or rather amalgamated to the all-powerful chief, solar and royal god Re (Ra) from about the middle of the Fourth Dynasty (c. 2566 BC). Horus became the morning star, the rising sun on the eastern horizon aspect of Re. The overall result was the human falcon-headed Re-Horakthe with a solar disk headdress and multiple functions. The pharaohs were now sons of Re, in addition to being the first falcon Horus.

The Osiris/Seth/Isis/Horus myth provided the second series of Horuses — Harsiesis, Horus the Younger. The child Horus was manifested in human form as Harpakhrad (Harpocrates), the son of Osiris and Isis, and was born on the floating island of Khemmis (Chemmis) in the western Delta marshes. He was usually represented with a shaven head (except for a side-lock of hair), with dimpled cheeks and sucking his thumb. The falcon-headed (or falcon) Harsiesis was the adult son of Isis who achieved his greatest glory as Her-nedi-itef (Harendotes), the avenger of his father Osiris, the god/King of Egypt and the victor over Seth who had killed Osiris. This victory transformed Horus into Sma-Tawy (Harsomtus), the unifier of the Two Lands, Upper and Lower Egypt, and Har-Paneb-Tawy, the Lord of the Two Lands, *Ta-Wy*.

At least from the Fourth Dynasty (c. 2566 BC), Horus, in Khem (Letopolis) in Lower Egypt, was the falcon Harmerti, or Horkhenti-Irti ("Horus of the two eyes") with his right eye being the sun and his left eye the moon, Mekhenti-er-Irti ("he who has no eyes") when the sun and moon were invisible and *Khenti-Irti* ("he who has eyes"), or *Khenty-Khem*, "the foremost of Khem," when the sun and moon re-appeared. Given the sky and solar aspects of these forms, these Horuses seem to have originated with the elder Haroeris form of Horus rather than his Osirisian form.

By the end of the Fifth Dynasty (c. 2494–2345 BC), and perhaps earlier, the reigning pharaoh was also the second Horus, the son of Osiris, while alive and Osiris when dead. By this time, Horus was also sometimes the hunting god Anhur (Onris), a form of Shu, the god of dryness, the atmosphere between the earth and the sky and the personification of sunlight. And by this time, Horus existed as Re-Horakthe and all the various forms of Horus both separately and together. In turn, during New Kingdom (beginning c. 1550 BC), Horus in his individual forms and in his Re-Horakhte form became aspects of Amun-Re, Egypt's new chief/creator/sun/royal god when Amun amalgamated all the gods beginning with Re. Amun-Re-Horakthe was most frequently represented in human form as a bearded man with a crown, a sun disk and two feathers.

Horus somehow concurrently became all the Horuses and the numerous individual Horuses and, notably, the falcon Horus and Horus, son of Osiris and Isis — who were utterly different from each other. Horus was separately and together and at different times a falcon emblem/totem, a sky god, an animistic sun and moon god, the god incarnated in the ruling divine pharaoh, a child in human form and the victor over Seth. He appeared with various names and various functions in several places as a local city or nome god as well as a god with national, or universal, attributes.

When the *sepat* (the nomes, or regions) were established during the Early Dynastic Period, c. 3100–2686 BC), three *sepat* — Edfu and Gebtu (Koptos) in Upper Egypt, and Damanhur in Lower Egypt — adopted falcon totem emblems. Horus falcon gods also flourished in several other cities, notably Gesa (Qus, north of Naqada), and Iunet (Denderah). At least from the New Kingdom, and especially from about 180 BC during the Ptolemaic Period, Kom Ombo was an important site for the worship of Horus in his Horus the elder Haroeris form, perhaps indicating that this might have been the case in the nearby ancient site of Nubt (Ombos). Many other Egyptian cities were directly linked to the falcon and/or to Horus in various forms, including Hut-hery-ib (Athribis), Djanet (Tanis), Mi'am (Aniba) in Wawat (Nubia), Ash, in the oasis area near the Libyan desert and during the New Kingdom, Egypt's old capital of Men-nefer (Memphis) became a center of Horus worship in the form of Horemakhet, "Horus in the Horizon," seen as being incarnated in Pharaoh Khephren's Sphinx in Memphis/Giza.

Egypt's oldest religious texts, the Pyramid Texts, the magical utterance-spells inscribed on the walls of the funerary chambers and corridors of at least ten pyramids, including one of a *hemet nisut weret*, a great royal wife, between about 2375 and 2125 BC, frequently illustrated Horus' linked role as an emblem/totem falcon, sky, royal and Osirisian god. Utterance 467 states: "I (the King) live on what Horus Lord of the sky lives on, by decree of Horus, Lord of the sky... I have soared to the sky as a heron, I have kissed the sky as a falcon, I have reached the sky as a locust..." and Utterance 468 states: "...may Isis cry out to you, may Nephthys call to you as Horus who protects his father Osiris."[8]

(The Pyramid Texts, first discovered by Heinrich and Emile Brugsch in 1881 in Pepy I's pyramid, are probably mankind's oldest elaborate written religious texts; at least, they are the oldest found to date. The most authoritative compiler of the Pyramid Texts, the British Egyptologist R.O. Faulkner (1894–1982) listed 759 utterances. By comparison, the early (-3000 BC) Sumerian clay tablets refer to the gods and their roles and religious feeling in only a cursory manner and the Sumerian Surupak and Tell Abu-Salabih tablets (c. 2600 BC) consist of difficult to understand fragments of rituals, theology and myths.)

Horus remained one of Egypt's main divinities from start to finish, from Predynastic times to the conventional end of Egyptian history in AD 395. He continued to be depicted in his various forms — falcon emblem/totem, winged sun disk, falcon-headed human, human and with headdresses of Egypt's *pschent* double crown of the Two Lands, the *atef* crown (a combination of the white crown of Upper Egypt, flanked by two red ostrich feathers) or a sun disk. He was one of Egypt's best-loved gods, combining in his various forms many beneficial and noble qualities — the sun, divine kingship, dutifulness, righteous and powerful vengeance, healing and protection, benevolence in the afterlife judgment court, the cuddliness and innocence of the child and the survivor of the immense difficulties and trials which are usually inflicted on the chosen child in mythology.

As early as the Pyramid Texts, the attributes and forms of the first series of Horuses, "Horus the Elder," became inexorably confused and merged with the second series of Horuses, "Horus the Younger" and with Re, creating a situation which defies any logical comprehension. Of all the Egyptian gods, Horus, with at least 17 different forms or aspects, was one of the most multiple and changing gods and probably the most confused for moderns to understand. In addition to his names as gods, he had more than 30 divine titles — "Horus, Lord of Mankind," "Guide of the Two Lands," "Foremost of Upper Egypt," "Horus on his papyrus," "Overseer of the Nether World," and others.

THE OLDEST DIVINIZED NATURAL ELEMENTS AND ANIMALS

Along with the falcon, one of the oldest and most complicated Egyptian examples of the divinization of animals was the cow, the *idet*. The cow was

---

8. Faulkner, R.O., *The Ancient Egyptian Pyramid Texts*, pp. 156 and 157.

linked to the sky, the *pet*, with the sky being represented as the divine cow, the *ahet*. The divine cow was the mother and the female and was also linked to the afterlife. Hesat and Mehetweret were celestial cow goddesses of the primeval "first time," the *zep tepey* — the "great flood" who emerged from the waters when everything was created. They were perhaps the prototypes of all the succeeding goddesses of motherhood, femininity, the sky and the afterlife. Hesat, Mehetweret, Bat, Hathor and Nut were probably the oldest and most important Egyptian cow goddesses linked to an element, a force, a function or a site.

It was Hathor who became "the first of the cows," and "the eye of the sun," more totally than these other goddesses. Hathor eventually integrated all the sky, mother and feminine principles. It is certain that she assimilated the functions of the "divine, celestial cow" Bat, whom rather than Hathor was perhaps depicted on the Narmer Palette (c. 3100 BC). There is also a possibility that Hathor evolved from Nut, the sky goddess of Egypt's oldest creation myth and ennead of gods and goddesses in Onu (Heliopolis), developed from older traditions by at least the Fourth Dynasty (c. 2613–2494 BC). Like Hathor, Nut was depicted as a cow who contained the sky and was linked to the afterlife, but she also had a kind of a bowl headdress. And like Nut, Hathor, as "The Lady of the Vulva," symbolized forms of sexuality with her father, the sun god Re. Like the divine white cow Hesat, Re, the sun, goes into Hathor's mouth at night and is born, or reborn, from her vulva in the morning.

Like Horus, Hathor had both local tutelary, henotheistic functions and a national destiny representing primordial characteristics and primordial societal functions. The origins of Hathor could go back to Naqada I (c. 4000–3500 BC) — rock drawings, apparently of Hathor, were recently found at Mount Nabta, 810 miles south of Cairo.[9] In any case, it is certain that at least from the Old Kingdom (c. 2686–2181 BC), Hathor was linked to Per-Hathor (Atfih), and Iunet (Denderah), the two cities in Upper Egypt named Aphroditopolis by the Greeks, and to many other cities, like Heliopolis, Edfu and Gebelein. In Memphis, Hathor was linked to the *nehet*, the sycamore tree and was known as "The Lady of the Sycamore." This could indicate, as we shall soon see, that she could have also been a prehistoric afterlife tree goddess. Over the centuries, Hathor's worship spread throughout Egypt and into Nubia and the Sinai, but Denderah maintained itself as the main site for Hathor's veneration in many forms linked to the mother cow. Especially during the New Kingdom (c. 1550–1069 BC),

---

9. Agence France Presse (AFP), 2/19/2001.

reverence for Hathor as "The Lady of *Amenta*," the West, the afterlife, was immense in temples on the Waset (Thebes) west bank of the Nile.

As Het-Heru (Hathor), "the house, or womb, of Heru," of Horus, she was the original mother and wife of Haroeris, the first Horus (Horus the Elder) and included the sky, the sun, the moon and the stars. And since Horus was incarnated in the reigning pharaoh, Hathor was the mother of the pharaoh, but this function was largely appropriated by Isis after the Osirisian myth rose to prominence from about 2375 BC. In fact, while Hathor always maintained her separate existence, Isis gradually became the great mother goddess of Egypt.

Hathor could be represented as a cow with a sun disk between her horns, as a cow suckling Horus, or as a human holding her son Ihy; or with a human face and cow's ears or horns, or as a human who was part of a tree; but her most usual form was a human wearing a headdress composed of cow-horns and a sun disk.

Hathor always remained basically representative of the main aspects of the very old concept of the Great Mother/Female. She was beauty, fertility, maternity and sexuality. As the mother of the Horus, she suckled him, but as his wife, she sailed upstream from Denderah to Edfu every year for the renewal of her divine marriage with him in the Festival of the Beautiful Meeting. She gradually accumulated a huge number of functions and names and especially those linked to the great mother and female principle. At times, she assimilated most of the powers held by many other goddesses, including childbirth, marriage, pleasure, music and afterlife protectress. Like all mother goddesses (until the Christian Mary), Hathor needed both to nurture children and to enjoy frequent sexual intercourse. Hathor was also prone to intoxication, anger and destruction. As such, and in lioness form, she was linked to the goddess Sakhmet and was a bellicose destroyer goddess, as we shall see in Volume II.

In meaning, Hathor was heir to the Venus female fertility figures (perhaps the very first divinities) 30,000 years earlier, although in form she was representative of the Egyptian slender feminine ideal rather than to the fat form of most Venuses. She also bears considerable resemblance to the Sumerian mother, love, fertility, war and sky goddess Inanna and to the nameless Sumerian goddesses who seem to have preceded Inanna. Like Inanna, Hathor was a beautiful woman oozing sexuality and pleasure, which is why the Greeks assimilated her with their own goddess of love, Aphrodite. Also like Inanna, Hathor loved violence.

While the Inanna profile, which emerged earlier than 3500 BC, might have influenced the Hathor profile, it seems likelier that Hathor was largely an indigenous Egyptian invention, an Egyptian form of the almost universal religious concept of the mother goddess.

In addition to the names of Hathor already mentioned, she had more than 30 names and titles including "Lady of Happiness," "Queen of the Stars," "House of the Sistrum," "Mistress of Fear" and "Eye of Re" (in her destroyer form), "Mistress of Drunkenness," "Lady of Byblos," etc.

The sun, *ra*, was always pivotal in the Egyptian religion. Horus, Tum (Atum), the creator god, Re the chief royal and sun god, Osiris, the King of the Dead, Amun-Re, the New Kingdom royal and chief god and many other gods were linked to the sun or became "solarized" when they attained national importance. In Heliopolis, at least from the building of the Heliopolitan sun temple, around 2660 BC, *ra*, the sun, and Atum were linked to the wagtail, and then the heron, or some mythical bird with a likeness to the heron. It came to be known as the *benu* and was perched on the original mound, on the *benben*, which in Egyptian mythology had emerged from the primeval watery chaos and was closely linked to the original rising sun. The *benu* was the carrier of perpetual sunlight from the gods to mankind in the daily resurrection of the sun and in rebirth in general. The *benu* became an aspect of Atum, was later the *ba*, soul, aspect of Re and afterwards was linked to Osiris. The Greek historian Herodotus (c. 484–420 BC) associated the *benu* on the *benben* with the Greek mythological Phoenix. Perpetual sunlight was carried from the gods to mankind.

The *ka*, the bull, was linked to Re, Ptah, Montu and to other gods, and to Heliopolis and other cities. In Heliopolis, the Mnevis bull, was an aspect of Re in the solar cult. Memphis was linked to the Apis bull as a form of Ptah. Iuny (Hermonthis) was linked to the Buchis bull as a form of the war god Montu. Hut-hery-ib (Athribis), Gebtu (Koptos) and Khent-min (Akhmim, Khemmis Panopolis) were some of the other major cities linked to bull gods, among other animal emblem/totems, and four nomes of Lower Egypt adopted the bull as part of their emblems.

Trees, *nehet*, in Egypt as in many other prehistoric and ancient societies, were together with the sun, the falcon and the cow among the oldest divine elements. Symbolizing life and the sun, subsistence in this life and in the afterlife, trees were the objects of elaborate ritual and intense worship particularly linked to several goddesses and gods — Nut, Hathor, Isis, Re, Osiris, Horus and Wepwawet (Upuaut).

Many cities especially revered the tree — there was a sacred *ished* (the persea tree) linked to the rising sun in Heliopolis, Memphis and Edfu, sacred *nehet* sycamores linked to the afterlife, Hathor and Re in Memphis and a sacred willow linked to Osiris in Abydos. The *ished* in Heliopolis was especially linked to Re and sometimes to the *benu* bird and was protected by the cat. The willow was also linked to the *ba*, one of the main souls in the Egyptian soul system. The *asher*, the tamarisk, was linked to resurrection and to Osiris and Wepwawet and the acacia to Horus. As we shall see later, the *djed* pillar, linked to Osiris' backbone, seems to have had some of its origins in prehistoric tree worship. Trees in general could have anthropomorphic attributes, particularly arms. (Of course, the saying, "touch wood," which we still use in the hope of good luck or to ward off evil, has its origin in tree worship.)

The lotus, the *seshen*, which shuts up during the night and opens again in the morning, was assimilated with the setting and rising sun, with death and rebirth, and with the Memphite god Nefertem, wearing a lotus headdress, or as a youthful sun god on a lotus. The lotus/*seshen* and the sedge reed plant, the *shema*, also became emblems and the name of Upper Egypt (*ta-shema*).

The papyrus cluster, the *mehyt*, was assimilated with the original primeval marsh, the four columns which held up the sky, and with the traditional Egyptian proclamation of praise for the pharaoh — *ankh, udja, seneb*, life, prosperity, health. The *mehyt* became the emblem and one of the names of Lower Egypt (*ta-mehu*).

In Nubt (Ombos), an indeterminate animal (perhaps a donkey, oryx, okapi, or a canine beast, or perhaps a mythical animal) and the god Seth constituted a very old tutelary combination. The Seth animal, the Setekh, can be traced back to the Naqada I Period (c. 4000–3500 BC). He was usually depicted with an indeterminate animal head and a human body, but also in his total animal form with a canine body, forked tail, square ears and long nose; and also sometimes as a pig, a hippopotamus or a donkey. Seth was "the *Nubty*," "he of the gold town of Nubt," much as Horus was the Nekheny of Hierakonpolis and Hathor, The Lady of Denderah. Seth, the *Nubty*, became a chaos, war, and storm god and then the great rival of both the falcon and human Horus. We shall soon deal very fully with the saga of Seth and his positive and then horrifically negative role in Egyptian mythology and religion.

Thebes, with its stylized zoomorphic scepter nome emblem, the *was*, may have first of all been linked to an indeterminate (a bull?) or mythologically invented animal (like the Seth animal may have been invented). By at least the

Sixth Dynasty (c. 2345–2181 BC), with the falcon war god Montu, Thebes was linked to the falcon, but also to the bull in Montu's manifestation as the Buchis Bull. In the New Kingdom, Thebes became the de facto city of the *ba*, the ram, the city of Egypt's greatest creator, royal chief and amalgamating/monotheizing god, Amun-Re.

Khmun (Hermopolis) was first of all a city of the hare, dedicated to "the swift one," the goddess Wenut, who may have also been linked to a snake. However, during the Early Dynastic Period (c. 3100–2686 BC), Hermopolis was *par excellence* associated with the baboon, the *ian*, then the ibis, the *heb*, and the moon, *ia-eh*, in the forms of Thoth (Djehuty), the god of wisdom and writing. Huge baboon colossi of Thoth were eventually sculpted, much like the falcon colossi of Horus and Re-Horakthe. Ba'h in Lower Egypt (one of the two cities named Hermopolis Parva by the Greeks) was also a city of the ibis linked to Thoth, and the ibis was also sacred in Abydos.

An indeterminate animal, a dog, or a jackal, the *ienpu* animal, was the manifestation of the death (and then embalmment and tomb protector) god Anubis. The Greeks called Cynopolis, (near Hardai, whose exact location is unknown) the city of the dog. The black dog, Khentymentiu, a god of the afterlife, was linked to Abdu (Abydos)

The wolf, or dog or jackal, was the emblem/totem of Zawty (renamed Lykopolis), the city of the wolf, by the Greeks) and became the jackal-headed god Wepwawet, opener of the road to the afterlife.

The goose was sacred to the earth god Geb — he was the "Great Cackler" and sometimes wore a goose headdress — and to the mighty and beloved Amun.

The cobra, the *iaret*, was the emblem/totem of the city of Buto, and became its henotheistic deity as the goddess Wadjit and later, as the uraeus, was a symbol of Lower Egypt and the pharaoh. The vulture was assimilated with the city of Nekheb (Eleithiapolis), the goddess Nekhbet, and Upper Egypt. The vulture, the *neret*, and the cobra, Nekhbet and Wadjit, became the royal protectress goddesses of the pharaohs of united Egypt.

Abu (Elephantine), Iunyt or Ta-senet (Latapolis, best known now as Esna) and Per-Banebdjedet (Mendes) were at various times linked to the *ba*, the ram, in the form of the potter-creator god Khnum. Mendes was also linked to the ram through its local henotheistic ram god Banebdjedet.

Mendes and Esna were also *ienet*, fish, cities. Mendes was linked to the sacred *schilbe* fish (the Nile carp, *lepidotus*) through Banebdjedet's wife/mother, the goddess Hatmehyt, "she who is before the fishes," who was depicted as a fish or with a fish headdress. Hatmehyt seems to have been the oldest original emblem and totemized goddess of the city and of the 16th fish nome of Lower Egypt of which Mendes was the capital. Esna was linked to the sacred *lates* fish (the *lates niloticus*, in the perch family) and eventually the Esna theologians linked the Sau (Sais) sky, war and dream guardian goddess Neith, whom they adopted, to the fish.

Sais was the city of the bee, *bity*, and especially linked to Neith and her temple, the *per-bit*, the "Castle of the Bee." The bee was also one of the terms designating Lower Egypt.

Esna as well as Tieny (This) were also cities of the lioness, the *mait*, of the war goddess Mehyt. Bast (Bubastis) was first the city of the lioness and then of the cat, the *miw*, of the music and dance goddess Bastet. She-Resy (Fayum) and its capital Hut-Sobk (Crocodilopolis) was the oasis zone of the crocodile, of the fearful god of the waters, Sobek. Khem (Letopolis), the capital of Second Nome of Lower Egypt, was linked to the scorpion goddess Hededet in addition to the falcon Horus, and so forth. Eighteen of Egypt's 42 nomes had animals, stylized animals or a part of an animal as their emblems.

TABOOS

Just as the totemistic, tutelary and emblematic functions of animals, plants and natural sites were sublimated into the functions of the divine, taboos were fabricated to designate the totem's enemies and prohibited behavior. Belief in taboos was particularly strong in Egypt. In a parallel movement, taboo animals became the basis of demons.

The Egyptians believed that taboos (*bewete*, abomination) were absolutely inherent in the universe, in some people, in some animals, in some objects and in some forms of behavior. Taboos were linked to some dangerous animals and to principles of interdiction anchored in totemistic religious beliefs, based on situations which would obviously cause conflict — such as incest, cannibalism within the clan, and contestation of the social order and its leaders.

However, as Sigmund Freud (1856–1939) noted in *Totem and Taboo*, a taboo was a mixture of the "consecrated" and "the disquieting, the dangerous, the prohibited, the impure," as well as of "fear and reverence." In practical terms, this meant that only the gods, the pharaoh-god or magician-priests could rectify a situation affected by taboo.

Perhaps the most obviously traceable totemistic taboos of the Egyptian religion were the prohibitions linked to alimentary laws and animal sacrifice. The identity bestowing taboo of the interdiction of the sacrifice and/or eating of certain animals was usually linked to the veneration and protection of a city or nome animal totem. This law was valid for all classes of society, but usually only the priestly class respected the corollary of not eating the enemy animal of the local totem, the local divinity, except when this enemy animal was ritually sacrificed. The Egyptian nome and priestly alimentary taboos developed into an extensive and complex system of good and bad foods and the non-use of the food utensils of other peoples. The Greek historian Herodotus (c. 484–420 BC), in *Histories*, describes the Egyptians' great aversion to eating meat "cut up with a Greek knife" or even "to use the knife, or a spit, or a cauldron belonging to a Greek."[10] *The Book of the Dead* indicates that a key factor in winning an afterlife was having not eaten taboo foods.

This system was at least as extensive and complex as the later systems of alimentary taboo which still survive in the Jewish (*kashruth*), Hindu/Buddhist (Brahman vegetarianism and *pakka* and *kakka* foods) and Moslem (*hallal*) religions.

The persistence and the exceptional emotional power of taboos concerning the consumption of certain divine animals can be verified at even very late periods in Egyptian history. This situation is illustrated by a well-known episode in the 5th century BC in Abu (Elephantine), a city protected by the ram-headed god Khnum. In Elephantine, as in so many other Egyptian cities in the Late Period (c. 747–332 BC), the local divine animal was never sacrificed and was mummified and buried for the purpose of attaining for it an eternal afterlife in much the same way as was done for humans. Sheep were never sacrificed in Egypt because one of the forms of the great chief god Amun was a ram. In Elephantine, reverence for the Khnum/ram at this time was so strong that rams were not only carefully mummified, but also extravagantly decorated and buried in stone coffins representing eternity. Despite their numbers and power, the Judean mercenaries of the Persian occupying army and the other Jews in Elephantine provoked a bloody, popular revolt in c. 410 BC with their insistence on sacrificing lambs as practiced in the Temple of Jerusalem. The Jewish Elephantine temple was completely destroyed. Both Egyptian and Hebrew totem and taboo were eminently illustrated in these events.

---

10. Herodotus, *Books I-II*, 2.41.3.

Of course, the frontier between totem and taboo was not always clear anywhere in the world. This was especially the case concerning Egypt's varied and complicated religious systems and was usually related to original, conflicting totemistic beliefs in different, and sometimes nearby, locations.

The Late Period theologians of the 16th nome of Upper Egypt dealt ingeniously with the contradiction between totem and taboo animals — they placed a falcon representing Horus in triumph above the original totem emblem of this nome, an antelope (oryx), which could be construed as both being sacred and representing the detested Seth.

As ambiguous as this might seem, it was probably the ideal solution since the antelope, notably in its gazelle form, seems to have been one of the most well-established totemized emblematic animals in Egypt, probably even before it became associated with Seth. The Predynastic king Scorpion's mace head, dating from at least before 3100 BC, contains carvings of gazelles, perhaps linked to the virtue of speed and perhaps also linked to the 16th nome emblem/totem or to the goddesses Anuket and Satis of Abu (Elephantine). The Denderah Sixth Nome of Upper Egypt adopted a similar solution by placing a red feather, representing Osiris and his "victory" over Seth, on the head of its crocodile totem/emblem.

From the New Kingdom and especially during the Late Period, a reliable indicator of the old and powerful divine emblem/totem quality of an animal was its breeding in a temple enclosure, its mummification upon death and its burial in a necropolis, a "godsland," as the Egyptians called it. However, the vast range of mummified animals, especially during the Late Period — rams, bulls, cows, lions, monkeys, cats, jackals, dogs, snakes, lizards, crocodiles, fish, baboons, ibises and even ichneumons and mice — virtually assures us that many animals were totem in some localities and taboo in others.

The contradictions between totem and taboo were particularly aggravated by the peculiar position occupied by Seth in Egyptian mythology and religion. Seth was probably one of Egypt's oldest gods, who probably began his career as the powerful henotheistic god of Nubt (Ombos) and achieved great power first in Upper Egypt and then throughout the country. This included being the patron god of some of the early pharaohs who saw in him not only great cunning but also the necessary representative of the forces of the night in the equilibrium of the world. However, by about 2375 BC, during the Fifth Dynasty when the Osiris/Seth/Isis/Horus myth was becoming firmly established, Seth became increasingly identified with treachery and evil as the murderer of Osiris, the persecutor of Horus the child, and the perpetrator of vile stratagems in his battles with Horus the avenger.

Esteem for Seth gradually declined, although he did make something of a comeback in the late New Kingdom with three pharaohs, beginning with Sety I (c. 1294–1279 BC), taking his name. By about the late Third Intermediate Period (c. 800 BC), he became thoroughly demonized.

In practical terms, this meant that the animals linked to Seth, especially the *shai*, the pig, and the *deb*, the hippopotamus, but also the donkey, the crocodile, the antelope, the goat, many types of fish and birds and reddish animals in general became taboo or their taboo condition was amplified. Pigs, donkeys and hippos were never mummified. During the Ptolemaic Period (c. 332–32 BC), at the annual Edfu Temple Festival of Victory, cakes in the form of a hippopotamus were cut up and eaten to signify the total destruction of Seth. Of course, the problem and the inextricable confusion in all this was that many of these animals were also incarnated in popular, beneficial gods and goddesses as totem emblems in many nomes and many of them were staple foods.

The black pig was one of the totemistic emblems of Seth of Ombos in his conflict with the falcon emblem/totem of Horus of Hierakonpolis, Khem (Letopolis) and Pe-Dep (Buto). This alone would have made the pig taboo, unclean, for the people of Hierakonpolis and other falcon Horus cities. However, the pig taboo became generalized throughout Egypt because Seth had taken the form of a black pig when he blinded Horus' left eye in one of their many battles.

This pig taboo was particularly strong in the Lower Egyptian Second Nome capital of Letopolis, where Horus took the form of *Khenty-irty*, the god "who has two eyes," after going through a *Mekekhenty-er-irty* phase, "without eyes," as the god of the blind. In Coffin Text Spell 157, Re declared that "The pig is detestable to Horus...the detestation of the pig came about for Horus' sake by the gods who are in his suite."[11] (The Coffin Texts were magical spells inscribed on inside of coffins of notables, first used in the Sixth Dynasty (c. 2345–2181 BC) and then generalized during the Middle Kingdom (c. 2055–1650 BC). Of course, detestation or no detestation, pigs were abundant, were a staple food of the peasants, were widely used to trod seeds into freshly ploughed land and even some temples raised them, presumably as food for their workers, servants and slaves. It is therefore no surprise that Coffin Text Spell 158 notes: "Not to be said when eating pork."[12]

---

11. Faulkner, R.O., *The Ancient Egyptian Coffin Texts*, Vol. I, p. 135.

Herodotus, in *Histories*, told much the same story of 5th century BC Egypt. He stated that pigs were so abhorred by Egyptians that if somebody "touches a hog in passing, he goes to the river and dips himself in it, clothed as he is" and that no Egyptian would "give a swineherd his daughter in marriage, nor take a wife from their women; but swineherds intermarry among themselves." Nevertheless, he notes that pigs were also sometimes ritually sacrificed and their flesh eaten on these occasions, "but they will not taste it on any other day."[13]

The most curious and complicated contradiction between totem and taboo animals was probably the crocodile, the *meseh*. Revered, detested or feared, it was better to have the crocodile on your side. The crocodile was a very old and basically chthonian totem and (in the form of the crocodile or crocodile-headed figure) god of the waters and fertility, Sobek.

The crocodile was widely feared for obvious reasons in ordinary, everyday life along the Nile. One of the reasons people worshipped the fearful Sobek was not to be destroyed, much as the Hindus worshipped Shiva. It is no coincidence that there were shrines for Sobek at places along the Nile, like Gebelein and Gebel el-Silsila in southern Egypt, where attacks by crocodiles were feared. The crocodile was also dreaded as one of the horrible monster-demon guardians in the *Duat* afterlife/underworld who, if not handled with the correct magic, could prevent a person from attaining eternal life. Geb, the earth god and father of Osiris, sometimes took a malefic crocodile form in the *Duat*. Furthermore, a crocodile was one of the companion god-animals of the evil god Seth, the crocodile whom the good god and divine hunter Horus killed; and the great demon of chaos, *Aapep* (Apophis), usually represented as a snake, was sometimes represented as a crocodile.

However, Sobek was also a form of Re as a beneficial sun god and frequently linked to the reigning pharaoh because of his awesome strength. The crocodile ate fish, an unclean animal for the priests and the pharaoh. Taweret, the goddess of childbirth and protectress of pregnant women, was widely revered; her composite makeup was partially crocodile and sometimes a crocodile was placed on her back (and of course, she was also a hippo).

The result of this mythological mishmash was a mishmash of totem and taboo. The crocodile became the revered emblem/totem animal of the *She-resy/*Fayum oasis region (and its capital was accordingly renamed Crocodilopolis by

---

12. *Ibid.*, p. 137.
13. Herodotus, *Books I-II*, 2.47.

the Greeks) and was also sacred in Gebel el-Silisa, Ombos, Denderah and Athribis. Several pharaohs in the 12th and 13th Dynasties (c. 1985–1725 BC) took Sobek/crocodile names. Crocodiles were bred in the sacred pool of the Fayum Temple. In Fayum, Ombos and Denderah, during the Late Period, they were mummified and buried in necropolises. Meanwhile, the people in Elephantine ate crocodiles, which must have been completely incomprehensible for the people of Fayum. In Edfu, the city of Horus, the crocodile was a hated, hunted, taboo animal, associated with Sobek and Seth, and was subject to execration rituals, spells and slaughter. From the New Kingdom, two clay statues of crocodiles were annually cursed and destroyed. From the Late Period, cippi, small talisman steles, frequently of Horus, have been found in Edfu and elsewhere portraying Horus standing triumphantly on two crocodiles, that is, Horus standing on Seth, Horus who has defeated Seth. Cippi, linked to defeating malefic forces, were widely used as protective talismans against dangerous reptiles, insects and other animals.

Fish, *ienet*, were another prime example of a mishmash in taboo and totem. Fish were a major element in the staple diet of the peasants despite the fact that they were generally considered to be unclean and sometimes associated with Seth. Ceremonies of "trampling the fish" took place in Edfu and other cities. On the positive side, the *schilbe* carp fish was the Predynastic sacred totem emblem of the city of Banebdjedet (Mendes) linked to the fish goddess Hatmehyt. The *lates* fish, linked to the sky, war, household crafts and dream guardian goddess Neith, was also sacred in Esna, which the Greeks accordingly renamed Latopolis. In the Late Period, in both Mendes and Esna, fish were mummified and buried. The Esna fish necropolis was exceptionally vast. An amuletic fish could also protect against drowning and the bulti fish symbolized rebirth.

Crustaceans, and notably the scorpion, were among the most hated, feared and evil animals. However, divinities like the goddesses Serqet and Hededet were protective scorpion goddesses, Isis and her child Horus/ Harpakhrad were protected by seven scorpion guards, and two Predynastic kings had scorpion names. Oysters symbolized health. The belemnite fossil shell may have been one of the early fetishes and totemistic emblems of the fertility god Min (*Menu*) before he was linked to a white bull. The Min belemite — if it was indeed a belemite, for there are several other interpretations of the odd design depicting Min on a palette dating to c. 3100 BC (now in the British Museum) — was integrated into the emblem/totem of the Ninth Upper Egyptian Nome of *Khent-Min* (Akhmim, Khemmis Panopolis).

The snake or the serpent, *djet*, was still another example of fundamental totemistic and religious ambiguity. Some snakes represented beneficial gods or goddesses (Wadjit), protected gods, or were used by them; and other snakes represented abominable gods and demons (notably Apophis and Seth) and were indeed snakes in the grass, enemies of the gods and man. Of course, not only in Egypt but throughout the world, the snake is one of the oldest chthonian symbols associated both with the supposedly taboo dark, demonic forces of the earth and wily behavior and savage aggressiveness and the totem beneficial forces of fertility, the sun, wisdom, transformation and resurrection.

The uraeus snake, the eye of the sun, was a key symbol and protector of royalty and as the fiery eye of the sun god Re, it could spray enemies with fire. Uraei also flanked both sides of the falcon-winged sun disk, the early Behdety form of Horus. The snake goddess *Mertseger*, "the friend of silence" (the friend of the dead), a form of the goddess Hathor, was the protector of the Theban Valley of Kings necropolis. The snake *Mehen* protected Re in his battle with the most terrifying of all the snakes, the giant *Aapep* (Apophis). Apophis was the key symbol of possible chaos and basic evil. Apophis had to be defeated every day before dawn by the sun god Re if the sun was to rise and life continue; drawings and wax figurines of snakes were burned to help Re.

Snakes were revered and feared, detested and hunted and then from the New Kingdom (beginning c. 1550 BC), hacked to pieces in model clay forms representing Seth, but also mummified. In short, snakes were divine or close to the divine, including the demonic snakes.

EGYPT'S ROYALTY AND THE TABOO OF INCEST

The taboo of incest is particularly interesting concerning Egypt. Although Freud believed that the taboo of incest based on the Oedipus complex was the act which founded the "collective neurosis" that is religion, this theory is open to considerable criticism concerning religion in general and Egypt in particular. It is evident that incest of all types, including son/mother incest, was frequent among the gods in many religious mythologies and that the interdiction of incest, seemingly a prime taboo, was not present either in Egyptian mythology or in royal practices. There is an enormous contradiction between the pharaohs' habitual practice of incest of all types (notably the marriage to sisters, but also sometimes to daughters) and Freud's theory that the taboo of incest was derived from the interdiction of incest by the father/leader.

What we find in Egypt was a glorification of brother/sister and son/mother incest, seen as the *perfectly natural* practice for gods and goddesses and pharaohs. Were this not a serious book, I would quite simply say that in ancient Egypt being a *kamutef*, "the bull of his mother," the bull/son consort of the mother/celestial cow, like the gods Re, Osiris, Amun-Min and others, was an eminent honor for a god. Moreover, for gods, goddesses, and the pharaohs and their entourages, brother/sister incest was in the natural order of things and father/daughter incest was frequent. Both Freud and Carl Gustav Jung (1856–1961) seem to have intentionally ignored or underestimated these realities.

In the main Egyptian creation myth — the Heliopolitan — the universe and mankind could not have been created without incest. The twins, Shu, the god of dryness, the atmosphere between the earth and the sky and the personification of sunlight, and Tefnut, the goddess of moisture and the eye of the sun, and their children, Geb the earth god and Nut the sky goddess, are all brother/sister/husband/wife couples, as were Osiris and Isis, the children of Geb and Nut. Osiris was also the lover of his other sister Nephthys (*Nebt-Het*). Osiris was sometimes referred to as "the father of his fathers" and according to *The Songs of Isis and Nephthys* (in the Bremner-Rhind Papyrus, written about 312 BC), Osiris was "a son who opened the body" (of his mother Nut). Nut herself was sometimes referred to as "the mother of her father" and "the daughter of her son." Horus was the son/husband of Hathor. In the Osirisian cycle, where Isis is Horus' mother, some magical spells say he "had intercourse with his mother Isis"![14] (Jung saw Horus as an archetype of the ambiguous son/lover/husband.) In Mendes, the goddess Hatmehyt is the mother/wife of Banebdjedet. One of the main titles of the virility and fertility god Min was *Menu-kamutef*, "Min, the bull of his mother." Min became an aspect of Amun, Egypt's great chief god in the New Kingdom (from c. 1550 BC) and they were sometimes referred to as Amun-Min-*Kamutef*. This list can be continued almost endlessly.

It is nevertheless difficult to decide whether godly and pharaonic incest constitutes a major invalidation of Freud's theories. Perhaps it represented the special privilege of royal, divine leaders, a voluntary, arrogant violation by the powerful, or the exceptions that proved that the rule existed. And a de facto rule

---

14. Borghouts, J. F., *Ancient Egyptian Magical Texts*, p. 88. From the Magical Harris Papyrus in the British Museum (10042).

did exist in Egypt, since the exogamous relationship was the norm for all classes in Egyptian society except for the pharaoh-god and his family. Yet unless one confers some kind of enormous overriding value and impact on the option of divine right and exception, it would seem that the taboo of incest should have been the general rule among the gods and pharaohs (whose origins, according to Freud, were so deeply rooted in the taboo of incest concerning the clan father). In fact, for the gods, goddesses, and the pharaohs and their entourages, it is not really possible to speak about oedipal desires, since they were not desires but fully assumed and openly expressed and exalted tenets of Egyptian religion and mythology.

Moreover, Freud's theories do not take into sufficient account the thirst for meaning that is part of man's nature, conscious, unconscious, collectively unconscious or social. Certainly the search for meaning, even if it was meaning through magic, seems evident from very early times in Egypt. In particular, meaning for the Egyptians implied a search for a solution to the problem of death. A clear illustration of the transformation of man's and society's needs into religious laws can be found in the history of mankind in Egypt. A huge proportion of early art and texts indicates that this was exactly what occurred in ancient Egypt — a system of meaning which, politically, meant the foundation of a united, theocratic, sacred nation; socially it led to precise, sanctified regulations concerning the role of all classes and men and women in society; and technologically it went hand in hand with the adoption of a religion favoring and sanctifying agriculture, irrigation and the Nile river.

However, even if some of Freud's views seem far-fetched, his general emphasis on totemism and taboos are indeed pertinent in many ways. Aspects of totemism and taboos seem to have played roles in the origins of Egyptian religion and many of their applications were remarkably persistent throughout its history. Freud's explanation concerning both the transformation of the primordial father, the great, first ancestor, into a totem god-the-father and the invention of divine kingship also seem highly apposite. Early Egyptian history seems to provide verification concerning both these points with primogenitor gods like Atum and the institution of the omnipotent father-like pharaoh-god.

Any fair examination of any religion must take into account the theories elaborated by psychoanalysis and sociology concerning the possible origins of religion and how they developed. Because of the antiquity of the Egyptian religion and the fact that no other early civilization has left us such an abundance of religious art, architecture and texts, the role of totemism and the origins of more elaborate religion concerning gods, theology, mythology, beliefs, taboos and societal organization are probably more traceable in Egypt than in any other society. Ancient Egypt is therefore an ideal terrain not only for the study of one of the major religions in history, but for a plunge into the origins of religion and into man's vast capacities of imagination.

HUMAN SACRIFICE AND ANIMAL SACRIFICE

Human sacrifice, linked to fertility, the appeasement of the divine forces, and expiation, was unquestionably widespread in all prehistoric societies. Cannibalism involving the eating of human flesh for reasons of necessity in times of food shortages and for reasons of taste probably preceded religious human sacrifice and religious cannibalism.

In raw form, and then linked to fire, human and animal sacrifices as burnt offerings to the gods and/or as totemistic meals may have been among the first elaborate rituals of most religions. The totemistic meal — the eating of the flesh and the drinking of the blood — of a sacrificed victim, human or animal, to absorb the victim's powers, seems to have had two forms: the evil or courageous enemy victim and the pure, innocent victim or the important victim.

The culminating point of the ritual of absorbing the qualities of the pure, innocent victim seems to have been the simulated — or according to some, like the esoteric teacher G.I. Gurdjieff (1866?–1949) — the real eating of the flesh and drinking of the blood of the most innocent victim of all, the "divine" Jesus, in order to supposedly establish with Jesus and his apostles "a connection between 'astral bodies' [which would not be] broken by death."[15] Of course, for the early Christians, the crucifixion of Jesus was a voluntary expiatory sacrifice.

The expiatory sacrifice of the innocent victim, without a totemistic meal, was one of the main methods of atoning, and appeasing the gods, and can be traced in most early societies including the Sumerian, Indian, Hebrew, African, Greek and Roman. In sheer numbers of people sacrificed, and at the very late date of AD 1487 when they founded the Tenochtitlán Temple City, the Mexican Aztecs seem to have gone furthest in the religious sadism of human sacrifice, with some sources stating that 60,000 prisoners were sacrificed and eaten.

---

15. Ouspensky, P.D., *In Search Of The Miraculous, Fragments of an Unknown Teaching*, Harcourt, Brace & World, 1949, pp. 96-98.

The preferred pure, innocent victims in most ancient societies were children and especially virgin girls; this was widely practiced in Amerindian societies. The ultimate important victim, the proof that in dire circumstances a leader was ready to atone for supposed faults and appease and manipulate the gods with the sacrifice of what was dearest to him, was the sacrifice of the leader's heir. This type of sacrifice was common throughout the ancient agricultural Middle East and two sacrifices of sons are noted in the Bible — King Ahaz of Judah (c. 735–720 BC) and King Manasseh of Judah (c. 687–642 BC); another by King Mesha of Moab (fl.c. 850 BC) is noted on the Moabite Stone (now in the Louvre Museum).

On the other hand, the sacrifice of enemies or foreigners in almost all early societies constituted both an appeasement offering to the gods and the possibility of totally wiping out the soul of an enemy in addition to the opportunity of acquiring the victim's qualities through totemistic cannibalism.

Fundamentally different from human sacrifice, be it of one's own people or of enemies, as appeasement offerings to the gods, was funerary sacrifice. In Egypt, Mesopotamia and everywhere it was practiced, it involved the notion of accompanying and continuing to serve a leader or a hero in the afterlife.

There is no clear evidence of the sacrifice of pure, innocent victims in Egypt, but labels from the reigns of Aha (c. 3100 BC) and Djer (c. 3000 BC) seem to depict forms of ritual sacrifice. It is unclear whether the victims were Egyptian or foreigners. Funerary sacrifice in which some of the officials and the servants, the *bakew*, of a ruler were sacrificed at his death was apparently practiced throughout the First Dynasty (c. 3100–2890 BC). Funerary human sacrifice was frequent throughout the history of Egypt's vassal state of Nubia and continued there right into Christian times between about AD 350 and 700.

Dozens of servants and slaves seem to have being sacrificed and buried near First Dynasty (c. 3100–2890 BC) rulers in Thinis/Abydos and Memphis, presumably so they could work for the king in the afterlife. It is reasonably established that at least 20 of Pharaoh/"Queen" Merneith's (c. 2950 BC) servants were sacrificed and buried alongside her in her Abydos and Memphis tombs.

After 3000 BC, statuettes of human figures were broken in mock sacrifice in what may have been a type of substitute for human sacrifice. Nevertheless, care must be exercised in such an analysis since we know that a similar magical technique was used at least from about the Sixth Dynasty (c. 2345–2181 BC), but probably from much earlier, for the opposite purpose — to cast a death spell against enemies. A large amount of smashed and buried human figurines and

41

pottery inscribed with so-called "execration texts" have been found. Here, the hope clearly was that named enemies, and notably foreign enemies, would die. The sacrifice or ritual execution of foreign enemies, usually Nubian and West Asian prisoners, seen as representing chaos, took place throughout most of Egyptian history.

There is some slim evidence, engraved on seals, that in these same Early Dynastic times (c. 3100–2686 BC) the Egyptians may have begun seeing the sacrifice of animals as a way of replacing human sacrifice, much as the later Hebrews seem to have done. The Greek priest/philosopher Plutarch (AD c. 45–125), in *Isis And Osiris*, reported an old tradition (related by the first century BC Greek historian Castor) of placing "a mark" on the sacrificed animal which "bore an engraving of a man with his knee on the ground and his hands tied behind his back, and with a sword at his throat."[16] In any case, the end of both ritual and servant human sacrifice occurred in Egypt at an early date compared to most West Asian Early Bronze Age agricultural societies.

The replacement of the killing, or sacrifice, of the primordial father by the killing of an animal in the totemistic clan might be, as Freud supposed, at least one of the bases of animal sacrifice. Surely stronger than such vague memories of the primordial father, as represented by his totem animal, were the pragmatic facts that the fetish animals (or animal emblems) of rival clans were feared, but ritually sacrificing and eating them meant not only assimilating their powers but pleasing one's own fetish animal-god. As in all totemistic or strongly totemistically influenced societies, in Egypt the ritual sacrifice of a rival animal totem meant killing an animal-god, the enemy of one's own animal-god. Such a sacrifice could only be carried out by priests and in everyday circumstances the enemy animal was unclean, unfit to be eaten as food by priests and was tolerated as food for ordinary people because it did not matter much what they ate.

In many ancient societies, the taboo of eating one's own totem emblem animal was lifted, usually once a year, to enable the communion with and assimilation of this animal's (god's) soul and powers. Freud believed that this practice of a totemistic meal was also an unconscious commemoration of the murder of the primordial father/leader. This type of taboo lifting sacrifice and totemistic meal does not seem to have been prevalent in Egypt, but it may have existed as an unconscious motive during the abundant animal sacrifices in the many annual festivals, notably during the New Kingdom. (Of course, the

---

16. Plutarch, *Moralia*, Volume V, *Isis and Osiris*, p. 77.

concept of an annual lifting of taboo (in innocuous form) still persists in our modern day carnivals.)

Early Egypt, although it practiced it in various forms, seems to have emerged as an early exception to the general trends in human sacrifice. Something fundamentally changed in relation to man's attitude toward human sacrifice, together with the elaboration of the notion that it could be replaced by animal sacrifice; just when and why this change took place cannot be answered satisfactorily in Egypt or elsewhere. Our strongest textual evidence that something had indeed changed in Egypt dates to the Middle Kingdom (beginning c. 2055 BC) and refers to an event in the Old Kingdom. It is the story of *The Magician Djedi* (in the Westcar Papyrus, now in the Berlin Ägyptisches Museum).

The papyrus relates how an old magician Djedi, despite the tempting promise of the Old Kingdom Pharaoh Khufu (Cheops, c. 2551–2528 BC) of a reward of great food and a great place in the *Duat* afterlife, refused to endanger the life of a human being. Djedi admitted that he was able to magically put back a man's head which had been cut off and that the man could live as before; but he refused to do so for the prisoner whom Cheops wanted to behead for a demonstration. Djedi humbly informed the Pharaoh that such a thing should not be done to a human being, somebody who belongs to "the noble cattle" (mankind).[17] Then, after three geese, an ox and a lion were beheaded, Djedi magically put back their heads and they lived. In much the same way, in Hebrew mythology, Abraham seems to have substituted a ram for his son Isaac.

In his account of the Osiris myth, in *Isis and Osiris*, Plutarch noted that "one of the first acts" of Osiris when he became ruler of Egypt was "to deliver the Egyptians from their destitute and brutish manner of living."[18] The British Egyptologist E.A. Wallis Budge (1857–1934) firmly believed that the rise of "The cult of Osiris set a curb on the cannibalistic tendencies of the Egyptians, but did not eradicate them, any more than it put a stop to human sacrifice and funeral murders."[19] Given the myth of the *civilizing* project of Osiris and the clear evidence of the widespread use of animals rather than humans (except for foreigners) in ritual sacrifices after the rise of the Osiris cult, by at least the Fifth Dynasty (c. 2494 — 2345 BC), this view seems to be partially plausible.

---

17. Lichtheim, Miriam, *Ancient Egyptian Literature, Volume 1*, p. 219.
18. Plutarch, *Moralia*, Volume V, *Isis and Osiris*, p. 35.
19. Budge, E.A.Wallis, *Osiris & The Egyptian Resurrection, Volume I*, p. 197.

However, when comparing Budge's view to available artistic and textual evidence, it seems that Budge exaggerated the continued extent of human sacrifice in Egypt.

The value of ritual appeasement sacrifices to curry the favors of Osiris as god of the afterlife rapidly became essential. Black pigs, goats, antelopes, or ducks were sacrificed because they were linked to Seth, who had killed Osiris. These sacrifices were carried out methodically and with great virulence. Several days in the year were set aside as festivals for killing Seth animals. In addition to the more or less usual and "normal" forms of slaughter of sacrificial animals, black pigs were hacked to pieces and birds and fish trampled to death as spells were recited, hymns sung and sistra clanged. The sacrifice of animals as food offerings for the dead — especially the ox, which was the Egyptians' favorite sacrificial animal — also played a key role in the funerals of people who could afford the entirety of the rituals which opened the way to the afterlife. Sacrifices of turtles, seen as being archenemies of the Sun god Re, were also frequent. One of the rituals practiced by the pharaoh was the stabbing of a turtle in the presence of Re.

However, the sacrifice of many species of animals was frequently extraordinarily ambiguous because of the extravagant contradictions between totem and taboo animals. Moreover, in all the Egyptian ritual animal sacrifices, except those directly related to Seth, repentance for killing an animal and its soul and a festive atmosphere coexisted. The animal to be sacrificed was decorated and incantations were recited. As to the feast, it was the priests who stood to gain most — since it was they who heartily ate most of the animal after the gods had consumed the invisible essence of the sacrifice and those who had offered the animals tasted it.

Perhaps a ritual confirmation of the ending of the practice of sacrificing people, which was often done so that they would accompany and work for a pharaoh or other notable in the afterlife, occurred in the Middle Kingdom (from c. 2055 BC) with the invention of the *ushabti* ("the answerers"). These *ushabti* statuettes were buried with the dead and magically did all their work in the afterlife. *Ushabti*-like figurines have also been found in Old Kingdom tombs, possibly indicating that this replacement idea was already germinating or emerging a few hundred years earlier.

It would seem that a whole set of factors ranging from the demonization of some dangerous animals and animals linked to Seth, fervor to please gods like Osiris and Re, the invention of the *ushabti* and a concern for the sacredness of human life — at least, a concern for Egyptian life, although not for foreigners — motivated the early Egyptians to end human sacrifice. Egypt appears to have been among the first societies to end the practice of sacrificing its own people to the gods.

CHAPTER 2.
THE EARLY TECHNOLOGICAL CONTEXT

SUMERIAN-TYPE INFLUENCES

Before the Neolithic Revolution reached Egypt, by about 5800 BC, Egypt seems to have been part of a fairly consistent cultural and technological zone all along the Nile River down into central and east Africa (although this remains difficult to definitively affirm due to the scanty available knowledge about Africa). By about 5800 BC, the main aspects of the Neolithic Revolution existed in Egypt — farming, animal raising, pottery and the beginnings of sedentary life. Agriculture probably arrived from West Asia and Mesopotamia (where it emerged from about 8500 BC). However, it is also possible that Neolithic agricultural values reached Egypt from Libya in the west and/or the African southern Nile Valley, where a transient period of proto-agriculture occurred in Nubia from c. 1200–10,000 BC during the Qadan Period. Over the next 2500 years, from c. 5800 BC, Egyptian Neolithic development was slower than in Asia. The key inventions of copper mining and copper smelting were introduced around 4000 BC from West Asia. Egypt mastered these techniques, but did not surpass the skill of Sumer.

It seems likely that Egypt, Libya and northern Nubia shared some common cultural and technological values at least until the end of the Naqada I Period (c. 4000–3500 BC), also called Amratian. Using the word "equipment" in which he includes "wardrobe," "penis-sheaths," "feathers" and elements of "royal insignia," A.H. Gardiner (1879-1963) — author of the magisterial *Egypt of the Pharaohs* —

tentatively concludes "that as regards equipment, which does not necessarily imply race, there was an affinity between Libyans, Egyptians and Nubians which confirms...the earliest culture of the Nile Valley as essentially African."[20]

Some archaeological finds indicate that the break away from the African cultural and technological zone and accentuated contacts with West Asia began before 3500 BC. After this break, Egypt's type of development in Naqada II, or Gerzean A (c. 3500–3300 BC), was culturally and technologically closer to the West Asian than to any other type of system. The following period, Naqada III (c. 3300–3150 BC), also known as Gerzean B, marked Egypt's final sprint from prehistory to history.

It seems certain that at any time between 4000 and 2600 BC, Egypt was still a relatively underdeveloped society compared to the world leader Sumer and the Sumerian West Asian zone of influence.

In Sumer, there were big villages (Eridu, Uruk, Ur, Lagash and Nippur) with temples earlier than 4000 BC and cities by 3500 BC with thriving craftsmen and merchants. By 3100 BC, Uruk was probably the biggest city in the world with perhaps as many as 25,000 people. Intensive agriculture was in full swing, pictographic writing was extensively used by the Sumerian elite and the land was being organized into city-states led by *ensi* ("great men"), rulers who presided over assemblies of elders.

With the exception of cities ruled by "great men," most aspects of this type of development did not exist in Egypt during these periods. There were permanent settlements in Egypt around 4000 BC, particularly in the south in the zone stretching from Hierakonpolis to Matmar, and in the north, at Gerza, Maadi, Omari and Buto, but as far as can be ascertained they did not match the extent of sedentary life in Mesopotamia. By 3100 BC, Egypt's great cities like Hierakonpolis, Abydos, Buto and Heliopolis probably had populations of less than 5000; Memphis was just being founded and Thebes was not even a village before the opening of the Old Kingdom (c. 2686 BC).

How did Egypt's break with Africa and the beginnings of its West Asian type of development occur? The archaeological evidence is insufficient to prove either an early Egyptian development totally dependent on Sumer and West Asia or a completely independent development. However, totally independent development was unlikely and at the least it seems difficult not to conclude that the West Asian zone significantly influenced early Egypt culturally, religiously,

20. Gardiner, Alan, *Egypt of the Pharaohs*, p. 392.

technologically and demographically. However, the debate on this subject remains ongoing with some Egyptologists asserting that Egypt did it all on its own.

Although the Egyptians later developed a solid hatred for the *Aamu*, or the *Setyu*, the Asians, in the Predynastic Period and right into the Old Kingdom (beginning c. 2686 BC), they already seem to have believed that the frontier between Asia and Africa was the eastern edge of the Nile Valley. It seems certain that while in conventional geographical terms Egypt was African, its cultural, religious, technological, economic and societal framework was more similar to a West Asian than an African model, at least from the late fourth millennium BC. Egypt virtually became a part of the West Asian sphere, albeit as an arrogant island in the sphere. The passing centuries accentuated both Egypt's participation in the West Asian sphere and its arrogant scorn for the "vile" Asians. By the New Kingdom (c. 1550 BC), like it or not — and the Egyptians usually did not like it — Egypt was part of a West Asia/Egypt continuum.

The period after 3100 BC, after the unification of Upper and Lower Egypt and up to the opening of the Old Kingdom (c. 2686 BC), was an era of stupendous changes which anchored Egypt's cultural separation from Nubia and Africa. Egypt was transformed into one of the most advanced societies in the world. She became a leader in many key areas — irrigation and intensive agriculture, urban life, Early Bronze Age implements, pictograms and then writing, the invention of a fairly efficient 12-month/365-day/24-hour calendar, the beginnings of centralized political organization and the beginnings of polytheistic religion with pantheons and chief gods. But at this time, Egypt continued to lag behind Sumer and other regions such as the Levant, Crete, Cyprus, Anatolia concerning trade, transport and technology in general, and bronze smelting in particular.

No Sumerian "Dynastic Race"

At least the catalyst of Egypt's sudden advance may have been a wave of Asian immigrants or invaders, the misnamed "Dynastic Race" of broad-headed peoples from West Asia, perhaps beginning after 3500 BC during the Gerzean A Predynastic Period and continuing sporadically into the late third millennium BC. At the same time, there also seems to have been considerable immigration of broad-headed peoples from Libya.

The archaeological evidence of Mesopotamian influence in Egypt at this time — from technology to architecture to art, seems to be too extensive to exclude a large presence of Sumerians or Levantines. These immigrants, or invaders, carrying Sumerian-type advanced agricultural and urban values, might have been mostly Semitic from Levantine Palestine/Syria rather than from Sumer itself. More than 400 objects of Palestinian origin were found in 1988 in the Predynastic (before c. 3100 BC) U-J Tomb in the Abydos "Mother of Pots" Necropolis.

However, there is no way to establish a fundamental Sumerian catalyst with certitude. There is even less support for the thesis of a "dynastic race," which most Egyptologists reject.

To begin with, the fusion of several ethnic types, including the broad-headed type, into the Egyptian type had probably already taken place before 3500 BC, as we shall soon see. A good case can also be made for the theory that there were rulers of at least parts of both southern and northern Egypt and rulers of groups of nomes in the south and in the north before the establishment of the First Dynasty around 3100 BC. This makes it doubtful that a new broad-headed type suddenly became the dynastic rulers of Egypt around 3100 BC, although an Egyptologist like W.B. Emery (1903–1971) could make such a claim. In *Archaic Egypt*, Emery postulated that broad-headed "invaders" whose "racial origin is not known" and whose "difference being so marked that any suggestion that these people derived from the earlier stock is impossible" meant that "the people known traditionally as 'The Followers of Horus' (the *Shemsu-Hor*) apparently formed a civilized aristocracy or master race ruling over the whole of Egypt." Emery believed that both Egypt and Mesopotamia had been influenced in their leap towards civilization by a similar source.[21]

There is no doubt that broad-headed Asians were constantly drifting into Egypt along the difficult but feasible 90-mile route in the Sinai from El Arish to Kantara to Pelusium (Tell Farama) and probably also across the Red Sea. The remains of broad-headed people dating from before 3100 BC which have been found in northern Upper Egypt contrast sharply with the remains of presumably indigenous long-headed people with less sturdy bodies found in both the north and the south. However, none of this is sufficient to assume "a master race" as

---

21. Emery, W.B., *Archaic Egypt*, Penguin Books, Harmondsworth, U.K., 1961, pp. 31-40 and 71-73.

Emery extravagantly does, rather than a mixture of ethnic groups and perhaps a catalyst coming from some of them.

Some Egyptologists, and notably A.H. Gardiner in *Egypt of the Pharaohs*, Cyril Aldred (1914–1991) in *The Egyptians* and Donald B. Redford (b. 1934) in *Egypt, Canaan and Israel In Ancient Times*, while basically rejecting the "Dynastic Race" theory, conclude that there must have been Mesopotamians in Egypt during the Gerzean Period (c. 3500–3100 BC).

Gardiner notes that "there seems good reason to think, the dynastic civilization owed much to Mesopotamian influence" and "nothing less than an infiltration into Egypt of Mesopotamian craftsmen can account for the introduction, at the threshold of Dyn. I, of the striking architectural and artistic innovations...Indirect trade relations are clearly insufficient...while actual invasion seems too much too assume."[22] Redford agrees that "there must have been more than Mesopotamian "intermittent and casual trade" and "incursions," but also that a "human component of alien origin is to be sought in the Gerzean demography of Egypt."[23]

Aldred, like many Egyptologists, sees "vigorous contacts from Western Asia" which led to "significant [technological] introductions" including writing, being "ultimately" traceable "to a Mesopotamia source, particularly to the Jemdet Nasr culture which extended as far as Syria by the end of the 4th millennium BC...These innovations coincided with a drift of broad-headed peoples, perhaps originally from Syria-Palestine, by way of the Nile Delta, into the Upper Egyptian sites, where they modified the slight, long-headed indigenes. Such immigration...does not necessarily indicate a military conquest."[24]

Nevertheless, many Egyptologists limit Mesopotamian influence to the cultural sphere and base it on trade relations rather than on a physical presence. The French Egyptologist Nicholas Grimal (b. 1948), author of *A History of Ancient Egypt*, perhaps the best history of Egypt since Gardiner, of course rejects the theory of a Mesopotamian invasion of Egypt, but he also resolutely rejects any Mesopotamian influence on Egypt, including cultural influence, and opts "for a slow process of evolution and not, as was long imagined, a brutal revolution involving the simultaneous appearance of new technology [essentially metallurgy] and new social structures [organization into agriculturally-based

---

22. Gardiner, Alan, *Egypt of the Pharaohs*, p. 36 and 397.
23. Redford, Donald B., *Egypt, Canaan and Israel in Ancient Times*, pp. 17- 24.
24. Aldred, Cyril, *The Egyptians*, p. 77.

cities and the proliferation of mud-brick buildings and writing]." Grimal rejects anything more than "commercial links" between Egypt and Mesopotamia, similar to those which Mesopotamia "also clearly established with Syria-Palestine, Libya and the African regions to the south of Egypt."[25]

On the whole, even if the debate cannot be closed as easily as Grimal postulates, it is indeed excessive to speak of a "Dynastic Race," either in northern or southern Egypt. Aside from a few northern cities like Buto, most of the advanced and major Egyptian cities during the Predynastic Period, like Hierakonpolis, Abydos/Thinis and Naqada, were in the south and their populations were basically indigenous people. They had powerful indigenous Egyptian rulers and indigenous gods. Around 3100 BC, it was a southerner, Narmer or Aha (the legendary Menes?), perhaps the King of Hierakonpolis or Thinis of Upper Egypt, who united Upper and Lower Egypt under the aegis of Hierakonpolis' falcon god Horus.

Nevertheless, as unproven as it may remain, an abrupt, transient and decisive Sumerian-type influence does seem to be a good bet for explaining the beginning of Egypt's linked technological, cultural and religious leap forward. Despite dissenting views, the minimal hypothesis seems to be a special, a significant Sumerian-type influence on early Egypt, certainly involving cultural and technological imports and a significant immigration of broad-headed peoples from West Asia.

It is possible that Egypt borrowed more than some core elements of a more sophisticated religion from Sumer, or Sumerian-influenced West Asian people in the Levant (or Anatolia); its technology and art, which formed the context of its religious development, also seems to have been significantly influenced by West Asia. Some archaeological evidence suggests that the main axis of Sumerian-type influence — political, religious, technological and artistic — was towards southern Egypt, Upper Egypt, and at least not exclusively through the northern Pelusium-El-Arish-Kantara route. In any case, Upper Egypt seems to have been more evolved than Lower Egypt around c. 3100 and seems to have influenced change in Lower Egypt. But around 3100 BC, Egypt's overall development still remained considerably less advanced than Sumer's.

Sumerian technological influence could have included advanced agricultural methods and artificial irrigation, canal and dam technology and management, plows, more efficient methods of grinding and polishing stone, the

---

25. Grimal, Nicholas, *A History of Ancient Egypt*, p. 29.

elaboration of improved pottery methods and the potter's wheel, more elaborate mud brick structures including tombs, new tools and weapons, improved copper smelting, bronze smelting and casting, seals, pictograms, writing, spinning, weaving, the cart wheel, oared seagoing boats and the development of trade. In any case, all of these technological advances first appeared in Sumer before reaching Egypt.

There is an undeniable and striking resemblance between Sumerian and Egyptian art in style and content at the end of the pre-historic period from about 3300 to 3000 BC. Palettes, pottery, cylinder seals, vases, labels, knife handles and statuettes show the same motifs of intertwined animals, broad headed human figures with big eyes, accentuated sexual characteristics, and bound prisoners being beaten and executed. The oldest completely intact Egyptian work of art ever found: The Palette of Narmer (dating to c. 3100 BC and now in the Cairo Museum), is indicative of Egypt's general evolution at this time — somewhere in a transition between West Asian artistic values and its own emerging values. King Narmer, his followers, servants and Asiatic victims, the falcon Horus and the cow-head Hathor or Bat are stylistically Egyptian and the beasts are stylistically Sumerian.

However, it is also possible to speak of at least some similarity in artistic approach across a huge swath of territory from Sumer and Elam in the east to Egypt and Libya in the west — especially in the sculpting of figurines — raising the question of whether Egyptian art largely, or independently, surged from a wide common approach.

Bronze smelting and casting probably reached Egypt around 2700 BC. Anatolia and the Levant had opened the Early Bronze Age, by about 3100 BC, followed by Sumer. The key inventions of bronze alloying and casting led to an enormous improvement in the manufacture of hard, durable and more varied tools and weapons which in turn led to an enormous overall improvement in architecture, carpentry, boat building and many of the objects of daily life. Skill in bronze metallurgy became one of the main indicators of a society's status. Egypt's production in crafts gradually rivaled that of the Sumerian city-states. However, Sumer continued to lead the way in the key field of bronze alloying and in the manufacture of wheeled vehicles. And so despite Egypt's strong overall position, Sumer remained the technological leader of the time.

By the mid-27th century BC, Egypt made its own great, revolutionary invention, the use of stone for monumental architecture. Over the next 160 years, this led to the building of pyramids which remained the most massive and tallest religious structures in the world for the next few thousand years.

Nevertheless, if Sumer was more advanced than Egypt in general and if some other regions were more advanced than Egypt in trade, transport and bronze alloying, the relative overall advance of both Sumer and Egypt over the rest of the world around 3000 BC can easily be verified.

At this time, the Levant and Anatolia were still in a religious period dominated by mother goddesses and fertility cults; North Africa and southern Europe were just beginning village life; northern and central Europe were in a phase of transition from hunting to farming culture, were still flaking stone implements, and their religion was probably dominated by the veneration of ancestors; Asia, from India to Japan, was a mixed zone of farming, hunting and fishing and villages and towns; and sub-Saharan Africa, North and South America and Australia were still in a period basically dominated by hunting and food gathering with scattered agriculture and very little sedentary life.

The revolutionary nature of the transformation centered in Sumer, West Asia and Egypt from about 3500 to 3000 BC can be better understood by its most spectacular consequence — a rapid increase in population, especially sedentary and urban population. It is generally estimated that from about 3000 to 2000 BC, the world's population doubled to 27 million and almost doubled again to 50 million by 1000 BC. (These extraordinary increases are probably only comparable to the quadrupling of the world's population in our own 20th century).

The regions practicing intensive agriculture based on irrigation, like Mesopotamia and Egypt, played key roles in this fabulous percentage and numerical population increase accompanying the entry into high civilization. First in Sumer and then in Egypt, intensive agriculture also led to even more radical revolutions — accentuated labor specialization, class differentiation and accentuated domination of the male over the female.

Key consequences of intensive agriculture — in Sumer as in Egypt — were a thriving advanced agro-sedentary surplus producing economy — notably cereals — and for the first time, because of this new, complex economy, a need to keep accounting records. Surplus accounting probably led to the adoption of writing in Egypt around 3100 BC. For the same reason, probably a century or two earlier, the Mesopotamian/Sumerians in the city of Uruk had been the first to invent pictoglyphic writing — a system which directly portrayed and named objects, things, and their numbers, and ideas.

It seems logical to assume that Egyptian writing was the result of Sumerian influence on late Predynastic Egypt (from c. 3300 BC), but the evidence for such direct influence remains flimsy — the apparent anteriority of the Sumerian system, the similarity of the use of combined signs to produce meaning and phonetics, the presence of Sumerian-type cylinder seals found in several places, and a similar artistic style to pictographically relate events on palettes and slates.

Gardiner sees "hieroglyphic writing" emerging in Egypt around 3100 BC as "an offshoot of direct pictorial representation" which was "clearly distinguishable from the surrounding purely pictorial representations" and "[i]n this respect it resembled the original Babylonian script, and indeed it is not improbable that there was an actual relationship between them, though it may have amounted to no more that hearsay knowledge that the sounds of language could be communicated by means of appropriately chosen pictures."[26]

However, a very credible argument can also be made for the independent development of writing in Egypt. Nevertheless, it is probably far too much to conclude, as Nicholas Grimal does, that "The question of whether writing was imported into Egypt or evolved there is easily answered by a consideration of the representations on Naqada-period pottery which apparently chart the gradual stylization of the plants, animals and religious dances depicted, eventually resulting in a set of divine symbols that are virtually hieroglyphic signs..." [27]

It is certainly true that in addition to Naqada pottery, pictograms on various objects found in Predynastic sites in Abydos also indicate that there were attempts to communicate meaning with story lines; but once again, this process was used earlier in Sumer. It is self-evident, as Grimal notes, that "Hieroglyphic writing brought together the pictogram, the ideogram and the phonogram."[28] It is also evident that the same cause, surplus agriculture and the need for accounting, could also have led to the same effect of writing in Sumer and Egypt. And despite important similarities, Sumerian and Egyptian writing are fundamentally different systems, with the Sumerian employing vowels and syllables while the Egyptian does not.

---

26. Gardiner, Alan, *Egypt of the Pharaohs*, pp. 20 and 22.
27. Grimal, Nicholas, *A History of Ancient Egypt*, p. 31.
28. *Ibid.*, p. 33.

Sumerian influence on Egyptian hieroglyphic writing could therefore have been limited to the Egyptian adoption of the Sumerian device of putting spoken language into writing, but this seems to be the minimal conclusion.

Egypt's hieroglyphic system seems to have almost immediately invented signs for both ideas and sounds and by Pharaoh Djoser's time (c. 2667–2648 BC) it could accommodate complex phrases using less than about a thousand signs. It was also a far more aesthetic system of writing than the Sumerian. Hieroglyphics and their cursive hieratic and demotic forms were more perfected than either Sumerian early (c. 3300-3200 BC) pictographic or later (c. 2800 BC) cuneiform writing. Egypt also invented a more efficient medium for writing — papyrus rather than clay tablets — by at least about 2950 BC, as unused papyrus rolls have been found, in Sakkara, in what was probably the tomb of Hemaka (3035 BC), an official of Pharaoh Den. The papyrus roll seems to be at the origin of the book form of writing. These inventions represented considerable progress over the levels reached in Sumer.

Nevertheless, it was in the field of language that the successor states of Sumer consistently maintained a clear lead over Egypt. Except for Nubia and parts of West Asia, and this in a colonial context, hieroglyphic writing hardly extended beyond Egypt's borders in the third millennium. Akkadian, written in Sumerian cuneiform characters, became the lingua franca of international diplomacy and culture in the West Asian Continuum throughout much of the second millennium until the Phoenician form of script superseded it.

The Egyptians believed that sign images, ideas and sounds were sacred images at the service of the gods, that they were *medu netjer*, "the words of the gods." A sign image was not just writing, not just an object; it was real and sacred and could magically produce what it represented. Eventually, the *medu netjer* became a highly complicated system of pictograms, ideograms and phonograms of phonetic and syllabic representation, these last images being not necessarily linked to the content of the image. The Greeks called Egyptian writing *hierogluphikos*, "sacred carvings" and this is the term which has persisted.

The hieroglyphic system greatly facilitated the teaching of religious concepts among the elite, but its complexity rendered it useable only by the elite. In the third millennium this literate elite probably did not account for even one per cent of the population, with some estimates putting the percentage of literate people at less than 0.4 per cent.[29] From the end of the Early Dynastic

---

29. Shaw, Ian and Nicholson, Paul, *The Dictionary of Ancient Egypt*, p. 164.

Period (c. 2686 BC), the use of the cursive "hieratic" form to write hieroglyphs in a rounded way on papyri made writing easier and quicker, but writing still remained confined to the very few. The invention of alphabetic writing by the Phoenicians about 1300–1100 BC and its non-adoption by the Egyptians even raises the question as to whether at any time the powerful and privileged Egyptian scribes had an interest in adopting writing systems which were easier to use by a great number of people.

In addition to the obvious breakthrough of being able to record events, information, knowledge and ownership of objects, writing enabled unprecedented political, economic and religious centralization and control, facilitating communications among the elite and the domination by the few who knew how to read and write. It provided a far more efficient tool than oral expression for refining, diversifying, finalizing and transmitting mythology and theology. It created a new mode of intellectual and emotional functioning inevitably involving new ways of perceiving, relating and imagining reality and inner life.

The Revolution of True Polytheism and Chief God Theology

The new technology and culture seem necessarily to have engendered a new religion, as technology and culture have always done and continue to do. Just as the Upper Paleolithic Period (from c. 35,000 BP) was a hunting culture and practiced a religion centered on animals and perhaps a hunting magic religion, just as the culture of abstract reasoning led to authentic monotheism (from the 6th century BC) and as modern industrial societies (with logical, soulless or soul-free machines) tend towards atheism, in Egypt, technology and culture, and especially agricultural technology, led to the adoption of an agro-polytheistic religion.

It seems probable that the Sumerian technological influence not only on Egypt but on the entire Levant, including Syria and the later Israel, was accompanied by Sumerian religious influence. Egypt may have maintained many Sumerian religious principles virtually unchanged, carrying some of them to their logical conclusions and also going its own extraordinarily original way in other religious domains. Egypt also seems to have exercised considerable religious influence on its close neighbors, including Israel, but it never seems to have exercised much influence on the religion of Sumer and its successor states, not even in the most original of its religious innovations.

Broadly speaking, it seems that we have to look towards West Asia to better understand the religious leap which began in Egypt, probably before the opening of the Early Dynastic period (c. 3100 BC). Egypt gradually became part of an Eastern Mediterranean religious continuum, before becoming its leading religious edge after about 2500 BC.

The new agro-sedentary society, one of the greatest cultural transformations man had experienced until that time, naturally led to a new revolutionary religious structure — this structure was true, or authentic, polytheism. At least by the second half of the Fourth Millennium, in both Sumer and Egypt, perhaps earlier, two major religions of the polytheistic type had emerged, the Sumerian and the Egyptian. They were similar, but not identical.

The new polytheistic religion had to deal with, and structure, the huge upheaval and accumulation of Neolithic and Bronze Age technological innovations. It also had to deal with their consequences — the immense population explosion and the vast migratory movements it facilitated, prosperous surplus economies, a new societal, political and sexual gender order, labor specialization and class differentiation, theocracy and a clear domination of the male over the female. All these developments converged and were sanctified by agro-polytheistic religious dogma.

The key defining element in the emergence of true polytheism was neither the multiplicity of gods in polytheism, as in the earlier religions, nor the consolidation into an organized pantheon and system of a large number of local tutelary gods. They were not what clearly distinguished true polytheism from the earlier forms of religion. True polytheism above all began as the religion of the agro-sedentary peoples with a corresponding set of theological values favorable to the economy, the technologies, lifestyles and aspirations of these peoples. The new economic and societal modes were the prerequisites of the new polytheistic religions. Whereas before authentic polytheism, the functions of gods and goddesses seem to have been limited to fertility, maternity, virility and perhaps animal, hunting and star personifications, emerging authentic polytheism organized the functions of a vast number of local gods and goddesses into systems which covered all walks of life in the new agro-sedentary society. This was the road which we know that both Sumer and Egypt took and which was probably taken by several other societies at that time.

As we have seen, the early Egyptian Nile Valley religion mixed local tutelary emblem/totem animal and animal-headed gods — theriomorphic gods — widespread representations of animals, nature religion, animism, mother goddess and fertility beliefs, various magical, local ritual and cosmological concepts and primary agrarian beliefs.

These older forms of religion continued to flourish, but were largely transformed. Rituals, taboos, zoolatry and the most ancient of all instruments of religion, magic, subsisted in almost uncountable forms. They were accentuated into a sophisticated system which was probably more extensive than any before it and certainly than any after it. Aspects of totemism, in the forms of animal and plant emblems of identity, protection, reverence and fear and their consequential henotheistic animal-headed and plant gods remained particularly strong throughout the history of Egyptian religion. The survival of elements from the older religions was much stronger in Egypt than in Sumer. The Egyptian version of polytheism especially remained more strongly laced with aspects of indigenous totemism than the Sumerian, but both cultures maintained a widespread use of magic and both continued to strongly believe in the animistic concept that the elements of nature had will and personality.

Gods and goddesses linked to agricultural fertility and irrigation, the crafts and urban lifestyles and then chief gods won places alongside the older animist, nature, emblem/totem and henotheistic divinities. Pantheons of gods, which attempted to reflect the totality of the cosmos, nature and man, were organized.

Man's increased mastery of nature engendered an anthropomorphization of the gods, a tendency to represent gods in human rather than animal or plant form. This general tendency was particularly evident in Sumer, where the first pantheons seem to have already been strictly human, and particularly absent in Egypt, where a system of animal, animal-headed and anthropomorphic gods and goddesses was concurrently developed.

The Egyptian religious leap to a largely West Asian type of polytheistic agricultural-based religion seems to have been relatively rapid and intensive — it prevailed after about 3100 BC and was certainly completely achieved by the opening of the Old Kingdom, around 2686 BC.

The environmental, psychological and technological starting points for Egyptian cosmogony and religion were the same as in Sumer — the omnipotence of water, in everyday reality and in creation myths, and the harnessing of water, the harnessing of the great Tigris-Euphrates and Nile Rivers. The Sumerians believed in a primordial sea before creation, the *abzu*, and like them, the

Egyptians believed in an original liquid chaos or primordial ocean or abyss, the *waret*, which was mastered by creation. Water contained the origin of everything, a view which Thales (fl.c. 580 B.C), the Greek founder of philosophy and science, at least 2500 years later, placed at the center of his system... a view which modern science, of course, has largely verified. The gods harnessed the *waret* and man harnessed the rivers. The technology of harnessing water, first in Sumer and then in Egypt, by the invention of artificial canals and huge dams provided the irrigation facilities for one of mankind's most important transformations — a new form of intensive agriculture which was a crucial victory in mastering the earth.

The needs and values of these societies, in Sumer and Egypt, were obviously similar. There was a common bed of occupations, preoccupations, capabilities and forms of expression, investigation and enjoyment. It was probably this similar cultural environment and technological context which enabled a Sumerian-type culture and religion to take hold and prevail in Egypt before undergoing a rapid independent development in its new home.

Given that the basis of this new society (Sumerian or Egyptian) with its new technology was agricultural, new beliefs and new gods were centered on how to favor the fertility of the land and the animal herds. This in turn led to the invention of Sumerian-type beliefs in death and resurrection inspired by the sequence of the seasons from winter to spring and the birth, harvest, death and rebirth of crops. These beliefs were probably adopted by Egypt, but they were independently adapted and extended in that resurrection was applied to the pharaoh and then to all people in addition to the Sumerian concepts of the annual resurrection of nature and the resurrection of a single god, Dumuzi.

In fact, this major difference in death/resurrection/afterlife beliefs between Egypt and Sumer was indicative of the major difference in their overall attitude and approach. Egypt was an optimistic society with life on earth taking place in a harmonious fashion according to the *maat* order given by the gods and life continuing forever in a positive manner after death. Sumer was a less optimistic, and even a pessimistic, society with man in an uncertain world as a tenant and plaything of the gods and death being a terrible reality for everybody: everybody in Sumer died and nothing, or almost nothing, of man remained in an indifferent afterlife realm.

Divine kingship was the pivot of the politico-religious system in Egypt (see Chapter 5); in Sumer, it did not exist or was only sporadically used.

Still another major difference was in chief god tendencies. Chief god tendencies existed from early times in Sumer and were probably disseminated from there among many West Asian religions, but Egypt rapidly carried chief god tendencies to more powerful levels.

Both societies were hierarchical in their approach to the gods and to man, but in Egypt the chief god was truly a chief and on earth, the divine king ruled alone; in Sumer, the chief god presided over a deliberative assembly of gods and the *ensi* leader presided over an assembly of elders.

Both early Sumer and early Egypt were impregnated with animistic nature religion beliefs which led to the divinization of the sky, the sun, the earth, water, mountains, valleys and fertility, weather, and so forth, as well as to ancestor/father and mother/love divinities. Both Sumer and Egypt also seem to have engaged in star and tree worship from early dates. However, in Egypt, emblematic totemism and animal worship were central; in Sumer, there are very few traces of animal worship and totemism after the mid-Fourth Millennium.

In Sumer, most of the nature divinizations became anthropomorphized gods and goddesses, seemingly without ever going through phases of animal or animal-headed gods and goddesses. The Sumerian leap towards the creation of divinities seems to have involved basically the creation of higher or superior human beings rather than the projection of animal qualities as in Egypt. The main Sumerian gods and goddesses frequently had animal companions, but do not seem ever to have been animals. There seem to be only two Sumerian cases of animals or monsters attaining near divine status — the bird/storm demon Zu and Gugalanna, the monster/Bull of Heaven who was the Underworld goddess Ereshkigal's husband before he died.

Both Sumer and Egypt also both produced an abundance of tutelary henotheistic gods. Sumer had anthropomorphic city-state gods and Egypt developed animal, animal-headed or strictly anthropomorphic nome gods. Forms of henotheism, in which a local god was appeased and worshipped, while the existence of other neighboring local gods was not rejected, were particularly widespread in early Sumer and Egypt. Both lands transformed some of their henotheistic gods into chief gods, into *nibs* of the gods, lords of the gods, lords of pantheons. From that time, the protection of gods in specific zones and towns was not only sought in preference to other local gods, but local henotheistic gods became chief gods linked to duos, triads and pantheons. The other gods in the pantheons were also appeased and worshipped, but the protective power of the chief god was clearly preeminent and the most potent.

Regional pantheons of gods and theologies co-existed with local gods and beliefs both in Sumer and in Egypt. Sumer's example seems to be the best bet for the Egyptian transformation of regional divinities, the system of nome local gods, into regional and national polytheistic henotheistic pantheons of gods supported by polytheistic theological concepts including chief god theology.

In both Egypt and Sumer, the people of various nomes and city-states basically shared the same type of polytheistic religious beliefs even if the names of their gods and theological niceties frequently varied even in neighboring nomes and city-states. The biggest differences were between the ruling elite and the people, who were separated by a strict class system and the resulting religious privileges and duties.

The basic political framework for the Egyptian pantheons and theologies also seems to have been the Sumerian theocratic model. However, Egypt quickly developed theocracy into a far more all-inclusive system.

And so, if, in an overall way, the Egyptian and Sumerian polytheistic religions were basically of the same type with their pantheons, systems of magic, animistic leanings and agro-sedentary preoccupations, they also had significant differences.

Sumer seems to have progressed from animistic nature religion and henotheism to the next phases in religious development — polytheism, the constitution of pantheons and chief gods — somewhat quicker. The early Sumerians do not seem to have engaged in as abundant a sculptural and pictorial representation of their gods and goddesses as the Egyptians and it is only with the invention of pictographic writing in Sumer that we can partially verify this leap to a more sophisticated polytheistic religious system in Sumer by about 3300 BC. Nevertheless, Egypt also took the road which led from henotheism to polytheism and its pantheons and chief god theology at a relatively early date, perhaps around 3100 BC.

Both polytheistic Sumer and Egypt grouped many of their tutelary henotheistic city and nome gods into pantheons personifying what they saw as the totality of the universe. Organized pantheons with global meaning probably constituted a major evolution from the simple existence of a multiplicity of gods without organic links as in previous religious systems.

This chief god concept, the concept of a god more powerful than, and ruling, the other gods seems to have been linked largely to the new hierarchical needs of emerging centralized religious and political agro-sedentary societies on both the regional and national levels. The existence of chief gods, lords of the gods, also provided a religious justification for the existence of political chiefs of several nomes, of a region, and then first in Egypt and later in Sumer, for a chief of the entire land, the king, the *nisut*, and then the pharaoh, the *per-aa*, and in Sumer, the *lugal*, the emperor.

It was the German philologist and historian of religions Max Muller (1823–1900) who invented the term henotheism (the worship of a sole god without denying the existence of other gods), mainly to account for stages of evolution between polytheism and monotheism; but the term is just as useful and perhaps even more apt for the understanding of many post-totemistic emblematic gods.

The tendency towards a preferred god, a more powerful god, a chief god, the most powerful god, was latent in the local god concept, or henotheism, right from its inception. Henotheism had a latently ambiguous aspect because by extolling the virtues of a local god it implicitly implied the possibility of a chief god.

The chief god concept had both immediate and long-range effects. Sumer and Egypt quickly adopted a new system in which chief gods became leaders of united polytheistic pantheons, the first and most powerful of a company of gods. However, in both countries, and especially Egypt, chief god theology opened another new possibility — the chief god could evolve into the sole omnipotent god, into the monotheistic god.

For the next 2000 years, Egypt (and Sumer to a much lesser extent) were faced with these possibilities, groped about for solutions, struggled and experimented with the possibility that the chief god could become the sole omnipotent god, the monotheistic god, and always ended up by opting for forms of polytheism. In Egypt's case, a brief 15-year period of Aten solar monotheism ensued in the mid-14th century BC, before being overthrown.

In many ways, chief gods were consecutively an adaptation of primitive henotheism, an element of synthesis with polytheism and a forerunner of monotheism. Three phases of development occurred — primitive, or local, tutelary henotheism; the chief god concept within the polytheistic system, which accorded preferential status to one god but encouraged polytheistic worship; and the much later Hebrew Yahweh and Persian Ahura Mazdah henotheisms, which decreed the sole worship of a national god who was more powerful than all the other gods and which set the stage for monotheism. Both local and national henotheistic and chief gods existed not only in Sumer and Egypt but at various dates existed almost everywhere in the world, but such powerful and exclusive national henotheisms of the Yahweh and Ahura Mazdah types existed only in Israel and Iran.

Chief god theology within the new polytheistic religions seems to have been a coherent response to the rise of centralized regional and national agro-sedentary societies and political needs that they engendered. It is important to note that the concept of one god more powerful than the other gods seems to have corresponded to the new hierarchical needs that emerged with this type of society. Moreover, chief god theology had the socio-political advantage of not eliminating the countless popular local gods and goddesses; a chief god reigned above the local gods and above other national gods and gods incarnating universal forces or functions and professions, but he had no need to eliminate them.

THE QUINTESSENCE OF THE NEOLITHIC REVOLUTION AND THE ERA OF HIGH CIVILIZATION

The quintessence of the Neolithic Revolution and the beginning of a new age, around 3000 BC, both in Sumer and in Egypt, are marked by the stabilization of the entirety of the developments of the agro-sedentary society: intensive agriculture, new technologies — including writing, new architecture and art, a new political and societal order, the new polytheistic religion and new funerary and burial practices

The Neolithic Age brought to a close hundreds of thousands of years of nomadic hunting and food gathering as the mainstays of an informal economy. Egypt and Sumer incorporated the accomplishments of the Neolithic Age and reaped its benefits better than any other societies. They opened a new era for mankind, the era of high civilization, the era of urbanism, labor specialization, metals, the wheel and the potter's wheel, seagoing boats and true polytheism. Five hundred years later only two other societies, Elam and to an even greater extent Mohenjo-Dara and Harappa in the Indus Valley, had joined Sumer and Egypt. The Indus Valley people practiced writing and had a flourishing agriculture, but their art and bronze alloying techniques were primitive compared to Egypt's or Sumer's and in religion there is little evidence of anything more than mother goddess fertility and animal cults. The breakthroughs achieved in these three zones were only partially present in other areas of the world which lagged behind them for much of the third millennium.

There were some critical differences in how Sumer and Egypt achieved high civilization, notably in political development. Around 3100 BC, Egypt was united into *Ta-Wy*, the Two Lands, Upper and Lower Egypt, while the Sumerians did not federate their city-states at an early date — even if one city-state often held military sway over some others. Sumer's political organization remained regional rather than national until about 2350 BC, when Lugalzaqesi of Umma and then Sargon forcibly created a single nation.

As we shall soon see, Egypt's precocious political and theocratic unification gave it an enormous capacity for centralization. It was probably one of the key factors that enabled Egypt to produce the world's vanguard religion and rapidly to surpass Sumer in theological innovation and religious art and architecture. Eventually, centralization enabled Egypt to become Sumer's rival in all domains, a modern regional power second only to Sumer throughout the third millennium BC.

Shortly after the opening of the Old Kingdom (c. 2686 BC), Egypt was well on its way to becoming the world's vanguard religious society. Its religious development had become largely independent within its specific technological, demographic, geographic, political, social, and artistic contexts. It had clearly surpassed Sumer in the innovativeness and complexity of its cosmogonies, myths, theologies and systems of rituals and in the corporate organization of its thousands of priests.

From about 2500 to 1500 BC, Egyptian political, commercial, trading and military power and urban life rivaled that of Sumer and its successor states of Akkad and Babylonia. During the reign of Thutmose III (c. 1479–1425 BC), Egypt the arrogant island ardently sought and achieved domination over West Asia, maintained an empire there for more than 250 years and continued to fight for an imperial role in Asia until at least the battle of Carchemish in c. 605 BC.

AGRARIAN VALUES AND THE NILE

Agriculture, the technological backbone of the prosperous Egyptian economy, was at the center of its lifestyles. Agriculture was synonymous with the Nile River and its water for irrigation and the fertile black topsoil it washed into the valley. The Nile was easily seen as divine. Herodotus commented that despite the fact that "there is no rain in their country," the Egyptians were very prosperous because "the river's gift" allowed them like "no people...in the whole world (to) live from the soil with so little labor"[30]; that may be a cliché, but it was quite simply true. When Herodotus wrote this, around 440 BC, Egypt was still wealthy but in economic decline relative to its past; it was in religious confusion and was on the wane politically and socially; his comment was probably truer yet during Egypt's periods of glory.

The Nile was both a divine gift and a divine mystery for the ancient Egyptians. They were unaware that the annual beneficial silt-bearing flooding of the valley originated with the water which came down from the sources of the Nile in Lake Victoria, Lake Albert Nyanza and the high plateaus of Ethiopia. The Egyptians divinely personified the Nile, its annual flood and the prosperity it bestowed on the land, first with Osiris and then with the god Hapi and his fat stomach symbolizing abundance, his woman-like breasts symbolizing fertility and his headdress of papyrus flowers (Lower Egypt, *Ta-Mehu*) or sedge reeds or lilies (Upper Egypt, *Ta-Shema*). The first fruits of the harvest always went to the temples and were especially dedicated to the fertility and virility god Min.

The Egyptians were also pragmatic and built so-called "Nilometers," staircases with markings which indicated exact flooding levels. They skillfully calculated that the beginning of the Nile's inundation would take place about on the equivalent of every July 19th, at the time of the rising of the dogstar Sirius (Sopdet, in Egyptian).

The Nile and the intensive agriculture it facilitated were so much at the center of Egyptian society that a system was invented of three four-month seasons based on the Nile's cycles and their agricultural consequences: *akhet* for the flooding and fertilization of the valley caused by the Nile and its irrigation canals in summer and early autumn, *peret* for "the coming forth," the spring re-emergence of the land after the flood waters receded, allowing planting and growth in October/November; and *shemu* for the harvest in the dry season from April.

The Nile was called *iteru*, (the river) in Egyptian, and also *Hep-Ur*, or "Great Hapi" after the god Hapi, before being somehow transcribed as *Neilos* in Greek.

---

30. Herodotus, *Books I-II*, 2.5.1 and 2.14.

THE EMERGENCE OF POWERFUL GODS AND THE RELEGATION OF WOMEN TO SECONDARY ROLES

Up until the opening of the Neolithic Age and the invention of agriculture, the primordial divinity for tens of thousands of years seems to have been the fertility goddess. She appeared in various human and animal-linked forms as mother and earth goddesses. Nonetheless, there can hardly be any doubt that the domination of the male over the female was a quasi-permanent fact whose origins are lost in the night of time. But clearly, with the emergence in the late fourth millennium in Sumer and then Egypt of intensive agriculture, advanced irrigation systems and polytheism, both a turning point in the hierarchy of the divinities and an aggravation of the female's condition had occurred.

Basically, the old great mother/fertility goddesses in both maternal and sexual versions — motherhood, and sensuality and joy — were maintained with reduced powers. The earth goddesses were almost eliminated and the royal father-type sky gods gained far more importance. Maternity, for a goddess or a woman, was exemplary but no longer a key to absolute power. Almost everywhere, the polytheistic religious and social customs which finally consecrated the transformation from a food gathering and hunting society to an agro-sedentary society seem to have resulted in a stronger affirmation of male domination and a decrease in women's roles and rights.

It is fairly clear that this happened in Late Neolithic and then Bronze Age Egypt. Among the earliest traceable deities, Horus, Atum, Re, Seth, Anubis, Osiris, Thoth, Min and other male gods were unquestionably the major deities. No comparison is possible between their powers and the powers of the most powerful early goddesses, Hathor, Sakhmet, Neith, Nekhbet Wadjit and Isis. Only Hathor, Nekhbet and Wadjit were royal patronesses of early cities. Hathor and Neith were sky goddesses, among other attributes, but much less important than male gods in the sky like Horus or Re. Goddesses like Hathor and Sakhmet were connected with a savage pleasure in trying to destroy mankind. Even the much loved, devoted and magically empowered Isis was also connected with negative characteristics such as fickleness, guile and indecision. It was only during the Late Period (from c. 747 BC) that she achieved an immense status as one of Egypt's greatest divinities. Other early goddesses seem to have begun their careers as practically nothing more than ministers without portfolio who were usually worshipped only in association with other divinities — i.e., "the mistress of the house," Nephthys, with Isis.

A similar shift in emphasis to male gods also clearly took place in Fourth Millennium Sumer and perhaps even earlier. While extensive lists of the hundreds of Sumerian gods and goddesses dating to earlier than about 2600 BC have not been found, it seems clear that these incomplete lists refer to very old classifications and that the love and fertility goddess Inanna was the only female divinity among the top Sumerian deities.

The early male gods were not only usually father-type gods, but they were also the city and regional patron gods, the creator, sky, sun, moon, earth, water, air, light, darkness, agricultural/ vegetation, death, virility and fecundation gods.

Human fertility was no longer uniquely represented by a goddess but also by gods, in contrast to the earlier phallic images which seem to have uniquely represented virility. In Egypt, Min, whose worship in the Predynastic Period before c. 3100 BC seems to have been linked to fetish fossil shells and lettuce and its sap which resembled sperm, became an ithyphallic human-headed god in the Early Dynastic Period. Min was both ultra virility ("the bull who opens females" and a *kamutef*, "the bull of his mother," seemingly the father of his own mother as well as her son) and the agricultural reproductive force, that is, annual renewal of the fertility of the earth.

The emergence of intensive agriculture seems to have consecrated male gods of the Min and Osiris types as gods of vegetation and crops when, theoretically, at least, goddesses could have played this role as an extension of their old earth and human fertility roles. In Egypt, Osiris became the main agricultural god but Min also played an important early role, proving that in the case of a male god, fertility was now across the board, human and agricultural. Min's double fertility and virility role led men to sacrificially offer lettuce to Min and then eat it to obtain super potency. Women would touch Min's penis in the hope of becoming pregnant (they still do, in modern Egypt). The pharaoh offered Min the first fruits of the cereal harvest and in the Ptolemaic and Roman Periods (after 332 BC) Min was offered the first stems of wheat which emerged from the earth.

What had been exclusively female — the miracle of birth through the female, through the miracle of the mother goddess — was now shared by female and male gods. The mother goddess maintained her preeminence in birth, but the male god was now not only simply a phallus — sexual virility — he was linked to birth through his fecundation role. On the human level, the male now controlled birth, or had the illusion of doing so.

The goddesses now had to share the human fertility function; and they had not secured a key role in agriculture, man's new main activity. In pre-agro/polytheistic times, the earth goddess, distinct from the mother goddess or in a composite form with her, was the origin of all growth, of everything in existence; but now males became earth gods, either alongside goddesses or in replacement of them. In Sumer, Enlil was both the air and earth god, even if his consort Ninhursaga remained a human and earth fertility goddess. In Egypt, the shift was more radical with the earth function — fertility and vegetation — being attributed to the green-skinned god Geb, his son Osiris, Min, and other gods. In short, the goddesses lost overall domination and, significantly, their role as the origin of nature and life.

The main male father gods became the great first ancestors of mankind, the primogenitors, the creators of the human species. In Egypt, Atum and then Re were early forms of self-created gods and primogenitors. Obliquely, this seems to indicate at least that the vision of who had the primordial role in the creation of mankind had shifted from the great mother goddess to the great father god. (It is interesting to note that when this agro-polytheistic vision shifted again with Hebrew agro-monotheism and a god, Yahweh, who was more of a transcendental, pre-existent creator than an ancestor/primogenitor creator, the agricultural vision nevertheless remained staunchly patriarchic and anti-feminine.)

Without going back 27,000 years earlier to Aurignacian, Gravettian and Magdalenian times and the Venuses (which, if perhaps not goddesses as later understood, certainly represented the magical qualities of motherhood and fertility), this turnaround and corresponding aggravation of the female condition are sufficiently evident in comparison to Catal Huyuk in Anatolia, probably the world's first city, when it was just entering the Neolithic agricultural age around 6250 BC. Catal Huyuk's main divinities were still unquestionably fat female fertility goddesses. The same situation prevailed around the same time in Mesopotamia, before it became Sumer. It is also interesting to note that the idealized physical appearance of the goddesses, and of women in general, in Egypt was slender, with very few exceptions like the birth and pregnancy protectress goddess Tawaret.

Until the consequences of the Neolithic Age and the invention of agriculture had fully taken hold, the father god seems to have been a shadowy figure in the background. This seems to have mirrored the relations between mother, father and child in which the child's mother was always self-evident, but the child's father was always open to doubt.

Some anthropologists and prehistorians believe that the male only fully understood his role in conceiving children after the invention of agriculture and the ensuing close observation of how offspring were conceived. According to this theory, farmers and shepherds now understood that the mystery of birth was not exclusively related to the female.

I have always had difficulty in accepting this theory; it has always seemed to me astounding if not implausible that, having achieved some kind of self-awareness and consciousness, man could continue like male animals not to understand his role in the conception of children. However, it does seem to be a fact that the agricultural age and then polytheism coincided with both increased domination of the male over the female and the father gods over the mother goddesses. At least among the deities, the roles seem to have been inversed — the father god became active and the mother goddess was relegated to a less important or shadowy role.

Nevertheless, I tend to think that the apparent dramatic decrease in women's rights at that time was probably a result of a convergence of many factors — new sexual, political and social values, labor specialization in agriculture and crafts and above all religious values, rather than a sudden awareness of the male role in conceiving children. The male drive for power must have also played a major role. As the earth, animals, pottery, transport, metals and crafted goods were all being domesticated or harnessed, the male passed on to the next domain to bring under his full control, the female, and consecrated his new power by rendering male gods primordial.

Another factor that has to be taken into consideration is the domestication of animals. Certainly, this enabled man to observe more closely the behavior of animals, might also have incited him to observe more closely the behavior of wild animals, the animals he hunted. In both cases, he would have observed that the male animal almost always dominated and exploited the female animal. As we have seen, in Egypt and elsewhere, the belief that animals were the repositories of the divine, the practice of divinizing animals and the use of animal behavior as a standard for human behavior were fundamental realities. This could have led the early Egyptians to downgrade the powers of goddesses and to religiously sanctify an inegalitarian system of male domination and supposed female inferiority.

It seems certain that at the very least a codification by numerous polytheistic systems sanctifying a decrease in respect for women and an affirmation of a system of female inferiority took place. The veneration of women and maternity as exemplified in prehistory, including the early Neolithic, by the "Venus" sculptures, the great mothers, was fundamentally dented. Women remained exemplary as mothers, but their creative roles compared to the food gathering and hunting societies were reduced and they were now also more and more seen as the epitome of weak, negative and even evil characteristics.

In Sumer, Egypt, and almost everywhere else, this overall attitude to women was apparently crystallized, sanctified and incorporated into religious law. The regional pantheons of gods and the body of magical, ritual, theological and cosmological concepts which emerged in Sumer around 3500 BC, and then in Egypt, clearly reflected the new domination of male gods in general and father gods in particular and the reduced religious roles for women. The extraordinary specificity of Egypt was that it attenuated the severity of the attitudes and religious regulations concerning women. However, in Egypt as elsewhere, discrimination against women became a religious norm. It remains a fact even today that the societies which most discriminate against women are those in which religion is part of the state's structures and those which are the most religiously based, in short, the societies in which religion has not become a matter of indifference or mere superficial social custom.

CHAPTER 3.
THE ETHNIC AND GEOGRAPHICAL CONTEXT

THE MAKING OF THE EGYPTIAN ETHNIC TYPE

It was probably at the beginning of the second half of the Fourth Millennium, when the consolidation of Egypt's early technology, society, religion and culture were underway, that its ethnic makeup was in the final phases of its constitution. The examination of human remains from before the beginning of the (Naqada III, Gerzean B Period, c. 3300 BC), suggests that a fusion of several ethnic groups into the Egyptian Mediterranean type was underway.

Between c. 4500–4000 BC (Badarian B), the vast zone including much of Egypt, Libya, Nubia, and perhaps beyond into Nilotic Sudan and East Africa, while it was culturally and technologically similar, seems to have been only partially similar ethnically. The Egypt of that time probably had five cultural and ethnic sources: (1) the Egyptian Nile Delta and Valley itself; (2) influences and immigrants that ever since the Sebilian Period, beginning at least c. 12,000 BC, came from the south — down the Nile River from Nubia and East Africa, (3) from the west — Libya and North Africa, (4) from the Saharan southwest (perhaps the Tassili-n-Aijer in what is now Algeria), perhaps beginning around c. 6000 BC, and (5) from the east (Asia, in an almost permanent trickle from before 5000 BC and continuing sporadically into the late third millennium BC). A.H. Gardiner (1879–1963) believed that in Predynastic Egypt (in his calculations, 3100 ± 150 BC), the people in the north were "tall" and "long headed" and with "a difference of race" from "the dwellers in Upper Egypt (the south)" who were "essentially African stock, a character always retained despite alien influences brought to bear on them from time to time."[31] As we have seen, it is also possible to assume a particularly important immigration of broad-headed Semitic peoples from West Asia, but it should be reiterated that there is no way to prove the existence of a "dynastic race" which supposedly came to Egypt from West Asia and became the ruling class.

Egypt was the haven where all these immigrants gathered — first during the Sebilian Period, for its abundant food gathering, hunting and fishing resources, and then in the Neolithic Period for its agricultural fertility and the great fresh water supply of the Nile. After 8000 BC and the end of the Pleistocene Ice Age, and with ups and downs, climatic conditions were better in Egypt than in the rest of North Africa and the Sahara, making Egypt a major center of immigration.

After about 3500 BC the Egyptian ethnic type, born of this vast fusion, seems to have already constituted both a Mediterranean type and something of an Egyptian island unto itself, mirroring the politico-religious island it would become. Although apparently different from them this early Egyptian type, especially in the north, seems to have been related to Hamitic North Africans, southern Europeans and eastern Mediterranean peoples. South of Thebes, in ancient times as now, the people were generally of a darker complexion than elsewhere in Egypt, indicating substantial Nubian origins — the Nubians themselves presenting a mixture of Negroid and Caucasoid features (Kushitic). Below the First Cataract of the Nile at Elephantine, on the border between Egypt and Kush, Egyptians cohabited with a significant black Nubian minority. In fact, Elephantine was originally an entirely Nubian city. Apparently, Egyptians did not penetrate into the purely Bantu areas of Nubia beyond the 4th cataract until Thutmose III's reign (c. 1479-1425 BC).

It seems that once this fusion occurred between the indigenous Nile Delta and Valley people, North Africans, Asians and Africans into the Egyptian Mediterranean type in most of the country, it persisted throughout Egyptian history; only a minority presence of distinctively non-Egyptian ethnic groups subsisted. Minorities included African *Nehsi* (notably, Nubian/*Iuntiu-setiu*) immigrants, prisoners, mercenaries, slaves (and sometimes conquerors), Semitic (West Asian *Aamu*, including Syrians, *Shasu*/Bedouins, *Apiru*/warrior-pillagers

---

31. Gardiner, Alan, *Egypt of the Pharaohs*, p. 392.

and *Heka-khasut*/Hyksos) and North African people (Libyan *Tjehenu* and others). None of these seem to have been present in sufficient numbers to significantly alter the basically established Egyptian composite type. During the 2500 years from predynastic times, including times of invasion and occupation, until the Kushite (Nubian), Assyrian, Persian, Greek and Roman conquests of Egypt (beginning c. 747 BC), the ethnic makeup of the Egyptians seems to have been perpetuated along the same lines as in late predynastic times.

However, all of these suppositions have to be tempered by a lack of definitive proof. While it is abundantly clear that from the late Predynastic Period the Egyptians were culturally a distinctive people, no clearly scientific definition of the early Egyptians' ethnic characteristics can be determined absolutely using the means now available to scientists. This is the conclusion which most scientists and Egyptologists using DNA samplings of bones, hair, nails and skin, X-rays of skeletons and mummies and craniological studies have reached; however, it must be emphasized that DNA sampling on ancient remains, including mummies, is in an early stage of development. Given the contamination with resins and bitumen in the mummification process and the danger of contamination by modern DNA in the environment, mummies rarely provide undamaged, clean DNA samples even when bone core or the inside of teeth is used. Moreover, arguing respect for dead bodies, especially royal bodies, the Egyptian authorities do not generally allow DNA bone sampling. They permit only analysis of pieces which have fallen off from mummies. Research to develop reliable DNA testing is continuing and seems to be especially promising at the Manchester Mummy Project in Britain.

The most recent DNA samplings, X-rays of skeletons and mummies and bone, tissue and craniological studies and endoscopies carried out on the remains of bodies dating from the Late Period (c. 747–332 BC) tentatively indicate a mixture of Mediterranean, Negroid and European elements. Of course, these results must be considered cautiously, but they generally coincide with most Egyptologists' suppositions about the Egyptian ethnic makeup from Predynastic and Early Dynastic times (c. -3100–2686 BC) — a Mediterranean type, which south of Thebes included notable Negroid characteristics.

It is interesting to note that the oldest so-called naturally preserved body — or natural mummy — of an Egyptian ever found, "Ginger," was of a "European" type with red hair. This body (now in the British Museum), dating from c. 3400 BC, was almost perfectly preserved in a shallow grave in the hot, dry sands near Gebelein (Per-Hathor) in southern Upper Egypt. In 1975 in Paris, a 105-member team of scientists led by Lionel Balout "restored" the mummy of Rameses II (c. 1279–1213 BC) and concluded, among many other points, that his hair was of the "European" type. Some Egyptologists even maintain that Rameses II's hair was also red, rather than dyed red.

Perhaps ancient Egypt's ethnic makeup is best summed up by the French historian of religions and Egyptologist Françoise Dunand and the X-ray specialist Roger Lichtenberg, who in *Mummies, A Voyage Through Eternity*, noted: "By studying hair, nails, skin and fingerprints (of mummies), we can learn a great deal about ethnic categories and gain a fairly good idea of what the ancient Egyptians actually looked like. Archaeologists have now established a method of scientifically measuring the bones of mummies on site using x-rays. They have also successfully carried out studies on mummified tissue. Their findings confirm the historical hypothesis that the ancient Egyptians were descended in roughly equal measures from Berber and Semitic peoples, with an increasing Negroid influence from the north to south of the country. It is particularly striking that, despite external influences at different periods of their history, the Egyptian people have remained remarkably unchanged to modern times." Concerning their own study of 200 mummies from the first century BC to the 5th century AD in Duch in the Kharga Oasis in the desert 75 miles west of Thebes, Françoise Dunand and Roger Lichtenberg concluded that "we are dealing with a population of Mediterranean type...pale skinned...almost identical in features to the population of the Nile valley." [32]

Recently Zahi Hawass, the Egyptian Egyptologist and Under-Secretary of State for Giza Monuments, has indicated that the DNA tests carried out by the Cairo Museum on some of the 600 skeletal remains he found in a Giza Pyramids workers' village will soon be published.[33] If these results are indeed made public, they could provide valuable additional information on the ancient Egyptian ethnic and physical makeup.

The difficulties involved in using the terms Afro-Asiatic, Semitic and Berber/Hamitic in other than a linguistic context, or Caucasoid or even Mediterranean types as physical categories, are self-evident. It is redundant to say that race is not a scientific concept; it does not, exist as such. But it is pertinent to reiterate that ethnic groups were formed from mixture. Egypt's

---

32. Dunand, Françoise and Lichtenberg, Roger, *Mummies, A Voyage Through Eternity*, pp. 89-90 (In the original French edition, Hamitic is placed in brackets after Berber.) and p. 118.

33. Zahi Hawass in www.guardians.net/spotlite/spotlite-hawass-2001.htm

language was basically part of the Afro-Asiatic linguistic family, a mixture of indigenous, Semitic and Hamitic elements whose core parent group may have existed some time between 12,000 and 6000 BC somewhere in what is now southern Sudan and Ethiopia. For want of better definitions, pragmatically it can be said that Egypt had early cultural links with the Africans (notably the Kushitic Nubians, Punt-Somalis and Gallas), the Semites (especially what is now called the enlarged Syrian family) and the Hamites (that is, the Libyans). Egypt's dominant physical type was more Mediterranean than anything else and its culture became distinctive in the late Predynastic Period.

Although the Hamitic, North African or Berber people in today's Egypt probably do not *stricto sensu* represent more than two percent of the population (perhaps they were much more in ancient times with the waves of Libyan immigration), the physical appearance of the majority of ancient Egyptians seems to have been close to what have come to be known as the Hamitic Berbers. This is probable, even though it is important to reiterate that the Egyptians were not Hamitic Berbers but rather that proto-Berbers were an essential element in their ethnic makeup. (The term Hamitic has become politically incorrect, but it nevertheless corresponds to what became and still is a de facto ethnic subdivision.)

As obviously incomplete and insufficient as these definitions are, they translate into an ethnic type which was, and still is, basically dark complexioned and dark-haired, with brown eyes, a mixture of long and broad heads and medium height and build. The ethnic mix throughout North Africa seems to have progressively become similar — the easily recognizable dark-complexioned Mediterranean type with African, European and West Asian Semitic influences and in all the southern parts of this region, darker people and the notable presence of African minorities.

And so with all its limitations, the best definition of the ancient Egyptians seems to be that they were a distinctive cultural group and a mixture of several ethnic groups. The result was one of the most fabulously original cultures in the history of mankind.

THE EGYPTIAN HUMANS, AND ALL THE "WRETCHED" OTHERS

From early dates, the Egyptians were very conscious of their own specific religious, political, cultural and ethnic identity. They saw themselves as neither

Asian nor African, nor Nubian, nor close to the despised *Tjehenu* (Libyans) whom they considered barbarians. Nevertheless, while most of the time the *Tjehenu* were depicted as different from the Egyptians, there are funerary temple murals dating from about 2500 BC which depict the *Tjehenu* and the Egyptians in a physically similar manner.

Broadly speaking, Egyptian art from the earliest times reflected the existence of several ethnic phenotypes and their permutations and combinations. These basic types were Egyptian, Libyan, Kushite (Nubian), Bantu and West Asian. While there is no way of establishing whether the Egyptian perception of their cultural and ethnic separateness was completely and faithfully translated into the strict color and design code in their art which was already in effect from the beginning of the Old Kingdom (c. 2686 BC), (see Chapter 7), it clearly corresponded to at least both idealized and caricatured realities.

Egyptian men in the prime of life were usually painted in brownish-red ochre, with a mix of long and broad heads, straight hair more frequently than curly hair (but often wearing wigs), frequently with projecting, aquiline noses but sometimes with large noses, with a mix of thin and thick lips, usually with receding jaws and slender bodies. Egyptian women were usually painted yellow and with the same general physiological characteristics as men, but usually with their feminine characteristics highly accentuated. Asians were frequently broad-headed and sturdier with light yellow skin, abundant hair held by a hairband, and pointed beards; Libyans were broad-headed with beards and a side-lock, depicted in pink or white; Nubians were black, with some Negroid facial and hair characteristics; and other Africans had clear Negroid features such as broad cheeks, fuzzy hair, large, flat noses, thick lips and prominent jaws. The peoples of the Aegean Sea, like the Cretans, Greeks, Cypriots and Sea Peoples, were depicted in much the same way as the Egyptians, in reddish-brown.

The early arrogant affirmation of Egyptian identity is clearly borne out by Early Dynastic Period art dated around or before 3100 BC, including The Palette of Narmer (now in the Cairo Museum), The Bull Palette (Louvre Museum) or "Scorpion's" Mace-head (Ashmolean Museum, Oxford). These works of art not only clearly distinguished between Egyptian, Libyan and Asian types; they seem to have accentuated these differences.

The distinct ethnic characteristics of the Egyptians and the Nubians were also frequently depicted. The miniature model of a group of Egyptian soldiers alongside a group of Nubian soldiers from the Twelfth Dynasty (c. 1985–1795

BC), now in the Cairo Museum, depicts different characteristics for each group with the Nubian soldiers clearly showing darker skins and thicker hair. There are literally dozens of battle scenes between Egyptians and Nubians in which the two peoples are sharply contrasted — reddish brown skin for the Egyptians and black skin for the Nubians. Scenes of Nubian captives, scenes of obviously non-Nubian Bantu captives and scenes of Nubians and other peoples bringing tribute offerings can be found on the murals of many temples and tombs throughout Egypt and they all portray sharp ethnic differences with Egyptians.

The Egyptians generally, but not always, saw the Nubians as considerably different from the Bantus; that is still the case concerning the differences between Peuls, Tuaregs, northern Sudanese, northern Ethiopians, northern Somalis, Eritreans and the less mixed Negroid peoples like the Bantus. The statuette of a young *baket*, a servant girl, holding a jug from Amenhotep III's time (c. 1390–1352 BC), now in the Gulbenkian Museum of Oriental Art in Durham, Britain, clearly portrays the facial features of an African who is not a Nubian. This is also clearly the case for the African prisoners depicted on the pavement in Akhenaten's (c. 1352–1336 BC) city of El Amarna/Akhetaten found by Petrie (*Tell el Amarna*, Plate II 1.20). However, there was also sometimes a tendency to depict enemy Nubians with marked Negroid features, for instance on Tutankhamun's (c. 1336–1327 BC) staff, chariot and footstool (in the Cairo Museum). Such depictions persisted right into the Late Period — for example, the pedestal of a statue of Pharaoh Nectanebo II (c. 360–343 BC), in the Louvre Museum, shows Negroid Nubian prisoners.

Numerous temple and tomb mural paintings, carvings and engravings and miniature model "installations" have survived which not only clearly differentiated between Egyptians, Nubians, Bantus and Asians, but sometimes did so in ways which would today be considered anti-black, anti-Arab or anti-Semitic. The painted reliefs found in the tomb General Horemheb built for himself in the Memphis necropolis of Sakkara, around 1319 BC, before becoming pharaoh, depict Asian and African prisoners in a hyper-realistic post-Amarna style verging on outrageous caricature. (These murals are now in the Bologna Museo Civico.)

Another well-known example of the ethnic separateness the Egyptians felt in relation to the Nubians, Bantus and Asians was depicted in the entrance murals of the Rameses II's (c. 1279–1213 BC) Abu Simbel Temple. Here we see Nubian, Bantu, West Asian and Libyan captives who are all being mistreated and whose differences to the Egyptian type are shown in disparaging ways.

Numerous tomb murals have been found picturing Nubians and Asians on trading missions, bringing offerings and paying tribute: the BH3 tomb of Khnumhotpe (c. 1950 BC), in Beni Hassan, north of Hermopolis, and in the New Kingdom (c. 1550–1069 BC), the western Thebes TT100 tomb of Rekmira, TT40 tomb of Huy, TT63 tomb of Sobekhotep, TT86 tomb of Menkheperra-seneb, and so forth. There are also numerous vignettes, especially in the New Kingdom *Book of the Dead*, of foreign prisoners being ritually murdered. One of the most classic Egyptian images from the earliest palettes to Late Period temple and tomb murals is the pharaoh ritually smashing the head of a foreigner (who looks like one!). In all these images physical characteristics, dress and accessories distinguish Egyptians and foreigners. The battle scenes we find on the walls of almost all the temples depict "wretched," "miserable" foreigners being defeated; they are all physically and sartorially easily distinguishable from the "noble" Egyptians.

Behind the depiction of the differences between peoples in Egyptian art and literature was the concept that the Egyptians saw themselves as *remet*, as "people," as full-fledged humans, blessed by the gods, while all others were the descendants of the enemies of the gods and at best could become serfs. The Egyptians believed that their region was ethnically, culturally, religiously and politically apart from and better than their neighbors'. They believed that they were the rulers of the entire earth and the only orderly people. In fact, for most of their history, the term *remet*, man, human, was only applicable to Egyptians. On the positive side, this attitude was frequently tempered by a relatively fair treatment of Nubians, as well as of Libyans and Asians, who were permanently established inside Egypt.

The Egyptians divided humanity into four races, or groups — themselves, the ideal, dark-skinned, dark-haired *remet*; the light-skinned *Tjehenu*/Libyans; the black-skinned *Yam* or *Nehsi*/Nubians and Africans; and the light brown-skinned *Aamu*/Asiatics. This theme of "four races" was frequently depicted on reliefs in the rock-cut tombs of the New Kingdom pharaohs in the Valley of Kings, notably in KV17 of Sety I (c. 1294–1279 BC) and KV11 of Rameses III (c. 1184–1153 BC).

The *khefty*, the enemies of Egypt, the enemies of the gods, were all usually grouped together as the *pedjet*, "the nine bows." At various times they included the *Iuntiu-setiu*/Nubian bowmen, the *Tjehenu* and *Tjemehu*/Libyans, the Asian *Shasu*/ Bedouin sand dwellers, the *Heka-khasut* (Hyksos) "rulers of foreign lands," the *Apiru*/nomad raiders and other "vile" Asians and the later *Meshwesh* and *Libu*/

Libyans. The exact list of enemy countries was subject to change according to necessity, but the designation of foreigners as "wretched" and "miserable" was standard practice. The Asians, in particular, during the New Kingdom (c. 1550–1069 BC) and especially during the Third Intermediate Period (c. 1069–747 BC) came to be seen as representatives of disorder and of the evil god Seth. The gigantic snake Apophis, the greatest threat to the maintenance of daily order, was also often seen as being Asiatic.

A related and frequently interchangeable term with *pedjet* was *khasut*, "the foreign lands," which usually designated the Asian countries but frequently also included the African countries. Any person in the *khasut* was systematically seen as a *khefty*, an enemy, and a *sebi*, a rebel. Perhaps it is easier to understand the negative connotations of the term *khasut* by noting its relationship to the later Hebrew term *goyim* (the peoples of the non-Hebrew nations, or gentiles), a term which could have been inspired by the Egyptian *khasut* doctrine. In turn, the early Christians used the term "gentiles" in the same derogatory manner as the Hebrews used *goyim* and the Egyptians used *khasut*, to designate non-Christians.

The Egyptian attitude to foreigners mellowed somewhat after they defeated and expelled the Asian Hyksos around c. 1550 BC and had more positive relations with Asians due to the constitution of their empire in West Asia. The Eighteenth Dynasty (c. 1550–1295 BC) *Hymn to Amun-Re* (Papyrus Boulaq 17 in the Cairo Museum) shows that as long as the Egyptian chief god Amun-Re, who had "made mankind and created the beasts," dominated, there was no contradiction with the tolerant view that "Atum...made the people...distinguished their nature...and separated colors, one from another."[34] The apotheosis in this more universalist view came with the proto-monotheist Pharaoh Akhenaten (c. 1553–1536 BC) in his *Hymn to The Aten*: "O Sole god beside whom there is none!...You set every man in his place...You supply their needs...Their tongues differ in speech, Their characters likewise; Their skins are distinct, For you distinguished the peoples."[35] However, it would be wrong to believe that this universalist philosophical attitude completely seeped down to Egyptian behavior concerning foreign soldiers and slaves; numerous contemporary inscriptions and artworks indicate that they were still seen as vile and part of the *pedjet*-enemies.

---

34. Wilson, John in *Ancient Near Eastern Texts Relating to the Old Testament*, pp. 365-366.

[35] Lichtheim, Miriam, *Ancient Egyptian Literature*, Volume II, p. 98.

35.

THE EARLY NOME STRUCTURES

Egypt before unification, about 3100 BC, probably consisted of 38 *sepat*, or nomes, composed of cities and their surrounding regions. Twenty-two were in the south and sixteen in the north. In any case, this was the situation at the time of the opening of the Old Kingdom (c. 2686 BC). Eventually, 42 nomes emerged, 22 in the south and 20 in the north, plus the oasis areas in the desert. Each had a chief, or henotheistic, protective god, as in Sumer. The emblems of the 42 nomes were placed on the walls of the temples.

The territories of the *sepat*-nomes were usually demarcated in function of irrigation canals. The early title of the *sepat* leader was *adjmer*, digger of canals, before becoming *hery-tep a'a*, "great overlord"/nomarch. These developments may have also taken place under the impetus of the West Asian traders, immigrants or invaders, or a bit of each. They may have been applying a city-state, regional and canal system which had already been fully developed in Sumer from at least about 3500 BC in city-states like Eridu, Uruk and Ur and elsewhere in West Asia.

These regions were transformed into provinces, the *sepat*, the nomes. The oldest Egyptian *sepat* nomes seem to have corresponded to the irrigated agricultural areas around some of the first major urban centers in Upper Egypt, like the twin cities of Nekhen (Hierakonpolis) and Nekheb (Eileithyiaspolis) in the Third Nome, Abdu (Abydos) in the Eighth Nome and Nubt (Naqada) in the First Nome, and in Lower Egypt, Sau (Sais) in the Fifth Nome and the twin cities of Pe-Dep (Buto) in the Sixth Nome.

The power of the most prosperous of these urban centers grew rapidly with towns holding sway over their surrounding regions. This in turn undoubtedly facilitated a hierarchy among the *sepat* in the emerging national geopolitical structures and engendered a transformation from local and regional beliefs to national beliefs.

AREA AND POPULATION ESTIMATES

The total area of Lower and Upper Egypt — the fertile nomes in the Nile Delta and the narrow Nile Valley — was relatively small and never covered more than a maximum of fifteen miles on either side of the Nile. It can be calculated at probably no more than 14,000 square miles; for purposes of comparison, today's Estonia is considerably bigger than ancient Egypt.

There is no way of reliably estimating population levels in 3000 BC, although some Egyptologists give an estimate of about half a million. Extrapolations from Egyptian documents and the estimates of later historians seem to indicate that around this time the main urban centers, and notably the nome capitals, probably had populations of more than 15,000. Two million is a figure frequently cited for Middle Kingdom Egypt (c. 2055–1650 BC) and 50,000 for the zone it controlled in Nubia. Bill Manley, in *The Penguin Historical Atlas of Ancient Egypt*, opts for a figure of 1.5 million before the New Kingdom (c. 1550 BC), rapidly increasing to 2.5 or even 5 million people during this period. If the 5 million figure is correct, cities like Memphis and Heliopolis might have had populations of a few hundred thousand inhabitants, making them the biggest cities in the world at that time. Population estimates for Thebes vary greatly from 20,000 to 50,000 in the Old and Middle Kingdoms to a startling and quite unverifiable one million during the New Kingdom.

K.W. Butzer in *Early Hydraulic Civilization In Egypt* estimated that the delta and parts of the Nile Valley had population densities of more than 200 inhabitants per square kilometer. This would have been the case for the area between Thebes and Elephantine, the zone around Hyselis (Sha-sehetep) and the area south and north of Memphis. Population density along the Nile in modern Egypt is 2,700 per square mile.

Many other population estimates for Egypt in various periods have been made by foreign historians and all of them appear to be guesses. The Hebrew Josephus (first century AD), in *The Jewish Wars*, made an estimate of 7.5 million, not counting Alexandria. The Greek Diodorus Siculus (probably in Egypt between 60 and 56 BC), in *Library*, spoke of 7 million in ancient times and about 3 million in his time. The Greek Hecataeus of Abdera (probably in Egypt around 320 BC) made an estimate of 7 million; but Herodotus, around 440 BC, postulated that it was only 3.5 million. At the late 4th century BC, equally unreliable population guesses for Assyria/Babylonia are 7 million; for Judea and nearby Jewish areas, 3 million; and for Greece and Greek speakers, 3 million.

NAMES OF EGYPT: FROM *KEMET* TO *AIGYPTOS*

The names the Egyptians used to designate their country seem to have originated with their new agricultural prosperity and especially with fertile black (*ar*) silt which the Nile River washed into the valley during its annual flood and which was the was the key to this prosperity. *Ar*, the black topsoil of the valley, could have led to the oldest known name of the region — *Kem* or *Kemet*, the black land. The Egyptians were the *remet-en-Kemet*, the people of Egypt.

Probably at about the same time, the sterile desert surrounding the fertile delta and the narrow band of fertile land along the Nile was named *Deshret*, the red land. Red frequently conveyed particularly detestable symbolic value for the ancient Egyptians — with the notable exception of the red-colored crown of Lower Egypt. Red was the color of the horrible god Seth; red ink was used to write harmful spells and the decree refusing entry into the afterlife. Red-haired people were seen at best as being special, but more usually as people not to be associated with because they were under Seth's evil influence.

The name for Upper Egypt, the land in the Nile Valley from the First Cataract near Abu (Elephantine) to just south of Men-nefer (Memphis), a few miles south of today's Cairo, was *Ta-Shema*, "the land of the sedge plant," or simply the south. The hieroglyph of a sedge-reed plant was also used to designate narrowness, thus making *Ta-Shema*, "the narrow land," in an obvious reference to the narrowness of the country.

For Lower Egypt, the Nile Delta to Memphis, the names were notably *Ta-Mehu*, the land of the papyrus clump, *Ta-Bity*, "the land of the bee," or simply the north.

In reference to the unification of Upper and Lower Egypt, *Ta-Wy*, the names "Two Lands", "Two Shores," "Two Shrines," "The Sedge and the Bee" followed between c. 3100 and c. 2600 BC. From the Middle Kingdom (c. 2055–1650 BC), the term *Ta-Mery*, the cultivated land of the people of the Nile, the beloved land, was also used to designate this union, but it was *Ta-Wy* which was most frequently used.

The Egyptians' geographical perception of *Ta-Wy* was the opposite of ours today. We see Cairo (Heliopolis and the Giza Necropolis, in the north), at the top of the country and Aswan (Elephantine, in the south), at the bottom. For the ancient Egyptians, it was the south, Upper Egypt, that was the top of their country, the *hat ta*, "the front of the land," and the north, Lower Egypt, was the bottom. Comparatively this would situate Miami at the top of the U.S. and New York at the bottom.

From at least about 1400 BC, the West Asian peoples referred to Egypt using forms of the Semitic word *Misr*, which means "the two territories." The Bible makes hundreds of references to Egypt as *Mitsraim*. In Arabic, Egypt is still referred to as *Misr*. The Greeks, after at least the 6th century BC, used the word *Aigyptos* for both the land and the Nile River. They perhaps derived this name from one of the Middle Kingdom titles of Memphis, the first capital of united Egypt — *H.wtk3pth*, *Hitkuptah* (the Mansion of the *ka* of Ptah, the Mansion of the soul-double of the god Ptah). In turn, from the Greek *Aigyptios*, Egyptians, came *Gypt*, Coptic, which first designated all Egyptians and then after the Moslem conquest in AD 642, and until today, designates only Christian Egyptians. Generally, it is the Greek invented names for Egypt's cities — like Heliopolis for Onu, or Hermopolis for Khmun — and the Greek deformations of names — Abydos for Abdu, Bubastis for Bast — which have survived in common usage to the detriment of the original Egyptian names.

The early Egyptians designated the land south of the First Cataract of the Nile, at Elephantine, as *Yam*, *Irem* and then as *Ta-Sety*, the Land of the Bow, the land of the archers. Many other names and sub-divisions followed including *Iuntiu-Setiu*, the nomadic archers, *Ta-Nehesy* and above all from the Middle Kingdom, *Wawat* for the northern part of this land and *Ka-sh* (Kush) for the southern part. These last two names were later usually replaced by the Arabic term, Nubia. The Egyptians also applied a host of derogatory names to the Nubians: *Iryshek*, *Ruket*, *Tua*, and so on.

The entirety of the land to the south and southwest, and also often the northeast, was called *Ta-Netjer* (The Land of the god). This usually included parts of what today are Sudan, Somalia, Eritrea, Saudi Arabia and Yemen. The land west of the delta (later Libya) was called *Tjehenu*. The lands east of the Two Lands, of *Ta-Wy*, but including the Sinai buffer zone, came to be known as *Retjenu*, which eventually included three districts — Canaan (from the Egyptian border to Byblos), *Amurru* (from Byblos to Ugarit) and *Upi* (including the Beka and the Anti-Lebanon) plus northern Syria and northern Mesopotamia. Palestine and Syria were also sometimes referred to as *Khor*. North of Lower Egypt, the Mediterranean and the lands beyond, and probably including the Delta marshes, was known as *Wadj wer* ("the great green").

As we have seen, the usual tendency was to consider the entirety of foreign countries, the *khasut*, as places of disorder and enemy territory with the term *pedjet*, "the nine arcs" (or *iunet*, the bows) being used to designate the direct enemies of the moment but almost always including Asiatics and Nubians.

EGYPT, AN ARROGANT ISLAND AND PART OF A WEST ASIAN/EGYPTIAN CONTINUUM

The Egyptians expended great efforts in creating military, political, ethnic and cultural buffer zones all around *Ta-Netjer*, *Tjehenu* and *Retjenu*. This policy was also applied to *Ta-Sety* (Wawat and Kush: Nubia) over which they believed they had natural colonial rights.

Kemet, *Ta-Wy*, *Ta-Mery*, became expressions of the concept of an arrogant island unto itself peopled by a superior ruler race in the northeastern corner of Africa. The German Egyptologist Siegfried Morenz (1914–1970), in *Egyptian Religion*, has called this stance "The Egyptocentric Attitude," noting that it is "impressively clear that the Egyptians regarded their country as the centre of the earth" and that "If Egypt was the nucleus and centre of the earth, the Egyptians were naturally its only legitimate inhabitants..."[36] Even the Egyptians in the *Aigyptos*, having been occupied, stripped of indigenous pharaohs and humiliated by the Greeks after the Greek conquest of Egypt in 332 BC and then by Romans after the Roman conquest in 30 BC, were imbued with a feeling of superiority.

However, as disconcerting as it may seem, it would be too simple to see Egypt as only an arrogant ethnic, cultural, religious and political island unto itself. At the same time, Egypt was a crossroads, a giver and a receiver of influences and progressively from about 3100 BC was part of a West Asian/ Egyptian continuum. If a single qualification has to be used to situate Egypt, it is the West Asian/Egyptian continuum that fits best. For most of its history, Egypt was basically a part of this continuum, looking more to the east, to West Asia — religiously, technologically, culturally, politically, militarily and commercially — than to the south, to Africa, or to the west, to Libya.

Over the centuries, this situation became increasingly accentuated and by the end of the New Kingdom (c. 1069 BC), Egypt was virtually a part of West Asia in everything but geography. In the 6th century BC, the Greek historian and geographer Hecataeus of Miletus (c. 540–490 BC) included Egypt in Asia in his *Ges Periodos* (Circumnavigation of the Known World). There was one notable

---

36. Morenz, Siegfried, *Egyptian Religion*, pp. 42, 45 and 47.

exception to this tendency: Nubia, which Egypt almost always tried to colonize and yet somehow integrate into its lifestyle.

SPECIAL RELATIONS WITH NUBIA

Egypt's relations with the African Nubian people to the south were the best illustration of this double exclusiveness and mingling with other peoples and cultures. Relations with *Ta-Sety*/Nubia (Wawat and Kush) were extensive from late Predynastic times (at least from c. 3500 BC) until well after the end of the 25th Kushite Dynasty which ruled Egypt from c. 747 to 656 BC.

There was clearly two-way influence and emigration between Egypt and Nubia; but except for the period of Kushite rule, relations between Egypt and Nubia were almost always based on Egyptian colonialism. The Egyptians were convinced that the Nubians were "naturally" vassals of the Egyptians. Annexation, domination and the imposition of an Egyptian-type system in all domains constituted what we would today call a typical colonial situation. The result was that over nearly 3,000 years, Egypt was on the whole a technological, cultural, political and religious influence on Nubia, a role model for Nubia, and rarely the contrary. Nubia, "The Land of the Bow," almost always found itself on the *pedjet*, "The Nine Bows," the list of the enemies of Egypt.

Following the break in cultural similarity between the two regions, between 3500 and 3000 BC there was a virtual disappearance of the early Nubians, the so-called Nubian A group, around 2800 BC. This may have been due either to a lack of adaptation to climatic and technological conditions or because they were largely eliminated by the Egyptians.

There is evidence of Egyptian incursions into Nubia right from the beginning of the Early Dynastic Period around 3100 BC. By the Fourth Dynasty (beginning c. 2613 BC), the Egyptians had established colonies in Nubia, notably at the site of the later Buhen near the Second Cataract, where the Nubian C group had settled, but these colonies were regained by the Nubians some 200 years later.

The early Egyptians often carried out military campaigns for loot — especially animals, gold, amethyst, jasper, granite, wood, incense, spices and herbs — and to create buffer zones and protect their African trading routes. From the Fourth Dynasty, there was a frequent use of Nubians as conscripted soldiers, police, laborers, servants and slaves. There is also considerable evidence that Nubians were frequently humiliated and ritually slaughtered.

Trade was consistently active between Nubia and Egypt, but from early dates Egyptian trade policy was based on protectionism and commercial domination. As far back at the Twelfth Dynasty (c. 1985–1795 BC), when Egypt regained control over much of Nubia, extensive documentation shows that they established severe regulations to prevent Nubians from settling or even travelling in Egypt for any other reason except trade and prohibited all navigation of Nubian boats down the Nile.

However, none of this seems to have stopped a permanent wave of Nubian emigration, especially in Upper Egypt, and a constant tendency for the Nubians to culturally and religiously Egyptianize themselves.

Nubia was a powerful, prosperous and autonomous society at various times, particularly during the 17th and 16th Centuries BC, but during the imperialistic New Kingdom (beginning c. 1550 BC), the Egyptians, and especially Thutmose III (c. 1479-1425 BC), reestablished tight control over most of Nubia. Nubia was now ruled by a resident staff of Egyptian administrators, headed by a so-called "King's Son of Kush." Heavy taxation of Nubians in goods, conscripted soldiers and slaves was particularly severe during this period. However, none of this altered a frequent Nubian threat to Egyptian rule, both in Nubia and in Egypt.

The Nubian threat to Egypt finally materialized with invasions into Upper Egypt by King Kashta (ruled c. 770–747 BC). Around 728 BC, the Kushite King Piye (c. 747–716 BC), ruling from Napata in Kush, established his domination and that of the 25th Dynasty over all of Egypt until 656 BC. For nearly a century, Egypt became a single state from the Mediterranean Sea to Meroe in what today is Sudan. But even during this period, the occupying Kushite kings were culturally and religiously Egyptian. They portrayed themselves in art with all the traditional Egyptian insignia and made major attempts to revive Egyptian culture and religion rather than to impose a Kushite culture and religion. Nevertheless, Egyptian resentment always remained strong.

Pharaoh Psamtek I (c. 664–610 BC), acting as something between an Assyrian vassal and an independent king, established the Egyptian Saite Dynasty in 664 BC and after the defeat of the Kushites by the Assyrians in 663 BC finally succeeded in repulsing the Kushite rulers from Egypt. The Kushites were forced to withdraw into their own land and gradually developed an independent religion, revived the Kushite language and developed a great African-type culture despite the persistence of Egyptian influence.

CHAPTER 4.
SYSTEMS OF GODS, DEMONS, COSMOGONIES, MYTHS AND MAGIC

THREE BASIC WAYS OF DEPICTING THE GODS

Between about 3300 and 3100 BC, the prehistoric and proto-historic cities and regions of Egypt seem to have gradually invented statues of gods and goddesses who were depicted in three basic forms — animal, human and animal-headed human forms. Frequently, the god or goddess in human form wore headdress emblems of their divine animal and plant totems. A same god or goddess had multiple forms of representation which were interchangeable. Only a small number of divinities were solely depicted in either animal or human forms.

A fourth form, common to many ancient societies but not as much used in Egypt consisted of combining animal powers and attributes in composite animal demons or divinities. The most feared of these Egyptian composites was Ammut, with a crocodile's head and a body that was half lion and half hippopotamus, who supposedly ate those among the deceased who could not pass the test of truth at the entry into the *Duat* afterlife. The goddess of childbirth Taweret, with a hippopotamus' head and body, lion's paws, a crocodile's tail and human breasts, was certainly the most loved composite goddess. Then there was the *Saget*, whose head was a falcon, its body and legs part lion and part bull or cow, with its tail culminating in a lotus. The *panthee*, usually linked to amuletic protection and healing, also had multiple features incorporating human and several animal characteristics.

The development of the three major forms for the divine and above all its most usual form — animal-headed human gods and goddesses — seems to have been strongest in ancient Egypt. Sumer and its West Asian zone of influence, despite that it operated within a similar animistic nature religion framework as Egypt, seems to have eliminated non-human representations of the gods and goddesses by the mid-fourth millennium. With rare exceptions, these West Asian gods were anthropomorphic, even if they had animal companions. Iran and India followed a similar human/animal divine representational path to Egypt, but perhaps more than 1300 years later. In Africa, representation in general, including the gods and spirits, was always primarily human and even hyperbolically human, with animal themes playing secondary roles.

In Paleolithic times, beyond the certainty that we are dealing with a religious mythology, it remains impossible to determine whether the artists were depicting divinities and whether they already situated themselves within an animistic system in which the divine was present in animals and nature. In any case, the Cro-Magnon imagination included all the types of depictions which were later transformed into divinities and were no doubt best illustrated in the Egyptian pantheon. In addition to the depiction of a huge number of animals, feminine forms ("Venuses," from c. 32,000 BP) and some vaguely drawn males, there are also some rare Paleolithic depictions of composite human-animals like the lion-headed lady (?) in Holhlenstein-Stadel in the German Swabian Jura (c. 30,000 BP), the bison-headed man in Gabillou, France (c. 15,000 BP), a bird-headed man in Lascaux, France (c. 15,000 BP) and of course several bison-headed men and the famous "sorcerer" in Trois-Frères, France (c. 15,000 BP) with bird, reindeer, bear, horse, feline and human attributes. Some Paleolithic composite animals have also been discovered, like the serpent with a bear's head in Baume-Latrone, France (c. 20,000 BP).

Given the strong influence of key aspects of totemism in Egypt, it seems logical that the early theologians could have believed that using the totem animal and the human form as composite gods could create stronger, more divine gods. Despite the combining of the animal and the human, the placing of an animal head on a human god was in a way the final, crowning theriomorphic stage. It was the transfer to man of the idea that the divine was manifested in animals, that animals were the repositories of the divine. Now, in the Egyptian mentality, the animal joined to man produced the supreme form of god. The surprise in all this is that Egypt clung to this system of human animal-headed gods for the entirety of its history, while all around them other nations adopted anthropomorphism and then abstract monotheistic concepts.

For the Egyptians, the manifestation of a divinity in strictly animal form or in composite human/animal form always remained central to the representation, worship, appeasement and manipulation of the divine. The British Egyptologist Carol Andrews, in *Amulets of Ancient Egypt*, has pointed out that the identification of many animal amulets is difficult because the desire to represent the gods in animal form led to the problem that "...there were so many deities that there were not enough types of animals to suffice."[37]

The Egyptians even added a fifth, ancillary category to the representation of the divine — human heads on animals: sphinxes with human heads and animal bodies, birds with human faces like the *ba* hieroglyphic representation of the soul, or with human attributes like the arms on falcons or human heads on serpents, like one of the representations of the Theban Necropolis goddess Meretseger. Here too, we find a Paleolithic antecedent — the animals with vaguely human faces in Trois-Frères, which some ethnologists have interpreted as a desire on the part of the artist to indicate that animals like humans had souls.

NAMEABLE DEITIES AND DEMONS

Egypt's emblem/totem animals, human and combined human/animal gods and goddesses in statue form, linked to specific zones, seem to have been transformed into Egypt's first nameable, henotheistic divinities. Over thousands of years, these deities were divided into several categories — universal gods, gods who represented forces which were a projection of what was perceived as the functioning of nature, chief gods, gods who had both national functions and status and universal qualities and local, or minor gods. The gods were divided into great gods and small gods, with the pharaoh and deified humans among the small gods. Demons were also subjected to categorization, with some of them being truly demonic, others both demonic and beneficial, and still others in whose cases it is unclear whether they were gods or demons or both.

---

37. Andrews, Carol, *Amulets of Ancient Egypt*, p. 14.

A great number of animal-headed gods and goddesses were named early on. They included the several forms of "the distant one," Horus — the falcon, king of the sky, or falcon-headed sky god with one eye being the sun and the other the moon, the falcon-winged sun disk, and the royal falcon god incarnated in the ruling pharaohs who were his avatars. Re, at first the sun itself, then the father of the pharaohs, then the falcon or falcon-headed sun god associated with Horus and then the great chief god who assimilated the powers of many other gods...Seth, the indeterminate animal, donkey, but perhaps okapi, jackal or donkey-headed sky storm and war god and then the chthonian god of the desert and metals, sometimes a powerful god and at other times the incarnation of darkness and evil...Anubis, the indeterminate black dog, or jackal-headed, god of death and then god of embalmment and protector of tombs...Khnum, "he who joins, unites, builds," the ram-headed creator and then sun and Nile flood god...Serqet, "she who allows the throat to breathe" and "the mistress of the beautiful house," the scorpion protectress goddess...Seker, the falcon-headed earth/fertility, mummified death god, god of the Men-nefer (Memphis) Necropolis and guardian of the gate to the *Duat* nether world...Hathor, "the house of Horus," the great female principle, the cow-horned/sun disk goddess of the sky, love, joy, drunkenness, female sexual fertility, motherhood and then death...the "two ladies," Nekhbet, "she of Nekhbet," the vulture goddess, patron of Nekheb (Eleithiapolis) and Upper Egypt and Wadjit, "the payprus-colored one," the cobra goddess patron of Pe-Dep or Per Wadjit (Buto) and Lower Egypt and then tutelary proctectresses of the *Ta-Wy*, the Two Lands and of the pharaohs...Taweret, "the great one," the goddess of childbirth, with a fat hippopotamus head and body, woman's breasts, lion's paws and a crocodile's tail...Sakhmet, "the most powerful one," the lioness-headed/sun disk goddess of war, fiery destruction and plagues and her benevolent counterpart, Bastet, Bast, "she of the ointment jar," the cat or lioness-headed goddess of pleasure, music and dance...Khepri, "he who is coming into being," the primeval, young scarab, or scarab-headed, god of the new rising sun, and more.

WEST ASIAN IMPORTS

Egypt may have also imported anthropomorphic gods from Sumerian and Semitic West Asia, or borrowed the concepts underpinning them and re-named them. An early import, before the Early Dynastic Period (c. 3100 BC), even could have included "he who sees the throne (?)," Osiris, the chthonian god of fertility, vegetation and its cyclic death and resurrection. However, Osiris owed much to the indigenous Egyptian Busiris agricultural god, "he of Andjeti," Andjeti, and the concepts concerning his lord of the afterlife role could only have been established in Egypt itself. "The throne"(?), Isis (Osiris' wife and sister, magician and mother goddess par excellence) may have been partially influenced by the Sumerian Inanna. However, here too, it seems certain that considerable portions of the Isis profile seem to have been purely indigenous to Egypt — Isis with the headdress of a solar disc between cow horns, as the mother/sky/celestial cow goddess, seems to have been grafted from early Egyptian goddesses like Bat, Nut and Hathor, and the Isis with a pedestal or a throne as a headdress is linked to her personification as the king's throne, as the mother of the god/king of Egypt.

"South of his wall," Ptah, the early Egyptian crafts, earth and creator god, bears a strong resemblance to the Sumerian chthonian god of the waters and crafts, Enki. However, Ptah's representation in human form suggests that he was not invented before the Early Dynastic Period and in all likelihood this resemblance could be simply due to the need in both societies of having a god with craft functions. Nevertheless, Enki could have been a model for Ptah as it is unquestionable that the emphasis on the crafts arose in Sumer before Egypt.

"He of Djehuty," Thoth, who was usually an ibis-headed human, but also baboon headed, or a baboon, or an ibis, or the moon, seems to be so closely related to the older Sumerian anthropomorphic moon god Nanna (Sin in Akkadian) that at least some kind of Sumerian influence seems possible. The Egyptians may have put an ibis and baboon head on Nanna to exemplify in an Egyptian way the same attributes of wisdom, writing, the calendar as measurement of time and the moon that the Sumerians assigned to Nanna.

Menu (Min), the old god of agricultural fertility, male virility and fecundation, represented with a huge, erect, circumcised penis and frequently seen as the legendary hero of orgiastic exploits was surely one of Egypt's oldest indigenous gods, perhaps first worshipped as a shell fetish, but his profile may have been modified by West Asian agricultural values. In any case, his New Kingdom (from c. 1550 BC) consort Cadet (Qetesh), the moon, mother and love goddess was certainly of Syrian Semitic origin and their son, the storm and war god Reshpu was of Levantine Amorite origin.

Also during the New Kingdom (from c. 1550 BC), Egypt imported the West Asian mother goddesses Astarte and Anat, as well as a West Asian demon, the *akhu*-demon or *samana*-demon.

The warrior goddess, "the terrifying one," Neith of Sau (Sais) in the Delta, was worshipped in Egypt at least from the First Dynasty (c. 3100–2860 BC) and she may have possibly been imported from Libya before these dates.

Bes, the bearded, big-headed dwarf, god of mischief, pleasure, war, protector against danger and protector of pregnant women and children, came from either Africa or West Asia around 1990 BC.

As we have seen, Seth became so intimately related to Asia and disorder that it was sometimes assumed that he was of Asian origin, as dubious as this seems in historical perspective. The case for an Asian origin of the demon Apophis, as popular as it was, seems equally dubious.

From about 330 BC, when the Egyptian religion was in decline, the Greek occupiers imposed (with limited success) Serapis, a mixture of several Greek gods and Osrapis, who was Osiris and the Ptah/Apis Bull in his afterlife form.

CATEGORIES OF GODS AND DEMONS

However, while it seems certain that Egypt's first gods and goddesses were animals, plants, stars and natural sites and forces, it is in no way possible to affirm, as some have done, that all the Egyptian human-headed gods, or their original models, were of imported, Asian, origin. The human animal-headed and the human depiction of the gods and goddesses were probably added to the animal representation of the gods in Egypt between about 3300 and 3100 BC. Some major Egyptian gods seem to have originated in human form or evolved from animal to human form or to multiple human and animal forms within the Egyptian sphere.

One of Egypt's main and most popular chief gods, "the concealed one," Amun, "mentioned for the first time in the Fifth Dynasty (c. 2494–2345 BC) Pyramid Texts 301 and 579,[38] began his career in Khmun (Hermopolis) where he may have been worshipped first in the form of a frog and then as the protector of those who died from suffocation. He changed appearances and functions several times. He was a goose linked to water before becoming closely related to the ram and its fertility symbolism. The ithyphallic Min, first worshipped in Gebtu (Koptos), north of Thebes, was one of his main hypostases (essential aspects).

---

38. Faulkner, R.O., *The Ancient Egyptian Pyramid Texts*, pp. 90 and Gardiner, Alan, *Egypt of the Pharaohs*, pp. 421-422.

The crowning manifestation of this assimilating process resulted in Amun becoming Amun-Re and incorporating Re's functions of a sky, sun and primordial creator god, as well as the functions of all the other gods who became his aspects.

Amun-Re was most frequently represented in human form as a bearded man with a crown, a sun disk and two feathers, the *shuty*. But he was also represented in the Min ithyphallic form, was often ram-headed or falcon-headed with a solar disk surrounded by a uraeus, and sometimes was a ram or a falcon. During the Ptolemaic Period (332–32 BC), he was sometimes extravagantly represented as a composite of a bearded man with the body of a scarab, four arms, the legs of a man and the claws of a lion.

Perhaps the earliest primordial god, "the all and the "nothingness," "he who is and is not," the creator god Tum (Atum), in Egypt's oldest creation myth from Onu, Heliopolis, was usually represented in human form but had numerous clearly local emblematic totemistic origins in Heliopolis. His earliest aspect seems to have been the solar *benu* bird, perched on the original *benben*, the mound, the pillar, which had emerged from the watery chaos and upon which Atum created the gods and man. In primeval, chthonian form, Atum was a scarab or a snake. He was also sometimes a mongoose, sometimes bull-headed and in amulet form was a lizard.

Atum's twin children — Shu, dryness, the personification of sunlight and the god who separated the earth from the sky and ruled the atmosphere in between, and Tefnut, moisture, and the goddess eye of the sun — were sometimes depicted as humans, sometimes as lion-headed humans and sometimes as lions.

One of Egypt's oldest goddesses, "the one who belongs to the red crown, the flood," Neith of Sais, was almost consistently human-headed despite some of the most numerous and contradictory changes of all the gods and goddesses. She sometimes took the form of a cow and was linked to the sacred *lates* fish, especially in Iunyt (Esna). Her headdresses varied from a shield with two crossed arrows and the red Lower Egypt crown to a weaving shuttle.

Over thousands of years, Neith was variously goddess of war and the hunt, sky goddess, creator, "mistress of the gods," patroness of household crafts and especially weaving, protectress in dreams, protectress of the embalmed stomach of the deceased and provider of bread and water to the dead. Neith was often simultaneously a war, hunting and mother goddess as well as a primordial female principle and a great virgin. Although notoriously aggressive and prone to anger, by at least the late New Kingdom (c. 1200 BC) Neith was attributed the role of "Divine Mother" of the Universe and was an *ahet*, a celestial cow. She was now "the Great, the divine mother" and a goddess of wisdom linked to the *maat* code whose advice was sought to solve difficult problems, including judging whether Horus or Seth should inherit Osiris' crown as Lord and King of the Two Lands. Despite her virginity, in Esna she was second consort of the creator god Khnum and in *She-resy* (Fayum) she was also the mother of the fierce crocodile god Sobek and was sometimes depicted suckling a crocodile. During the Greek occupation of Egypt (Ptolemaic Period, 332–32 BC), she was assimilated with Isis.

There were also gods known as *panthees* who had multiple features incorporating several animals, usually linked to sun incarnations like the ram, the monkey or the falcon and aggressive animals like the crocodile, the lion or the dog. The *panthees* often wore terrifying masks and had double or many heads and/or multiple headdresses, a human body, arms with wings, many eyes, and so forth. All this may have indicated that the attributes of several gods had been superimposed to better serve the *panthee's* main function in amulet form: magical, prophylactic protection from danger.

One of the most popular *panthees* was Bes, who protected pregnant women and children. He was frequently portrayed in small statuettes, amulets and steles, both in households and temples. The Louvre Museum has an extraordinary bronze and gold statuette of Bes dating from Psamtek I's reign (c. 664–610 BC) in which he wears a multiple headdress of snakes over a terrifying and jovial mask with a lion's mane, has four hands with wings and a massive, erect penis; he is trampling snakes.

There were also other double gods like "the bender," Aker, the double lion, the guardian of the east/west junction, the junction between the world and the underworld and the day and night sun. In the Late Period (from c. 747 BC), it was believed that Aker enveloped the world and was "yesterday and today." Another double god was Antaios, the double falcon god, who was later assimilated by Horus.

There was a small category of gods and goddesses who personified major abstract functions and usually had no specific temples. The most notable of these was the goddess Maat, "order, truth and justice," portrayed in human form. Maat played a central role in Egyptian theology and cosmology and will be thoroughly discussed, especially in Volume II. Sia, perception, and Hu, divine creative utterance (the word), are other major divinities who play important abstract roles.

A very large number of minor gods and goddesses represented a totemistic protective force for local clans; they evolved into gods of cities and/or a deified aspect of nature. These gods had their places of worship in one or several localities in the same nome or in several nomes. Usually, their power did not extend beyond their home zone, but sometimes these minor gods became at least temporarily important while remaining intimately linked to other gods. This was notably the case for "he was on his lake," Heryshey (Harasaphes), the ram-headed creator, sky and war god of Henen-Nesut (Heracleopolis), capital of the 20th Nome of Upper Egypt, who had his moment of glory during the First Intermediary Period (c. 2181–2055 BC) when Heracleopolis was the capital of Egypt. Despite his new importance, Harasaphes remained linked to Re, Osiris and Amun.

Deified humans constituted still another category of gods. The foremost of these gods was Imhotep (fl.c. 2660 BC). He was the inventor-architect of the first pyramid, Pharaoh Djoser's Step Pyramid at Sakkara on the west bank of the Nile near Memphis, a high priest of the Heliopolis Re-Horakhte Temple, a vizier, in the central administration in Memphis and a medical doctor. According to the Egyptian priest/historian Manetho (fl.c. 300 BC), Imhotep was the inventor of the art of building with cut stone. He is also sometimes credited with improving mummification techniques and linking them to afterlife concepts. He apparently wrote several *sebayt* (wisdom texts). Imhotep was not only one of the rare commoners in ancient Egypt to have become a high official, but he is also among the few humans, aside from the pharaohs, to become a god. Imhotep (whose name means "in peace") was deified as the son of Ptah, probably during the 26th Saite Dynasty (c. 664-525 BC).

Amenhotep son of Hapu (c. 1430–1350 BC) was another of Egypt's foremost deified humans. He was Amenhotep III's (c. 1390–1352 BC) chief architect and as such he supervised the building and artistic projects of one of Egypt's greatest builders. He also built a large cult temple for himself and a tomb (TT368) in Thebes and was almost immediately deified after his death.

At the top of the category of human gods was the ruling pharaoh, the *ntr.nfr*, *netjer nefer*, a "perfect god," but this status was not enough for some pharaohs who sought to be fully-fledged "great gods."

A god or a goddess was either a "great god," a *ntr.aA* or a *wr*, a *wer* — this included gods and goddesses like Horus, Hathor, Re, Ptah, Osiris, Isis, Thoth,

Amun and many others — or a "small god," the *ndsw*, *nedsew*, the "small ones" — and this included a huge number of minor and local gods and goddesses. A "great god" could also be an "All-god," a *nb-r-dr*, a *nib-r-der*, a "Lord of all," like Re or Amun, or a *nesu netjeru*, the "King of the gods," like Amun.

Belief in the demons and their powers was a central reality in the Egyptian religion, as in all ancient religions. Just as the gods were everywhere, the demons, hundreds of them, were everywhere — in the sky, on the earth — and especially in the desert — in the Hall of Two Truths afterlife judgment court and in the *Duat* afterlife. The demons wreaked illness, misfortune, death, and destruction, tried to prevent the sun from rising and tried to prevent the deceased from entering the *Duat*. However, demons also protected Osiris, the temples and tombs, helped the pharaohs win wars and cured those who revered them. The demons were believed to have numerous animal, human, human/animal and multiple animal forms, the most usual being snakes, scorpions, reptiles and insects.

It is often difficult to establish which demons were originally gods who personified the negative aspects of nature and gradually came to be seen as evil gods, as demons with powers similar to the gods. This was particularly true of the 42 assessors who assisted Osiris in "The Hall of Two Truths" afterlife court after it was invented about 2180 BC. These ferocious demons clearly went deep into Egyptian prehistory and history. Among them were Fire Embracer, Swallower of Shades, Fiery Eyes, Doubly Evil, Demolisher, Owner of Faces, and Eater of Blood. "The Swallower of the dead," Am-mut, the female lion/hippopotamus/crocodile who supposedly ate the heart of the deceased who failed the test of eligibility for the afterlife, was one the most terrifying demons in the Egyptian system. The baboon Babi was both a beneficial god and a murderous demon of darkness — his phallus was the door-bolt of the *Duat*. Identification with his phallus ensured good sexual intercourse and he chased off snakes, but he lived on human entrails and unless tamed by magical spells, killed without warning for this purpose. Shezmu, in human, lion-headed or falcon form, was the god of the wine-press, but he also drew out the blood of those who had been rejected in "The Hall of Two Truths" and cut up and cooked gods in the afterlife for Pharaoh Unas (c. 2375–2345 BC).

Was Nehebklau, the serpent with human arms and legs (sometimes with two heads, one at each extremity) who guarded the entrance to the *Duat* afterlife and who threatened both the gods and humans, but sometimes gave food to the dead, a god or a demon or both? Was the lioness-headed goddess Sakhmet more important in her aggressive, destructive, plague bringing aspects, or in her aspects of plague curing, protection, righteous wrath, fire spewer in war and as the wife of the good god Ptah? The case of Seth is the most ambiguous of all — he was one of the most powerful, full-fledged gods, but also the most demonic divinity.

The huge, spiraled serpent, "the roarer," Apophis, 450 cubits long (about 765 feet), who every day tried to prevent the sun from rising, was the most terrifyingly powerful of the demons. Apophis was also sometimes depicted in his equally terrifying aspect of Akhekh, an antelope with a bird's head, three cobra uraei and wings. But there were also Am-heh, with a hunting dog face, who lived in the Lake of Fire in the *Duat* and was the "Devourer of millions" and who could only be tamed by Atum; and the Red Fiends, the Crusher of Bones, Apshai, the scarab who ate the deceased and the cobra Hetepes-Sekhus and her team of crocodiles who slaughtered the enemies of Osiris.

A demon could have his "tongue in his anus" and "eat the bread (excrements) of his buttocks"; he could be a crocodile whose "teeth are a knife," or a snake who has "eaten a mouse...and chewed the bones of a putrid cat"; he could be a "Male...whose head Thoth has cut off" and who has "swallowed an ass"; he could be a "scorpion...with its sting erect."[39] In the *Duat*, guarding the entrances to the twelve sections, were serpents with three heads, serpents with human heads and four legs, serpents who spewed fire and poison, lion, crocodile, scorpion and winged demons.

The "great," or national (or universal) gods, were worshipped everywhere while the power of the "small" local gods often did not extend beyond a few square miles. Polytheism gradually systematized meanings for all these gods and goddesses, but confusion, contradictions and frequent changes in the characteristics and names of the gods persisted in ancient Egypt right until the end.

INEXTRICABLE SYNCRETISM

More than any other society, ancient Egypt adopted a syncretic approach to its divinities. The fact that a god could emerge from another god and assume

---

39. Borghouts, J. F., *Ancient Egyptian Magical Texts*, pp. 17-18. Faulkner, R.O., *The Ancient Egyptian Book of the Dead*, Spell 31, p. 56; Spell 33, p. 58; Spell 40, p. 61. Borghouts, J. F., *Ancient Egyptian Magical Texts*, p. 77.

an earlier god's functions under a new name was common to all societies, but only early Egypt adopted a syncretic system which preserved the names and functions of combinations of gods. Egypt amalgamated its divinities without exclusion or repudiation, creating an inextricable theological mess, but also a pragmatic capacity to face any situation. This system existed in Egypt from the rise of the ennead, the *pesedjet*, the grouping of nine divinities, which can be dated at least from the Fourth Dynasty (c. 2613–2494 BC) and probably much earlier. In Mesopotamia it was not until the 18th century BC that a similar situation arose with the theologians of the chief god Marduk proclaiming that almost all the gods were his manifestations.

A powerful god assimilated the functions and name of another god, while each god maintained some of his exclusiveness and attributions. One of the most astounding example of amalgamation, changes and multiple identities, accompanied by the continued coexistence of several individual identities, was the god Horus. But of course, Horus was far from alone in going through the multiple changes which render clear profiles impossible. Re almost equaled him and became Atum-Re, Re-Horakthe (a composite form of Re and Horus, but also implicitly including Atum and Khepri), Sobek-Re and Khnum-Re and then the "All-god." Hathor, Ptah, Osiris, Neith and others were no slouches when it came to adopting new functions and names. Egypt's greatest chief god, Amun, pursued a career over 2600 years into Roman times which involved fabulous changes taking him from an obscure local frog, goose and ram god to becoming Amun-Re *nesu netjeru*, Amun-Re, the "King of the gods" in which all the other gods were his aspects.

Moreover, if the main tendency was to impute the functions of other gods to a chief god while allowing these other gods to continue their existences and functions, there was also an incredible overlap in the number of gods exercising the same function. A single example serves to illustrate this situation: the gods and goddesses connected with the Nile. Andjeti, Osiris, Re, Ptah, Amun, Hapi, Khnum, Anuket, Satis and others were all divinities of the Nile in one way or another.

The amalgamation of two or several gods into a unit and the superimposition of contradictory layers of mythology concerning them frequently also represented a pragmatic need. The introduction of new gods and new concepts obviously required name and appearance changes for some of the Egyptian gods and corresponded to the real and changing needs of society. Even at an early date, it also clearly had something to do with a unifying tendency, and a trend toward monotheism which the Egyptians with their deeply ingrained polytheistic spirit never managed to carry to its logical conclusion. However, it also had much to do with which great chief god and which great temple were in positions of domination. The changes carried out this way solved both theological and power conflicts and clarified the role of the leading god and the leading temple.

Without neglecting the possible pertinence of Henri Frankfort's interpretation (which will soon be discussed) that these changes were coherent "multiple approaches and answers," it can nevertheless be neutrally said that inextricable syncretism was the natural tendency of the Egyptians. It governed not only the changing nature of their gods but also their mythology and theology. Whether it was an individual god, the amalgamation of two or more gods into one in a chief god dynamic, religious innovations or new twists to old myths, these changes were usually incorporated into the system and presented as having always existed.

DUOS AND TRIADS OF GODS AND GODDESSES

As in Sumer, in Egypt the divinities were almost always grouped into duos. The most primary form of the duo owed nothing to amalgamation but was quite simply the couple; a god necessarily had a goddess consort and vice versa. There were also well-known duos in which association was the key: this was the case for Horus and Seth; the "Two Ladies" Nekhbet and Wadjit, the tutelary protectresses of Upper and Lower Egypt; and the two sisters of Osiris, Isis and Nephthys.

In a further projection of human and animal behavior and as the essence of fruitful multiplication, the divine couple had a child and became a triad, a trinity. The trinities thus formed were almost systematically composed of a god, his goddess consort and a youthful god, usually male. For the Egyptians, the triad seems to have constituted some kind of a permanent principle that transformed the contradictions of duality into coherent connection. It is therefore not surprising that the family triad, in which the duality of the couple is resolved in the child, was clearly the most usual form of triad.

If the principle of transforming the contradictions of duality in the triad, in the child, were extraordinarily illustrated by the qualities Horus inherited from Osiris and Isis, the same cannot be said for many of the other Egyptian triads which frequently constituted artificial combinations. Moreover, in the case of the multiple Horus, of course nothing was ever simple and he was also part of a triad composed with his first mother/wife Hathor and their human-headed son Ihy, a god of creation in his youthful phase as player of the sacred sistrum rattle. Denderah, the city of Hathor, was the main cult center of this triad.

The family triads were usually identified with a city or a nome. One of the leading family triads was in Thebes, capital of the Fourth Nome of Upper Egypt, with "the concealed one," Amun, "the mother," the vulture or human or lioness-headed sky and mother goddess Mut and "the wanderer," the youthful moon, protector/healer god Khons with a child's side-lock of hair and a moon-and-crescent headdress. However, this Thebes triad seems to have originated as an artificial or symbolic family triad since Khons was both a universal god and part of the triad in Ombos with Sobek and Hathor; it was the snake goddess Amaunet who really was the wife of Amun, before being replaced by the until then obscure vulture Mut in the descriptions of the Theban triad. Nevertheless, it was the Amun/Mut/Khons triad which in the Eighteenth Dynasty (c. 1550–1295 BC) became one of the most powerful in Egyptian history. Amun was the divine father of the reigning pharaoh and his consort Mut was the greatly revered divine mother of the pharaoh, linked to one of his wives or his mother and mother of the future pharaoh.

In Memphis, the capital of the First Nome of Lower Egypt, the ruling triad was the crafts and creator god Ptah, the lioness-headed war/destroyer goddess Sakhmet and Nefertem, the primordial *seshen* (lotus) which emerged from chaos and shuts down like the sun at night and re-emerges in the morning. This triad seems to be a near-perfect illustration of Egyptian dualism composed of harmonious opposing forces resolved in a positive result.

In Esna, capital of the Third Nome of Upper Egypt, the original ruling triad was the ram-headed creator god Khnum, the goddess guardian or "mistress" of the local territory, probably Nebetu'u and the god and personification of magic in child form, Heka. The lioness-headed goddess Menhyt may have been a second wife and may have replaced or assimilated Nebetu'u as Khnum's consort and Heka's mother. The primeval cow goddess Mehetweret fits in somewhere in this confused triad which eventually stabilized into Khnum, the war and mother goddess Neith and Heka.

Further south, in Elephantine, capital of the First Nome of Upper Egypt, Khnum also became the omnipotent god of the First Cataract of the Nile and here ruled in triad with the human-headed goddesses Satis, Guardian of the border with Wawat/Nubia, with a headdress of the Upper Egyptian crown and antelope horns and Anuket, with a headdress of a crown of feathers. This triad provided the refreshing waters of the inundation and the nourishment of fields.

Another well-known triad stemmed from both the family system and star worship — Sah, Sopdet and Soped. Sah was the personification of the Orion Constellation, Sopdet was the goddess who personified the Dog Star Sirius, first represented as a celestial cow; and their son was Soped, a star and the falcon god of the eastern border. But, of course, Sah was Osiris and Sopdet was Isis and so this triad was linked to the Osiris, Isis and Horus triad and Soped was also Har-Soped.

The triadic system was not utterly systematic and also was evolutionary. Triads emerged which were based on what were seen as composite universal realities, combined functions. In this manner and over perhaps 2300 years Ptah, at first the god inventor of the crafts and a creator god, "the opener" and powerful henotheistic god of Memphis, joined at a early date during the Old Kingdom (after c. 2686 BC) with the mummified falcon or human headed crafts and god of the dead of Memphis, Seker and then in the Late Period (c. 747–332 BC), the two were joined with Osiris to form the funerary composite Ptah/Seker/Osiris. Together this triad represented the single function of the Kingdom of Death.

Above all, as the chief god tendency strengthened, duos, triads and several gods were fused into unities, usually to the benefit of Horus, Re, Osiris, Ptah or Amun. This evolutionary capacity of the triadic concept culminated in the royal, totalizing, monotheizing, organic unity triad of Amun/Re/Ptah in the early 13th century BC. In this triad, the unity of all the gods through the combination of the three major state gods, Amun, Re and Ptah, was ordained. Amun was concealed, but his face could be seen in the sky as the sun Re, while on earth his body was Ptah. How much of this theology was authentically unitary and how much of it was related to amalgamating the gods to give the greatest power to a single god, Amun, while somehow maintaining diversity is a very difficult question.

Another kind of triad in which three functions were constantly associated was constituted by Heka, Sia and Hu, the gods who personified magic, perception and divine creative utterance. They participated in the creation of the universe, constantly accompanied Re and helped him defeat darkness and chaos as represented by Apophis and aided the ruling pharaoh/god to maintain the orderliness of creation.

ENNEADS, CREATION MYTHS AND THEOLOGIES

At the summit of the Egyptian pantheon was a group of nine gods called the *pesedjet*, the ennead. It was first established by the clergy in Heliopolis, capital of the 15th heron, *benu* bird, nome of Lower Egypt (and today a suburb of Cairo). The ennead of gods and goddesses and its theology were probably underpinned by myths going back beyond 3000 BC. It probably appeared in detailed form during the Fourth Dynasty (c. 2613–2494 BC) and was consolidated during the Fifth Dynasty (c. 2494–2345 BC) when references to the ennead and its creation myth and theology in the Pyramid Texts (c. 2375–2055 BC) were frequent.

The Heliopolitan Ennead postulated a series of nine primordial gods and goddesses, perhaps based on the magical concept that three triads, three times three, constituted a nine which supposedly embodied the totality of existence. The ennead supposedly mirrored the multiple families, triads, of harmonious universal forces and explained the origins of the world. Diversity was the fundamental reality of the Heliopolitan and succeeding enneads, but at the same time there was indeed an attempt at crude unity in plurality and diversity, an attempt to make an addition of the "millions," *heh*, in universality, sacred completeness and totality.

Over more than a thousand years, the original Heliopolitan Ennead was significantly modified in Hermopolis, Memphis and Thebes. These modifications had the curious result that, except for the Heliopolitan Ennead, none of the newer enneads was ever permanently composed of nine divinities — they ranged from seven divinities in Abydos to fifteen in Thebes.

The Heliopolitan creation myth declared that the earth (a primeval mound, the *benben*) and life emerged from Nun, the personification of the *waret* watery realm of chaos. Nun was sometimes called the father of the gods. Atum, who was "the all and the nothingness" (completed being and non-being), the creator and the sun, surged out of the liquid chaos with the primordial *benben*. Pyramid Text Utterance 600 says: "O Atum-Khoprer...you rose up as the *bnbn*-stone (the *benben* primeval mound) in Onu (Heliopolis), you spat out Shu, you expectorated Tefenet..." Utterance 527 says that "Atum is he who (once) came into being, who masturbated in Onu. He took his phallus in his grasp that he might create orgasm by means of it and so were born the twins Shu and Tefenet." The Bremner-Rhind Papyrus (written about 312 BC) says that Atum after "copulating with his hand" (the female principle), "sneezed" Shu and "spit" Tefnut.[40] The Egyptologist David Lorton on the Net, using the Bremner-Rhind

Papyrus says it was auto-fellatio.[41] The first gods were thus created — the twin couple of lions, brother and sister and lovers, Shu, the god of dryness, who then separated the earth from the sky and was the personification of sunlight, and Tefnut, the goddess of moisture.

The children of Shu and Tefnut were Geb, the green-skinned earth god, and his blue-skinned wife/sister Nut, the sky goddess. Nut was most frequently depicted slender and naked, with stars on her body, hands and feet touching the two edges of the earth and arched like the vault of the sky, but also as a celestial cow. Geb was often depicted beneath Nut, sometimes with his erect penis pointing upwards to her, and alongside her father Shu who had separated the earth from the sky. Geb and Nut were the parents of Atum's four great grandchildren, Osiris, Isis, Seth and Nephthys. After the creation of these nine gods and goddesses, universal order and human life were created.

Atum was the prototype of the three generations of his immediate descendants and of all the succeeding gods. These gods were the great first ancestors of mankind, the primogenitors, the great fathers. The Heliopolitan Ennead, theology and creation myth from at least the Fifth Dynasty (c. 2494–2345 BC) were dominated by the sun god Re, as Atum-Re, who assimilated Atum's powers. Heliopolitan theology decreed that before the pharaonic dynasties of "human gods," Egypt was ruled by the nine deities of the divine Heliopolitan Dynasty — beginning with Re-Atum and ending with Geb, Osiris, Seth and Horus.

At least before the end of the Old Kingdom (c. 2181 BC), a second "great and mighty ennead" (but also sometimes called the "Lesser Ennead"[42]) led by Horus, as the son of Osiris and Isis, plus Thoth, Maat, Anubis and other less important gods, was added in Heliopolis.

In the justice-hungry Middle Kingdom (c. 2055–1650 BC), the Coffin Text Spell 1130/1031 version of the Heliopolitan creation myth was significantly altered. Now Re had "made the four winds that everyone might breathe in his lifetime...the great flood so that the poor as well as the great might be strong...I made every man equal to his fellow, and I forbade them to do wrong, but their

---

40. Faulkner, R.O., *The Ancient Egyptian Pyramid Texts*, pp. 246 and 198 and the Bremner-Rhind Papyrus, British Museum (10188).

41. Lorton, David, *Autofellacio and Ontology*, 1995, www.geocities.com/Athens/Academy/1326/ontology.html.

42. Faulkner, R.O., *The Ancient Egyptian Pyramid Texts*, Utterance 606, p. 250 and Ut. 219, p. 47.

hearts disobeyed...I created the gods from my sweat, and mankind from the tears of my eyes."[43] (Many Egyptologists have noted the interesting correlation between the Egyptian words for man — *remet* — and tears — *rimi*.)

The Heliopolitan Ennead and its theology always remained the most influential in Egypt. The theology and creation and geopolitical myths propagated by Heliopolis always remained essential centralizing factors in Egyptian religion and society.

The Heliopolis clergy seems to have been at the root of many major religious innovations. Many of the magical utterance-spells of *The Pyramid* Texts, which contained the fundamental aspects of early Egyptian religion and were the forerunners of *The Book of the Dead*, seem to have been their work. Over thousands of years, this clergy was at the root of many major politico-religious innovations such as the decrease in the pharaoh-gods' powers, the amplified feudal powers and afterlife privileges of the ruling elite, the unification of the dogmas of the rival Re-solar and Osiris-afterlife myths and finally, primitive monotheism in the mid-14th century BC with Pharaoh Akhenaten's Atenism.

However, while the Heliopolitan creation myth was the oldest and the preeminent one, more than ten creation myths were invented, each identified with the theologies of a great city. Three other enneads and theologies played key roles in Egypt — the Hermopolitan and the Memphite (both with ancient local origins, but apparently consolidated after the Heliopolitan system) and the Theban (beginning with the New Kingdom, c. 1550 BC), which was a kind of amalgamation and apex of Egyptian beliefs.

In Hermopolis, capital of the 15th hare nome of Upper Egypt, the *pesedjet*, "the ennead," was in fact a *khmun*, an ogdoad. The Egyptian name of Hermopolis, Khmun, means "Eightfold." With its four couples of divinities, the Hermopolis Ogdoad described original chaos, tumult and concealment before creation occurred. The gods and goddesses of the Ogdoad ruled creation during a golden time before dying and going to live in the afterlife. The Ogdoad was said to have already been in existence before the emergence of the primeval mound, the *benben*, which supposedly arose in Hermopolis and not Heliopolis.

The four gods in the Hermopolis Ogdoad were frogs or frog-headed and the goddesses were snakes. Nun and Naunet were the personifications of the formless primeval waters. Heh and Hauhet were infinity, never-ending space, and eternity. Heh as a god and as a hieroglyph — a squatting human figure with

---

43. Faulkner, R.O., *The Ancient Egyptian Coffin Texts*, Volume III, pp. 167-168.

an upraised knee and arms uplifted to the sky — represented eternity and the "millions," millions of years and millions in general. Kuk and Kauket were darkness. Tenem and Tenemet were twilight. There were several versions of the Ogdoad, including later ones in which Amun and Amaunet represented concealment.

The Hermopolis Ogdoad could become an ennead when the ibis or baboon-headed god of wisdom and writing, Thoth, whose main place of worship was Hermopolis, was added to the list. Thoth's wife was sometimes said to be Maat, the goddess of primeval order, truth and justice; and together they are sometimes referred to as the parents of the eight Hermopolis divinities.

Despite its emphasis on the primordial situation before creation, the end result of the Hermopolis creation myth was the same as in the other Egyptian creation myths: at some stage, Re (or Re-Atum), the sun, created himself on the primeval mound and then in a chain reaction of fission created the other gods and goddesses in pairs of opposites, the earth, the annual inundation of the Nile and humanity.

Four different versions of the creation of the world from the *benben* were developed in Hermopolis: a great egg was laid on the *benben* by a cosmic goose (containing Re as sun and light who then created the world); an ibis (Thoth) laid the cosmic egg; a lotus stemming from the waters of the Sea of Two Knives in Hermopolis opened and gave birth to the solar child Re; a scarab, the rising sun and the eye of Re, was inside the lotus and was transformed into a crying boy whose tears became mankind.

Extrapolating from a few Pyramid Texts (Utterance 301 which refers to Nun, Naunet, Amun and Amaunet together), the reference to Hermopolis as the "Unu (Heliopolis) of the south" (Utterance 219) and references to "chaos gods" (Utterances 558, 406), the Hermopolitan Ogdoad appears to have been Egypt's second oldest grouping of divinities. However, its theology and creation myth are mainly known from inscriptions in the surviving Theban Karnak Temple (after c. 1550 BC) as there are no surviving remains of the Hermopolis Temple.

The ennead in Memphis, capital of the first white wall nome of Lower Egypt, was led by the preeminent local crafts and creator god Ptah. Memphite theology features aspects that set it apart significantly from both Heliopolitan and Hermopolitan theologies, but there is great difficulty in dating when it attained its plenitude. Only a single document amply describes Memphite theology — the Shabako Stone (in the British Museum since 1800 and first reliably translated by James Henry Breasted only in 1901). The Kushite Pharaoh

Shabako (c. 716–702 BC) claimed that the Stone's contents had been faithfully copied from a "worm-eaten" Memphis Ptah Temple text dating to the Old Kingdom (c. 2686– 2181 BC). Unfortunately, for the sake of truth, there are many reasons to doubt this claim and only a few to support it.

Memphite theology as contained in the Shabako Stone postulated that the entire Heliopolitan Ennead was an aspect of Ptah and that Ptah preceded Atum and was greater than him. Ptah was pre-existent to the creation of the universe; he was Ptah-Nun, part of original chaos, part of the personification of the primeval waters, *Nun*, from which everything emerged. By his desire, with his *ieb*, his heart (which for the Egyptians was the "mind," the seat of intelligence, knowledge and emotion) and his tongue, the word, Ptah created the universe and everything in it including the earthly elements and man. Ptah's mind thought out creation and his tongue materialized it. Ptah, or rather Ptah/Nun, was the Egyptian version of the first principle, the first cause and the primogenitor of mankind. These notions of pre-existence and the creative power of will and the word bear a startling resemblance to Hebrew and Christian theology and to the Greek *logos* — and the concept of all the gods being aspects of Ptah seems to be close to a kind of crude multiform monotheism.

In addition to Ptah, the Memphite Ennead included another local god, "risen land," Tatenen, the god of the bowels of the earth, with a headdress of ram's horns and a crown. Tatenen was a form of the self-created Ptah who had emerged with the primordial mound of earth from chaos. Nun and Naunet were the primeval waters of chaos and Atum, in the form of a serpent was the active agent of creation. The four other gods in this ennead were probably, but not certainly, Horus, Thoth, Nefertem and a serpent god. Ptah embodied all these eight gods.

The story of the Shabako Stone/Memphite theology is one of those chestnuts that abound in Egyptian lore. However, despite its folkloric aspects, Memphite theology is of immense importance — perhaps almost as important as Heliopolitan theology — in understanding man's evolution from polytheism to monotheism.

Was it a "worm-eaten" copy of a very ancient papyrus? If it was, much in its theology constituted early examples of abstract reasoning concerning a god's will and creation, a unifying tendency and a totalizing or amalgamating process regarding the divinities, that is, their reduction to a single god with the other gods constituting his aspects (of course to the advantage of the local god Ptah).

As such, Ptah/Memphite theology would be an early tendency toward monotheism.

It can be supposed that the inclusion of gods from the Heliopolis and Hermopolis Enneads in the Memphis Ennead could have had strictly theological reasons for amalgamating the gods, but it could have also been an attempt to avoid irritating the powerful clergies of Heliopolis and Hermopolis. Moreover, the key constitutive elements in Memphite theology — creation by the heart/mind and the tongue/word — could have been a radicalization of the Heliopolitan concept that Atum was self-created with the assistance of god Sia, the personification of perception, and the god Hu, the personification of creative utterance. At the same time, Ptah's existence before Atum as much as it can be seen as a theological concept of divine pre-existence, also can easily be interpreted as a sign that the Memphite Temple sought to dominate the older Heliopolitan Temple. Despite claims that the Memphite Ennead and theology were the oldest in Egypt, it seems that the inclusion of gods from Heliopolis and Hermopolis and the development of Heliopolitan theological concepts would logically make it posterior to these latter enneads.

Was the Shabako Stone an archaizing, manipulative retrospective document written in Pharaoh Shabako's time? Did Shabako attempt to instill some of the glory of the Old Kingdom into his Kushite regime? Was Shabako attempting to promote peace, reconciliation and unity in his day by promoting the idea that the Kushite pharaohs were continuing an old Ptah tradition of peace and reconciliation in the Horus-Seth confrontation? Was he highlighting rising moral considerations, as we shall see in succeeding chapters? Was Shabako attempting to gain the favors of Memphis and its clergy, which was still very powerful in the late 8th century BC and which had ardently resisted his brother Pharaoh Piye's (747–716 BC) military takeover of Egypt?

Breasted, who was the first to understand the immense "philosophico-religious" importance of the Shabako Stone, first ascribed an early Eighteenth Dynasty (shortly after c. 1550 BC) origin to its contents, before definitively opting for an origin in "the Pyramid Age" (for him c. 2980–2475 BC).[44] Other eminent Egyptologists, like Adolf Erman (1854–1937) also pushed the origin of the Shabako Stone back to "about the beginning of the Old Kingdom" (which in his chronology was c. 2830 BC).[45] Henri Frankfort dated it to some time "in the

---

44. Breasted, James Henry, *Development of Religion and Thought in Ancient Egypt*, pp. 46-47.
45. Erman, Adolf, *La Religion des Egyptiens*, p. 117.

third millennium BC."[46] John A. Wilson (1899–1976), in *The Intellectual Adventure of Ancient Man*, 1946, concluded that "the language and typically early physical arrangement of the text" proved that it was "a document which comes from the very beginnings of Egyptian history..." Wilson saw strong geopolitical reasons for this Early Dynasty Period (from c. 3100 BC) origin: "The text in question is part of a theological argument of the primacy of the god Ptah and thus of his home, Memphis."[47]

Many modern Egyptologists now tend to believe that the Shabako Stone/ Memphite theology was invented in Shabako's time or they attribute a late New Kingdom date (c. 1200 BC) to its contents. This supposition is primarily based on the philological analysis made by Friedrich Junge in 1973 who believes that the Shabako Stone was adapted from late New Kingdom sources and deceptively used archaic language and style to make it appear to be a copy of an ancient document. This view is accepted by some modern and eminent Egyptologist/ translators, notably the Israeli/American Miriam Lichtheim (b. 1914) who in 1980 revised her earlier firm opinion of an Old Kingdom origin of the Shabako Stone and concluded that "generations of Egyptologists...[had been] misled [by] the strongly archaizing language of the text..."[48] However, this view is not accepted by other modern and eminent Egyptologists like Nicholas Grimal (b. 1948), who wrote in 1988 that "The original version...obviously dates to the Old Kingdom...probably...more specifically to the Fifth Dynasty"[49] (which Grimal dates as c. 2510–2460 BC).

Perhaps the most reasonable view is held by the Canadian Egyptologist Donald Redford (b. 1934). He deplores that the period between 725 and 525 BC "has never been adequately explored by scholars," but concludes that that the "impact" of Memphite theology could only have occurred during this period. "[N]o one can deny," states Redford, "that the contents became known [again?] only at the beginning of the Kushite period around 710 BC and were disseminated during the following two centuries...[when] the entire eastern Mediterranean including the Aegean found themselves thrown together in a cultural, an economic, and, more importantly, a spiritual community of interests."[50]

---

46. Frankfort, Henri, Ancient Egyptian Religion, An Interpretation, p. 126.
47. Wilson, John A. in The Intellectual Adventure of Ancient Man, pp. 55-56.
48. Lichtheim, Miriam, *Ancient Egyptian Literature, Volume* III, p. 5.
49. Grimal, Nicholas, *A History of Ancient Egypt*, p. 45.
50. Redford, Donald B., *Egypt, Canaan and Israel in Ancient Times*, pp. 399-400.

It seems that while the arguments for an 8th or 13th century BC date of the contents of the Shabako Stone are indeed convincing, it has nevertheless not been sufficiently demonstrated why its archaic language, style and layout, reminiscent of the Old Kingdom Pyramid Texts, are necessarily fakes. The legitimate argument that the policy of the entire 25th Kushite Dynasty (c. 747–656 BC) in everything from politics to religion to art was to make its decisions, beliefs and production appear to be ancient or the continuation of ancient traditions does not seem to fully answer this objection. Moreover, the political considerations which plead in favor of a late 8th century origin are even more applicable to an Old Kingdom origin; as Wilson has noted, it would have been perfectly coherent to elevate Ptah, the henotheistic god of Memphis, to the foremost divine creator role and endow his ennead with a new, dominant theology mirroring the celebration of the new role of Memphis as the capital of Egypt, united for the first time.

Beyond purely linguistic questions, other questions have to be asked, even if they cannot be answered.

Could Memphite theology have been created almost *ex nihilo* at relatively late dates or was it at the least the culminating point of ideas already inherent in Ptah/Memphite and other Egyptian theologies? The least that must be said is that even if Ptah is not often mentioned in the Pyramid Texts, the basic Heliopolitan and Hermopolitan concept of a primordial time before creation is found in many Pyramid Texts, some going back as far as c. 2375 BC, and that this was indeed the pre-existent situation in which Ptah-Nun was part of original chaos. Ptah is frequently mentioned in the Middle Kingdom (c. 2055–1650 BC) Coffin Texts, but not a single Coffin Text spell refers to a heart/tongue creation role for him. On the other hand, *The Hymn to the Nile* (*Hapy*), which most probably dates to the Middle Kingdom, metaphorically considers Ptah as "the fashioner" of everything. This hymn describes Hapy, the god of the Nile Inundation, as being of "the like of Ptah," The might that "fashions all…"[51] Breasted saw Ptah as having evolved "into master-workman of the universal workshop" in the early New Kingdom (c. 16th century BC). He cited a *Hymn to Ptah* of this time in which it is abundantly clear that Ptah "is the mind [heart] and tongue of the gods," who "wills" everything into existence.[52] Siegfried Morenz (1914–1970) noted that the

---

51. Lichtheim, Miriam, *Ancient Egyptian Literature, Volume I*, p. 207.

52. Breasted, James Henry, A History of Egypt, From The Earliest Times To The Persian Conquest, p. 299-300.

Berlin Papyrus 3048 from Sety I's time (c. 1294–1279 BC) refers to Ptah as "fashioner of the earth."[53] Rameses III's (c. 1184–1153 BC) *Prayer to Ptah* (in the Great Harris Papyrus, (c. 1153 BC, found in a Theban royal craftsman's tomb in Deir el-Medina, now in the British Museum and, at 133 feet long, the biggest surviving Egyptian papyrus) referred to Tatenen (the earth aspect of Ptah) as "father of the gods, great god of the first time, former of men, maker of gods, beginning that became the first primeval being, after whom happened all that came to past, who made the sky after the conception of his mind...who formed the earth by that which he himself did...who made the nether world...men live by that which comes out of his mouth..."[54]

It is therefore clear that whether or not some of Memphite theology's steps toward monotheism go back to the Old Kingdom, the concept of Ptah as "the fashioner" of everything who operated with the will of his mind/heart, and the action of tongue was only well anchored in the New Kingdom (c. 1550–1069 BC).

This legitimately poses another question: Was the main thrust of Shabako Stone/Memphite theology not Old Kingdom concepts, but the New Kingdom Theban theology of Amun-Re, the totalizing, monotheizing, pre-existent creator god concepts adapted from Heliopolitan solar theology and 14th century BC Atenist proto-monotheism? Even if this were so, the Memphite concept of the power of the word, at whatever date it was established, would still constitute a major theological invention.

Of course, the tale of the Shabako Stone has to be finished by noting that it was apparently used as a millstone for more than a thousand years before being discovered in a badly damaged state. Poor old Breasted complained that "with a better light than it is possible to get in the [British] museum gallery, more could in places be gotten out."[55]

The 15-god "ennead" in Thebes, capital of the fourth *was*, scepter, nome of Upper Egypt, went further in one-upmanship than all the other enneads, theologies and clergies. Its goal was clearly to render Thebes, its god Amun, and his theology more important than all the other major Egyptian cities, enneads, theologies and clergies. However, in a first stage, it probably also attempted to reconcile the southern and northern halves of Egypt by incorporating the Heliopolitan god Re and his solar theology into Theban theology.

---

53. Morenz, Siegfried, *Egyptian Religion*, p. 92.
54. Breasted, James Henry, *Ancient Records of Egypt*, Vol. 4, 308, pp. 162-163.
55. Breasted, James Henry, *Development of Religion and Thought in Ancient Egypt*, p. 47.

Around 2100 BC, towards the end of the conflict-ridden First Intermediate Period, Thebes imported several gods. These included the mighty fertility and virility god Min from Koptos, but also a minor Hermopolitan air god, a god who protected those who had died from suffocation, that is Amun. Amun's name (*imn*) means "the concealed one" and he achieved great popularity as the god who acted in a concealed way through the air or the wind, as the god who knows all and acts secretly and wisely.

The fortunes of Amun rose steadily after the victory of Thebes, led by Pharaoh Mentuhotep II (c. 2055–2004 BC), over Herakleopolis for the control and reunification of all Egypt. Opening the new Twelfth Dynasty (c. 1985–1795 BC), Amenemhat I (c. 1985–1955 BC), which means "Amun is at the head," was the first pharaoh to take an Amun name, indicating that by this time Amun had taken over as chief god of Thebes from "the savage one," the falcon war god Montu. Amenemhat I continued the policy of his Mentuhotep predecessors by also adopting a Re name, Sehetepibra, "He who appeases the heart of Re," as his praenomen throne name. The Re solar theology of Heliopolis was now also the theology of Thebes, but under the direction of a new composite chief god Amun-Re, "King of all the gods." The absolute preeminence of Amun-Re's ennead and theology were established after the opening of the New Kingdom (c. 1550 BC). Amun-Re became, and remained, Egypt's main god, although after the sack of Thebes by the Assyrian Emperor Assurbanipal in c. 663 BC, his popularity steadily declined.

The Theban creation myth developed during the New Kingdom decreed that in the beginning *Kem-atef*, a snake destined to live only a certain time, gave birth before dying to Irta, the creator of the earth. Irta gave birth to the eight divinities of the Hermopolitan Ogdoad, including Amun and his consort Amunet. Amun now was the original *Kem-atef* serpent, as Amun-Re; as Min-Amun, he was the serpent Irta; as the Ogdoad, he was reborn; and as the solar child who emerged from the Hermopolitan lotus, he was Re. In this new schema, the consort of Amun was no longer Amunet but the mother goddess Mut. Their son was the moon god Khons and one of Amun's main aspects was Min.

Thebes was now the original primeval mound, *the benben*, which had emerged from Nun, the formless primeval waters. Amun, in both his concealed and air deity capacity inherited from the Hermopolis ennead, had created himself on the Thebes *benben* and he amalgamated the Heliopolitan Ennead including Re and Osiris, the entire Memphis/Ptah ennead and the entire Hermopolitan ennead. The Leiden Papyrus I 350, from Rameses II's time (c.

1279–1213 BC), tells us that "Thebes is *normal* beyond every (other) city. The water and land were in her from the first times. (Then) sand came to *delimit* the fields and to create her ground on the hillock; (thus) the earth came into being."[56]

In a chief god and monotheizing dynamic, the Theban clergy literally amalgamated all the gods, all the enneads, all the theologies, all the creation myths and all the cosmogonies as aspects of Amun. In fact, a new doctrine which can be called Amunism was created. The Eighteenth Dynasty (c. 1550–1295 BC) *Hymn to Amun-Re* (Papyrus Boulaq 17 in the Cairo Museum), but already partially inscribed on a statue dated to the Thirteenth to Sevententh Dynasties (c. 1795–1550 BC), N° 40959, now in the British Museum), gave Amun a host of superlative titles and functions the "UNIQUE," the "chief of all the gods," the "father of the gods..."the lord of the gods whose shrine (name) is hidden"; "the sole one who made [all] that is." Amun-Re even "supplied the needs of the mice in their holes."[57] Re came to be considered Amun's son and the eye of the Thebes ennead and of course, Amun-Re was also incarnated in the ruling pharaoh who was his son. Above all, Amun, Re and Ptah were amalgamated into an organic unit, into a great triad of creation and total sovereignty.

During the New Kingdom, the Thebes Ennead was the major ennead and its clergy the most numerous, powerful and richest in Egypt. It consecutively constituted the strongest totalizing, amalgamating chief god theology ever developed in Egypt, the apex of Egypt's monotheizing tendency, the stage which directly led to Akhenaten's brief period of Aten primitive solar monotheism in the mid-14th century BC, the rejection of this monotheism, the anchoring of chief god solar theology within an exuberant polytheistic system and the root of extreme religious fundamentalism in the Twentieth Dynasty (c. 1186–1069 BC) (more on this in Volume II.)

In Elephantine and Esna, in Upper Egypt, the ram-headed creator-potter god Khnum modeled nature and man from clay. This myth bears a strong resemblance to how the Sumerian water god Enki created man. Khnum was sometimes represented with four heads as the symbol of the union and totality of creation — Re for the sun and the sky, Shu for the atmosphere between the earth and the sky and for sunlight, Geb for the earth and Osiris for the underworld. The Khnum creation myth was also obviously linked to the creative virility of the

---

56. Wilson, John in *Ancient Near Eastern Texts Relating to the Old Testament*, p. 8.
57. *Ibid.*, pp. 365-367.

ram and the annual Nile inundation and silt from which pottery was made. It could go back to the Early Dynastic Period (c. 3100–2686 BC), but was certainly embellished, especially in Esna, with the building of the Ptolemaic Khnum Temple (after c. 180 BC).

During the Roman occupation of Egypt (after 30 BC), a creation myth arose in Esna centered around the goddess Neith as a sexless great cow who was part of Nun, the watery chaos, and who created thirty other gods by merely naming them in Ptah/Memphite theology fashion. She also created her son Re from an egg, as well as the giant snake Apophis, the necessary force of evil counterbalancing the good Re. Humans were then born from Re's tears and Khnum's potter's wheel and Neith left Esna to live in Sais in Lower Egypt. This myth not only indicates the amalgamation of many of Egypt's key creation beliefs, it also illustrates the constant theological rivalry between Egyptian cities, as it is abundantly attested that Neith as a sky, war and hunting goddess was one of Egypt's oldest goddesses whose origin goes back to Sais and Abydos from at least the First Dynasty c. 3100–2890 BC).

In Edfu, a creation theology arose, which naturally favored the beloved local and national god Horus, mainly in his primeval falcon form, although all the forms of Horus had been amalgamated in Edfu. This creation theology could have arisen during the building of the Ptolemaic Horus Temple in Edfu (c. 237–57 BC), but perhaps it originated during the New Kingdom (after c. 1550 BC). It decreed that two deities had emerged from chaos on a primeval mound and stuck a stick into it; a falcon flew onto the stick and caused light to appear in the darkness of chaos; the mound became the earth and its central sacred place was the stick which became the first temple, the temple of Horus the falcon in Edfu.

MAGIC UNDERPINS EVERYTHING

Magic was ubiquitous in ancient Egypt. *Heka*, magic religion, was already a central reality in the Predynastic Naqada III period (c. 3300–3150 BC). It was consolidated into the most elaborate and complex system of magic ever invented, probably in the Early Dynastic Period (c. 3100–2686 BC). There is no way of knowing whether the god of magic, Heka, had been invented to personify magic in Predynastic times, but by the Old Kingdom (from c. 2686 BC), he occupied this role. He was usually represented as a man with loosely hanging hands, sometimes holding snakes, with a short beard and a *nemes*, royal headdress, marked by the hieroglyph for a lion's backside; sometimes Heka was represented as a child.

The entirety of the system of deities, demons, cosmogonies, theologies and the afterlife was underpinned by *heka*. *Heka* was at the very heart of creation myths, the operation of the universe, temple rituals and contact, appeasement and manipulation of the gods, the combat against demons, art and architecture, political power, international relations, oracles, personal protection, healing, medicine and life after death. Wherever we turn, everything was subjected to what today generally would be considered crude techniques and rituals of magic. Indeed, magic to prevent personal trouble and harm and to threaten and curse others probably constituted the core of religion for ordinary Egyptians.

Heka was the force used by the creator god Atum. Then, the regent of the earth, the ruling pharaoh, was divinely empowered with the greatest *heka*. The *heb-sed*, royal jubilee, ceremony periodically re-affirmed the pharaoh's magical prowess and his right to rule. Incantations and rituals were used every day by the priests in the temples to maintain creation within the cosmic *maat* order and prevent *izfeh*, disorder, to manipulate the gods to obtain favors or appease their fury or fickleness and to correct demonic and/or negative situations. Spells (some of them still used today), frequently linked to sexuality, and involving an incredible variety of incantations, amulets, material techniques and vegetables, animal parts, beverages and dejections, were constantly cast by the priests and ordinary people to at least impede the horrible deeds of hundreds of monstrous demons.

Hieroglyphs, sculpture and painting were alive and were the essence of the substance of life and not mere representations of ordinary reality. Execration texts written on statuettes or pottery and then smashed were used by notables and ordinary people to eliminate enemies, rivals or detested people, whose names and often the names of their fathers and mothers were specified.

Magical amulets were literally revered; they were invaluable both in life and in the afterlife. Amulets were called *nehet*, *meket*, *sa* — words linked to protection — and perhaps most often w*edja*, linked to healing and welfare because the w*edjat*, the "Eye of Horus," was Egypt's most popular and potent amulet. Amulets, in Egypt as elsewhere, sunk their roots deep into prehistory and were frequently linked to animal fetishes and then associated with gods and goddesses. They were believed to provide protection, the annulment of evil powers, welfare, healing and the transfer of qualities, like the strength or swiftness of animals, to the wearer or user.

The Egyptians probably invented the biggest and most varied collection of amulets in the history of mankind. Over thousands of years, literally millions were fabricated, usually in faience, shell, ivory, precious stones like lapis lazuli, jasper, alabaster, turquoise, silver, gold and later in bronze. The extensive use of amulets and their importance can be measured by the fact that 143 amulets were found in the wrappings of the minor pharaoh Tutankhamun (c. 1336–1327 BC). The MacGregor Papyrus lists 75 different amulets, most of which can be seen at the Louvre Museum in one astounding display case. In 1914, W.M.F. Petrie listed 275 amulets in his book *Amulets*. In *Amulets of Ancient Egypt* (1994), Carol Andrews gave an explicative description of more than 500 amulets. Using Petrie's basic system of classification, Andrews divided them into several specific categories such as "gods, goddesses and sacred animals, protection and aversion, scarabs for the living and funerary scarabs, amulets of assimilation, amulets of powers, and offerings, possessions and amulets of property."[58]

Andrews goes right to the centrality of amulets in Egyptian life. "[A]mulets and jewelry incorporating amuletic forms were an essential adornment...The Egyptians made amulets with the intention that their magical powers should last forever. Even for those forms whose primary purpose was to be worn in life, the ultimate resting place was on the mummy in the tomb to be of use in the Afterlife."[59]

Some of Egypt's principal "positive" amulets were the *wedjat* Eye of Horus — a human eye with the traits of a falcon, symbolizing being complete, protection, healing and rebirth; the *kheper* resurrection and heart scarabs — a scarab linked to the morning resurrected sun god Khepri, also systematically used from the beginning of the New Kingdom to prevent the heart from testifying against the deceased in the afterlife Hall of Two Truths; the *ankh* — a kind of a "T" surmounted by an oval figure and representing the force and breath of life; and the Osirisian *djed* stability pillar — a column with four flat, lateral, protruding sections symbolizing stability, strength and permanency.

Amulets depicting disabled animals supposedly annulled their dangerous and evil powers. The use of amulets and various objects to annul evil powers often used a curious reverse logic from that of protective amulets. The wearing of a hippopotamus or donkey figure, representing Seth, was believed to enchant the animal and prevent it from using its evil powers. Small steles, cippi, of various

---

58. Andrews, Carol, *Amulets of Ancient Egypt*, p. 5.
59. Ibid., pp. 6 and 106.

gods and goddesses and especially of Horus standing triumphantly on two crocodiles, that is, Horus standing on Seth, were believed capable of defeating malefic forces. Cippi were also used as prophylactic protection against venomous stings from scorpions and snakes and bites from crocodiles. Protective figurine amulets in dwarf form with a falcon's or a ram's head, or a bald head, probably representing Ptah, and called *pataikoi* by the Greeks, seemed to have appeared in the late Old Kingdom (c. 2686–2181 BC) and were especially widespread after the beginning of the New Kingdom (from c. 1550 BC). *Pataikoi* protected against dangerous animals and were often depicted as eating snakes.

Amulets, statuette/fetishes of the gods and goddesses, magical papyri, concoctions to be eaten or applied to the body, magical drawings and words, and hundreds of spells and counter spells were employed by everybody for just about everything that could happen in a lifetime and in the afterlife. This included warding off evil; protection from demons, dangerous animals (especially crocodiles, snakes, scorpions and lions); protection in childbirth and for the family; prevention of pregnancy; and against bad fortune and illness — even nightmares and headaches; spontaneous healing and medical treatment; and communication with the dead. Spells were cast for gaining the affection of others and to break others' spells. Pierced statuettes, the breaking of pottery, cakes of phalli wrapped in meat and given to a cat to eat, the repetition of incantations (usually four times), spitting, trampling, and burning wax figurines were ways to cast spells on others and to wreak revenge. Curses and threats against those who spoke badly of the gods or robbed tombs were frequent. Incantations and rituals accompanied medical treatment and mummification. Water poured over statuettes of healer gods and goddesses inscribed with magical formulae was drunk to obtain cures from illnesses.

The Dutch Egyptologist J.F. Borghouts (b. 1939) has probably made the most extensive study and translation of Egyptian spells, which he qualifies as "everyday magic" in contradistinction to state and temple magic. He qualifies them as "individualistic compositions, more or less like hymns," "verbalized core matter of the rite," "an immediate, unmythical confrontation between the magician or sufferer and an enemy," using a "linking mechanism" to the divinities which can "be broken up by the reluctance or refusal on the part of the divine or demoniac powers involved."[60]

---

60. Borghouts, J. F., *Ancient Egyptian Magical Texts*, pp. VII, IX and X.

A person's name, the *ren*, had profound magical quality and power. For Egyptians, as for many ancient peoples, this was not just a name; it was one of a person's souls, his identity and essence. No magical protection from evil or misfortune and no projection of such misfortune was possible without reciting the person's *ren* in spells; and no afterlife with the same privileges as had been enjoyed in this life was possible for any Egyptian unless he had a name. When a person's name was chipped out of an inscription, it signified a second death for the victim — that is, eternal elimination. It meant obliterating a person from among the living, both in this life and in the afterlife.

Magical techniques were used to provoke controlled dreaming and perhaps for meditation and esotericism. Magical utterances/incantations and rituals in the funerary texts, and notably the Pyramid Texts, the Coffin Texts and *The Book of the Dead*, guaranteed an afterlife. *Ushabti* statuettes did the menial work in the afterlife and the paintings of food in the tomb could become real food.

During the Old Kingdom Fourth Dynasty, when Re became the greatest god (c. 2566–2558 BC), the god Heka accompanied Re in his solar barque and helped him in his fight against Apophis, the eternal enemy of solar order. Heka was sometimes described as the first-born child of Re.

But order for the Egyptians was not just cosmic order; by the New Kingdom (from c. 1550 BC) it was the order of Egypt as the imperial ruler of the world. Here, too, the correct use of *heka* was essential. The pharaoh drew up the lists of enemy countries and together with his sorcerers performed the execration rituals and spells that assured their enemies would be rendered powerless and Egypt would be victorious.

When the words: "all the Asiatics — of Byblos, of Ullaza, of Iy'anaq...of Jerusalem...their strong men, their swift runners, their allies..." were inscribed on a bowl and the bowl was smashed, it was certain that these Asiatics would become powerless and even die. When the priest in charge of conducting the temple service uttered: "The Eye of Horus drives away enemies [for] Amon-Re, Lord of the Thrones of the Two Lands,"[61] he believed what he was chanting. When the priest/doctor prescribed "water of pig's eyes with honey" and accompanied this with spells, he was sure the treatment was efficient. A man believed that when he was dead he would be able to make visits out of the afterlife by using Spell 17 of *The Book of the Dead*: "...going out into the day, taking

---

61. Wilson, John in *Ancient Near Eastern Texts Relating to the Old Testament*, pp. 329 and 325.

any shape in which he desires to be...and going forth as a living soul by the Osiris N (the name of the deceased)."[62] Threats were made: "any man who shall rip out any stone or any brick from this tomb...I will seize his neck like a bird and I will cause all the living who are upon earth to be afraid of the spirits who are in the West (the afterlife),"[63] and there was indeed cause to fear that this could happen. When it was proclaimed that the self-created creator god Atum created the god Shu (dryness, the atmosphere and sunlight) and the goddess Tefnut (moisture and the eye of the sun) by masturbating or by spitting and sneezing, neither version was doubted. A great magician "selected from an infinite number...whose name is not known," even considered himself capable of provoking an upheaval in the natural elements: "I will cause the earth to be invaded by a flood and then the south will be the north, and the earth will turn itself."[64]

As difficult as it may be to understand today, Egypt's love and extraordinary development of magic was not a manifestation of crudeness, hysteria and ignorance; it was the manifestation of a vanguard society. It is much too simplistic to label ancient Egypt as a crude society governed by magic as we understand the word today. First of all, magic had been the main vector of what was later called religion for tens of thousands of years everywhere among mankind. Putting religious *heka* at the center of its system did not make Egypt a retrograde society, as magically dominated societies are today; at the time, it made it the lucid continuator of one of the main inventions which had advanced man's knowledge of himself.

The Egyptians, like other peoples of the time, did not view magic as *magical*, as miracles. *Heka* was not irrationality and superstition; it was a force, an energy, a tool of knowledge, creativity and power, much like our science and technology. Magical techniques using rituals, objects and words, and spells were seen as an efficient, pragmatic way of manipulating existence, the universe and the gods. Although we loosely translate the term *heka* as "magic," its meaning seems to have been closer to the concepts of power and creativity. In addition to the term *heka* and the usual terms associated with magic, such as "casting spells," "sorcery," "art of the mouth," "conjuration" or "exorcise," the Egyptians also

---

62. Faulkner, R.O., *The Ancient Egyptian Book of the Dead*, p. 44.

63. Wilson, John in *Ancient Near Eastern Texts Relating to the Old Testament*, p. 327.

64. Borghouts, J. F., *Ancient Egyptian Magical Texts*, pp. 87-88. From the Magical Harris Papyrus in the British Museum (10042).

employed many empirical terms in their practices, terms like "influence," "power," "greatness" or "protection."

Egyptian *heka* sorcerers displayed the same self confidence (and sometimes arrogance) and confidence in their methods as do modern scientists. Magic was, so to speak, *scientific*. In fact, the Egyptians were a highly pragmatic people and they fervently believed that magic was truth.

This vital, complex system of magic religion constituted the soul, the exuberant driving force and efficient tool for the building of a modern, prosperous country. However, when the false and illusionary nature of crude magic — or rather classical magic — had become abundantly apparent, perhaps around the 6th century BC, especially in Greece with science and in Israel and Persia with monotheism, for the Egyptians it nevertheless remained a key part of the permanent divine laws.

Heka remained at the very heart of Egypt and, contrary to most other societies which gradually differentiated between magic and religion or pretended that they were against magic, Egypt always maintained the centrality of *heka*. The Egyptians clung to a mixture of primitive magic and rituals (alongside pragmatic, materialistic techniques) and even accentuated magic from the Late Period (c. 747–332 BC), in times when magic was beginning to take on the negative and silly connotations it has today.

CHANGE WITHOUT CHANGES — THE CORE MEANING OF THE EGYPTIAN RELIGION

Nobody in ancient Egypt ever admitted that theological or political change had occurred. Yet changes were being made all the time, resulting in immense confusion — and to a modern mind, immense contradictions; but the Egyptians never acknowledged them. They merely heaped layers of meaning atop one another, amalgamated one or many gods with another god, assigned functions to gods which were already being fulfilled by other gods, let stand side by side rival and contradictory creation myths and lumped together seemingly incompatible theological concepts.

The Egyptians had a passion to change, synthesize, and preserve all at the same time. They seem to have loved change...without changes. A substantial part of the constant changes in the status of their gods and their theologies seems to have to do with this attitude. In particular, the extent of change in the appearance and characteristics of the divinities was almost automatically amplified by the vast possibilities of form open to the theologians and artists — the animal, animal-headed and human forms of the gods and goddesses could be combined in countless ways.

Permanency — *unchangeability* — was the fundamental declared characteristic of the Egyptian system of gods, demons, cosmogonies, myths, theologies, magic, time, nature, humans, animals, language, art, political and social systems and the afterlife. The divine was immanent in everything in the universe. The system was a description of the *truth* of the origins of the universe and its nature and man and his role and duties. The operation of the universe — the *maat* primeval order of truth — which the gods had created — absolutely described what the pharaoh-god and man should believe and the correct and only way for the pharaoh and man to behave in the recurrent daily dualistic struggle to maintain the *maat* harmony.

All this had been given at the time of creation, at *zp-tpj, zep tepey,* "the first time" or "first occasion" and it had been decreed for *nuheh,* for all time, for endlessness, for eternity and for *shenu,* for all around, millions, encircling, eternity. The universe and everything in it lasts for *heh,* "the millions," infinity, and it was unchangeable. Progress was a totally irrelevant term — the ancient Egyptians would have been incapable of understanding the later Moslem Koranic concept of newer, "better verses," better answers after a first answer had been given.

Despite the many differences and contradictions in the theologies and cosmogonies of the various enneads, the numerous local variants and powerful local gods and goddesses and the great divide between the royal religion and the commoners' religion, there was a common bedrock of approach and beliefs. Centuries of theological speculation eventually led to a basic Egyptian concept of the universe, which seems to have been expressed in elaborate written form for the first time in the Pyramid Texts (c. 2375–2055 BC). It was composed of an above, the sky, the heavens (the *pet*), ruled by Re in "lightland" (Ra *netjer-aa-neb-pet,* "Re, the great god, Lord of the Sky"); an earth, in which *ta* ("the land", Egypt), that is *Ta-Wy,* the Egypt of the Two Lands, united by Horus and ruled by a pharaoh-god (*sa* Ra, the son of Re), was the center and "the nine arcs (*pedjet*), or "foreign lands" (*khasut*), was the periphery and usually *khefty,* enemy, territory; and a below, "the divine subterranean place" (*Khert-Netjer*), the land of the nether world living dead, (the *Ta-Duat*), ruled by Osiris (the *Wnn-nfr, Wennefer,* the completed, eternally or continuously good being).

The orderly and harmonious cosmos and the earth, divided by the Nile, were surrounded by the *izfeh*, the disorder of the *waret* primeval watery chaos. The *pet*, the sky, was held in place by four pillars, usually depicted as mountains or women with outstretched arms. The sun (Re) and stars, as gods and goddesses, traveled across the horizon, the *akhet*, from east to west during the twelve daylight hours in the *Mandet* solar boat, "the barque of millions of years" (770 cubits long, about 1324 feet) which cruised across the watery sky of the universe like a boat on the Nile. It was on "the barque of millions of years" that the gods governed the universe. The sun, Re, set in the form of the tired, old god Atum. Re then switched to his *Meseket* night solar boat, became the night sun Osiris, lord of the *Duat* underworld, and traversed the *Duat* in twelve hours. Re then re-emerged and engaged and always defeated the demon serpent, "the roarer," *Aapep* (Apophis), in the daily deadly primordial battle in which Apophis tried to prevent the sun from rising. Re was reborn, to rejoicing, in the east as the rising sun in the form of the youthful sun, the scarab-headed god Khepri.

Once these notions were established, they were declared to be permanent and unchangeable dogmas which could not be openly contradicted. Nevertheless, like any religion or metaphysical system, change was in fact not only possible, but ongoing.

This basic context of *change without change* must be borne in mind when examining the emergence and the evolution of the Egyptian religion. This mixture of conservatism and de facto radicalism resulted in the non-elimination and superimposition of contradictory layers of theology and mythology and the fusing of several gods into single gods as his aspects in order to respect the fiction of permanency and *unchangeability*.

A first major change in the system occurred towards the end of the Old Kingdom (c. 2181 BC), when everybody (and not just the reigning pharaoh) was granted the right to have souls and an afterlife. The culminating point in the situation of permanency and change came in the New Kingdom with Amunism, Amun Theban mythology and theology, in which the previous Horian and Re systems were simultaneously eliminated and maintained.

The key question is: Was all this sophisticated or holistic coherency, or was it utter confusion, a confusion which was rationalized as magic or even hypocritically accepted "truth"? Spell 17 in the New Kingdom *Book of the Dead* (c. 1550 BC) illustrates this problem: "I am the Great god, the self-created. Who is that? The Great god, the self-created, is water, he is Nun, father of the gods. Otherwise said: He is Re...Who is he? He is Atum, who is in his sun-disc.

Otherwise said: He is Re when he rises in the eastern horizon of the sky...I am Min in his going forth, I have set the plumes on my head. What does this mean? As for Min, he is Horus who protected his father...As for his plumes on his head, it means that Isis and Nephthys went and put themselves on his head..."[65]

Indeed, *what does this mean?* To consider that there was some kind of sophisticated coherency in these numerous forms or transformations of the gods and in Egypt's constant theological transformations in general seems to be fundamentally wrong. If there was any kind of coherency, it seems to have had more to do with the Egyptians deeply believing or feeling that there were many ways to skin a cat — while somehow not killing the cat. If there was coherency, it was in the Egyptian capacity not to be put off by contradiction.

The elusive idea of a coherent core meaning for the Egyptian religion has been sought ever since Herodotus wrote *Histories* in c. 440 BC. As will be discussed in Volume II, from the Italian philosopher Marsile Ficin (c. 1433–1499) to the Freemasons even today and including people like Giorando Bruno, Isaac Newton and Friedrich Schiller, the assertion of such a core meaning often revolved around a *prisca theologica*, a god-given first secret, permanent religious knowledge and a hocus-pocus proclamation of a hidden monotheism. This imaginary vision succeeded in defying commonsense for centuries.

From the late 19th and early 20th centuries, generations of Egyptologists were influenced by the sincere but motley evaluation of the one of history's pioneer Egyptologists, E.A. Wallis Budge. Budge was one of the leading representatives of the 19th century attempt to attribute coherency to the Egyptian religion, but at the price of an imaginary construction and Christian prism which has since largely been disproved across the board. Budge simultaneously accepted that from "the standpoint of Christian spirituality...Egyptian rites were cruel, bloodthirsty, and savage, that the legends of the gods are childish, and are the outcome of debased minds and imaginations"...which are "the relics of a barbarous and half-savage period in Egyptian history"; but that "Nothing...can alter the fact that beneath such rites, legends, and beliefs there lay...wonderful religious and moral conceptions," that "all its [the Egyptian religion] fundamentals remained unchanged throughout the Dynastic Period," but that after "the New Empire, its spiritualities became buried under a mass of beliefs which were purely magical in character," that "the Egyptians believed in the existence of [a monotheistic] god Almighty and that

---

65. Faulkner, R.O., *The Ancient Egyptian Book of the Dead*, p. 44.

his behests were performed by a number of 'gods' or as we might say, emanations, or angels."[66]

A first turning point came with the German Egyptologist Adolf Erman, who attempted to employ a scientific, impartial approach to Egyptian society and religion. In Erman's *Life In Ancient Egypt* (*Aegypten und ägyptisches Leben im Altertum*) (1885), somebody with a good understanding of the Egyptian language for the first time swept away much of the prevailing romantic, mystical and adulatory approach to Egyptology. He concluded that there was "unparalleled confusion" in the Egyptian religion and "This chaos was never afterwards reduced to order; on the contrary, we might almost say that the confusion became even more hopeless during the 3000 years that...the Egyptian religion 'flourished.'"[67] In 1905, in *Die ägytische Religion* (*A Handbook of Egyptian Religion*) and in its much revised 1934 final, third edition as *Die Religion der Aegypter* (*La Religion des Egyptiens*), Erman submitted Egyptian religion to an analysis based on the study of a vast number of documents as well as climatic, geographic, political, economic and social conditions, international relations and human nature and psychology.

Perhaps above all, Erman saw the Egyptian religion (like any other religion) formed by the need for the "divine...the fantastic and the supernatural," "fantasy...chance occurrences...barbarity" leading to "ceaseless transformations (and) strange...and great confusion...and contradictions." Furthermore, he saw the long development of the Egyptian religion as being even more affected than other religions by a lack of "any solution of continuity." Erman concluded that "In the Egyptian religion, tradition remained stronger than in other religions and we always note with surprise how this people cultivated, side by side, things of the present as of the most remote past, even if one was in flagrant contradiction with another." Erman simply asked: "Are not a lack of clarity and contradictions the inevitable lot of any religion?"[68]

The process of clarification begun by Erman was given a big boost in 1961 with the publication of *Egypt of the Pharaohs* by Sir Alan Gardiner (1879–1963). Gardiner did for Egyptian history what Erman had done for Egyptian religion — he provided as clear as possible a view, untainted by romanticism.

---

66. Budge, E.A. Wallis, *Osiris & The Egyptian Resurrection, Volume I*, pp. 348, 349, ix, xii, xiv.

67. Erman, Adolf, *Life in Ancient Egypt*, p. 261.

68. Erman, Adolf, *La Religion des Egyptiens*, pp. 21-30.

However, between Erman and Gardiner, the search for Egypt's core meaning and the evaluation of its role in history headed off in many wild directions.

1912 was an important date for the elaboration of a positivist variant in the evaluation of ancient Egypt, in *Development of Religion and Thought in Ancient Egypt* by James Henry Breasted (1865-1935), who had been a student of Erman. Breasted, the eminent founder of American Egyptology and the Oriental Institute of the University of Chicago, was among the first Egyptologists who attempted to appreciate the Egyptian religion for what it was, even if he was frequently dithyrambic. Only two years after the publication of the first reliable edition of the Pyramid Texts by Kurt Sethe (1869-1934), Breasted became the first Egyptologist to draw major conclusions from the vast amount of material therein — "[T]he oldest chapter in human thinking preserved to us, the remotest reach in the intellectual history of man which we are now able to discern." Noting that the Pyramid Texts "are chiefly concerned with the *material* welfare of the departed in the hereafter," he also saw that they contained "the earliest chapter in the moral development of man as known to us." With *The Admonitions of Ipuwer* (which he dated to c. 1906-1887 BC), he saw the emergence of "the earliest crusade for social justice...[and t]he appearance in this remote age of the necessary detachment and the capacity to contemplate society." Breasted drew worldwide attention to the "non-national, universal faith" which was that of Akhenaten, when "for the first time in history monotheism dawned."[69]

Undoubtedly Breasted, perhaps because of his deep Christian sense of history, went overboard. Although he was right to see that a struggle for moral evolution had taken place, he attributed considerable success to it followed by a relapse into magical decadence from the 16th century BC when in fact it now seems clear that the ancient Egyptians' greatest concern all along was order and decent behavior in society and not high moral values. Breasted also indeed saw that the "social, moral and religious aspirations" of the 6th century BC Hebrew prophets had "overtaken" the aspirations of Akhenaten, but he nevertheless assumed that "the general drift of the religious development in Egypt is analogous to that of the Hebrews...We have seen the Egyptian slowly gaining his honest god."[70]

---

69. Breasted, James Henry, *Development of Religion and Thought in Ancient Egypt*, pp. 84, 165, xvii, 215, 6.

70. *Ibid.*, pp. 343, xiv, 369.

Around 1946, an extraordinary adventure centered in the Oriental Institute of the University of Chicago began; it eventually constituted the biggest turning point of all in the study of Egypt. The key actors were the Dutch Egyptologist and archaeologist Henri Frankfort, his art historian wife H.A. Groenewegen-Frankfort and the American Egyptologist John A. Wilson. The groundwork was laid with a series of lectures which were published as *The Intellectual Adventure of Ancient Man*. Here the two Frankforts outlined what they called "the logic of mythopoeic thought" as it applied to the ancient Near East and how it "admit(ted) the validity of several avenues of approach at one and the same time" and how this approach did not mean "inconsistencies." In the specific section concerning Egypt, Wilson declared that "Within Egypt the most divergent concepts were tolerantly accepted and woven into what we moderns might regard as a clashing philosophical lack of system, but which to the ancient was inclusive." Wilson advanced the concept of the "consubstantial" and "complementary" nature of the Egyptian approach in which phenomena and gods could have "a different form of appearance for a different purpose" while remaining coherent in an overall manner. Wilson noted that in the Amon/Re/Ptah trinity, "Three gods are one and yet the Egyptian elsewhere insists on the separate identity of each of the three." [71]

In 1948, in *Ancient Egyptian Religion*, Henri Frankfort integrated all these ideas and adamantly concluded that there was indeed a coherent, core meaning to the Egyptian religion. What I have described above as haphazard and probably confused, the ongoing transformation and the tendency of change without change, the Egyptian ability to skin a cat in many ways while somehow not killing the cat, Frankfort more eloquently described as the Egyptian system of "multiplicity of approaches," "multiple answers," "several separate avenues of approach" and "meaningful inconsistency." Frankfort strongly supported the concept that *unchangeability* was one of the central Egyptian theological and political "assumptions" and claimed that there was only an "apparent confusion" since "Ancient thought...admitted side by side certain *limited* insights, which were held to be *simultaneously* valid, each in its proper context, each corresponding to a definite avenue of approach."[72]

---

71. Frankfort, Henri, Groenewegen-Frankfort, H.A. and Wilson, John in *The Intellectual Adventure of Ancient Man*, pp. 10, 20, 19, 33, 62-66.

72. Frankfort, Henri, *Ancient Egyptian Religion, An Interpretation*, pp. 4, 20, 91,19, viii, 3, 4.

Frankfort was the first to see things this way and to ascribe a coherency to the contradictions and changes in Egyptian theology, which in his mind were of course not contradictions and radical changes. In a mere 180 pages, Frankfort not only advanced his theory of coherency but also magnificently cut straight through to the essentials and main motivations in the Egyptian religion and probably defined its main concepts better than had ever been done previously. He opened new and multifaceted ways of understanding which have increasingly become mandatory in any study of the Egyptian religion. There could no longer be any doubt that the Egyptian religion was multiple, complex and incapable of being reduced to a single rigorous interpretation. It has become exceedingly difficult to make any analysis of Egyptian religion without it somehow being in relation, for or against, Frankfort's views.

Nevertheless, there was both something profoundly true and profoundly false in Frankfort's concept of "multiplicity of approaches and answers." This concept gave order to the Egyptian religion; perhaps too much order. It does not by any means account for what can only be considered as real contradictions and obvious and frequently diametrical changes over thousands of years. There certainly was a "multiplicity of approaches and answers," but it goes beyond that — there were thousands of cases where such a system of coherency in multiplicity cannot possibly be applied. A few fundamental examples would be: the multiple and frequently contradictory forms, functions, transformations and amalgamations of gods like Horus, Re and Amun; the reverence for the animal manifestation of a god in some cities and the profanation of the same animal manifestation in other cities; and the numerous changes and contradictions in afterlife beliefs. The overlapping, contradictory episodes in much of Egyptian mythology, which nevertheless constituted a key basis for theology, are still other examples showing that Frankfort's theory cannot work globally — to choose only a single startling example in mythology/theology, the Pyramid Texts (c. 2375–2125 BC) portray the god of wisdom and writing Thoth as having conspired with Seth to kill Osiris, while from the New Kingdom (c. 1550–1069 BC), texts of the myth portray Thoth as a champion of Osiris' views and the defender of his son Horus.

Real changes, contradictions, confusion and a good dose of haphazard development mark the Egyptian religion, as they do all religions.

Frankfort's views, nevertheless, represented the key turning point in the interpretation of many outstanding questions. Such an achievement and honor should have been enough for any man, but he accompanied it with cruel criticisms of some of his predecessors and perhaps did not attribute sufficient credit to his then wife, H.A. Groenewegen-Frankfort, in the establishment of his central ideas. His evaluation of Erman as somebody who "gave in 1905 a masterly but patronizing account of weird myths, doctrines, and usages, while the peculiarly religious values which these contained remained hidden from his lucid rationalism" was excessive. His evaluation of Breasted as somebody who "described in 1912 a 'Development of Religion and Thought in Ancient Egypt' towards ethical ideals which pertain to biblical but not to ancient Egyptian religion"[73] put the focus on a partial misconception in Breasted's vision to the detriment of the vast and often correct picture of the Egyptian religion and history that Breasted was sketching out in many pioneering books at that time. And his own conclusion that there was coherency in the Egyptian religion was excessive, in itself.

It was certainly legitimate to criticize Erman's systematically rationalistic approach — or more precisely, his insufficient consideration of the emotional and poetical factors in religion, and Breasted's anticipations and over-evolutionary approach. But in turn Frankfort must face the criticism of frequently rationalizing the irrational and vastly underestimating at least some of Erman's and Breasted's perceptions. Moreover, Frankfort underestimated or rejected political, economic and sociological factors. His analysis that the rise of Amun-Re to the position of Egypt's supreme god was a coherent theological process and that it is irrelevant to link it to the enormous political power of the city of Thebes, is simply astounding.[74]

Frankfort also seems to have accepted much in Egyptian religion at face value. He seems to have assumed a coherency and a logic in Egyptian theology — albeit what he called a "mythopoeic" logic — which may have only been partially there and sometimes was not there at all. The word "magic" is mentioned only once in Frankfort's book and he angrily dismisses any possibility that the Egyptians might have "held a number of incompatible ideas in a hazy or muddleheaded confusion."[75] Nevertheless, imaginative magical attitudes — which make anything feasible — and their paradoxical consequences of pragmatic workability and muddleheadedness are indisputably as much characteristics of the entirety of the history of religion — and especially their

---

73. *Ibid.*, pp. v and vii.
74. *Ibid.*, pp. vi, 22.
75. *Ibid.*, pp. 91, 4.

early phases like those in Sumer and Egypt — as intentional efforts at understanding and expressing reality.

The debate on the "multiplicity of approaches" and the "multiple answers" was magisterially advanced into "complementary propositions" by the Latvian Egyptologist Erik Hornung (b. 1933). In 1971, in his best known work, *Conceptions of the Gods in Ancient Egypt: The One and the Many*, Hornung gracefully acknowledged his debt to Frankfort and proposed a framework of meaning concerning the Egyptian approach to religion and the gods which has indeed further opened the road to greater clarity in the analysis of the nature of the Egyptian religion. Hornung also modestly acknowledged that "Anyone who takes history seriously will not accept a single method as definitive; the same should be true of anyone who studies belief seriously."

Hornung prudently sees Egyptian formulations of the divine "as one and almost absolute and then again as a bewildering multiplicity" as part of "the one and the many as complementary propositions, whose truth values within a many-valued logic are not mutually exclusive, but contribute together to the whole truth." He sees an impossibility in choosing between Egyptian thought and theology as "undeniably 'illogical' or 'prelogical'" or perhaps being "a different type of logic which is not self-contradictory, which can only be a many-valued logic." He concludes that "the Egyptians strove earnestly after a system"; that "...they certainly did not proceed carelessly in their thought"; and that "So long as the intellectual basis of a many-valued logic remains uncertain, we can indicate only possibilities, not definite solutions. If the basis is not established, Egyptian thought and all 'pre-Greek' thought will continue to be open to charges of arbitrariness or confusion."

Hornung, contrary to Frankfort, does not believe that Egyptian thought "as a whole was 'mythical' or mythopoeic'." He states that a "metalanguage" is "necessary" to understand how the Egyptians described their systems of divinities and "their continually changing combinations," and that "global truth," perhaps linked to quantum mechanics rather than "the arbitrary or confusion"[76] is probably the key to the Egyptian way of thinking.

We are dealing here with a great genius, perhaps with the greatest living Egyptologist, who has perhaps best decorticated the Egyptian religion. Hornung probably has come closest to providing a complete picture of ancient Egyptian

---

76. Hornung, Erik, *Conceptions of God in Ancient Egypt, The One and the Many*, pp. 11, 237-243, 257.

religion and the beginnings of a global, coherent vision. Nevertheless, his basic position was that the Egyptian approach to the gods and religion was a matter of "complementary propositions" and the "one and the many" suggests some kind of an equal importance of the two factors, when in reality it would seem that the "many," infinity in diversity, was always the fundamental Egyptian vision of the universe — the primeval and enduring Egyptian center of gravity was *heh*, "the millions," infinity.

Moreover, Hornung's opinion that Egyptian thought represented some kind of alternative "metalanguage" logic, some kind of well thought out complemental system, leads me to add a caution similar to that which applies to Frankfort's "multiple approaches and answers": Hornung's "complementary propositions and many-valued logic" certainly go far towards better understanding aspects of the way the Egyptians thought, but by no means do they eliminate the great mass of obvious contradictions and real confusion in Egyptian theology. Above all, they do not eliminate the strong likelihood that the successive and frequently haphazard syntheses in Egyptian theology were largely the fruit of the way the Egyptians thought — that is, mythologically, magically and therefore indeed, "illogically."

In some ways Frankfort, especially, but also Hornung seem to apply a kind of reverse interpretation to Freud's definition of the id as the primitive, inherited characteristics which drive the unconscious, which includes contradictory impulses and inclinations and which operates without logic or organization. Frankfort with his "mythopoeic thinking and multiple approaches and answers" and Hornung with his "complementary propositions and many-valued logic" may be saying some of the same things as Freud, in other ways. The essential difference seems to lie in the logic, the coherency, which Frankfort and Hornung project onto a phenomenon which Freud saw as illogical and incoherent, subject only to the satisfaction of needs and wishes and expressed in dreams (i.e. fantasy) and unconscious gestures and slips of the tongue.

Freud's theory may be helpful in understanding the nature of the mythological, magical type of thinking used by the Egyptians, even if it does not answer all the questions. The more instinctive a person is, the more will he express contradictions and not be fussed by such contradictory expression; the same is true of a society's culture. To what degree the Egyptians mixed a basically illogical instinctive approach and a basically logical rational approach is a matter, which is not about to be credibly determined by anybody. And to what degree, some Egyptologists are ultimately saying that what is felt is true and others are ultimately saying that only what is well thought out is true also must be considered. Perhaps, some kind of answer lies in a mix of rationalism and feeling and in the knowledge that both thoughts and feelings can be either true or false. In any case, it is doubtful that systematically assuming holistic meaning for the Egyptian religion can lead to authentic understanding of its core meaning.

In the final analysis, Frankfort could not resist the temptation to impose a master key — *a great explanation* — in Egyptology and Hornung prudently proposed a similar one. Especially for Frankfort, what should have been proposed as one avenue of approach among many largely became a sole, obligatory road to Egypt. A master key to mythological and magical thinking does not open the door to coherency; at best, it shows that the key somehow does not fit into the lock, or like Freud's id it only opens the door to better understanding the largely arbitrary and confused nature of such thinking.

Erman's work was certainly marred by biases of Eurocentricism, Christian criteria, Prussian ideals of order and virility and the denial of even a modicum of coherency to most of Egyptian theology. However, somewhere down the line he was also right, or at least more comprehensive than Frankfort and Hornung — all religions, including the Egyptian, necessarily leaned heavily on magic, fantasy and mythology, while at the same time belonging to the world of "impressions and feelings" whose "deep meaning...still escapes us."[77] In short, religions are sincere, awkward attempts by man to understand the sacred, the world and himself.

It cannot be denied that the Egyptian type of thought, mainly mythological and magical, was eventually discarded in favor of Greek rationalism because it was indeed "open to charges of arbitrariness or confusion." Even the major religions that followed adopted a rationalistic approach or an approach disguised as rationalism.

Hornung also made the extraordinarily obtuse judgment that: "If we are to comprehend the world we still need the gods." Hornung seems to be an incorrigible believer in the need for religion, almost any religion, although preferably a "pluralist" religion.[78] This is much the same type of logic as that which Frankfort (and Jung) used and cannot be accepted as an inevitable premise in any examination of religion.

---

77. Erman, Adolf, *La Religion des Egyptiens*, p.19.
78. Hornung, Erik, *Conceptions of God in Ancient Egypt, The One and the Many*, pp. 259, 254.

In the 1980s, the great German Egyptologist Jan Assmann (b. 1938), in *Moses The Egyptian*, attempted to expand Hornung's view of "oneness" and "the millions" within a framework of comparison between the reality of ancient Egypt with the memory of Egypt as it was artificially constructed in Europe. Assmann leans towards the concept that Egyptian pantheistic solar theology coherently solved the problem of unity and plurality in religion: "the one in the many," "the postulate of the oneness of god does not exclude the existence of other gods," "a 'hidden unity' in which all living plurality on earth has its origin," "The predication 'the One who makes himself into millions' means…all of the gods are comprised in the One."

However, Assmann also believes that "in the course of Egyptology's establishment as a discipline of its own in the context of Classics and Orientalism, its original questions fell into oblivion and the growing gap between Egyptomania and Egyptology created a no man's land of mutual incomprehension." He sees the "positivistic" work of Ermann and Gardiner as "immensely" important, but also sees it as "marginalizing" Egypt. He sees the reaction to positivism by Egyptologists like Eberhard Otto, Siegfried Morenz and others in the 1950s and '60s, as involving a "more or less unconscious hope of gaining insight into the fundamentals of moral and religious orientation" and attempting to "colonize the no man's land between Egyptomania and Egyptology."[79]

Despite all these attempts, perhaps there was really only one period in history when the task of finding the core meaning of the Egyptian religion was pragmatically possible. This was in the early third century BC, at the beginning of the Greek occupation, when Egyptian religion, although decadent, had not yet succumbed to Hellenism and sunk beneath the sands and Egyptian priests sometimes talked to foreigners about their religion. At that time, it may have been possible for somebody — an Egyptian or a Greek — to write an analytical book or books on Egyptian religion and history, much as has been done for the world's later religions. And somebody was indeed appointed by the Greek ruler of Egypt Ptolemy I Soter to complete the task — the Greek-influenced Egyptian priest/historian Manetho (fl.c. 300 BC). Manetho produced *Aegyptiaca*, a book written in Greek and now lost; fragments survive, notably in the writings of the Judean historian Josephus (c. AD 37–100) and in the works of the Christian

---

79. Assmann, Jan, *Moses The Egyptian, The Memory of Egypt in Western Monotheism*, pp. 198, 193, 206, 22. See also, Assmann, p. 204 and Hornung, p. 170 on "oneness" and "millions."

historians Julius Africanus (c. AD 180–250), Eusebius (c. AD 260–340) and George Syncellus (fl. late 8th century AD). These fragments constitute a mix of highly useful information, misleading statements, and Greek influence, but very little analysis. They raise the question as to whether Manetho really understood what was essential in the Egyptian religion. What a difference it would have made, if some of the great Greek rationalists contemporary to Manetho, like Epicurus (c. 341–271 BC) or Zeno (c. 336?–264? BC), had undertaken to learn the Egyptian language and given us their analysis of the Egyptian religion!

In short, unless one opts for a kind of simplistic Zen-like *it means what it means*, the question of the core meaning of the Egyptian religion remains to be solved. We now possess a considerable amount of Egyptian theology which we can understand, including its contradictions; considerable descriptions of theology which we can partially understand; and a considerable amount of syncretic amalgamations and superimpositions which we cannot even begin to classify reliably as either confusion or forms of imperceptible coherency.

Perhaps the core meaning of the Egyptian religion will forever be out of our range of understanding, or more precisely, perhaps we will never be able to understand how the Egyptians thought and felt. Certainly, with or without Frankfort and his followers, it is evident that the mythological, magical approach of the Egyptians makes it difficult for a modern mind to grasp what in many instances might have indeed been holistic coherency.

Nevertheless, it seems inescapable to conclude that imagination, an enormous frenzy for religious experimentation and magical and aesthetic manipulations without regard for coherent results seem to have played far greater roles in the changes in the theologies and in gods than any theological logic or sophistication. Perhaps one day somebody will undertake the gargantuan task of sifting out what indeed were sophisticated, coherent "multiple approaches and answers," "complementary propositions" and "consubstantiality" from the great mass and maze of real diametrical changes, contradictions, fantasy and "unparalleled confusion."

Until such a hypothetical time, Hornung and Frankfort have perhaps unfairly sent Egyptologists like the rationalistic Erman and the evolutionist Breasted into limbo and have, perhaps more fairly, propelled Egyptologists who ardently sought forms of permanent, coherent monotheism within Egyptian polytheism, like Budge, de Rougé, Emile Brugsch and Morenz, into outer space.

SUMERO-EGYPTIAN VERSUS HEBREW APPROACHES TO THE SACRED —
IMMANENCE AND DIVERSITY VS. TRANSCENDENCE AND UNITY

With many (if not most) religious concepts, what a people believes is truth matters less than the approach a people adopts, because it reveals their deep nature and deeply influences overall efficiency.

The underpinning of the entire Egyptian religious and societal system lies in a magical, immanent, animist, unchangeable, multiple, material, artistic, hierarchical and pragmatic approach to the sacred. There was nothing transcendental or supernatural in the Egyptian religion; all the gods were immanent in nature — in the sky, on the earth or inside the earth, in animals and in the divine pharaoh. All the gods were represented in material idols and mythologically expressed in images and words. Nature was made of *hch*, of millions, of diversity, and all the diverse parts were immanently divine, powerful and possessed will. And the Egyptians believed that they had solved the problem of negative forces and disorder — the demons — by their daily defeat in a system of ultimate harmony, the *maat* order. Diversity in ultimate harmony was the heart of the Egyptian approach.

Basically, this Egyptian approach did not differ from the Sumerian system, but it considerably consolidated and extended it. The Egyptians instituted a more complex organization of the pantheon and its artistic representation in human, animal and combined human-animal forms, added divine kingship, decreed the sacred nature of the nation, invented a positive afterlife as the central goal of the living and created a system of harmony.

The Sumerian and Egyptian approaches were a continuation and an extension of man's previous history anchored in magic, rituals, plastic arts, mythology, diversity, dualistic forces, immanence, animism, emblematic totemism and henotheism. In the few centuries before and after 3000 BC, at the beginning of the Early Bronze Age, both Sumer and Egypt had anchored the polytheistic system and gave it its distinctive attributes. This included the transformation of the previous systems of local and rival gods and theological concepts into a system of co-existing gods and goddesses and national, or universal, concepts.

The Sumero-Egyptian system was man's first complex and coherent approach to the sacred, the approach which evolved from a synthesis of past beliefs and fully took into account new agricultural and urban values and organized the whole into a credible framework. The cultural transformation represented by the Sumero-Egyptian system was earth-shaking.

The Hebrew approach to the sacred, as described in the Bible, represented a radical turning point in the history of religion. A transcendental, absolutely monotheistic god above nature and the elimination of a divine presence, or gods, in the elements of nature, the interdiction of the plastic arts, elaborate ethics, human free will and the emergence of a "humanististic" personal god represented an approach which was diametrically opposite to the Sumero-Egyptian approach. These inventions were revolutionary, at whatever date they were made.

However, while we may have a fairly clear idea of the Sumero-Egyptian approach from about 3000 BC, comparisons with the Hebrew approach are complicated by the lack of Hebrew relics before the late 10th century BC. Two verses of the *Tanach* (the Bible) from the 7th century BC and the quasi entirety of the Bible from the first century BC are as far back as we can go. As best as reasonably can be established, the Israelite nation emerged in the 13th century BC Late Bronze Age/Early Iron Age, together with a probably legendary leader named Moses. The Bible and the Hebrew system were elaborated from about the 10th century BC. The struggle against polytheistic tendencies, nature worship and idolatry were only strongly engaged in the 7th century BC under King Josiah (c. 640–609 BC) and authentic or full-blown monotheism emerged with Deutero-Isaiah and Jeremiah in the 6th century BC.

It is frequently said that the fundamental difference between the Sumero-Egyptian and Hebrew approaches to the sacred was the belief in many gods or a single god and the declared falsehood of all the gods except Yahweh; in fact, this was only one of the basic differences. The Hebrew view started from the approach of taking the divine out of nature and putting it above nature. It is this transcendental approach that is the key to the Hebrew view and it is more fundamental and more radical than the invention of monotheism. For the Hebrews, nature was a beautiful hymn to god, but it was not sacred, the divine; god was not in the sun, the winds or the rivers, god was not in the elements of nature, the elements of nature were not divine and god was not in the animals. The Hebrew notion of the divine, of god, was above nature, man and the animals. Yahweh told "man" to "have dominion...over all the earth" and to "replenish...and subdue it..."[80]

---

80. Genesis, 1.26-30.

Of course, both the Sumerian and Egyptian religions also reflected an earnest ambition to dominate nature, which had become a general movement with the invention of agriculture. But, unlike Hebrew monotheism, the Sumerian and especially Egyptian gods primarily expressed an animistic vision of nature. The Sumero-Egyptian gods were immanent in nature and its diverse elements therefore had will, purpose and personality. And for the Egyptians, the gods had animal forms.

For the Hebrews, a sole transcendental god implied that diversity was not intrinsically deeply diverse; it was an all which was immediate unity, oneness, which had come from god, from the one, *echad*. The Hebrews further reasoned that rather than any kind of struggle between order and disorder in nature or any pre-determined harmony, there was a struggle between good and evil, which alone could produce individual harmony and eventually harmony for mankind. The Hebrew approach was transcendental, non-animist, unitary, spiritual, ethereal, proto-egalitarian, idealistic, abstract and literary.

A single people — the Hindus, or the Aryans — spontaneously, and probably operating independently, combined the two approaches, minus egalitarianism. Another people — the Persian Zoroastrians — were the first to propose an ethical end to the dualism of positive and negative, good and evil. Still another people or religion — the Christians — struggled with the validity of the two approaches and eventually combined them, albeit ambiguously.

Unquestionably, the counterpoint to Egypt's extraordinarily elaborate polytheism was Israel's extraordinarily subtle monotheism. Both systems created an imaginary construction, but their methods and consequences were deeply opposed. The Hebrew system (with or without Moses) was more a matter of revolution than evolution.

The *modus operandi* of the Hebrews was an early form of abstract reasoning and manipulation, which was a kind of halfway house between the Sumero-Egyptian approach and the later crowning achievement of 6th century BC Greek abstract rationalism and clarity. Without ever abandoning the faith and intuitive belief of the Sumero-Egyptian type, the Hebrews, over the centuries, developed abstract reasoning and a questioning attitude which was a timid precursor of the later Greek rationalist approach.

Even if the early Hebrew system continued to abundantly employ magical, mythological reasoning, its element of abstract reasoning already gave it infinite possibilities and especially the possibilities of imagining anything and linking anything with anything. The Hebrews remained anchored in an intuitive, uncritical, magical, mythological world vision in which man served, praised and appeased god and in which nature was god's creation. However, their definition of a transcendental, invisible god who was not present in the elements of nature and of man who had "dominion" over nature and the animals were the result of non-animistic abstract reasoning.

This mixture constituted a radical break with the Sumero-Egyptian system — and indeed with all the other systems and peoples. The Sumero-Egyptian system imagined that it was accurately describing what is, starting with the presence of the divine in nature. The Hebrew proclamation that the divine was not in nature but above it constituted a radically new departure in man's approach to the sacred. Taking the divine out of nature and putting it above nature was a first rough recognition of the mechanist, amoral nature of nature, and of the relativity of man and his free will. Man was beginning the adventure of critical moral judgment and freedom, values which Protestant Christianity would eventually exemplify in the type of daily life it fostered.

The Hebrew religion seems to owe much to the Egyptian religion, but perhaps never in human history have the nature of two religions and two approaches to the sacred been so fundamentally opposed to each other. Over thousands of years, and despite the attempt by many Renaissance philosophers and Egyptologists to find a common ground between the Egyptian and Judeo-Christian religions, or to see an esoteric monotheism or forms of monotheism within polytheism in ancient Egypt, this opposition has persisted. This deep enmity resulted in the extraordinarily intolerant view by mainstream Jews, Christians and Moslems that everything before the Mosaic Revolution, and notably Egyptian "paganism," was false and only monotheism was true and had been "revealed" by the true and only god. It also resulted in Egyptian hostility to the Jews at least from the late 5th century BC and initial Egyptian reticence to Christianity in the first two centuries of our era before monotheistic Christianity overwhelmed the Egyptians.

It is a cliché to state that the Hebrew system — the Mosaic Revolution — constituted a radical turning point in the religious and cultural history of mankind, but this simple statement must be made.

However, it must also be stated that the frequent Jewish, Christian and Moslem perception that there were no such things as authentic religion, an authentic god and ethics and authentic religious "revelation" before the Mosaic Revolution must be rejected. This arrogant and intolerant view which puts down everything before Moses as "paganism," "idolatrous culture" and "magic" is simply ridiculous. Unlike all other ancient texts, the Judeo-Christian Bible has not only been more frequently and arrogantly proclaimed as factual and truth, but as the only source of god's "revelation." This extraordinary opinion has only recently been challenged successfully. Fortunately, most scholars now reject the notion that many parts of the Bible are automatically true merely because they are in the Bible.

A turning point in the history of religion, rather than "revelation," is perhaps the most neutral way of describing what occurred.

This turning point in the history of religion is called "the Mosaic distinction" by the German Egyptologist Jan Assmann. In *Moses The Egyptian. The Memory of Egypt in Western Monotheism*, Assmann demonstrated "the counter religion" nature of Judaism and the "confrontation, antagonism, hatred" that it generated. For Assmann, between Egypt and Israel, there is "a tale of two countries," an "intercultural estrangement" (and the impossibility of) "translatability" born from the radical Mosaic distinction. Assmann states that over the centuries, this situation developed into "The Israel-and-Egypt constellation" becoming "the model of mutual abomination."

Assmann devotes considerable attention to the several Renaissance philosophers and to Freud who attempted "to dissolve and overcome...the problem of antagonism" between Egypt and Israel by "dismantling" the "barrier" of "Moses and the One against Egypt and the Many" and tracing the "idea of unity back to Egypt."[81] However, we shall soon see that aside from the gradual emergence of monotheizing tendencies in Egypt and Akhenaten's (c. 1352–1336 BC) 15-year period of primitive monotheism, there seems no way of basically concluding anything else than the invention of two radically different approaches to the sacred — the Egyptian and the Hebrew.

These two approaches came into head-on collision and perhaps it could not have been otherwise.

The priority of the Sumero-Egyptian approach was ritual correctness and the priority of the Hebrew approach was moral purity, even if in practice the Hebrews frequently relapsed into ritual correctness. The Egyptian approach tended towards holism and favored types of achievement and particularisms in lifestyles and goals which were not strictly within logical, ethical and spiritual domains: notably joyousness, refinement and pragmatic, hierarchical, complex

---

81. Assmann, Jan, *Moses The Egyptian, The Memory of Egypt in Western Monotheism*, pp. 1-8, 55, 217, 209, 168.

and frequently contradictory solutions to existential and metaphysical questions. The subtlety and pre-rationality of the Hebrew approach proved to be a more efficient vector for the invention of simple and less verifiable religious concepts, higher ethical goals and a more open-ended existential and metaphysical search. Nevertheless, each approach to the sacred had its advantages and disadvantages and much in common. In both cases, the result was complicated theologies and fabulous mythological richness.

Manipulative magic was mankind's basic approach to religion. The center of the Egyptian system was *heka*, magic. Magic was the key to maintaining cosmic order and obtaining protection and an afterlife and the Egyptians elaborated the most complex system of magic ever invented.

The Hebrew system was the first to undermine the basis of magic. The prohibition of manipulative magic in favor of a subtler magic — the belief in an invisible god who could not be moved by anything except ethical behavior — engaged a battle against magic and mythological thinking, which represented an even greater cultural upheaval than the introduction of the Sumero-Egyptian polytheistic system. The consequences for world history of the simple commandments in Exodus 22:18, "Thou shalt not suffer a witch to live," and in Leviticus 19:26, "neither shall ye use enchantment [magic], nor observe times [look for omens]," are still being felt.

Nevertheless, magic and religion are always inseparable. The common ingredient of magical thinking — the intuitive belief in gods or a god and their, or his, supposed consequences — remained unchanged in Israel and in Egypt. What changed with the Hebrews was that magical thinking was packaged in a different way. The Hebrews were probably the first people who perceived the need to proclaim a difference between religion and magic, who perceived the need to prohibit the use of manipulative, material, magic to obtain what could not be obtained by righteousness and prayer.

The different approach they adopted constituted spiritual magic. The Hebrews adamantly pretended that this approach was truth. They eventually succeeded in constituting a system which while fundamentally magical and mythological in its own way could nevertheless credibly appear to be non-magical and non-mythological. Possibly one of Moses' greatest strokes of genius was to understand that the existence of a spiritual, invisible god and ethics could not be credible if it were based on crude, undisguised magic. Subtle, unverifiable magic was the answer.

The Hebrews obviously believed that manipulative magic worked, but because they saw it as unethical and unspiritual they condemned its use and condemned magicians to death or banishment. In practice, the Hebrews were simultaneously disdainful, envious, and tempted by the Egyptian magical system. They were proud of their great magicians like Aaron and Joshua; they never ceased to extol Moses as a greater magician than any Egyptian; and the Talmud (c. 300 BC–AD 500) admiringly admitted that "Ten measures of sorcery descended into the world; Egypt received nine, the rest of the world one."

It is clear that there was more spiritual and ethical content in the Hebrew religion than in any other religion before it, but it is just as clear that the Hebrews disguised a considerable amount of extravagant, manipulative magic and the extensive use of protective and healing amulets and rituals as unverifiable spirituality.

Just as radical and new was the Hebrew ideal of *tsadaquah*, righteousness and justice. For the Hebrews, righteousness was dependant on man's free will, on man as the creator of his own destiny, rather than the Egyptian *maat* correct way of behaving based on permanent conformity to the supposed operation of primeval nature. The Egyptian belief in *maat* conformity to nature deeply meant conformity to *the way things are*, to nature with its good things and dangerous things, to nature that is neither moral or immoral.

In their search for understanding, the Egyptians' main tendency was to scrutinize the nature of nature; they believed that nature did not tell lies. The main tendency of the Hebrews was to scrutinize the nature of human nature; they believed that *natural nature* had to be respected, but that its functioning could not be a basis for human morality, which had to be above *natural nature*. As early as the early 8th century BC with the prophet Amos, *tsadaquah*, or more simply ethical behavior, social justice and proto-egalitarianism, linked to god's absolute sovereignty over mankind and nature, was in the process of becoming a value which god applied universally and fairly and not just to the Hebrews. In a similar vein, the Hebrew adoption of the non-animistic belief that god was not in but above nature eventually resulted in an overall aim of truth and justice rather than an description of an unchangeable *modus operandi* of the divine, the cosmos and man.

The Hebrew interdiction of "graven images" or the non-representability of Yahweh greatly accentuated the fundamental opposition between the Sumero-Egyptian polytheistic approach and the Hebrew monotheistic approach. The Egyptian approach to the sacred naturally found its epitome, its deepest magical religious expression and explanation, in the plastic arts and architecture; the Hebrew approach naturally found it in literature.

The Egyptians, with their deep feeling for magic, materiality and divine immanence, plunged into the mystery and magic of art and architecture. They exuberantly manipulated the mystery which enables man to artificially but concretely create meaning and reality which are at best paradoxically more meaningful, realer and more poignant than reality. Egyptian art and architecture probably provide the best insight towards understanding why the Hebrews prohibited sculpture, had a reticence towards temple architecture (they built a single temple) and poured their immense concern for the sacred into a non-plastic realm, into literature.

For the Hebrews, entirely centered in transcendency, only the sole, invisible, omnipotent god, Yahweh, supposedly possessed the meaning, the poignancy, the mystery and the power which sculpture and architecture expressed and which Egyptian art and architecture epitomized. According to Hebrew tradition, Abraham's father Terah was a sculptor and Abraham destroyed his father's idols. The Hebrews correctly reasoned that sculpted idols in stone or wood could not be gods but could nevertheless compete with Yahweh and powerfully sway people by their magical meaning. The Hebrews linked the prohibition of images to a concept, but *a contrario* they validated the Egyptian and so-called "pagan" perception that sculpted gods were somehow indeed eminently meaningful, indeed magically "real" and indeed "gods."

However, if the Hebrews exemplified the reasons why material idols could not be gods, one can also imagine that like many nomadic peoples the primitive Hebrews mundanely exercised a de facto prohibition of sculpture because of the problems involved in transporting them. Without over-generalizing, one can also reason that nomadic peoples tended towards societies without images and then sanctified this choice largely born from necessity, while highly sedentarized peoples like the Egyptians tended towards massive architecture and sculpture and also sanctified their choice largely born from possibility. The early sedentary Sumerians were a curious exception to this generalization — they built great temples, and the statues of the divinities in these temples were considered to be real divine presences as in Egypt, but apparently they did not engage in a similar and vast sculptural representation of their gods and goddesses as did the Egyptians.

The Africans, using a similar approach of divine immanence to the Egyptians, but without the same overriding pragmatic attitude, probably carried sculpture to its highest levels of frank meaning, notably with their masks and statues of humans whose role was to intervene with the gods in favor of individuals. The Hindus combined the two approaches, the plastic arts and literature, and together with the Egyptians became the greatest and most varied image-makers of the gods in history. Eventually the Christians, after overcoming their intransigent Hebrew anti-image heritage, also combined the Hebrew and Egyptian approaches and probably produced the most all-inclusive art. The reasoning of the Moslems in the seventh century AD concerning figurative art was similar to the Hebrews, but the Moslems attenuated the Hebrew abstract sensitivity and found their artistic identity in magnificent temple architecture and artistic decoration.

In the domain of ethics, the two basic approaches to the sacred naturally produced very different consequences. Egypt struggled with the problem of ethics, but could not solve it. In the ancient rough-and-tumble world, ethical progress seems to have only been possible in liaison with spiritual concerns. The Egyptians mundanely sought to live well and to continue to live well in the afterlife; they had few of what the monotheists and most people today would qualify as spiritual concerns, even in their relation to the gods. The Egyptians did not waste much time speculating why they were on earth, but devoted immense energy to devising magical, materialistic technology to survive after death. For the Egyptian, life like death was strictly material; there was no evident spiritual quest involved either in life or in death. Decent or correct behavior in society was stressed, but in this life and in the afterlife magic, not ethics, was the key.

In this approach they were obviously deeply dissimilar to the later monotheistic Hebrews and Persians and even more dissimilar to the later Christian monotheists. A central aspect of the monotheistic approach to the sacred was the attempt to link ethics and religion and justify it by the will of the sole transcendental invisible god. It is no surprise that the monotheists made this link more successfully than the Egyptians, who could achieve no more than a brilliant ethical theory linked to the *maat* primeval order. Hardly anybody from the mighty pharaoh down to the simple Egyptian peasant considered it necessary to genuinely apply those ethical concerns in preference to magical, primeval concerns.

Throughout the ancient world the search for a unifying principle within what seemed to be infinite diversity and a basic dualism was a central aspect of the approach to the sacred. Many peoples — the Sumerians, the Egyptians, the Babylonians, the Hebrews, the Persians, the Hindus, and the Greeks — actively sought this unifying principle. All of them, with the exceptions of the Hebrews (and Christians) and Persians, found this principle in forms of diversity in nature and in forms of a polytheistic organization of a vast number of local gods, with no unifying principle ever becoming strong enough to justify an abandonment of polytheism.

The Egyptians, together with the Sumerians, the Hindus and the Greeks, embraced a complicated unifying principle — a system which simultaneously considered the diversity of hundreds of gods with varying powers (more than 30,000 for the Hindus) as the various aspects of the entirety of the harmonious universe and the hundreds of demons as a menace of chaos, but gods and demons led by a chief god nevertheless formed a whole. Perhaps, more than for any other people, the Egyptian unifying principle was constituted by the notion of diversity in ultimate harmony.

Without abandoning the key tenet of polytheism — diversity — in the New Kingdom (c. 1550–1069 BC) the Egyptians invented the strongest forms of syncretic chief god theology. But even when the greatest of these chief gods, Amun-Re, assimilated all the gods and all the forces they represented as his aspects, thus unquestionably constituting a monotheizing tendency, Amun-Re remained immanent in everything, in *heh*, in "the millions" and especially in the air and the sun. From the Nineteenth Dynasty (c. 1295–1186 BC), several texts and temple inscriptions refer to Amun as "the one who made himself into millions," but the millions, *heh*, and the existence of the many gods remained the central reality. Whatever system of ultimate unity was concocted, the Egyptian system always operated on the basis of polytheistic diversity. Henri Frankfort astutely saw that "Polytheism is sustained by man's experience of a universe alive from end to end. Powers confront man wherever he moves, and in the immediacy of these confrontations the question of their ultimate unity does not arise."[82]

All this was fundamentally dissimilar to the monotheistic unitary approach to the sacred, to the Hebrew "one," *echad*, and its consequences.

In Egypt, the only exception to a concrete, animistic approach was the minority Ptah/Memphite theology which probably did not reach its plenitude before the late 8th century BC. However, if Ptah created the universe in an abstract manner by his heart (mind) and tongue (word), Ptah himself and all the other elements in the Ptah/Memphite theology remained overwhelmingly

---

82. Frankfort, Henri, *Ancient Egyptian Religion, An Interpretation*, p. 4.

immanent, multiple and animistic in its approach to the gods, nature and human existence.

The Egyptians and the Hindus saw the entirety of nature and life as a permanent dualistic struggle. The Egyptians and the Hindus shared a deep belief in the immutability of the world and its laws, in the impossibility of change, in the eternal conflict between opposites of the day/night and good/bad types and in the necessity of appeasing both the good and bad forces and gods. However, although their basic belief in the principle of diversity was similar, for the Egyptians, the good, the positive — *maat* order and harmony — always triumphed if the correct magic was applied, while for the Hindus the victor in the struggle was always variable and perfect equilibrium for man and the world was impossible. The consequences drawn by the Egyptians and the Hindus were radically different, with the Egyptians adopting an optimistic approach and the Hindus a pessimistic approach.

However, whether it is Egyptian or Hindu, or any other polytheism, it is essential to see that viewing reality as diversity is as valid a theoretical option as the monotheistic option of unity. In the imaginary world of religion, polytheistic views are no less valid a way of interpreting and rationalizing reality than monotheism — there seems to be no compelling reason to choose between a unifying principle of diversity in ultimate harmony and one which immediately sees the all as unity. The problems generated by the polytheistic vision are elsewhere; they are the near impossibility of separating and concretely evaluating magic, nature, gods and demons; the inflation of needless gods; and the innate weakness of creating gods with the same or overlapping functions. All this created an unwieldiness which made it difficult for polytheism to incorporate subtler human needs like strict ethics and rendered it incapable of coming to terms even partially with rationalism and science. It is difficult to imagine any innate hierarchically based polytheistic system, including the Hindu, being able, like Christian monotheism, to adopt ideals of absolute forgiveness and love.

Nevertheless, despite their basic vision of diversity, with Amun-Re theology in all its ambiguity the Egyptians struggled with the problem of a *unitary* unifying principle. And for a brief 15-year period, under Pharaoh Akhenaten (c. 1352–1336 BC), Egypt crossed the Rubicon and sketched out this primitive *unitary* unifying principle, a monotheistic principle. The heretical Akhenaten may have been the precursor of the second, Hebrew, unitary approach to the divine, but as we shall see later his attempt at proto-monotheism failed and was seen as out of character with Egyptian religious aspirations by all the succeeding generations until the advent of Christianity. The ancient Egyptians adamantly clung to a multiple approach to the sacred which could accommodate nothing more than a strong chief god and ultimate harmony rather than immediate unity.

The Hebrews and the Persians were the first peoples who adamantly drew the opposite conclusion. They considered it to be a self-evident conclusion which the others somehow could not accept or perceive — the simplest, most concrete unifying principle was a unity itself, a *unitary* unity, monotheism, rather than any kind of syncretism. They saw that this also favored the thirst for ethics and justice. Unwittingly, they also created systems which proved better equipped to at least confront rationality and the mechanical nature of the universe. Moreover, the unitary way of looking at the universe and existence not only did not alter any polytheistic truth about the diversity of universe; it made it simpler to grasp and permitted the development of equality within diversity.

However, while the monotheists came up with the simplest, most obvious and open unifying principle, its theological applications evolved into a mess compared to the polytheistic view which despite all maintained an inner coherency and an apparent unchangeability.

Despite the "truth" of a sole god and its implications, each of the monotheistic peoples developed their own brand of theology: unitary monotheism for the Hebrews and the Arabs and plural monotheism for the Persians and for the Christians. In Persian monotheism, matters were further complicated by the principle of evil, Ahriman, who was nearly as powerful as the sole god Ahura Mazdah before he would be finally defeated. In Christian monotheism, god was subdivided into three and religion became the religion of the "Son," who had been temporarily immanent, rather than that of the transcendental "Father."

But as messy as all this was, the unitary unifying principle of the monotheistic Hebrews, Christians, Persians and Arabs had the advantage of not just establishing a completely different view based on the concept of a sole god, but eventually underpinning this view with the goodness and perfection of this invisible god in addition to his omnipotence. A major implication of this kind of thinking was that things could be no other way — the unity of all existence and humanity and god and a bright divine plan came to be seen as self-evident. Eventually, the polytheistic concept of the permanent struggle between order and chaos was abolished by the monotheistic concepts of a present world which was perfect insofar as it could be and a future perfect world. The Christian concept of a future perfect world quickly found its expression with the Apostle John (fl.c. AD 90) in millennianism, a future one-thousand-year reign of Jesus, and the Apocalypse followed by a perfect and just existence for the good few of all times. The Christian idea of the present eventually found its ultimate definitions in Descartes' (1596–1650) self-evident perfection of the universe, Leibnitz's (1646–1716) "best of all possible worlds" and "why is there something, rather than nothing" and Newton's (1643–1747) "clock-maker" order and perfection of the universe.

The principle of justice was a central concern in all the forms of polytheism and monotheism, but its meaning was fundamentally different and inevitably led to different consequences.

In polytheism, justice was based on gracefully assuming a predefined role in relation to a divinely ordained hierarchy and universal natural harmony. Egyptian polytheism developed one of the stiffest hierarchical systems from the near-omnipotent chief gods to the divine, theocratic pharaoh, to the ruling class of privileged notables, to the pure high priests, to the commoner craftsmen and peasants and to the inferior status of women, all with different rights and subject to different sanctions.

The exception to the general polytheistic hierarchical concept was Hinduism, which elaborated a pessimistic system of stiff, inegalitarian hierarchical rules and selective justice in this life with a very long-range type of overall equality and individual justice. The final reward for the Hindus, after successive reincarnations determined by one's *karma*, the result of one's accumulated moral worth, was the extinction of suffering through the extinction of rebirth, *samsara*, in *Nirvana*. The daughter of Hinduism and Islam, Sikhism, from the early 16th century AD, rebelled against this system and established a new monotheistic religion without castes and without idols, but continue to believe in *karma* and *samsara*.

Persian near-monotheistic Zoroastrianism, perhaps as early as the 13th century BC (although its flowering and influence has to be dated from the 6th century BC), conceived a new system of justice involving the eventual and final victory of good over evil and the moral reward of a paradisiacal afterlife for all good people. This revolutionary concept — so opposed to polytheism and permanent, recurrent dualism in general and to the Egyptian religion in particular — deeply influenced the Hebrew and especially Christian versions of monotheism.

Possibly from the outset of its establishment in the late 13th century BC, and certainly by about 800 BC, the Hebrew system was the radical vector of both the immediate necessity of ethics, ethical equality and justice and a collective moral and material reward, the happiness and prosperity of Israel.

Nevertheless, a stiff hierarchy also existed in the Hebrew system beginning with the concept of the most omnipotent god ever invented, Yahweh, and continued by the division of society into priests (*Cohanim*), temple assistant/ guardians (*Levites*), the people (*Yisrael*) — whose males were conscripted soldiers, and women, whose status was lowest. However, this system was tempered and finally undermined by a proto-egalitarian law code (including for foreigners), national fraternity and the requirement of all members of society to respect the same form of *tsadaquah* (righteousness and justice). As transcendental as he was, Yahweh gradually emerged as a personal god who not only intervened in the destiny of the nation but also in the lives of individuals as a father who rewarded righteousness.

Christian love, ethics, forgiveness, and international fraternity further tempered the Hebrew hierarchical system. Jesus, the son of Yahweh, emerged as perhaps the most affectionate, just and personal god ever invented. (The aggravated status for women in Christianity in relation to the already severe Hebrew system was one of the few hierarchical and judicial aspects of the Hebrew system that was not tempered by Christianity.) Together with Greek proto-democracy, Judaism and Christianity became the forerunners of justice in daily life, the democratic system.

It seems clear that a standard form of polytheism, like the Egyptian, was eventually unable to compete with either the monotheistic or the Hindu systems because it failed to credibly quench one of the central thirsts of man — equitable justice in this life or at least the promise of equity in the afterlife. It is also clear that religion — monotheistic or polytheistic — eventually faltered and enabled the rise of atheism, agnosticism and secularism due to its basic failure to make a genuine attempt to provide justice in the here and now.

From at least the time of the Greek philosopher-scientists in the 6th century BC, the problem of providing justice in the here and now was complicated by the equally basic problem of the credibility, the "truth," of religion. Whatever the approach to the sacred — Sumero-Egyptian, Hebrew, or Hindu — despite some hesitations, they all pretended to provide fundamental answers to all the fundamental questions, including what happens after death. The theories of some Greeks (but not the mainstream), that is, most of the philosopher-scientists, implicitly postulated that this was impossible and that what was at stake was a search for clear, non-mythological, material truth. For these Greeks the central principle of truth was materialistic, anti-magical, or atheistic rationalism and science. Intolerance and persecution forced the gradual abandonment of this view in favor of rigorous Greek polytheism. Atheism was reborn in 17th and 18th century Enlightenment Europe as a humanism which transformed the Greek ideal into the naïve assurance of constant progress and the eventual attainment of truth.

The modern atheistic movement constitutes a revolution that may yet turn out to be a greater upheaval than monotheism or polytheism. However it, too, like Sumer-Egyptian polytheism or Hebrew monotheism, is often based on an exclusive, central way of looking at things, even when it denies that it is doing this; it is often based on nothing less than finding absolute truth, even if this "truth" is nihilistic, or "non-truth," as opposed to the Greek Socratic ideal of an endless search. Nevertheless, atheism has grown into a force which could eventually destroy all religion, polytheistic or monotheistic. The Sumero-Egyptian and the Hebrew systems had represented immense cultural changes, but the atheistic movement begun with the Greeks has gone even further — it has finished the job of undermining magic and opened the road to undermining the very basis of religion.

And so, in 5000 short years, man invented two basic approaches to the sacred — the Sumero-Egyptian and the Hebrew — and the utter opposite of both, Greek and European atheism. In 5000 short years, man has encompassed what seem to be all the religious possibilities open to his understanding and imagination — from many gods to one god to no god and from Sumero-Egyptian presumed conformity to nature, to Hindu pessimism, to Hebrew morality, to Persian ultimate justice, to Christian love, fraternity and forgiveness, to Moslem *umma* communitarian identity and conquest and to atheistic rational, emotional and pragmatic respect of nature, morality, justice, love and identity without the divine, identity with a stratum of nihilism where no absolute truth is possible. And yet somehow, more than the concepts of many gods, one god or no god, it was the Sumero-Egyptian and Hebrew difference of approach concerning whether the divine was in the diversity of nature or above unitary nature which was the watershed. In the final analysis, only two basic and radically dissimilar approaches to the sacred were invented by man, the Sumero-Egyptian and the Hebrew, the immanent *heh*, "the millions" and the transcendental "one," *echad*.

CHAPTER 5.
THE THEOCRATIC AND POLITICAL CONTEXT

DIVINE KINGSHIP AND THE PRACTICE OF THE *HEB-SED*, THE ROYAL JUBILEE

In retrospect, it is easy to see how the Egyptian approach to the sacred as divine diversity within ultimate harmony led to the invention of divine kingship, to a divine person on earth who guarantees harmony. It is just as easy to see why the Hebrews rejected this, before eventually inventing a quasi-divine kingship concept with the messiah king.

The Egyptians, operating from the basis of vibrant animist and totemistic influences, transformed the concept of the powerful clan leader into god-the-Father and into immanent divine kingship. The Egyptian divine king was the fatherly provider, the immanent but distant chief god/man of a united but pluralistic human society, mirroring the polytheistic pantheon.

The Hebrews, at much later dates, were unable to do this because nobody but the god Yahweh was a divine king. This view made them hesitate to even establish a kingship. Likewise, despite their hierarchical class societal structure, the Hebrews leaned towards proto-democratic equality in human society.

It must have been a considerable revolution and a seemingly brilliant and logical deduction when the Egyptians invented divine kingship, probably before 3000 BC. This revolution was so considerable that it still marginally survives in our modern world.

The earliest historical evidence of the ruler-god concept is clearly in Egypt. Kings, leaders and sorcerers had probably been mediators between man and the divine for tens of thousands of years and some ancestral rulers had probably been deified after death in an extension of ancestor worship.

Despite their anteriority as a polytheism, an advanced agricultural society and a high civilization, the Sumerian city rulers (the *ensi*, or *lugal*, the "great man") ruled as representatives, as mediators, of the gods and as the "landlord" of the gods' properties on earth. Almost all the kings of the Sumerian city-states received their inspiration and power from the gods, but were never totally living gods on earth like the Egyptian pharaohs.

There were a few exceptions to this general rule in Sumer, but they all seem to have occurred after divine kingship was invented in Egypt. The legendary king-god Gilgamesh, who ruled the city-state of Uruk at about the same time as Djoser ruled Egypt (c. 2660 BC), was said to be born of the goddess of buffaloes, Ninsuna, and the human King of Uruk, Lugalbanda. Gilgamesh was said to be two-thirds divine. However, the attributes of divinity for Gilgamesh and the deification of his human father Lugalbanda seem to appear for the first time only in the Sumerian Kings List, dated to about 2100 BC. Sargon of Akkad (ruled c. 2340–2305 BC) declared a special relation with the divine as the goddess Ishtar's (Inanna) lover.

In fact, the Sumerians were never systematic about divine kingship; a king who was a god or who was deified were exceptions, like Naram-Sin (c. 2254–2218 BC), who saw himself as the king of the universe and the god of Akkad. Naram-Sin preceded his name with the *dingir*, the "star" ideogram indicating the divine, as did his son, Sar-kali-sarri (c. 2217–2193 BC). Perhaps this development was due to Egyptian influence, but even after these two the Mesopotamian kings never attained the degree of divinity accorded to the Egyptian pharaohs and they essentially remained mediators of the gods.

The Sumerians toyed with the idea of divine kingship. The Egyptians invented a system of divine kingship and carried the process to its logical conclusion. The human pharaoh became a god in addition to being a representative and a mediator between the gods and man. He was responsible for assuring the correct functioning of the *maat* order of harmony. From this lofty position, a short step took the pharaoh-god beyond the status of the Sumerian *ensi* as a proxy landlord to being the divine owner of everything.

In Egyptian Predynastic times, kings seem to have variously been mediators between the gods and man, representatives of the gods, gods in their own right and always powerful magician/sorcerers. With the Early Dynastic Period (c. 3100 BC), the pharaoh assumed all these attributes as the "good god" who was the incarnation of the falcon god Horus. Horus was divine kingship, the unifier and god of *Ta-Wy*, the Two lands, Upper and Lower Egypt and also god of the entire world; and the pharaoh was Horus. At least from about Pharaoh Radjedef's (Djedefra) time (c. 2566–2558 BC), the Pharaoh was not only Horus but he had no human father, his father being the god Re who magically impregnated the royal wife (like the later Jesus, whose father was Yahweh and his mother the human Mary).

The Pharaoh as god-incarnated was a sign of the power that the Egyptians believed that a human could wrench from the gods. In turn, this indicated enormous confidence both in man's and society's capacities and may have played a role in Egypt's precocious political development. Of course, it also indicated great daring on the part of the early pharaohs. They may have consciously exploited man's yearning for the gods to come into the human domain, for a superhuman presence among humans, an immanent god/man who could lead, reassure and comfort.

The pharaoh's incarnation as a god — as the falcon Horus, and later as Horus, son of Re, and as Osiris upon death, and then in the New Kingdom (c. 1550–1069 BC) as the son of Amun-Re — was therefore a key instrument of his political power, of his theocratic rule. No doubt the early pharaohs' perception that deification gave them more clout was one of the main origins of their divinity. Deification removed the pharaohs from the league of humans, removed them from the constraint of answering to human criteria and even sometimes enabled them to vie for the favor and the fervor of the people alongside the other gods.

In Predynastic and Early dynastic times, the pharaoh's divinity was also exemplified by the facts that only the gods and the pharaoh had souls and only the pharaoh had the privilege of afterlife immortality. And throughout Egyptian history, the pharaoh alone was the governor of the *maat* principle of cosmic order. Without the pharaoh and his status as a divinity and a magician-sorcerer, existence for all other people could not proceed in an orderly manner, there could be no prosperity, agricultural or otherwise, and there could be no protection from cosmic disorder, *izfeh*, or foreign conquest.

Divinity for the pharaoh was certainly implied from his birth and in some hyperbolic versions of his divine kingship of Egypt it was implied even from all time, or before time. Pyramid Text Utterance 571 states: "...the King was fashioned by his father Atum before the sky existed, before earth existed, before men existed, before the gods were born, before death existed..."[83]

It was believed that Horus increased the power of Re's son, the future pharaoh, and the love he received from his human father, the reigning pharaoh, until the day Horus' chosen, the Horus on earth, was crowned. This divine birth was first confirmed when the reigning pharaoh announced who was his heir; this heir was then known by the title "Horus in the nest," in addition to his nomen birth name. The new pharaoh's coronation was "certified" by a vast system of royal titles, emblems and amulets which were active during his reign and in his afterlife. The coronation event was called the *kha,* "the appearance," as were all the succeeding public appearances of the pharaoh, usually on special balconies in the palace or a temple, called the "window of appearance." One of the glyphs designating the king, the pharaoh, was now the same as one of the glyphs designating a god — a seated, bearded figure with upraised knees. The crowned king was also linked to Isis as mother of the god/king and to her glyph with a pedestal or a throne as a headdress as her personification of the king's throne.

The inscription on the statue of Pharaoh Horemhab (c. 1323–1295 BC) and his "great royal wife" Mutnedjmet (now in the Turin Museo Egizio) gives us a good description of the pharaoh's divinity from birth to the coronation ceremony. This description of Pharaoh Horemhab's *kha* coronation ceremony, as the culminating phase in his designation as a god, as the divine certification of the pharaoh as a god, was most likely not very different from those of the pharaohs right from the Early Dynastic Period — except that Re had become Amun-Re. This is especially true because Horemheb's claim to the throne was tenuous and he therefore had to prove that he corresponded to all the traditional criteria.

The inscription on the Horemheb statue states that "he [Horemheb] already came out of his mother's bosom adorned with the prestige and the divine color..." This means that he had the color of the future pharaoh's skin, which was supposedly gold or blue, the color of the gods and goddesses.

At an elaborate, secret coronation ceremony in the Luxor Temple in Thebes, Amun-Re, who had engendered the child he had chosen to become pharaoh, revealed the identity of his pharaoh/son, Horemheb. Amun-Re then "intertwined" himself with the new pharaoh and the divine *ka* souls which flowed in his body were transmitted to his pharaoh/son. The son of Amun-Re,

---

83. Faulkner, R.O., *The Ancient Egyptian Pyramid Texts,* p. 226.

the new Horus, now ruled *Ta-Wy*, the Two Lands, in accord with all the gods and goddesses who rejoiced.

The Pharaoh Horemheb was now the "Superior Mouth of the Land," the theocratic ruler, who "fixed the law of the Two Shores [the Two Lands of Egypt]" in accordance with the cosmogonic order of the goddess Maat and all the gods and goddesses of Egypt and who "walked along the road of the goddess [Maat]...who assured his protection for the duration of eternity." Horemheb was now the chosen representative of the gods.

Horemheb, wearing the conical white crown of Upper Egypt (the *hedjet* of *Ta-Shema*) and the peaked red crown of Lower Egypt (the *Deshret* of *Ta-Mehu*), intertwined into the *pschent*, the double crown, then appeared as the magnificent omnipotent pharaoh-god before the rejoicing people gathered in the temple outer courtyard: "[A]ll the people of Egypt were contented and their shouts reached the heavens...the entire country was in exultation."

Quite naturally, the notables only approached the divine Pharaoh Horemheb in "a bent," submissive posture and the rulers of the foreign lands, "the Nine Arcs," the *pedjet*, submissively "stretched out their hands to him" or even prostrated themselves face downwards, "honoring him like a god."[84]

As usual, the Egyptians were utterly thorough in their magical thinking concerning the pharaoh or any other aspect of life. The transmission of Re's (or Amun-Re's) *ka* into the body of the pharaoh and his designation as Horus and as the son of Re, Sovereign of *Ta-Wy*, the Two Lands, were considered insufficient to permanently maintain his status as a worthy pharaoh-god, divine certifier of the union of the Two Lands.

After the pharaoh had ruled for 30 years — but frequently well before — the *heb-sed*, the royal jubilee ritual, was enacted. The *sed* seems to have been linked to the jackal god Sed, who himself was linked to the wolf or dog-headed opener of the way to the afterlife, the god Wepwawet. The pharaoh made offerings to all the gods of Egypt, each represented by a model of his temple. A gigantic wooden *djed* pillar, symbolizing resurrection and Ptah-Seker-Osiris, was raised. The pharaoh then supposedly ran up and down the length of a predetermined course, proving that he physically mirrored the strength required to maintain the gods' *maat* order in Egypt. With more than a little duplicity on the part of the officiating priests, even elderly pharaohs always emerged from

---

84. Lalouette, Claire, *Textes Sacrés et Textes Profanes de l'Ancienne Egypte, I, Des Pharaons et des hommes*, pp. 44-48.

this test with flying colors. The pharaoh was once again crowned with the double *Pschent* Crown of united Egypt and received homage from his entourage. The *heb-sed* symbolically confirmed his status as divine king, as pharaoh-god of *Ta-Wy*, the Two Lands.

The pharaoh was now regenerated; he was resurrected with renewed strength. Perhaps in earlier Egyptian local kingship, and certainly in later African systems, the king would be ritually murdered if he failed to accomplish the physical tests.

The *heb-sed* was then carried out every three years until the pharaoh died. Legend, archaeological remains and murals in Pharaoh Djoser's Memphis Step Pyramid precinct (built c. 2660 BC) indicate that the *heb-sed* was carried out much like a similar ceremony first supposedly performed by Menes, the supposed uniter and first pharaoh of Upper and Lower Egypt. In any case, we know from the scenes depicted on an ebony label of an oil jar found in Pharaoh Den's tomb (c. 2950 BC) in Abydos (and now in the British Museum), that the *heb-sed* as a confirmation of divine kingship over the Two Lands, including homage to the pharaoh and running a course, was practiced from at least this very early date. The *heb-sed* jubilee attained its greatest splendor in Thebes during the New Kingdom.

The Egyptian coronation and *heb-sed* ceremonies bear considerable resemblance to the Sumerian coronation and *Zag-muk* New Year celebrations which were often held simultaneously. The Sumerian *lugal* (king) played the role of the legendary King of Uruk, Dumuzi, who had been deified as a vegetation, fertility and spring renewal god, and a priestess played the role of his wife, the mother and love/dying-resurrecting goddess Inanna. The return, the resurrection, of Dumuzi from the nether world and his ensuing sacred marriage with Inanna guaranteed the reigning *Lugal's*, or new *Lugal's*, prosperity and the spring fertilization/resurrection of the land.

However, unlike the pharaoh who was a god, who was Horus and the son of Re, the Sumerian *Lugal* mimed the role of Dumuzi; he was neither Dumuzi nor any other god.

And so, the earliest traces of the absolute divine right of kings which was to cause so many ravages throughout the world are found in Egypt. As we shall see later, the Egyptian divine kingship and resurrection concepts may have produced variants in Africa and in Persia and probably influenced the Hebrew Messiah-King concept. It was developed to the imaginative high point of the Christian Son of God, Resurrection and Trinity concepts and probably played a role in divine-right, or essence of the divine, emperors and kings in Rome and Europe.

POLITICAL UNIFICATION: THE BIRTH OF "THE TWO LANDS"

At dates earlier than 3100 BC there is no solid evidence — only mythological legends — to substantiate the existence of two kingdoms or federations. Nevertheless, it is reasonable to suppose that two distinctive regions, Upper Egypt and Lower Egypt, gradually grouped some of their nomes around Nekhen (Hierakonpolis) in the south and Pe-Dep (Buto) in the north. There are some indications, for instance references in the later Pyramid Texts, to suggest that these two loose federations of nomes may have existed — but there is no certainty that structured federations existed. Much depends on what interpretation is made of terms such as the "Souls of Pe," the "Souls of Nekhen" and the *Shemsu-Hor*, "the followers of Horus"[85] — are they strictly religious terms or do they also refer to kings?

Nobody is about to solve this mystery, much less identify exactly who were the *Shemsu-Hor*. On the one hand, they seem to be the legendary demigods after Horus' rule of Egypt and before Menes' time described in the Turin Canon and in Manetho's Kings' List. On the other hand, in numerous utterances in the Pyramid Texts, they seem to be these legendary kings or demigods, and at the same time they are very similar to the *henmemet*, the solar retinue, the sun folk, guards and attendants of the king in his resurrection process in the sky.

Other loose federations of nomes, sometimes in rivalry and sometimes linked, may have also existed in Predynastic times before unification. These loose federations seem to have included the zones around Tieny (Thinis)/Abdu (Abydos), Naqada and Elephantine in Upper Egypt and Sau (Sais) in Lower Egypt. Another good possibility is that there were kings who ruled over segments of both Upper and Lower Egypt from at least 3200 BC. The distinctive names for Upper Egypt, *Ta-Shema*, the land of the sedge-reed plant, the land of the south, and for Lower Egypt, *Ta-Mehu*, the land of the papyrus clump, the land of the north, or *Bity*, the land of the bee, may have existed before unification.

---

85. i.e.: Utterances 574, 580, 474, in Faulkner, R.O., *The Ancient Egyptian Pyramid Texts*, pp. 229, 235, 162 and Gardiner, Alan, *Egypt of the Pharaohs*, pp. 421-422.

Around 3100 BC, it seems that centuries of battles for domination between Upper and Lower Egypt came to an apex with the unification of the Two Lands, although the royal titularies of the kings right until the end of the Second Dynasty (c. 2890–2686 BC) clearly indicate that there were numerous ups and downs in this process. Nevertheless, the first unified kingdom and the first nation in the history of mankind was in existence.

This naturally led to the establishment of a national religion with national pantheons and myths, even if local systems of beliefs continued to be widespread and the deep differences between the royal religion and the various local religions of the commoners persisted.

In religious and theocratic terms, the falcon sky god Horus became the main god, incarnated in the incumbent pharaoh. In geopolitical terms, after ruling from Thinis during the first two dynasties (c. 3100–2686 BC), the pharaohs of united Egypt seem to have made Ineb-Hedj, the white walled city which later came to be known as Men-nefer (Memphis) in the first nome of Lower Egypt, their official residence, the *khenu*, at least from the beginning of the Third Dynasty (c. 2686 BC). In mythological terms, peace and unification of the two regions was expressed as both the victory of Horus and reconciliation between Horus and Seth.

In legendary terms, a pharaoh known as Menes of Upper Egypt (who may have been Narmer, Aha, or Scorpion) was the founder of the First Dynasty and the unifier of Egypt, ruling from Thinis in Upper Egypt. The Turin Royal Canon (dating from Rameses II, c. 1279–1213 BC and now in the Turin Museo Egizio), lists the ten god-kings from Ptah, Re and Shu who ruled Egypt until a human, Menes, became king, and then all the kings until Rameses II's time. Manetho, who established a list of kings in his lost book *Aegyptiaca*, stated that Menes was the first human-god king of Egypt following the rule of the prehistoric god/kings.

Not enough is known about this period to separate myth and legend from real history. It is impossible to determine if a Menes really existed, if the Narmer relics actually have the meaning usually attributed to them, and if indeed Aha was the first king of a united Egypt. The unification of Egypt might not have been the result of a great war and might have been a largely peacefully development taking place over a few reigns, including a so-called "Zero Dynasty" preceding the reigns of both Narmer and Aha (c. 3100 BC). Aha, whose name means "the fighter" and who may have also had the title of Menes or "Men," is frequently cited as being the likeliest first pharaoh of a united Egypt. It seems possible that Aha organized a *heb-sed*, a divine kingship royal jubilee, and worked for reconciliation with the north and may have built a temple to the northern goddess Neith in Sais. However, The Palette of Narmer and some of the Abydos Umm el-Qa'ab Necropolis relics also constitute a strong case in favor of Narmer as the victor and unifier, as the Menes.

The unification of *Ta-Wy*, the Two Lands, certainly represented a political and probably a military upheaval. However, it is clear that it was a logical development since despite the many (but not all) different local gods there was a similarity between Upper and Lower Egypt in systems of religious beliefs and structures and in art and lifestyles. Tools, weapons, stone jars, tablets, labels, furniture and clay seals found in both Upper and Lower Egypt and dating from around 3000 BC bear great similarity. Barter in goods and produce seems to have been extensive, as many objects fabricated in the south have been found in the north and vice versa. In short, the political, religious, technological and artistic synthesis which took place in Egypt around 3000 BC was the logical result of a largely common background.

If indeed some kind of great war took place between Upper and Lower Egypt, it would not be a surprise that the victor was Upper Egypt. Archaeological evidence makes it clear that Upper Egypt was far more evolved at that time. That being said, there are some Egyptologists who claim that the north conquered the south and others who claim that the north conquered the south and then collapsed and was conquered by the south.

In any case, it seems that about 800 years after unification, the Egyptians themselves believed that the south had won a battle over the north. Pyramid Text Utterance 239 in Pharaoh Unas' (c. 2375–2345 BC) pyramid in the Sakkara Necropolis (Memphis) states: "The White-crown goes forth, having swallowed the Great One..."[86] This clearly means that the "white-crown," Upper Egypt, won over "the Great," over the land of the snake goddess Wadjit of Buto, protectress of Lower Egypt and its red crown.

And if indeed there was a final military victory of Upper Egyptians over Lower Egyptians at Memphis or elsewhere, it was perhaps this victory and/or preceding, concurrent and succeeding victories against Asiatics and Libyans which were celebrated in a series of carved palettes and mace-heads dating to around 3100 BC. These objects provide us with a sketchy view of the early political and theological history of Egypt.

---

86. Faulkner, R.O., *The Ancient Egyptian Pyramid Texts*, p. 57.

The most famous of these objects is the carved slate known as The Palette of Narmer, dating to about 3100 B.C, and apparently designed for use in mixing cosmetics (although by this time palettes seem to have had religious meaning). The Palette of Narmer was found in 1898 in the so-called Upper Egyptian Hierakonpolis hidden "main deposit" by the archaeologist J.E. Quibell (1867–1935).

The reverse side of The Palette depicts Narmer, under the protection of a falcon, presumably the god Horus, and an *ahet*, a divine cow, presumably the goddess Hathor, or Bat or another cow goddess, perhaps Mehytweret. Narmer's royal *serekh*, his emblem of sacred identity as the incarnation of Horus (perhaps as "Horus Nar, the raging catfish") is depicted between two celestial cows and his name. Narmer is assisted by his sandal-bearer. He is killing an enemy with his mace (perhaps a Libyan and in any case, a northerner), above a scene of already dead Asiatics. The front side of The Palette shows Narmer's followers holding military totemistic standards, stacks of dead victims, two long-necked intertwined beasts and the bull form of Narmer knocking down a walled city and killing an Asiatic.

There is hardly any doubt that the battles depicted in The Palette of Narmer took place in Lower Egypt, perhaps in the Buto region, and that Narmer was acting as King of Upper and Lower Egypt, at least separately and perhaps even concurrently. The victorious Narmer is wearing the conical white *hedjet* crown of Upper Egypt on one side of the slate and the peaked *deshret* red crown of Lower Egypt on the other side. This could either signify that he is the ruler in both Upper and Lower Egypt or even that he is the ruler of *Ta-Wy*, the united "Two Lands."

But rather than the final victory at Buto, Memphis or elsewhere (or only the final victory), The Palette mainly seems to be celebrating and telling the story of a series of victories of Narmer, presumably of Hierakonpolis (but perhaps from Thinis), in battles with bearded Lower Egyptian, Asiatic and probably Libyan enemies. The reverse side of The Palette, showing the falcon Horus with a human arm holding a rope attached to a clump of *mehyt* (papyrus) with a bearded human head indicates that the land of the papyrus, Lower Egypt, *Ta-Mehu*, and its people have been conquered and that Horus is giving Lower Egypt to the white-crowned Narmer of Upper Egypt. The front side of The Palette, showing Narmer wearing the red crown of Lower Egypt and followers carrying poles topped by totemistic military emblems (or perhaps even the emblems of early *sepat*-nomes), clearly indicates that these followers, perhaps representing *sepat*, paid allegiance to Narmer and participated in battles against his enemies. Since Narmer is wearing the red crown, these followers could well be Lower Egyptians participating in battles against Asians.

This early work of art is already confusing in what will become a typical Egyptian fashion. It certainly tells the story of conquest, but does not clearly indicate unification. If a Narmer, under the protection of Horus as royal god of Hierakonpolis conquered Lower Egypt and unified the Two Lands, why is he separately represented as King of Upper Egypt and King of Lower Egypt, rather than as wearing the intertwined double *pschent* crown of the King of a united Egypt? And why is Horus not represented as the royal god of all Egypt, the lord, protector and unifier of *Ta-Wy*, the Two Lands? It may well be that the concepts of unification and of the falcon-headed Horus as the ancestor of all the pharaohs and incarnated in the ruling *Ta-Wy* pharaoh wearing the double crown as god of all Egypt were inventions which were made after Narmer's time, after Narmer's phase of conquest. In any case, the earliest known portrayal of a pharaoh wearing the double *pschent* crown symbolically intertwining Upper and Lower Egypt is on an ebony label found in Den's (c. 2950 BC) Abydos Umm el-Qa'ab tomb by W.M.F. Petrie in 1900.

In addition to The Palette of Narmer, the mace-head of a King "Scorpion" also found in the Hierakonpolis "main deposit" by J.E. Ouibell in 1898 and dated from c. 3150 BC sheds considerable light on the late Predynastic Period. This mace-head (now in the Ashmolean Museum in Oxford) is called "Scorpion" because of the scorpion carved near the king's face. There is an important difference between the mace-head and The Palette — the "Scorpion" King is solely depicted as wearing the white conical crown of Upper Egypt, the *hedjet*. Therefore, although he is the conqueror of the north, he saw himself as solely the king of the south.

The mace-head, like The Palette, clearly indicates that peoples of the north, of the Delta, and foreigners were vanquished. Lapwing birds (*rekhyt*), the usual hieroglyph for captive people until the beginning of the Old Kingdom (c. 2686 BC), are tied to military standards topped by *sepat*/nome totems. These *rekhyt* seem to represent Lower Egyptians. The foreign peoples vanquished by the "Scorpion" King are represented by the bows (*iunet, pedjet*), the symbol for foreign enemy peoples or lands (the lands of "the nine arcs," the *pedjet*), tied to Egyptian banners.

The central scene on the mace-head depicts the "Scorpion" King holding a tool in what could be a temple building ceremony or the opening of a dike at the end of the Nile inundation period. (The temptation here is to jump to the conclusion that this could be the temple building ceremony in the new *khenu*, the official royal residence, of the Two Lands, Memphis. However, almost no pictorial evidence authorizes such a conclusion except for the fact that like in The Palette of Narmer, a victory over northerners is being celebrated and therefore the scene of action depicted on the mace-head was in all likelihood in Lower Egypt.)

Another interesting question is raised by both the "Scorpion" mace-head and Narmer's Palette: do the followers carrying standards represent the *Shemsu-Hor*, "the followers of Horus," the *Shemsu-Hor* allies? This is possible even if a Min belemnite shell fossil and a Seth animal are included among the standards on the "Scorpion" mace-head. Clearly, these standards represented the nomes that were allied to "Scorpion" of Hierakonpolis and its god Horus.

Several other palettes, mace-heads and other objects found mainly in Hierakonpolis and Abydos bear witness to a troubled but exalting political and military period in which *Ta-Wy*, the Two Lands, was born. These votive objects feature battles with northerners (foreign and Egyptian), a union between at least some sepat-nomes of the south and the north and the divine omnipotence of the early kings of *Kemet* or *Ta-Wy* (represented as powerful emblematic totemistic bulls, jackals or lions) and their desire to hold sway in enemy territory, over their foreign neighbors in the *pedjet*, in the "nine arcs" or "bows."

The Bull Palette (now in the Paris Louvre Museum) depicts a bull (the king) killing a man wearing the traditional Libyan beard and penis-holder. Poles topped by the totemistic emblems of nomes in Upper and Lower Egypt indicate a union or an alliance at least in this battle. The poles are attached to a rope presumably binding prisoners who are not shown on this surviving fragment of the Palette. The other side of The Bull Palette obviously indicates that two cities have been captured.

The Battlefield Palette (sometimes called The Vultures' Palette (found in Abydos and in three fragments now in London, Oxford and Lucerne), depicts a lion (the king) killing an enemy. Vultures and crows are killing other enemies and emblem/totem standards of Lower Egyptian nomes are holding prisoners.

The Libya Palette (now in the Cairo Museum) clearly depicts battles in Libya in which victory, perhaps by "King Scorpion," had led to a great deal of booty in the form of cattle, donkeys, rams and plants. The reverse side depicts walled cities being destroyed.

The hippopotamus tusk handle of the Gebel el-Arak knife found in Hierakonpolis (and now in the Louvre) presumably depicts hunting, war, a creation myth, victorious and/or defeated nomes and totemistic animals or animals. On one side, a man, perhaps a king, is firmly holding two lions. He is above two dogs who seem to be protecting an egg, perhaps the mythical primordial egg of creation, and various other animals including rams (perhaps the god Min) and dogs.

The other side of the handle depicts warfare, dead bodies, the pole standards of several nomes on a boat and a symbol of a rope-bound town which has obviously been captured.

The least which can be concluded from these early works of art is that kings of Upper Egypt sought to conquer Lower Egypt and to dominate Egypt's neighbors. Perhaps the union of Upper and Lower Egypt into *Ta-Wy*, the Two Lands, was also a goal of these early kings. It is very tempting to conclude that effective union had already taken place, perhaps as early as about 3100 BC. In any case, it is clear that some kings reigned over Upper and Lower Egypt before 2950 BC and that there was a natural, spontaneous and positive vision of the unification of Upper and Lower Egypt. The union of Upper and Lower Egypt was quickly glorified.

At least from the time of Pharaoh Den (c. 2950 BC), the concept of *Ta-Wy* was also illustrated by Den's use of the title *nisut* and *bity*, "he of the sedge and the bee" (he of Upper and Lower Egypt). Early Egyptian works of art, *serekhs, shenu-cartouche* emblems, amulets, hieroglyphic inscriptions, incantations, sacred texts and ritual ceremonies all consistently symbolized, commemorated, extolled and divinized unification and reconciliation. The defense of the land of Egypt was also a key theme — an ivory label found in Abydos (now in the British Museum) shows King Den slaying an Asiatic enemy with a mace-head in a pose similar to that of Narmer on The Palette. This slaying of the *khefty*, the enemy, pose was adopted by all succeeding pharaohs as a symbol of the pharaoh's role as the great warrior of Egypt.

Reconciliation, unity and peace between Upper and Lower Egypt could not have been an easy task. Anedjib (c. 2995 BC), "he who is bold of heart" was the first to use the *nebti*, "Two Ladies" titulary, indicating rule over the south and the north under the protection of Nekhbet, the vulture goddess of the south and Wadjit, the cobra goddess of the north and under the protection of Horus and Seth. Hetepsekhemwy (c. 2890 BC), the founder of the Second Dynasty, also obviously wanted peace as clearly indicated by both the meaning of his name —

"The two mighty ones are at peace," that is Horus and Seth — and his *nebti* title — "The Two Ladies are at peace" — the north and the south.

However, a crunch in the process of reconciliation seems to have occurred during the reign of Peribsen (c. 2700 BC). Until his time, all the *serekhs* of the pharaohs depicted the falcon Horus, but Peribsen's *serekh* was surmounted by a Seth animal. It seems that Peribsen began his reign as a partisan of both Horus and Seth and in favor of north-south peace and reconciliation. His later adoption of Seth in his *serekh* and in his name — "Seth, the one who has come forth from (them?)" could indicate both a temporary resumption of the conflict between Upper and Lower Egypt and a new mythological and religious struggle between Horus and Seth.

In any case, after some initial hesitation, the *serekh* of the next pharaoh Khasekhemwy (c. 2686 BC) — "the Two Powers are crowned" — depicted both the falcon Horus and a Seth animal in an evident show of reconciliation and union between the north and the south, perhaps after more fighting in which the south once again defeated the north. The succeeding pharaohs' fourth divine and first *shenu*-cartouche name, the *nisut-bity* or coronation throne praenomen, all cited them as rulers of the united Two Lands.

The celebration of national unity was a central aspect of the coronation ceremony for every new pharaoh, as it was during the *heb-sed* jubilee ritual. Every two years, the pharaoh and his entourage, in a ceremony called "the following of Horus," sailed down river to Lower Egypt in a reenactment of the voyage and feats of Horus and Narmer uniting *Ta-Wy*, the Two Lands.

HISTORY'S FIRST NATION AND FIRST SACRED NATION

Egypt was the first centralized state in the history of mankind and the first nation to proclaim its sacred nature. Divine kingship naturally implied the divinity of the land of Egypt. *Ta-Wy* was not only the first united kingdom and the first nation in the history of mankind, it was also the first sacred nation. *Ta-Wy* was the first nation to implicitly proclaim its sacred nature by proclaiming that it was directed by a god, the pharaoh, who was also, as the incarnation of Horus, the god of the world, and that its people were superior to all others.

The founding of a nation was indeed revolutionary; the great civilization of Sumer did not found a nation until Sargon of Sumer-Akkad (c. 2340–2305 BC), who established both a nation and history's first empire, stretching from what is now Iran to the Mediterranean.

The Early Dynastic pharaohs, and perhaps even the Predynastic rulers, seem to have had a deliberate politico-religious plan which involved the belief that they were building something unique and great in a divinely ordained way and not just securing a place for Egypt in a rough-and-tumble world. The Sumerians had considered the gods as omnipotent landlords and themselves as "cousins of the gods," but they did not transfer divinity to the concept of the nation until the reign of Naram-Sin, at least 700 years after the establishment of the Two Lands. It would take another 1200 years before the Hebrews, around 1200 BC, articulated the concept of *Eretz Yisroel*, the holy god-given "Land of Israel."

Whether the Egyptians understood that they were building the first nation in the history of mankind and how stupendous a political development this was is, of course, open to considerable doubt. The very notion of a "nation" was probably not immediately evident and it was probably the uniting of the people living in the numerous *sepat*, into *Ta-Wy*, the Two Lands, which was the perceptible goal. It is also doubtful that the Egyptians fully understood the economic implications of what they were doing. By establishing the first nation, the Egyptians were the forerunners of politico-economic centralization, of the vastly increased political and economic clout resulting from the merger of clans, tribes, city-states and *sepat* provinces.

The Egyptians generated bountiful resources with this new centralized system. They financed an immense building program of temples, palaces, granaries, warehouses, workshops, towns, ports, canals, dams and roads for their "first economy" — the economy of the living — and an even greater building program of mastaba and pyramid tombs, temples and fabulous works of art and furnishings for life in the afterlife for their "second economy" — the economy of the living dead.

And, of course, the Egyptians could not know that by establishing the sacredness, the divinity, of the nation, they had established a concept which would survive in various forms for almost 5000 years until the 1789 French Revolution when a new transfer was operated — the transfer from the divinely ruled nation to the "sacredness" of secular rule in the nation-state. It can even be argued that remnants of the Egyptian concept of the divinely ruled, divine nation still linger on today in countries like Saudi Arabia and with concepts such as

"God bless America" and the divinity of the Japanese Emperor — even if hardly anybody takes these notions seriously.

Much like the Sumerians before them and the Hebrews and Greeks after them (and indeed, like all peoples who forge major cultures), the Egyptians cultivated the phantasm that they were different and better than all other peoples. They were deeply imbued with a feeling of superiority and self-designated themselves as the only people blessed by the gods. They saw themselves as the oldest and most religious people, as the ideal people, as the center of the world. As we have seen, Egyptians were *remet*, humans, literally "people," the only people blessed by the gods, and other peoples were not quite up to the Egyptian standard. It was probably this attitude which had favored their proclamation of the sacred nature of the Egyptian nation and people. This proclamation gave them a virtual "Chosen People" status, a notion that was later even more extravagantly and explicitly developed by the Hebrews who proclaimed themselves as "the Chosen People."

When we speak of patriotism and love of one country's today, these terms seem pale compared to the deep reverence and physical and emotional love expressed for *Ta-Wy* in so many steles and temple mural inscriptions, emblematic amulets, weapons, holy ornaments and papyri.

From 3100 BC, hieroglyphically and emblematically united Egypt was powerfully and physically expressed by a pictogram called *Sma-Tawy* (unite the two lands), frequently engraved under the pharaohs' name on his throne, on carved reliefs and paintings in temples and barques and on steles. The *Sma-Tawy* depicted a trachea-artery and lungs binding together sedge-reed (*shema*) or lotus (*seshen*) representing Upper Egypt and a cluster of papyrus flowers (*mehyt*) representing Lower Egypt. Sometimes, the strong desire for harmonious union, for an avoidance of conflict between the old tutelary gods of the north and the south, led to depictions of a *Sma-Tawy* in which Horus of the north and Seth of the south together tied the knot of the *Sma-Tawy*. This occurred even among pharaohs of the Middle Kingdom, like Senwosret I (c. 1965–1920 BC), when Seth although still feared was abhorred (as depicted on a statue found in Itjtawy (modern El-Lisht) and now in the Cairo Museum).

We know from the Palermo Stone (copied around c. 710 BC, supposedly from another source dating to at least 2400 BC, a big fragment of which is now in the Palermo Archaeology Museum) that the holy crowning ceremony of each new pharaoh involved rituals celebrating the divine union of the Two lands and was an occasion for great rejoicing, both for the gods and the people. The *heb-sed*, royal jubilee, ceremony also extolled divine union. After his coronation the pharaoh, wearing the *pshent* double crown of the Two Lands, was delegated by the gods as the father and guarantor of order and prosperity for Ta-*Wy*.

The New Kingdom *Book of the Dead* (c. 1550 BC) extolled the sacred, awesome, ideal nature of the unification of the Two Lands and the peace and reconciliation which had been achieved. Spell 17 declares that all this had been divinely decided upon from eternity under the aegis of Re "...on that day in which the foes of the Lord of All [Re] were destroyed and his son Horus was made to rule...The battleground of the gods was made in accordance with my command." Spell 183 lauds Osiris' role who "pacified the Rival gods...stopped the raging and the tumult...and the Two Lands are peacefully reconciled...The gods of the sky and the gods of the earth have entrusted the earth to your son Horus..."[87]

THE FLIP SIDE OF THE SACRED

However, the reverse side of the coin of this great reverence, patriotism and love for the Two Lands was exacerbated nationalism and militant arrogance, underpinned by the conviction that the people and the land of Egypt were sacred. From the earliest times of the Old Kingdom, obviously premeditated politico-religious concepts expressed in thousands of texts, steles, statues and temple murals depicted the Pharaoh not only as the god-provider of the Two Lands but also as the ruler and guardian of the equilibrium of the entire world. The Pharaoh was always "victorious" in battle and his enemies were always "wretched." And as natural as the Pharaoh's strength and the vileness of Egypt's enemies, was Egypt's right, given by the gods, to wreak immense destruction and rule over all the foreign countries, and especially the *pedjet*, Egypt's enemies.

Of course, this philosophy was partially magical wishful thinking, buttressed by execration texts written with a repetition of derogatory terms, which supposedly made the wish come true and facilitated victory in combat. Nevertheless, the use of *heka*, magic, in this manner was the faithful mirror of Egypt's deep disdain for its neighbors.

The *natural* Egyptian right to rule also involved the natural right to conscript soldiers from Nubia, Libya and elsewhere, utterly pillage and devastate

---

87. Faulkner, R.O., *The Ancient Egyptian Book of the Dead*, pp. 44 and 183.

the lands they attacked and take prisoners who became slaves, servants and concubines. This general attitude was evident in early as well as later times. After being a relatively peaceful people until about the Middle Kingdom (beginning c. 2055 BC), or rather having no powerful enemies inclined to challenge them, the Egyptians evolved into an eminently bellicose and imperialistic people.

The autobiographical inscriptions on the wall-stele of the mastaba tomb in Abydos of Wenis (fl. c. 2280 BC), the Nomarch of Hierakonpolis, priest, overseer of the royal estate and general of Pepy I's army (and perhaps Merena's army), concerning his military campaigns against "the Asiatic Sand-dwellers" (the *Shasu* Bedouins) in Sinai and Canaan were already a "soft" version of what would follow. Wenis sings that his troops had "cut-down its (the *Shasu's*) figs, its vines...thrown fire in all its [mansions]...slain its troops by many ten-thousands."[88]

The hard military and magical version of what usually happened during these wars can be found in numerous execration texts and in a hymn of praise for Pharaoh Senwosret III (c. 1874–1855 BC), who may have organized Egypt's first large standing army. The hymn states: "Hail to you *Khakaure* (Senwosret), our Horus, Divine of form! Land's protector who widens its borders...Who smites foreign countries...Fear of whom smites the Nine Bows. Whose slaughter brought death to thousands of Bowmen (Nubians)...When he felled thousands who ignored his might. His Majesty's tongue restrains Nubia, His utterances make Asiatics flee."[89]

Ahmose, son of Abana, the captain of the ship "Appearing in Memphis," under three 16th century BC pharaohs (Ahmose I, Amenhotep I and Thuthmose I), had a particularly active career of killing, mutilating and looting, especially during the "sacred" task of expelling the Hyksos from Egypt. In his autobiography, on the walls of his tomb in Nekheb (Eleithiapolis), he triumphantly and candidly told the story of looting, massacres, mutilated bodies and male and female prisoners: "I made a capture and I carried away a hand...The Gold of Valor was given to me...Then Avaris [the Hyksos capital] was despoiled. Then I carried off spoil from there: one man, three women...Then his majesty gave them to me to be slaves." And on and on goes Ahmose's tale with more despoiling, carnage, cut off hands, countless prisoners and gold as rewards.[90]

88. Lichtheim, Miriam, *Ancient Egyptian Literature*, Volume I, pp. 19 and 20.
89. *Ibid.*, p.198.

This bellicose attitude was most virulent during the New Kingdom. The general attitude is well illustrated by a stele erected by Egypt's greatest conqueror, Thutmose III (c. 1479–1425 BC), in the Amun-Re Temple in Karnak (and now in the Cairo Museum): "I [Amun-Re] gave you valor and victory over all lands. I set your might, your fear in every country..." The immense text — "The Annals" — inscribed by Thutmose III on Pylon VI in the Karnak Temple refers to all the people it cites, whether from Gaza, Megiddo or Kadesh, as "wretched enemies" to be rightfully "overthrown" in order to "extend the borders of Egypt" in conformity with the "command" to "conquer" from the "father [Amun], mighty and victorious" of the King. It lists the booty won in Megiddo: "Living prisoners: 340. Hands: 83. Horses: 2401...Chariots of his wretched army: 892...Sheep: 20,500..." North of Megiddo, Thutmose' army added greatly to the booty. "The women of the vile enemy and the princes...474 people...the Children of that enemy and of the princes with him: 84...Male and female slaves and their children: 1796...Total: 2503...bowls of costly stone and gold, and various vessels...a statue of ebony...with a head of lapis lazuli...Sacks of wheat: 207,300..."[91]

The statue of Pharaoh Horemheb, referred to above, states: "The Nine Arcs were under his sandals." Pharaoh Merenptah (c. 1213–1203 BC) declared on his stele (found by Petrie in 1886 in Thebes and now in the Cairo Museum) nothing less than: "Not one of the Nine Bows lifts his head: Tjehenu [Libya] is vanquished, Khatti [the land of the Hittites] is at peace, Canaan is captive with all woe. Ashkelon is conquered, Gezer seized, Yanoam [in south Lebanon] made nonexistent; Israel is wasted, bare of seed, Khor [Syria] has become a widow for Egypt. All who roamed [the *Shasu* or the *Habiru*?] have been subdued."[92]

This outpouring strikes us today as excessive nationalism, arrogance, hostility and aggressiveness, but such an attitude was the norm throughout Antiquity. To say the least, the contemporary Babylonians, Hurrians and Hittites of Thutmose III and the later Assyrians, Hebrews, Greeks and Romans were just as cruel as the Egyptians.

This generalized cruel, no-nonsense attitude is perhaps best paradoxically illustrated by the Hebrews, a people who sought to place morality at the center of their system of belief. Despite this goal, Hebrew morality was usually relative

90. Wilson, John in *Ancient Near Eastern Texts Relating to the Old Testament*, pp. 233-234.
91. Lichtheim, Miriam, *Ancient Egyptian Literature, Volume II*, pp. 36 and pp. 30, 33-34.
92. *Ibid.*, p. 77.

and selective. There are terrifying tales in the Hebrew Old Testament of wiping entire cities off the map with fire, killing enemy soldiers, impaling kings, slaughtering horses and cattle — tales of "Joshua [who] smote all the country...utterly destroyed all that breathed, as the Lord god of Israel commanded." Even the generally morally-minded Moses, supposed author of the revolutionary commandment "Thou shalt not kill," ordered the soldiers fighting the Midianites to "kill every male among the little ones, and kill every woman that hath known man..." As to the Hebrew warrior/kings, like Saul and David, Saul did not want "any dowry, but an hundred foreskins of the Philistines" from David for his eldest daughter; David promptly obliged with 200 foreskins of Philistines he "slew."[93]

MEMPHIS, THE FIRST CAPITAL CITY AND FIRST HOLY CITY

Egypt established the first capital city and the first holy city — Memphis — in the history of mankind. Memphis was the first city where the government of an entire nation was centralized. It was also the first city which epitomized an entire people's religion. It was a holy capital long before Babylon, Knossus, Jerusalem, Varanasi, Teotihuacàn or Rome attained such a status.

If a great war did take place and if Lower Egypt lost it, then in choosing Memphis as the new capital of the united land the early Egyptian kings were both magnanimous and politically shrewd in managing their military victory. They clearly had no desire to humiliate Lower Egypt. The building of the new city at Memphis, just inside Lower Egypt, was a symbol glorifying unification and national unity. Memphis was an ideal and shrewd geopolitical choice for a capital city since it was near the border with Upper Egypt and thus in a central position and might have also been the site of the supposedly decisive victory over Lower Egypt. Cairo is now located 15 miles north of ancient Memphis.

With ups and downs, from Narmer's, or Scorpion's, or Aha's time, or whoever was Menes, Memphis first became a sacred Egyptian city and then gradually became one of the greatest Egyptian cities and one of the greatest cities of Antiquity. It remains uncertain whether the First and Second Dynasty "Thinite" pharaohs (c. 3100–2686 BC) were buried in their Abydos or Memphis

---

93. Joshua 10.40, Exodus 20.13, Numbers 31.17, I Samuel 18. 25-27.

tombs. The national political role of Thinis was eliminated at the beginning of the Third Dynasty (c. 2686 BC) when the pharaohs stopped ruling from there and Memphis succeeded it as Egypt's main politico-religious center. Abydos gradually declined into a strictly religious center. At this time, the Memphis Ptah Temple was certainly one of Egypt's greatest temples, before being surpassed by the size and above all the renown of the Heliopolitan theologians, especially from the mid-Fourth Dynasty (c. 2566 BC).

However, the nation continued to be governed from Memphis and most of its major politico-religious ceremonies, including the pharaoh's coronation and *heb-sed*, jubilee, were celebrated there. Memphis became the main port on the Nile, the administrative center of all Egypt and a key economic center. By about the early part of the Fourth Dynasty (c. 2613–2494 BC), a central and coordinated national administrative system and civil service were set up in Memphis, making Egypt the first nation to devise such a system. Until the establishment of Sargon's Sumero-Akkadian Empire about 250 years later, Egypt was the only country in the world to have achieved such a central administration.

Memphis' population was among the largest of all the Egyptian cities, with tens of thousands of civil servants, traders, craftsmen, sailors, artists and priests. Until the rise of Greek Alexandria in the late 4th century BC, Memphis was probably also the most cosmopolitan city in Egypt, with thousands of foreigners. During the New Kingdom (c. 1550–1069 BC), Syrian and Canaanite traders and craftsmen built several temples in Memphis to their gods Baal, Anat and Astarte.

Memphis rapidly became, and remained, the symbolic city of sacred Egyptian national unity. By the Middle Kingdom (beginning c. 2055 BC), in addition to being Ineb-Hedj, the white walled city, it was often referred to as *ankh-Tawy*, "the place which binds together the Two Lands." At the beginning of the New Kingdom (c. 1550 BC), Memphis became known as Men-nefer, the name of the Pepy I (c. 2321–2287 BC) Pyramid in Sakkara. Men-nefer was transliterated into Memphis in Greek.

Memphis' main god, the god of crafts, Ptah, also became a creation, royal patron and funerary god. He was depicted as a mummy with shaven head and a cap and his hands emerging from the bandages holding a rod topped by the *was* scepter (divine dominion) above a *djed* pillar (stability) and an *ankh* (life force). A beard was added to his portrait during the Middle Kingdom (c. 2055–1650 BC). As god of the Holy capital of Memphis, Ptah became one of the main gods of Egypt and maintained this position throughout its history, consecutively pontificating alongside Horus, Osiris, Re and Amun-Re. Ptah also played an immense role as a popular protector in his amulet dwarf pataikos form. During the New Kingdom (from c. 1550 BC), Ptah also had a major international role, especially with a temple in Ashkelon, in Canaan, where he was known as the "Great Prince of Ashkelon" and, of course, in Nubia with temples in Abu Simbel and Gerf Husein.

Concurrently to Ptah in human form, the cult of the Apis Bull — Ptah in his earthly, animal incarnation — was immensely important, perhaps as early as Narmer's or Aha's reigns around c. 3100 BC.

Certainly, the political and at least some of the theological implications of Ptah's and Memphis' roles were evident early on. However, the plenitude of Memphite/Ptah theology, promoting Ptah as the pre-existent creator of the universe, was probably not achieved before the Late Period (c. 747–332 BC).

The Memphite clergy consistently attempted to instrumentalize Ptah as one of the greatest and oldest of Egypt's creator gods. The importance of the crafts at least from c. 3100 BC; Memphis' role as a center of the crafts and Ptah's role as the patron of the crafts must have facilitated this task. Memphis as the symbol of the unification of the Two Lands also enhanced the role of the city and its main god. The Memphite clergy consistently sought to impose their city as the holy theocratic capital of the Two Lands and their god Ptah as the chief god to the detriment of the other great temple-cities and especially Heliopolis and the chief and creator god of its Ennead, Atum-Re. However, neither Memphis nor Ptah ever fully succeeded in this enterprise, even if Memphis constantly grew in splendor and Ptah in importance.

Over the centuries, Memphis was embellished with monumental architecture for the living and for the dead. Vast palaces and administrative offices, libraries, warehouses, workshops and magnificent temples dedicated to Ptah, Hathor, Nefertem and Seker-Osiris were built. The immense Memphis Necropolis stretched out more than 18 miles along the west bank of the Nile from Abu Roash and Rasetau (Giza) in the north to Dashur, south of the city. In Sakkara (a Grecized version of Seker's name), facing Memphis, thousands of tombs and mastabas dating from the Early Dynastic Period (c. 3100–2686 BC) to the Roman Period (30 BC–AD 395), 15 pyramids, and the *Serapeum* catacomb tombs for Apis bulls with *dromos* of sphinxes have been found (as well as an immense network of tunnels dug over centuries by thieves). In all, 32 pyramids, including the Step Pyramid in Sakkara, the Great Pyramids and Great Sphinx at Giza, the Bent Pyramid and the first "true" pyramid at Dashur, Re sun temples in

Abu Ghurab and Abusir and a huge number of First Dynasty mastaba tombs for royal wives and high officials in Abusir have been found in the Memphis necropolises.

Memphis was the epitome of the Old Kingdom Egypt and even after the definitive loss of its role as political capital of the Two Lands (c. 2181 BC) Memphis always exercised considerable religious and political importance. It remained the capital of Lower Egypt, a residence of the pharaohs and above all it was seen as the religious/geographical foundation of the Two Lands, the holy city of *Ta-Wy*, throughout Egyptian history.

CHAPTER 6.
THE FOUNDING MYTHOLOGICAL CONTEXT

THE OSIRIS/SETH/ISIS/HORUS TALES AS THE FOUNDING MYTH OF THE NATION. THE ADVENTURES OF THE GODS AND GODDESSES

Once it became a central belief in its Osirisian version, perhaps around 2375 BC, the Osiris/Seth/Isis/Horus tale constituted the founding myth of the sacred nation of Egypt. Its importance was as a model of identification and imitation for resurrection and the afterlife for the reigning divine pharaoh. The central elements of this great myth found their way into Egyptian theology, religious rituals, art, magic, politics and life and then gradually the afterlife for everybody and not just the pharaoh. Right into the first centuries of our era, the central point of reference of Egypt always led back to the Osiris/Seth/Isis/Horus myth.

The many and succeeding versions of the myth provide us with a unique insight into the daily life of the gods of the Great Heliopolitan Ennead and by extension the other Enneads. In all its versions, the gods were a magnification of human qualities, strengths and faults which resulted in brave, wise, noble and moral behavior, but also in frequent wily, fickle, indecisive, fearful, cowardly and immoral behavior.

Egyptians theologians' vision of the life of their gods and goddesses was hardly different from other polytheistic visions, like the earlier Sumerian or later Hindu, Greek or Roman polytheisms. The gods and goddesses were vibrant, adventurous, raucous, sensual, sexually hyperactive, barely spiritual and fundamentally concerned with maintaining primeval concepts of cosmic harmony and order.

This contrasts sharply with the austerity, the fire and brimstone revenge when righteousness was not practiced and with the morality, love, ethereal spirituality and asexuality of later Hebrew and Christian monotheisms and even considerably contrasts with the halfway house represented by Persian near-monotheism.

Several key theological and political principles occurred in all the versions of the myth — resurrection, the afterlife, the innocence of the victim Osiris, the struggle between might and right in its primeval and then its moral forms, the potency of magic and the sacred nature of a united Egypt.

These general principles were accompanied by some sort of present victory for Horus and posthumous justification and victory for Osiris. Almost equally important was the elevation of Isis to the epitome of motherhood ("mother of the god" Horus and later, in the New Kingdom, from c. 1550 BC, "mother of all gods"). Isis was also elevated to being the perfect wife, involving faithfulness to her husband, warmth, magnanimity and consolation despite occasional lack of strategic judgment and an irresolute nature.

Osiris, the main character in the myth, was mythically presented as the affectionate, good, intelligent, perfect teacher of the people, instructing them in knowledge of the gods and religion, the *maat* (order), harmony and what's right for the universe, but also what's right in human behavior. He was the god who led the Egyptians out of their primeval, savage state into civilization and gave them agriculture, food laws and taboos. He was also the perfect tall, handsome husband and the caring father. In short and for the Manichaean needs of myth, Osiris was known and loved by all.

Concerning the villain of the myth Seth, younger brother to Osiris, the norms for the oldest versions of the myth were defeat and a form of disrepute, but reconciliation between Horus and Seth and the maintenance of great power for Seth. This situation led to reverence and royal patronage status for Seth before he was definitively rejected. Seth was always respected for his great physical power and feared for his ability to do evil and, in these roles, he always remained a respected force who had to be reckoned with.

However, Seth consistently played the loser's role, the role of disorder, night, darkness, the desert, sterility, storms (and eventually, evil), but it was an absolutely necessary dualistic Manichaean role. Over the centuries, Seth was increasingly depicted as the personification of evil, trickery and aggressive heterosexual and homosexual behavior, as the murderer of his elder brother, a fellow god, and as everything horrible implied in the color red. However, before the Late Period (c. 747–332 BC) versions of the myth Seth was not designated as the epitome of evil.

It is also clear that Seth was utilized not only to amplify Osiris' qualities but also in relation to one of the core meanings of what Osiris stood for — resurrection. Just as there could be no resurrection of Jesus without the betrayal by Judas, the religious opportunism of the High Priest Caiaphas and the political expediency of the Tetrarch Pilate, there could be no resurrection of Osiris and resurrection in general without the murder of Osiris by Seth and the succeeding physical and moral defeat of Seth.

FIRST PROTOTYPES FOR ARCHETYPAL FIGURES?

With Isis, the good girl aspect was introduced into the saga. This was done using the same Manichaean techniques. Isis' powerful, positive feminine qualities — her fierce loyalty to her husband Osiris, her protective role as "mother of the god" Horus and her immense magical powers — were an unbeatable recipe.

In all the variants of the myth, Horus played the winner's role, the epitome of the perfect, brave, intelligent, dutiful, avenging son who gloriously fulfills the promise placed in him. Horus was the good little guy who beats the bad big guy; he was order and light.

Here, within a framework of raucous adventure, we are dealing with the earliest known version of the good guy — bad guy saga. The hero must go through trials and tribulations and usually temporary defeat, but in the end wins definitively, while the anti-hero after temporary success is permanently defeated. Of course, this is how things turned out in Egypt. Osiris eventually became the popular savior god, the *Wennefer*, the innocent, pure, eternally good, compassionate god, offering an afterlife to all. Seth was eventually ruined by Egypt's founding myth and became the permanent personification of guilt and evil (and one of the possible prototypes for Satan and then for the devil).

The founding Osiris/Seth/Isis/Horus myth has several variants. Viewed together, the succeeding variants do not give us even a minimum of coherence concerning the main events and the identities of the main characters, but rather result in one of the most confused tales (and also one of the most fabulous) in the history of mythology.

The earliest extant written fragments and episodes of the Osirisian cycle of the myth can be traced to many utterance-spells in the Pyramid Texts (c. 2375–2125 BC) and then to the spells in the Coffin Texts in the First Intermediate Period (c. 2181–2055 BC). During the New Kingdom (c. 1550–1069 BC), major episodes of the Osiris/Seth/Isis/Horus myth were included in *The Book of the Dead*, the central Egyptian religious text, composed largely from the Pyramid Texts and the Coffin Texts. *The Great Hymn to Osiris*, on the Stele of Amenmose (in the Louvre Museum), the Karnak Temple's Chief of Cattle Herds, perhaps around 1400 BC, contains one of the fullest Egyptian versions of the myth but it is an incomplete summary and lacks a blow-by-blow description of events.

We find this detailed description in what is often referred to as *The Contendings of Horus and Seth*, composed during Rameses V's reign (c. 1147–1143 BC) and now in the British Museum as the Chester Beatty I Papyrus. Another Ramesside version is contained in the Sallier IV Papyrus (now in the British Museum).

Numerous versions and fragments of the myth were copied from earlier texts or composed during the Late Period (c. 747–332 BC), including the Memphite/Ptah version on the Shabako Stone (late 8th century BC) which added significant elements of morality and accentuated the aspects of divine and political reconciliation of the original myth. Magical spells like those on the Metternich Stele (c. 380–362 BC) and now in the New York Metropolitan Museum are other important sources.

Other important versions, fragments and episodes of the myth date to the Ptolemaic Period (c. 332–32 BC). They are contained in the late 4th century BC *Lamentations of Isis and Nephthys* (Papyrus Berlin 3008) and in *The Songs of Isis and Nephthys* (Bremner-Rhind Papyrus, now in the British Museum), *The Divine Battles and Judgment* on the 1st century BC Jumilhac Papyrus (now in the Louvre Museum), the inscriptions and reliefs on the walls of the Edfu Horus Temple (c. 237–51 BC) and in *The Book of Breathings* (notably in the Louvre and in the British Museum), probably the final compendium of Egyptian afterlife beliefs.

The Egyptians never compiled and unified the scattered myths, tales and legends concerning Osiris, Seth, Isis and Horus. The task of compiling the Osirisian cycle was undertaken only some 2300 years into the game, by the Greek priest/philosopher Plutarch (c. AD 45–125) in *Isis and Osiris*.

Plutarch seems to have made this compilation fairly; it seems to have corresponded to Greek-influenced Egyptian beliefs during the first century AD. However, we must also take into account that Plutarch was writing at a time when Christianity was emerging, that he was a staunch supporter of Orphic polytheism and a priest at the Delphi Oracle dedicated to Apollo, whom the Greeks had assimilated with Horus, and that one of his main goals was to demonstrate the validity of polytheism. Plutarch saw Egyptian mythology through a Greek prism and he superimposed Greek religious and moral ideals and rationalism onto the Egyptian tale. He had a mania for attributing Greek semantic origins to the names of the Egyptian divinities and sought to emphasize the common identity, under different names, of the ancient Egyptian gods and the Greek gods. Plutarch was particularly favorable to the cult of the "exceptionally wise and lover of wisdom," Isis, which in his time had spread throughout the Greco-Roman Mediterranean world.

According to Plutarch, Osiris (Dionysus) from birth was order and benevolence, "the Lord of all that is good" and the epitome of "creative moisture" who taught the Egyptians "the fruits of cultivation [agriculture], [gave] them laws," taught them "to honor the gods" and "traveled over the whole earth civilizing it." Typhon (Seth) was "diseased and disorderly," "dry, fiery and arid," "irrational and truculent," "confused by his wickedness" and "prompted by jealousy and hostility...filled the whole earth, and the ocean as well, with ills..." Typhon/Seth invited Osiris to a banquet and tricked him into placing himself in an extraordinarily beautiful cedar chest inlaid with gold, silver, ivory and ebony and painted with images of the gods. Typhon/Seth had noted the exact height of Osiris and announced that he would give the beautiful chest to the person whom it fitted perfectly. Of course, the chest was only a perfect fit for Osiris, who gleefully claimed it as his, but once he was inside it Seth and his 72 accomplices and Aso, the Queen of Ethiopia, shut it tight and then threw it into the Nile.

The chest floated to the Mediterranean Delta papyrus marshlands city of Chemmis and then to the Levantine city of Byblos (*Djaty*). Here it was enclosed and protected by an *asher* tree, the tamarisk, which became so beautiful that the local king cut it down and had it sculpted into an ornamental pillar for his palace. Isis (which Plutarch mistakenly believed was a name of Greek origin — "hastening with understanding,"[94] when we now know that the likeliest

---

94. Plutarch, *Moralia*, Volume V, *Isis and Osiris*, pp. 9, 33, 121, 81, 35, 81, 121, 35, 123, 65, 143.

meaning of Aset is throne), the loving, faithful sister and wife of Osiris, with great difficulty and many adventures, but unrelenting resolve and as the supreme magician, sought out and found her husband. She brought the chest containing the corpse back to Buto in the Delta where she was nurturing Arueris (Horus the Elder, Apollo), the child born from her union with Osiris while both were already in love in the womb of their mother Rhea (Nut), the goddess of rhythmic flow, whose husband was Khronos (Geb).

With Osiris dead, the rebel Typhon/Seth had become the Lord of Egypt. While out hunting boars at night (he particularly loved the night), discovered the chest in the Delta marshes where Isis had hidden it. He ripped Osiris into 14 parts and cast these remains throughout Egypt. Typhon/Seth pretentiously believed he had now triumphed, that he had killed his brother Osiris. However, he did not take into account Isis' divine motivation, immense magical powers, and great love for her husband.

Assisted by her guard Anubis, Isis embarked on her second quest for Osiris' body. Plutarch says that Anubis was the son of Osiris and Nephthys (Aphrodite) the sister/wife of Seth, and sister of Isis and Osiris, and some Egyptian texts also claim this, although the most usual version is that Anubis was the son of Seth and Nephthys. According to Plutarch, Nephthys disguised herself as Isis, made love with Osiris, Anubis was born of this affair and Nephthys fled from Seth in fear. This version of an affair between Nephthys and Osiris seems coherent with other aspects of the myth, given, as we shall soon see, Nephthys' sexually tinged lamentations for Osiris.

Osiris' status as the good guy/perfect husband is not really dented by this interpretation, since his behavior was within the norms for Egyptian gods — there was no transgression. Pyramid Text Utterance 356 says that it was Geb, the father of Osiris and Isis and Nephthys, "who brought your two sisters to your side for you,"[95] and in the *Lamentations of Isis and Nephthys*, which opens with the proclamation "To soothe the heart of Isis and Nephthys,"[96] Isis and Nephthys ardently lamented Osiris together without a trace of jealousy.

According to Plutarch, Isis found every single piece of Osiris' body, except his penis which had been eaten by a fish. Isis fabricated an imitation penis for Osiris and an imperfect child, weak of limbs, Harpocrates, was born (the

---

95. Faulkner, R.O., *The Ancient Egyptian Pyramid Texts*, p.114:
96. Lichtheim, Miriam, *Ancient Egyptian Literature, Volume II*, p. 116.

Egyptian Harpakhrad, the child manifestation of Horus). Isis then buried all the pieces of Osiris in the places where she had found them.

Horus was secretly raised by Isis in the sacred floating island of Chemmis in the papyrus marshes of the western Delta. Isis nurtured Horus with the help of the royal and guardian goddess of Lower Egypt, Buto (Wadjit), and Aphrodite/Nephthys. She protected Horus and with magic spells fended off the serpents, scorpions and demons Seth sent to torment him. (The child Moses, in a much later period, seems to have gone through a very Horus-like experience of this kind. Horus the child was also clearly a prefiguration of Jesus the child and the Isis mother aspect, a prefiguration of Mary.)

The Metternich Stele, which is a cippus talisman of Horus against venomous bites, dating to Nectanebo I's reign (c. 380–362 BC), adds another twist: One day, when Isis was away from Chemmis, a scorpion sent by her "evil brother" (Seth) stung and killed the concealed child Horus, the "innocent" future "avenger of his father." Isis cried out to the heavens for help. The god of wisdom Thoth urgently descended from his "barque of millions" in the sky and with immense protection from many deities and magical words brought Horus back to life so that "revenge" against Seth could one day occur.[97]

According to Plutarch, from time to time Osiris returned to earth to teach his son Horus noble behavior and the art of war so that he could one day avenge his father and assume his rightful position as Lord-god of Egypt. Plutarch seems to be dealing here with "Arueris," Horus the Elder, as a child, rather than the child Harpocrates (Harpakhrad), while in the Egyptian tradition, it was Harpakhrad who was brought up by Isis in Chemmis and all the forms of Horus were lumped together as his aspects. Plutarch also introduces an anachronism here when he says that Horus will use a horse in his future battle with Typhon/Seth, although the time frame for the myth is around 3000 BC and horses only appeared in Egypt in the 17th century BC when the Hyksos brought them there.

When he became a young man, Plutarch's "perfected and complete" Horus engaged Typhon/Seth in battle and won, but Typhon/Seth "smites the eye of Horus...or snatches it out and swallows it, and then later gives it back to the Sun"...while Horus "cut out" the "privy members of Typhon."[98] Plutarch then confusedly re-introduced Harpocrates/ Harpakhrad at the trial in which Typhon/Seth accused Horus of being an illegitimate child, born after Osiris'

97. Borghouts, J. F., *Ancient Egyptian Magical Texts*, pp. 62-69.
98. Plutarch, *Moralia*, Volume V, *Isis and Osiris*, pp. 133, 135, 133.

death; but with the help of Hermes (Thoth), Horus was declared legitimate. Two more battles between Typhon/Seth and Horus then ensued.

Plutarch did not deal extensively with two major points in most of the Egyptian versions of the myth — the mummification and resurrection of Osiris and the details of the trial. The most popular Egyptian version of Osiris' resurrection portray Isis as working an even greater miracle than that of her quest — using magical incantations and techniques, she resurrected Osiris, and breathed life back into him by flapping her wings. This vision of a winged Isis was frequently used in funerary art in which she was shown hovering over the deceased. In other Egyptian texts, it was Re or Horus who resurrected Osiris and Anubis who made the first mummy, that of Osiris' body. The trial between Horus and Seth eventually became a vital element of the myth as expressed in the mid-12th century BC Chester Beatty I Papyrus.

According to more than 25 utterances in the Pyramid Texts, Osiris was tricked, murdered and drown by his brother Seth, with the help of Thoth. Nut saved her eldest son Osiris from rotting in the water and re-assembled his bones and put back in place his head and his heart. Osiris' two sisters Isis and Nephthys, after a great quest, found Osiris' body and brought it back to life. Isis had a child, Horus, with Osiris. Horus grew up and engaged the battle against Seth, castrating him. Horus lost an eye in the battle, but retrieved it after his victory and gave it to his father Osiris, giving Osiris power over spirits. Osiris' father Geb convoked the Heliopolitan Ennead to decide what had to be done. Horus pushed Seth beneath Osiris and Seth was condemned to carry Osiris on his back forever. The resurrected Osiris, who had received sovereignty over the earth from Geb, was reinstated as king, but he then took his place in the sky where he became the "Foremost of the Westerners" (the dead) and the pharaoh upon death ascended to the sky and became Osiris. Horus became "lord of the Two Lands" of Egypt.[99]

In the Egyptian texts, Osiris gradually came to be seen as the "King of the Dead," but Plutarch, in a typically Greek anti-body, idealistic manner, wrongly believed that Osiris was not associated "with the bodies of those that are believed to have reached their end"; he was "far removed from the earth, uncontaminated and unpolluted and pure from all matter that is subject to

---

99. Faulkner, R.O., *The Ancient Egyptian Pyramid Texts*, Numerous Utterances, notably Ut.572, p. 227, Ut. 218 and 219, pp. 45-47, Ut. 593, p. 243-244, Ut.447, pp. 148-149, Ut.357, pp. 114-115, Ut.33, p. 7, Ut.570, p. 225, Ut.366, p.120, Ut.356, pp. 113-114, Ut.532, p. 200, Ut.677, p. 291.

destruction and death." For Plutarch, Osiris was rather the "leader and king" of the "souls...set free in the realm of the invisible and unseen, the dispassionate and the pure corruption of death."[100] Of course, nothing could be more untrue concerning the Egyptians, for whom the afterlife above all meant *wehem ankh*, repeating life, with one's earthly body.

In the Pyramids Texts, Osiris ruled from the celestial afterlife in the sky and then is located both in the sky and in *Amenta*, the West, the *Duat*, "the beautiful place in nether world," the underworld land of the afterlife dead. The "Introductory Hymn to Osiris in *The Book of the Dead* says that Osiris, "King of Eternity, Lord of Everlasting...The Two Lands are marshaled for him as leader" now "rules the plains of the Silent Land (that is, the land of the dead)." *The Great Hymn to Osiris* on Amenmose's Stele says: "Hail to you Osiris/Lord of Eternity, king of gods..."[101]

At least from the Middle Kingdom (c. 2055–1650 BC), the so-called "mysteries of Osiris" — of his death and resurrection — were acted out annually in the Osiris Temple in Abydos. From the 4th century BC, the deeply moving *Lamentations of Isis and Nephthys* and *The Songs of Isis and Nephthys* were also enacted. Two young women with completely shaven bodies and wearing wigs and who were virgins ("not yet opened") played the roles of Isis and Nephthys. They sang and pleaded for the return and resurrection of their beloved Osiris: Isis, in *The Songs of Isis and Nephthys*, proclaims: "O being with such a handsome face and whose love is great...Come back in peace, O our master, so that we can see you, so that the two sisters can unite with your body in which there is no more activity...Unite yourself to us like a male...Your son Horus will protect and avenge you...O Bull who fecundates the cows...Lord among the women...I'm your sister Isis...flooding this land with tears...Seth is in the place where he will be executed...Come back to your house without fear...O my brother, O my Lord, you who have gone to the Land of Silence [the nether world], come back to me in your first form..." Nephthys, in *The Lamentations*, cries out: "Your two sisters...Call for you in tears!...Our faces live by seeing your face!...I am with you, your bodyguard, For all eternity!"[102]

---

100. Plutarch, *Moralia*, Volume V, *Isis and Osiris*, p. 183.

101. Faulkner, R.O., *The Ancient Egyptian Book of the Dead*, p. 27 and Lichtheim, Miriam, *Ancient Egyptian Literature*, Volume II, p. 81.

102. Lalouette, Claire *Textes Sacrés et Textes Profanes de l'Ancienne Egypte*, II, *Mythes, Contes et Poèsie*, Papyrus Bremner-Rhind, pp. 74-88 and Lichtheim, Miriam, *Ancient Egyptian Literature*, Volume III, Papyrus Berlin 3008, pp. 117-118.

After such loving lamentations by two superb women, who wants to doubt that Osiris was resurrected?

However, Isis also embodied what has come to be seen as the standard, hackneyed feminine shortcomings. Nevertheless, Isis (and Hathor) were basically a reflection of the relatively more egalitarian attitude to women which the Egyptians held compared to other peoples in Antiquity. Neither was submissive; they were strong-willed, spoke their minds and were capable of the type of action usually associated with the male. Hathor's sexual behavior was what today would be called emancipated and to some extent this was also true for Isis. A similar attitude of freewheeling sexuality can be found in the Sumerian mother and love goddess Inanna and the underworld death goddess Ereshkigal, but Sumerian women were notoriously submitted to men and as the playthings of religion were forced to periodically prostitute themselves in the temples. The Judeo-Christian tradition gave us only one positive archetype of a really free, strong-willed woman — Deborah — and imposed the archetype of the asexual, submitted and self-effaced woman — Mary.

The earlier fragments of the myth depicted Osiris insisting that his son Horus inherit his crown as part of a natural, clannish harmony with the *maat* laws of the cosmic order, but the later versions became more revolutionary. The c. 1400 BC *Great Hymn to Osiris* is a warm, moral tale from start to finish in which the positive characters — Osiris, Isis and Horus — are lauded, and win their rightful places and enduring esteem. *Maat* (as order, but also as truth) is "set...throughout the Two Shores [Upper and Lower Egypt]" and "Evil is fled, crime is gone/The land has peace under its lord."[103] The mid-12th century BC Chester Beatty I Papyrus depicts Osiris, Thoth and some of the other gods and goddesses, insisting that the *maat* aspect of doing what was morally right was as important as the concept of clannish primogeniture as expressed by the birthright of Horus. The versions of the myth that were "copied" or composed just before or during the Late Period (from c. 747 BC), like the Shabako Stone and the Jumilhac Papyrus, accentuated these tendencies. These versions of the myth illustrate how, over the centuries, the idea of the *maat* was gradually transformed from a primeval concept of a so-called natural cosmological order to also include the ideal of a moral order and justice. By the Late Period, this attitude — even if it remained more theoretical than real — had become

---

103. Lichtheim, Miriam, *Ancient Egyptian Literature, Volume II*, pp. 81-85.

widespread in Egyptian society and was reflected in the new versions of the myth.

We are now also dealing with several Horuses with various names and various attributes before the founding Osirisian myth, during the main action of the myth, and afterwards when all the Horuses were virtually combined while simultaneously continuing to have separate existences. There are the early falcon Horuses of Upper and Lower Egypt. There are the Haroeris "Horus the Elder" forms. There are the Harseisis "Horus the Younger" forms as the son of Osiris and Isis: Horus in human form as the child Harpakhrad (Harpocrates), Horus Harsiesis, the grown son of Isis and Osiris, and the successors of Hariesis in the form of Har-nedj-itef (Harendotes), who was the obedient, duty-minded avenger in the Osirisian cycle of the myth and who won the final battle against Seth, and Heru-Sma-Tawy (Harsomtus), uniter and Lord of the Two Lands.

At least from the Fourth Dynasty (c. 2613–2494 BC), the combined "old" Horuses" of the Horian cycle and "new" Horuses of the Osirisian cycle were incorporated into a "secondary ennead" in Heliopolis alongside Atum-Re's solar cult. In this secondary ennead, Horus was the son of the Sky goddess Nut and Re, who was also the mother of Osiris, Seth and Isis.

In typical Egyptian fashion, Horus, in his combined form, at specific periods or all at the same time, was therefore the several forms of the falcon "Horus the Elder" and the nephew of Seth, the brother of Seth and the son and brother of Osiris and Isis, as well as the seventeen or so individual forms of Horus. All these Horuses are identified with the original falcon Horus — they are all the same as the original Horus — and yet they are also different and not the same as the original Horus — they all have separate identities. Moreover, Re as Re-Horakthe, the amalgamation of Re and Horus, not only includes "Horus the Elder" but also "Horus the Younger."

The Middle Kingdom (c. 2055 BC) Coffin Texts already amply illustrated the amalgamated nature and role of Horus. Coffin Text Spell 148 (sometimes called *The Birth and Flight of Horus*) indicated that even when "Horus son of Isis" was in the stomach of his mother Isis, "pregnant with seed of her brother Osiris"and therefore an "Osirisian" Horus, he was already linked to the "Horian" falcon Horuses — "in this your name of falcon" — and to Re-Horakhte — "you shall always be in the suite of Re of the horizon in the prow of the primeval bark for ever and ever." Spell 148 is also perhaps the epitome of how the amalgamated Elder solar Horus and Younger Osirisian Horus were seen during the Middle Kingdom (beginning c. 2055 BC): "I am Horus, the great Falcon...of the mansion of Him whose name is hidden (Re). My flight aloft has reached the horizon...I have overpassed the gods of sky. I have made my position more prominent than that of the Primeval Ones [the old Heliopolis Ennead]. There is no god who can do what I have done...I am aggressive against the enemy of my father Osiris, he having been set under my sandals." Horus is "lord and heir of the Ennead" and Isis promises that "What he shall rule is this land...what he shall kill is Seth."[104] The clear meaning is that Horus amalgamated with Re defeats the negative forces embodied in Seth and therefore maintains cosmic harmony in Egypt. For the dead person who has this spell inscribed on his coffin, identification with this powerful Horus is the perfect choice to ensure an afterlife.

Horus' loss of an eye in the battle with Seth was a major recurrent theme in every version of the myth and seems to be primevally linked to the temporary loss of light to night and the appearance of the moon as a lesser light, with phases. In the Egyptian system, Horus' eye also represented several other key aspects — divine kingship, power over the world of the dead and magical protective and healing capacities. Numerous utterances in the Pyramid Texts refer to this loss of an eye in several different manners — Seth "snatched it," "trampled" it, "pulled" it out, or perhaps Horus' eye is still in fairly good shape, "for little is that which Seth has eaten of it," although Seth's followers "licked" it.[105]

In the Edfu temple mural inscriptions of the myth (c. 246–51 BC), and probably in the story's antecedents farther back in history, the Horian and Osirisian aspects are gaily mixed. Horus acts as the son of Re in his Behdety winged sun disk sky god form, but he fights Seth in his hippopotamus form after the latter murdered Osiris. Horus loses an eye to Seth and his troops that were transformed into demonic crocodiles and hippopotami. The tradition of Re, the sun, losing an eye fits into this version and Horus wages a battle for the return of his father Re's eye. At the same time Thoth, in his moon god form, had received an eye from Re and returned Horus' eye. In the Coffin Text Spell 157 episode of the myth, "Seth...transformed himself" into a fiendish, fierce "black pig...[and] projected a wound into (Horus') eye," but Re healed his blindness. In the Chester Beatty variant, Seth pulled out both of Horus' eyes and the goddess Hathor restored and healed them with gazelle's milk and magic. Most of the first

---

104. Faulkner, R.O., *The Ancient Egyptian Coffin Texts*, Volume I, pp. 125-126.

105. Faulkner, R.O., *The Ancient Egyptian Pyramid Texts*, Ut.57-o, p. 13, Ut.111, p. 24, Ut.121, p. 25, Ut.166, p. 31, Ut.145, p. 29.

212 utterances in the Pyramid Texts say that Horus' eye was given to Osiris and thus to the pharaoh who became Osiris upon death — "O Osiris the King, take the eye of Horus..."[106] In other versions, Seth returned the eye to Horus, who gave it to Osiris. Meanwhile, Re had replaced his lost eye with a cobra, who was the goddess Wadjit. This *uraeus* became the "eye of Re," and was used by Re to destroy enemies.

The cobra *uraeus* became the insignia of the reigning pharaohs and spewed poison on enemies. Horus' healed eye, as the *wedjat*, the "Eye of Horus," became one of the most popular and potent amulets of Egypt. (In some texts, it was the sound eye that was the *wedjat*.)

The final trial phase of the Osirisian myth, or rather what seems to be the final superimposition of the Horian, Re and Osirisian myths, is best described in the mid-12th century BC Chester Beatty I Papyrus.

This final phase features Horus as the avenger of Osiris. Horus was now an adolescent, a divine youth. He appeared together with Isis before the Great Ennead of Heliopolis that had been enlarged to the thirty members of the traditional Egyptian court. Horus called on the Ennead to give him his birthright as King of Egypt, as the son and heir of Osiris. The arguments, interspersed by decisions, counter-decisions, battles between Horus and Seth, hilarious events, eroticism, graft, trickery, vile and noble intentions and incredible errors of magic dragged on for eighty years.

The air and sunlight god Shu immediately ruled in favor of Horus, declaring, "Right rules might." The wisdom god Thoth jubilantly added: "That is right a million times." That's the same Thoth who in the Pyramid Texts had conspired with Seth to kill Osiris, had not mourned Osiris' death, and was threatened with punishment from a resurrected Osiris. The gods of the Ennead seemed to side with Horus, but this aroused Re's wrath; after all, he was the chief god and it was up to him decide alone.

Seth argued that he was the eldest living son of Nut, the daily destroyer of Re's enemy, the giant snake Apophis, the most powerful of all the gods, and that all this clearly gave him the right to rule. He proposed to "step outside" with Horus and settle matters. Thoth said there was no way of giving the "office of Osiris to Seth while his son Horus is there." This greatly irritated Pre-Harakhti

---

106. Faulkner, R.O., *The Ancient Egyptian Coffin Texts*, Vol. I, Spell 157, p. 135 and Faulkner, R.O., *The Ancient Egyptian Pyramid Texts*, Ut.26, p. 5.

(Re as the amalgamation of many gods). He was clearly lukewarm to the notion of Horus becoming ruler of Egypt and favored Seth because of his great strength.

Atum called in the god of Mendes, Banebjedet, for advice. Banebjedet wanted the Ennead "not to decide in ignorance" and proposed consulting Neith, the great divine mother. A letter was sent to Neith asking for her opinion in the name of Re-Atum, Thoth and Hapy, combined as Re-Harakhti. Neith had no doubts about the matter — the throne should go to Horus and Seth should be appeased by doubling his goods and giving him the foreign goddesses Astarte and Anat as wives. Neith furiously threatened to bring the sky down on the earth if the Ennead committed "big misdeeds" by not awarding the throne of Egypt to Horus. But the All-Lord Re still believed that the function of King of Egypt "was too big" for the "feeble youngster" Horus, whose "breath smells bad [of milk?]."

Pre-Harakhti was now insulted by the minor god Baba, and was angry and despondent. Hathor, presumably in her goddess of love and pleasure aspects, did a striptease for Re to relieve the tension, but this succeeded only momentarily. The gods continued to dillydally, torn between "right" and "might." Seth threatened to "take my scepter of 4500 pounds and kill one of you every day!" until he got his way. The fearful Ennead was now deadlocked, with some of the gods favoring Seth. Seth then threatened to withdraw forever from the court if Isis was permitted to stay. Pre-Harakhti, also deeply irritated with Isis, decided that the court, without Isis, would sail up to the "Island-in-the-Midst" (Pi-aaleq, Philae), where a final decision would be taken.

We are now dealing with Re as he somehow maintains his own individual characteristics while also appearing as the All-Lord, Re or Pre-Harakhti who combines many gods. Atum takes decisions that anger Re, but Atum, as Re-Atum, is one of Re's aspects. Re, as Re-Harakthi, not only contains all of the Horuses, but by the time of the writing of the Chester Beatty version of the myth (the mid-12th century BC), Re himself was also part of Amun-Re (who had amalgamated all the gods including Horus). And Onuris (Anhur), who had the gift of supremely irritating Re, was a form of Shu and Horus.

Of course, Isis used magic, trickery and graft and succeeded in getting to the island of Philae. Once again, she played a key role in turning the tide against Seth. She transformed herself into a beautiful young widow and immediately attracted the attention of the lustful Seth. She wept bitterly and told Seth her story — she had taken a stranger into her home and fed him after the death of her shepherd husband and after a few days the stranger had confiscated her dead husband's herds — while their son was still alive. Seth promised to avenge the beautiful widow and her son, as it was absolutely unheard of to "give the cattle to a stranger while the man's son is here...One must beat the intruder with a stick, and throw him out, and set the son in the place of his father." Isis transformed herself into a kite, flew into a tree and roared, "Weep for yourself...Your own cleverness has judged you." Isis' magic and parable had confounded her brother Seth into admitting that Horus was the rightful King of Egypt. Seth was furiously resentful of his sister's betrayal, but Pre-Harakhti himself now ruled that Seth had, indeed, judged himself. The Ennead then placed the white crown of Upper Egypt on the head of Horus.

Seth's rage against this decision was beyond the boiling point. He proposed that Horus and he transform themselves into hippopotami and plunge into the sea, with the first to emerge above the water being disqualified from becoming king.

Isis was outraged and fearful. She concocted a magical harpoon to kill Seth and tossed it into the water where Seth and Horus were fighting as transformed hippopotami. But in trying to help her son, Isis made matters worse. The harpoon hit Horus and Isis had to employ more magic to revive her son. Finally, the harpoon hit the hippopotamus Seth, but he begged his sister to have pity in the name of their mother. So, instead of letting him die, Isis felt overwhelming pity for her brother Seth and saved him with more magic. This infuriated Horus, who cut off her head.

The Behdety winged sun disk Edfu version states that a 12-foot tall Horus, wielding ten 30-foot harpoons with 6-foot wide blades, killed a gigantic Seth in the form of a red hippopotamus straddling both banks of the Nile, with ten blows to different parts of his hippopotamus body. The Sallier IV Papyrus states that Horus and Seth fought first as men and then transformed themselves into bears and fought for three days and three nights. Horus finally got the upper hand and put a tied-up Seth into Isis' custody. Isis, feeling pity for her brother Seth, freed him. Horus then cut off Isis' head and Thoth, using great *heka*, great magic, restored it as a cow's head. For Plutarch, it was not Isis' head but her diadem which was slashed off and replaced by Hermes/Thoth with a cow's head headdress. Whatever the version, and there are still others, the point is that Isis is being clearly linked to the great mother, the *ahet*, the divine, celestial cow, much like the earlier Nut, Bat or Hathor.

Pre-Harakhti decided to punish Horus for cutting off Isis' head. He ordered the Ennead of gods to search for Horus. Seth found him, ripped out his two eyes and buried them. Hathor found a weeping Horus the next day. She caught a gazelle and poured its milk into Horus' eyes and healed them.

The All-Lord Re and the Ennead now decreed that Horus and Seth should stop quarreling: "Leave us in peace," and go eat and drink together. Seth invited Horus to his house. In the evening, Horus and Seth lay down together to rest. Seth tried to sodomize Horus, to prove to everyone that Horus was a puny, effeminate softy and unworthy of being King. Without Seth's knowledge, Horus caught the sperm in his hand before it could penetrate him. Isis then spread some ointment on Horus' penis, masturbated him and placed his sperm on some lettuce which they knew Seth would eat. Seth ate the lettuce. With more magic, Isis and Thoth got this sperm to talk from inside Seth's body, humiliating Seth and proving that Seth, and not Horus, was an effeminate softy who had been sodomized.

An angry Seth insisted that the Great Ennead of Heliopolis authorize still another contest with Horus, this time a race in stone ships, with the winner being given the crown of Osiris. Horus cheated, and built a boat of wood disguised as a boat of stone. Seth's stone ship sank, but Seth, transformed into a hippopotamus, attacked Horus' ship and sank it. The Ennead stopped the contest just as Horus was about to kill Seth.

A final decision was once again in the offing. The Ennead again favored Horus. Thoth convinced the All-Lord Re to write a letter to Osiris, addressing him with the five titulary names of the King of Egypt, to judge between Horus and Seth. Of course, Osiris immediately replied in Horus' favor and added an insult against Re. Pre-Harakhti then sent an insulting letter to Osiris. Osiris' stinging reply was that he would unleash the demons of the Underworld against the Ennead: "The land in which I am (the land of the dead) is full of savage looking messengers who fear no god or goddess. If I send them out, they will bring me the heart of every evildoer, and they will be here with me!...Who among you is mightier than I?"

The Great Ennead finally decided that it had had more than enough of battles, tricks, threats, discussions and trials to decide who was the heir to Osiris' crown. The quarrel had to be ended. In the Chester-Beatty I version, Seth wanted still another fight with Horus, but then, after being brought bound in fetters by Isis before Atum, Seth surprisingly accepted that Horus should succeed Osiris as King. Isis was overjoyed. Pre-Harakhti decided to affectionately take Seth into the sky "and be my son," naming him god of storms so that "he shall thunder in the sky and be feared." Horus was now the ruler of Egypt and "all lands for ever and ever!"[107]

In the Shabako Stone version, Geb, the President/Judge of the Ennead Court, first gave Horus sovereignty over the north, Lower Egypt, and Seth sovereignty over the south, Upper Egypt, and reconciled them. Geb then changed his mind, seeing that it was wrong to give the same "portion" to his grandson Horus and to Seth. He named Horus as sole king and uniter of Upper and Lower Egypt and Horus and Seth "were reconciled and united...their quarreling ceased...being joined in the House of Ptah..."[108] In the Sallier IV version, Seth is sent into the *Deshret* red land as god of the desert.

Just as various versions of the myth took into account the moral evolution of Egyptian society, it seems certain that they all also took the political options of Egypt into account — notably the need for reconciliation, national unity and peace — at the times they were composed.

Politico-religious manipulation is perhaps clearest in the version of the myth inscribed on the Shabako Stone, and this whether its origin was a papyrus from the Old Kingdom (c. 2686–2181 BC) Memphis Ptah Temple or whether it was composed in the late 8th century BC. If the Shabako Stone was really a copy of an Old Kingdom text, then it would illustrate how the Memphis theologians added still another twist to the myth — a clear political as well as a physical victory of Horus over Seth while accentuating the element of reconciliation, under the patronage of the chief god of the Memphis Ennead, Ptah in his Tatenen earth god form. The key intentions were to laud a united and peaceful Two Lands and Ptah's and Memphis' roles. The door of the Ptah Memphis Temple was adorned with sedge reeds, symbolizing Upper Egypt, and papyrus, symbolizing Lower Egypt. Horus and Seth were pacified and united in the House of Ptah, "the Balance of the Two Lands," just as the Two Lands were united, pacified and happy.

All this could date the original "Shabako" papyri far back into the Old Kingdom, when it was politically and religiously expedient to promote Ptah as the *netjer ah* (*ntr.aA*), "the great god," of the holy capital of a peaceful Two Lands.

---

107. Quotations from the Chester Beatty I version of the myth, in Lichtheim, Miriam, *Ancient Egyptian Literature, Volume II*, pp. 214-223 and on Thoth in the Pyramid Texts who conspired with Seth to kill Osiris, Faulkner, R.O., *The Ancient Egyptian Pyramid Texts*, Ut. 218 and 219, pp. 45-47. Also Sallier IV Papyrus, British Museum (10184).

108. Quotations from the Shabako Stone version of the myth, in Wilson, John in *Ancient Near Eastern Texts Relating to the Old Testament*, pp. 4-6.

However, the strong likelihood is that the Shabako Stone version of the myth was a politico-religious manipulation inspired by the Kushite Pharaoh Shabako (c. 716–702 BC), for his own purposes of political and societal reconciliation, which in many ways (as we have seen in Chapter 4) obeyed the same type of logic as that which may have prevailed at the beginning of the Old Kingdom.

In any case, no version of the myth changes the fact that after the Early Dynastic Period, Seth's fortunes gradually declined both mythologically and politically, even if that occurred ambiguously and involved both disrepute and a revival of respect for Seth, notably in the New Kingdom (c. 1550-1069 BC). During this period, ceremonies in which Seth animals — pigs, antelopes, snakes, fish, birds, etc. — were hacked to pieces, took place during the darkest season of the year, when Seth's power was believed to be strongest. However, offerings were also made to appease Seth, to convince him not to undertake evil actions.

Nevertheless, the status of Seth and exactly what happened to him always remained unclear.

The oldest fragments of the myth in the Pyramid Texts (c. 2375–2055 BC) generally portray Seth as a principal element of reconciliation, worthy of assistance, powerful and an example for the pharaoh to follow. Utterance 34 says "...what Seth spits out is *zmin* (a pleasant substance), what reconciles." Utterance 667A states: "...that Horus may be cleansed from what his brother Seth did to him, that Seth may be cleansed from what his brother Horus did to him...Utterance 215 says "pick up the (castrated) testicles of Seth, that you may remove his humiliation...," but Utterance 327 says "The king eats Seth's testicles." Utterance 215 also states that "You are conceived, O Seth, for Geb, and you have more renown than he, you have more power than he." Utterance 271 states: "Horus and Seth take hold of my hands and take me to the Netherworld." Utterance 483 says, "May Seth be brotherly to you." Utterance 81 says, "...cause the Two Lands to dread this King even as they dread Seth..."

Is Seth alive and prosperous? Where is he? Is he dead?

Utterance 390 says, "Seth is hale of his body..." Pyramid Texts Utterance 61 says that Horus had "torn off" Seth's "foreleg." Utterance 277 says Seth "crawled away" from the battle because of "the loss of his testicles." Utterance 357 says "...he [Horus] has smitten Seth for you [Osiris], bound..." Utterance 571 states that "Seth escaped his day of death." Utterance 25 tells us that "Seth has gone to his double [to his *ka* soul in the afterlife]..."

Spell 15 in the New Kingdom *Book of the Dead* states: "The rebel (Seth) has fallen, his arms are bound, a knife has severed his spine..." The "Introductory

Hymn to Osiris" in *Book of the Dead* celebrated Osiris as a father who should be proud of his avenger son Horus: "Osiris...Lord of Everlasting...May your heart which is in the desert land (the land of the dead) be glad, for your son Horus is firm on your throne...The Two Lands flourish in vindication because of you."[109] Ah, what greater Manichaean satisfaction could a father hope for from a son!

The *Book of the Dead* was consistently laudatory toward Horus and contradictorily prudently respectful and severe with Seth. Seth was among "the foes of the Lord of All," but surprisingly he was also among "the Lords of Justice." The bottom line on Seth (and Horus' superiority to him) in *The Book of the Dead* was Spell 17: "Save me from that god who steals souls, who laps up corruption, who lives on what is putrid, who is in charge of darkness, who is immersed in gloom, of whom those who are among the languid ones are afraid. Who is he? He is Seth. Otherwise said: He is the great Wild Bull, he is the soul of Geb." "What does this mean? This means the day when Horus fought with Seth when he inflicted injury on Horus' face and when Horus took away Seth's testicles....he is Horus the eyeless. Otherwise said: It is the tribunal who took action against the foes of the Lord of All...Who is he? As for him who was entrusted rulership among the gods, he is Horus, son of Isis, who was made ruler in the place of his father Osiris on that day when the Two Lands were united."[110]

In the Turin Papyrus (Nineteenth Dynasty, c. 1295–1186 BC), Seth tries to aggrandize himself: "I am Yesterday, I am Today, I am Tomorrow which has not yet come," before Horus gets him to admit that his real name is "Evil Day."[111]

However, *The Lamentations of Isis and Nephthys* in the late 4th century BC Bremner-Rhind Papyrus seems to indicate that it is safe for Osiris to return to his loving sister/wife Isis and his sister/mistress Nephthys, because Seth is dead: "Your foe is fallen, he shall not be!"[112]

Seth was banished to the desert, as a god of sterility and evil. After the final battle in Edfu, Horus retrieved sovereignty over all Egypt, which Seth had usurped from his father Osiris. He was now the unifier, the Heru-Sma-Tawy (Harsomtus in Greek), of *Ta-Wy*, the Two Lands — Upper and Lower Egypt. Seth was not only castrated and thoroughly disgraced, but any kind of reconciliation has been eliminated.

---

109. Faulkner, R.O., *The Ancient Egyptian Pyramid Texts*, pp. 7, 281, 42, 105, 79, 171, 19, 128, 14, 85, 114-115, 226 and 4. Faulkner, R.O., *The Ancient Egyptian Book of the Dead*, pp. 40 and 27.

110. Faulkner, R.O., The Ancient Egyptian Book of the Dead, pp. 44-50.

111. Borghouts, J. F., *Ancient Egyptian Magical Texts*, pp. 74-75.

112. Lichtheim, Miriam, *Ancient Egyptian Literature, Volume III*, p. 118.

It is the version of the myth inscribed on the first century BC Jumilhac Papyrus that raises the most intriguing questions. The Jumilhac Papyrus not only assimilated Seth with disorder, sterility and evil, but also utterly excluded any possibility of reconciliation. It decreed justice in its fullest form for Seth and this included death, mutilation and an impotent existence in the sky. The Jumilhac Papyrus drops the key Egyptian concept of ambivalent respect for Seth. In its moral thrust, it is therefore Greek-influenced and very similar to the preoccupations expressed in Plutarch's version of the myth, in which Seth pays "the penalty" for his "terrible deeds."[113]

However, in the Jumilhac Papyrus Seth is killed no fewer than eight times and somehow he always returns to fight again, suggesting that Seth is never really destroyed and always returns to exercise his destructive intent against order, against Horus. Plutarch also reported in the first century AD that the Egyptians believed that Seth is never destroyed.[114] The implication is that the forces of evil and darkness eternally continue a dualistic coexistence with the forces of good and light.

The goal of Seth and his allies in the Jumilhac Papyrus is to steal the innards of Osiris, which Anubis has mummified, and to regain power over Egypt. Seth never succeeds more than temporarily — Isis hacks him into pieces by cutting him to the bone with her teeth. Seth in the form of a panther is burned to death by Anubis (with Re and the other gods enjoying the smell of Seth's burning flesh) and then Anubis uses his panther skin as a cloak; Seth, in the form of a bull, pursues Isis with sexual advances, but she transforms into a dog with a knife in its tail; Seth cannot catch her and O! abomination for a bull, according to Isis, he ejaculates on the ground in the desert. Isis then transforms herself into a snake and bites and kills him. The killings and the returns of Seth go on and on — his phallus and testicles are chopped off, he is speared to death... Anubis, as a falcon, recovers Horus' eye and with the help of Thoth mummifies and resurrects Osiris. A trial is held and Thoth rules that Horus should succeed his father Osiris as King of Egypt and Seth should be banished to the desert. Seth and his allies attack again and steal Thoth's writings, before finally being killed by Horus in a great battle. Horus devastates Seth's cities and nomes, erases his name, destroys his statues, cuts off his hand and sends him to *Meskhetiu* (the Great Bear

---

113. Plutarch, *Moralia*, Volume V, *Isis and Osiris*, p. 65.
114. *Ibid.*, p. 105.

Constellation) in the sky where demons guard him and prevent him from navigating with the other gods.[115]

Perhaps this composite description of the Osiris/Seth/Isis/Horus myth is merely the least awkward way of obtaining some kind of a vaguely consistent story. It is evident that no real coherence in plot, chronology, characters and roles can be attributed to the myths and individual and composite gods which were artificially amalgamated, with many contradictory written and artistic versions, over at least 2300 years. Some of the ensuing confusion and contradictions defy the most elementary logic and are intellectually insurmountable. The feel of what the Egyptians were driving at only seems attainable by spontaneously accepting what defies ordinary logic as we do in extraordinary dreams, by surfing over contradictions.

It is indeed something that is only possible in mythology that all these problems posed no particular problem to the Egyptians at any period in their history. They never sought to unravel the intricacies of the precise degree of authority and family status and who did what and with which and to whom. The multiple identities of the gods and the superimposed layers of mythology and religion apparently were acceptable to them; at the most, one can imagine that there might have been a quickly repressed question of how this could all be — much as a religious Christian today might be briefly troubled about the logic of the Trinity or a religious Hindu might wonder about how at least ten avatars of Vishnu can coexist.

It can also be surmised that the religious fervor of the Egyptians, more than most ancient peoples, was so intense that they were ready to accept any kind of tale in the name of religion, and this over thousands of years. Confusion and contradictions were not issues. They were part of the structure of Egyptian religious belief, which was deemed to be unchangeable, but in which disguised change, contradiction and superimposition were in fact methodical. This was the atmosphere in which the Egyptian theologians who later interpreted the myths over centuries, if not thousands of years, operated. They may have been tacitly encouraged to let their imaginations run wild — as long as they remained within a strict overall system.

The Osiris/Seth/Isis/Horus tale has its place alongside the greatest myths that the human mind has fabricated. As an efficient, magnificent and awesome

---

115. Lalouette, Claire *Textes Sacrés et Textes Profanes de l'Ancienne Egypte*, II, *Mythes, Contes et Poèsie*, Papyrus Jumilhac, pp. 104 -109.

national founding myth and as the establisher of archetypes, it is at least the equal of the Sumerian Gilgamesh and Sargon myths, the Hebrew Moses myth, the Christian Jesus myth, the Aryan Rig Veda hymns and the Hindu Mahabharata, the Greek Iliad and Odyssey and so many others.

The Osiris/Seth/Isis/Horus saga works marvelously as religious mythology, and as a tale that defies ordinary logic; it delivers the kind of deep, metaphoric message that the heart would like to believe is the truth.

UNIVERSAL PRIMEVAL DUALISTIC CONCEPTS AND REVOLUTIONARY CONCEPTS OF RESURRECTION, THE AFTERLIFE AND PROTO-MORALITY

The revolutionary Osirisian aspects of Egypt's founding myth were clearly combined with older concepts and myths concerning primeval dualistic antagonism, *seba*, star, worship, probably earlier tales about Horus, Seth and Re and Heliopolitan solar theology and cosmogony. There are many indications that the primeval bedrock origins of the Osiris/Seth/Isis/Horus myth were in the quasi universal primeval concept of a struggle between light and darkness, between what was seen as the inevitable positive and the inevitable negative.

All the main players in the myth were linked to stars or planets from at least the beginning of the Early Dynastic Period (c. 3100 BC) and probably earlier. Osiris was Sah (the Orion Constellation). Seth was the *Meskhetiu* (the Great Bear Constellation). Isis was Sopdet (the Dog Star Sirius), the brightest star in the sky with its rising in mid-July connected to the start of the Egyptian year and the annual life-giving inundation of the Nile; thus Isis was also linked to agricultural prosperity. Horus was no less than three planets, Mars, Jupiter and Saturn.

The early Egyptians viewed the sky as divided into four parts, with two halves (north and south), and filled with the *Ikhemu Seku*, "The Imperishable Stars" — the stars which never seemed to move and were therefore eternal — and the *Ikhemu-Weredu*, "The Stars which Never Rest" — the stars which were always in motion. Logically enough, Osiris/Orion was in the bright south and Seth/Great Bear was in the dark north. Just as logically, both Osiris/Orion and Seth/Great Bear were among "the imperishable stars" with inevitable behavior and in primeval opposition. Horus was among "the stars which never rest" (which were, of course, really planets) and this too corresponded to a reality, to Horus' character as a man of action.

The earliest Horian and Re/Apophis mythology can be compared to any number of similar myths or doctrines including early Sumerian, Shamanistic, Hebrew, Persian, Aztec and Taoist tales and practices. Early aspects of the Egyptian myth particularly resemble the later Hindu *Hari-Hara* and Taoist *Ying Yang* dualistic struggle between seemingly antagonistic opposites, between day and night, light and darkness, summer and winter, fertility and sterility, vegetation and desert, life and death, feminine and masculine, hot and cold, wet and dry, sweet and salt, and so on, that is, the two basic opposites frequently seen as being required to maintain life.

In Egypt, a major additional layer of dualism came into play — the particular and mysterious situation of the Nile River. Unlike most major rivers, the Nile flows south to north and before the Aswan High Dam was built (1964), it flooded annually despite the fact that it flowed through the hot desert. In a country with very little rain, the annual Nile inundation was the unique means ensuring agricultural prosperity. Insufficient flooding meant food shortages and surely gave birth to fears that the floodwaters would not return and consequently to the rituals and spells ensuring that they would. Of course, the ancient Egyptians did not know that it was the rainfall 4100 miles upstream around the Ethiopian, Sudanese and Lake Victoria sources of the Nile — and not good/bad dualism of the summer-fertility/winter-sterility type and manipulative magic to ensure the return of the inundation, of fertility — that was the cause of the Nile's strange behavior.

Unquestionably, the cycles of the Nile were a key element in forming the Egyptian dualistic vision, but just as fundamental were the cycles of the sun. For the Egyptians, more than any other people of the Egypt/West Asian cultural sphere, the sun within its predictable cycle was the surest and most unchanging element in nature. The Egyptians interpreted darkness and night as a threat to the power and light of the sun. In a version of the dragon myth which we find in almost every religion right back into prehistory, the Egyptians imagined that the sun must vanquish, must burn up, the awesome enemy snake Apophis in order to rise again after night. Victory meant the return of the sun; temporary defeat meant storms or an eclipse; and permanent defeat would mean the end of the world.

The Book of Overthrowing Apophis, which dates from the late 4th century BC Bremner-Rhind Papyrus but in all likelihood comprises very old beliefs, relates that the sun (Re) eternally wins this battle to prevent him (the sun) from crossing the sky and rising, resurrecting in the morning. But it is implicit in the myth that it is a constantly renewed daily battle — Apophis is "tied and bound and put on the fire every day."[116] Apophis always loses; he is always burned up; but he is immortal, he is always reborn and fights again. There can be no rebirth of the sun without the defeat of Apophis, but Apophis is permanent and necessary; he is like Seth in relation to Osiris. These primeval concepts almost certainly existed before being superimposed on the main characters in the Horian, Re and Osirisian myths and their combinations.

It would be logically satisfying if we could place the Edfu Horus/Re/Seth version of the myth before the Osirisian version. The indications point to the contrary, but it cannot be excluded that it preceded, at least orally, and/or partially, the Osirisian version. What seems certain is that as early as the First Dynasty (c. 3100–2890 BC), the Egyptians seem to have taken for granted the basic concepts and aspects of the Horus/Re/Seth variant of the myth. A situation anterior to the rise of the Osirisian cycle of the myth was being depicted which clearly implied conflicting primeval notions of light, the sun, and darkness, the night...Horus and Seth were seen as enemies and there was a battle between the north and south. At that time, Re was the god/King of Egypt and Horus, as Haroeris, Horus the Elder, and Seth were his sons. Haroeris was a falcon-headed god of the sky and light with his right eye being the sun and his left eye the moon. Seth rebelled against Re, and Re sent his son Horus in his winged sun disk Behdety form to combat and defeat him.

The Egyptian type of dualism, expressed in the daily struggle for the victory of the *maat* harmonious universal order over disorder, now culminated in Osirisian goodness, the gift of the afterlife. Universal primeval concepts of order and disorder also began evolving into the proto-moral aspects of Osiris and Horus and the proto-evil aspects of Seth.

These new Osirisian aspects in the myth constituted a revolutionary attempt to solve the problem of dualism and a revolutionary turning point for Egypt and for humanity.

The immensity of this shift can be seen by the fact that the Hindus never resolved the problem of dualism; for them, there was always a dominating aspect in the dualistic struggle and the universe went through *Yugas*, ages or cycles, in which sometimes the good and sometimes the bad dominated. It was only from about the 6th century BC that the Zoroastrians took a fundamental step beyond Egyptian concepts (if indeed Zoroastrianism was founded at in the 6th century

---

116. Wilson, John in *Ancient Near Eastern Texts Relating to the Old Testament*, p. 7.

BC and not the 13th century BC, as some scholars postulate); for the Zoroastrians, the battle between good and evil, Ahura Mazdah and Ahriman, was no longer just part of the description of the *modus operandi* of the universe, as it was in the Egyptian system, it became a conflict in which good and the sole god, Ahura Mazdah, were destined to win a permanent victory over evil and the destructive spirit, that is the devil, Ahriman. The Hebrew 3rd century BC to 1st century AD Essenians (or Qumran sect) Master of Light and the Master of Darkness doctrine and the Christian (still to come) final victory of Jesus in the role of Master of Light seem to stem from these Zoroastrian concepts.

All of this mythology was fabricated from much the same sequence of events — from primeval dualistic concepts to heroes and gods incarnating these concepts. Perhaps the Egyptians invented the point of equilibrium in dualism, while the Zoroastrians gave moral meaning to the entire process.

Looking at agricultural functions and contents and its anthropomorphic aspects, the origin of parts of the Osirisian myth might have been foreign: they might have originated in the older agricultural societies of Sumer or Sumerian-influenced West Asia. The Osirisian fertility god principles of incarnating the yearly resurrection of vegetation, personal divine resurrection, and immortality, and light, were much the same in Egypt and Sumer. The Sumerians (and perhaps other peoples before them, without written records) had concluded that a mother goddess, Inanna, could be resurrected from the clutches of darkness and death in the *Kur* underworld ("the land of no return") and that her consort, the deified king Dumuzi, died and resurrected annually in agricultural spring renewal. Some of the attributes of Inanna and Dumuzi and Isis and Osiris were similar.

The Sumerian Inanna tales are probably the oldest light/darkness, winter/spring, and death/resurrection myths developed in the Neolithic agricultural age. Inanna and the deified Dumuzi were the first dying/resurrecting divinities in recorded history. Similar myths were developed throughout Sumerian-influenced West Asia. Thus it is only a slight, plausible, but unprovable leap to situate the origins of the Egyptian Osirisian myths in Sumer. It is easy enough to suppose that Osiris, the god mythologically credited with the invention of agriculture, was modeled after the agricultural Dumuzi and the chthonic aspects of Inanna or other West Asian gods of the Dumuzi and Inanna types. It can be surmised that West Asian immigrants and traders brought the agricultural/dying/resurrecting concept with them. This concept may have then been superimposed on the Egyptian Naqada III Period (c. 3300–3150 BC) agricultural underworld and dead/former ruler god Andjeti of Busiris, before being transferred to Osiris.

However, given the universality of the concepts involved, linked to the Neolithic discovery of agriculture and its cycles of winter, spring planting, summer growth, and autumn harvest and its possible analogies with human sleep and wakefulness, death and resurrection, it is basically only anteriority which pleads in favor of a Sumerian origin of the Osirisian myth. Even the notion of anteriority is a complicated matter due to the existence of only scattered Sumerian fragments from before 2600 BC, which presuppose the existence of earlier myths and beliefs. In fact, a case can almost equally be made that Osirisian myth emerged independently in Egypt. In any case, the Egyptian Osirisian system merged and carried forward to new conclusions its own and/or the Sumerian observation of natural cycles like the succession of night and day, the daily rebirth of the sun, winter sterility and spring rebirth and summer fertility.

With Osiris, the predictable result of natural phenomena as well as the annual Nile inundation, were transferred to the individual sphere and became rebirth after death. These ideas could date to the Second Dynasty (c. 2890–2686 BC). It can be reasonably supposed that they were incorporated into the dominant Heliopolitan theology at least from the Fourth Dynastic Period (c. 2613–2494 BC) — notably Osiris being "alive" as a dead former king of Egypt, like Andjeti — that is, resurrection and afterlife. However, an Osirisian afterlife was apparently not applied to a pharaoh before the Fifth Dynasty Pharaoh Unas (c. 2375–2345 BC).

The Egyptians had possibly imported a myth, or aspects of a myth, but they did not do only that; they added original afterlife and savior concepts. The Egyptian Osirisian concept was contrary to the bleak, or lucid, Sumerian view that a human could not be immortal no matter what magic he employed. With Osiris, the death-rebirth concept gradually evolved from the invention of an analogy with the daily, seasonal and agricultural cycles for a god to analogical consequences for a human god — the pharaoh — and then to consequences for all humans. The closest the early Sumerians came to the concept of immortality with a human (in the first half of the Third Millennium) was the exceptional case of Ziusudra (Utnapishtim), the Sumerian Noah who was granted immortality after the Great Flood. But Ziusudra was such an exceptional case that even the legendary king of Uruk and two-thirds god, Gilgamesh, despite his great efforts and the use of great magic, could not gain immortality.

There is no denying that in many ways Osiris was a typical West Asian dying-resurrecting vegetation god. However, his afterlife-savior function for humans was so clearly of Egyptian origin that he is set apart from the Sumerian Dumuzi or any of the other West Asian resurrecting-vegetation gods (like the Hittite Telipini, the Syrian-Canaanite Adonis, the Anatolian-Phrygian Attis, and more). Osiris did not only die and rise again as a god; he eventually represented resurrection and immortality in the body and soul in the afterlife for all humans, or at least all Egyptians. With Osiris, first the pharaoh and then everybody who applied the preparations which had been applied to Osiris — embalmment, mummification, a tomb and magical spells and rituals — could be resurrected to an afterlife as an Osiris in the *Duat* nether world. A person could repeat this life, *wehem ankh*, for eternity in the *Duat* if he was properly "equipped" — if his tomb and accessories had been correctly built, if *hetep* and *aut*, offerings, by the living to his body and souls were continued or if he nourished himself from the paintings of food on the walls of his tomb which could magically become real food. None of this was Sumerian.

The principal Egyptian religious dogmas obviously could not have been conceived without the concepts of resurrection and the afterlife as enunciated in the new Osirisian cycle of the myth. The belief that mummification, funerary rituals and magic as used on Osiris could be used for others with the same goal of resurrection and afterlife would have been impossible without the founding Osirisian myth. Likewise, from Pharaoh Unas' time (c. 2375–2345 BC), the ruling pharaoh could not have become Osiris when dead without the founding myth. In short, much of the specificity of the Egyptian religion — its central pillars proclaiming a solution to the problem of death and divine kingship even in the afterlife — was dependent on the development of the Osirisian aspects of the founding myth.

Moreover, over the centuries, the proto-morality aspects of the myth were developed. What began as a question of ensuring so-called natural primeval *maat* cosmic harmony and order in the struggle between opposite forces evolved into an ethical debate on might and right. The question in relation to the brute force of "might" evolved into a debate concerning the nature of "right": was "right" merely a problem of deciding who was the heir to Osiris' crown, Horus or Seth, or did it also involve a more subtle interpretation of the *maat*, doing the right ethical thing? The idea of the *maat* was gradually transformed to include the ideal of a moral order and justice.

All these elements, superimposed on primeval concepts and the older Horian and Re myths, went into creating a definitive version of the Osiris/ Seth/ Isis/Horus myth, at least in its main thrust. The process of defining, refining (and distorting) the beliefs in these myths spanned at least 2500 years.

THE ORIGINS OF OSIRIS

The rule of Osiris over the earth is a consistent theme in Egyptian mythology, as part of a schema in which the gods directly ruled Egypt and the earth before the pharaoh-gods (beginning with Menes) took over. Atum was frequently depicted as a divine pharaoh, wearing the *Pschent* double crown of the united *Ta-Wy*, the Two Lands. Re, who assimilated Atum, ruled on earth before getting old, tired and fed up. Then the other gods of the Great Heliopolitan Ennead ruled, including Shu, the god of dryness, the atmosphere between the earth and the sky and the personification of sunlight, and afterwards the earth god Geb. When he became an adult, Osiris received sovereignty over Egypt and the earth from his father, Geb. Osiris was god/king of a mythical "Pan-Egypt," as the Pyramid Texts (c. 2375–2125 BC) abundantly described.

In real terms, the first descriptions of Osiris as a chthonian god of the spring rebirth of vegetation and the annual inundation of the Nile valley seem to date to the Second Dynasty (c. 2890–2686 BC). This role may have begun as far back as Naqada II Period (c. 3500–3300 BC). He then can easily be traced as the henotheistic god of *Djedu* (Busiris) in the Delta of Lower Egypt, who took over from the agricultural, underworld and dead/former ruler and royal god Andjeti. In any case, Osiris probably adopted many of the attributes of Andjeti. Osiris' totemistic emblem/fetish was sheaves of wheat, clearly representing grain which is buried/planted and rises/resurrects as stalks of wheat. This agricultural fertility role, seemingly appropriated from Andjeti, was coupled with the chthonian, agricultural shepherd's crook, the *awet*, also appropriated from Andjeti. The *awet* became the *hekat* symbol of the royal guardian/shepherd of the people, together with the *nekhakha*, the royal flail symbolizing majesty and dominion, which may have started out as Andjeti's fly swatter!

Osiris was also deeply linked to Abydos, in the 8th Nome of Upper Egypt, whose capital was Tieny (Thinis) and whose emblem/fetish was a primeval mound on a pole topped by two feathers. This fetish was called the *ta-wer*, "the oldest land," and became associated with Osiris, perhaps from the Fourth

Dynasty (c. 2613–2494 BC), as the container/shrine in Abydos containing his head. And so, even before becoming a personage in the Osiris/Seth/Isis/Horus myth, Osiris probably already represented inundation, agricultural fertility and spring resurrection. His succeeding characteristics were perhaps due to the importation of Sumerian-type divine death and resurrection concepts linked to the cycles of nature.

However, there are also views that Osiris was of African origin — the British Egyptologist E.A. Wallis Budge, and the Senegalese historian Cheikh Anta Diop (1923–1986) firmly believed this. Such views are basically unverifiable since we cannot know the substance of Early Bronze Age African history and theologies. Reasonable consideration of a possible foreign origin for Osiris, or for some of the beliefs associated with him, has to be limited to the above speculation about hypothetical West Asian links.

The physical appearance of Osiris may have been stabilized during the Old Kingdom (c. 2686 — 2181 BC), but only a few statues and reliefs of him have been found which date to this period. By the New Kingdom (beginning c. 1550 BC), he was usually represented as a mummified human with a beard, sometimes with ram's horns, and his color was white (like his mummy bandages), blue (divinity), black (Nile, giving fertility) or green (resurrection, eternal renewal). He held the *nekhakla*, flail, and *hekat*, crook, of sovereignty and wore the *atef* crown composed of the white conical crown of Upper Egypt flanked by two red ostrich feathers symbolizing Busiris and Lower Egypt. The fetish container/ shrine in Abydos containing his head was often used to symbolize him, as was the *djed* pillar. He could also take the Form of Khnum-Re, the Nile inundation, fertility, and potter-creator god and in this form was represented with a ram's head, like Khnum and like the early Andjeti. As the night sun aspect of Re, Osiris carried a solar disk between the horns of his ram's head.

When the Osiris/Seth/Isis/Horus myth began to have major political and theological consequences, from the Fourth Dynasty (c. 2613–2494 BC), its core meaning revolved around Osiris. On the whole, as fundamental as was Horus' archetypical role and as great as was his popularity throughout Egypt's history, Osiris was even more fundamental to Egyptian religion and society for the simple reason that the central aspect of the Egyptian theological system was the afterlife — and without the savior, Osiris, there was no afterlife.

Despite the fact that the resurrected Osiris remained fundamentally chthonian, ruling from the *Duat* "Other Land" in the Underworld as the undisputed god of the dead, King of the "Other Land" and savior, he became, by the Sixth Dynasty (c. 2345–2181 BC), second in power only to the Sun god Re. Volume II describes how Osiris recuperated most of the afterlife functions of Re and became a combination of all the characteristics attributed to him in the Osiris/Seth/Isis/Horus myth as well as his earlier characteristics.

The enduring fervor and awe for Osiris throughout Egyptian history is well illustrated by the fact that fourteen cities claimed parts of Osiris' body and were sites of pilgrimage. Busiris claimed that Osiris' spinal column was buried in its temple. Abydos claimed it possessed his head and hair, Khem (Letopolis) claimed the neck, Mendes claimed the phallus (although how this could be, given that a fish had eaten it, is anybody's guess), and the Biga Island "pure mound" Osiris tomb across from Pi-aaleq (Philae) claimed it had a leg.

SETH — FROM REVERED GOD TO THE PROTOTYPE OF THE DEVIL

Chapter One showed that Seth was one of Egypt's oldest gods, going back to the Naqada I Period (c. 4000–3500 BC) and then was the powerful henotheistic god of Nubt (Ombos) in the Fifth Nome of Upper Egypt as "the *Nubty*," before being linked to violence, chaos, war, the desert and storms. Seth was a god eminently connected to Upper Egypt, to southern Egypt, but many localities in the eastern Delta were dedicated to his cult. The earliest representation of a Seth animal, dating to the Naqada I Period (c. 4000–3500 BC), was found on an ivory comb in tomb (H29) at El Mahasna, southwest of Tieny (Thinis) in Upper Egypt. Seth is generally said to have been born in Ombos, and his power base was unquestionably there as the henotheistic god of the city, although the Shabako Stone says he was born in Su, near Hierakonpolis. Nevertheless, Seth has a primeval connection to the northern stars, to the night and to dark regions.

It is impossible to escape the fact that Seth's role changed several times, like so many other Egyptian gods'. The various versions of the Osiris/Seth myth did not coherently take into account the early and later functions and Seth's royal powers before his gradual degradation and demonization. He began as other gods, deeply revered and with powers, qualities and faults; he went through periods of ostracism, decline, recovery and ambivalence and then finally became one of the major symbols of evil in the history of religion. His role as the personification of evil, as the great villain, fear inspiring, guilty, and nasty, bad character and ornery disruptive creature *par excellence*, probably took more than 1500 years to fully construct.

Initially, Seth was sculpted and painted in a standard manner and not as a terrible beast. His indeterminate form — donkey, jackal, okapi, etc. — might even indicate that his original representation was a mythological invention much like the Magdalenian unicorn painted on the walls of Lascaux about 10,000 years earlier. All of Seth's forms — the indeterminate animal with a canine body, forked tail, square ears and long nose, the animal-headed human form and his form as a pig, a hippopotamus or a donkey — came to be gradually seen as malefic.

Certainly, the early Seth was cunning and crafty — but not necessarily evil, according to the conceptions of the time. Even in later times, most of his dirty tricks were no dirtier or trickier than those practiced by most of the other gods, including Re.

The Predynastic king "Scorpion" did not seem to have a problem with Seth — his mace-head includes a Seth animal. Right from Narmer's time (c. 3100 BC), while a Horus falcon was usually pictured above the pharaoh's *serekh* emblems, the names of the Early Dynastic (c. 3100–2686 BC) kings often referred to both Horus and Seth as joint royal patron gods. More significantly, Peribsen's (c. 2700 BC) *serekh* was surmounted by a Seth animal indicating that he was the sole royal patron god and Khasekhemwy's (c. 2686 BC) *serekh* depicted both the falcon Horus and a Seth animal. When the coronation ceremony for the pharaoh of the united Egypt, the Two Lands, was designed in Memphis, perhaps around 3000 BC, it was Seth who presented the red *deshret* crown of Lower Egypt to the pharaoh while Horus presented the white *hedjet* crown of Upper Egypt. In later times Seth, like Horus, was sometimes depicted as a symbol of the unity of Lower and Upper Egypt and wore the intertwined *pschent*, the double white and red crown of united Egypt.

Even in the New Kingdom (beginning c. 1550 BC), Seth was considered to be a major, respected god who could trick Egypt's enemies and powerfully help the pharaohs in battle. Three pharaohs (Sety I, c. 1294–1279 BC, Sety II, c. 1200–1194 BC, and Sethnakhte, c. 1186–1184 BC) again adopted Seth titles and Rameses II (c. 1279–1213 BC) also prudently encouraged his worship. For a long time, confusingly enough, Seth even played a key role on Re's solar barque as the only god together with Re with enough power to harpoon the monster Apophis. This Seth actively participated in the daily ritual in the Amun Karnak Temple in which the gods and goddesses massacred Apophis.

But it was also during the New Kingdom that consideration and worship of Seth declined and a rise in popular fervor for Osiris occurred, following the period of Osiris' banning under the monotheistic Ankhenaten (c. 1352–1336 BC). Despite the favor of some pharaohs, the "fact" that Seth had murdered Osiris could never be forgotten.

Sometime during the Third Intermediate Period, perhaps around 800 BC, Seth's career began to be limited to that of an evil divine being who was reviled, as an outlet for people's hatred and violence. By the end of the 22nd Bubastite-Libyan Dynasty (c. 715 BC) in the Third Intermediate Period, Seth statues were widely destroyed and he was considered to be the origin of evil.

The episode of the Shabako Stone in the late 8th century BC was probably the last attempt to reconcile Seth and Horus. It was during this Late Period (c. 747–332 BC) that Seth reached the abyss of his religious and political disgrace. In addition to all his other faults, as the god of the desert he was now considered to be the god of Asian foreign countries — at a time of Asian invasions. By the first century BC, Seth reached the apex of his reputation as the personification of guilt and evil. He was now seen as somebody in favor of *izfeh*, disorder, and against *maat* natural harmony and justice, as a homosexual, and as somebody associated with hated invaders. He was even identified with the demonic snake Apophis, whom he had previously been credited with heroically fighting.

However, it is obvious that as powerful and revered as he was in early times, Seth probably was never a very positive god, incarnating as he did the necessary "negative" in the primeval synthesis and then being the murderer of Osiris and the treacherous villain in his attempt to defeat Horus the avenger. The fact that the hated foreign Hyksos rulers, between c. 1650 and 1550 BC, revived Seth as their virtually henotheistic national god not only further disgraced Seth in Egyptian eyes, but added further questions as to his exact identity, specifically concerning possible Asian-Semitic or foreign connections.

The Greeks in the first century AD and in particular Plutarch saw Seth as the archetype of their own Typhon, an evil monster who was neither a god nor a man and who had been slain by Zeus. Plutarch, in *Isis and Osiris*, superimposing Greek concepts of rigid morality, imputed even more evil intentions to this Typhon/Seth than the ancient Egyptians did.

However, Seth cannot be confused with the devil concept. He was not responsible for the evil in the world, even if at times he personified or pursued it; but he seems to have been a prototype of both Satan and the devil. The forging of Satan, the Hebrew Yahweh's hatchet man, might have borrowed attributes from

Seth alongside Humbaba and other Sumerian monster-men. The Seth concept might have also influenced the invention of the first authentic devil, or independent responsible force of evil, the Persian Zoroastrian Ahriman, around the 6th century BC. Like Seth, envy was one of Ahriman's chief characteristics. In turn, Ahriman most certainly influenced the Hebrew apocalyptic writers and sects from about 250 BC and then the early Christians as they forged their notions of the devil.

THE ORIGINS OF ISIS, AND ENDURING LOVE FOR HER AND FOR HER SON HORUS

As for Isis, love for her was always the norm in ancient Egypt, an enduring love that over the centuries went from peak to peak and then engulfed the Greco-Roman Mediterranean world. She is first mentioned in the Pyramid Texts (c. 2375–2125 BC), but she certainly goes back further as an *ahet*, a divine, celestial cow. Her origins appear to be in the Delta, but she could have been a graft on to the indigenous Egyptian cow/mother and female principle goddess Hathor.

Like Osiris, some West Asian influences may have been present in the Isis profile, for instance those associated with the Sumerian Inanna. Like Isis, Inanna was beautiful and thirsted for supreme magical power. However, Inanna had a far more impulsive and violent nature than Isis and was far more concerned with raw sexuality. Above all, in order to save her own skin, Inanna condemned her husband Dumuzi to the *Kur* nether world and tried to kill Gilgamesh because he refused her marriage proposal, which the fiercely faithful Isis never would have dreamed of doing to Osiris. The motherly/sisterly Isis even sometimes had pity and compassion for the horrible Seth, and according to Plutarch, treated Anubis, the son of her husband Osiris and her sister Nephthys, like her own son.

It is far from clear who actually was first featured — Hathor or Isis — in the oldest oral fragments of the myths. Certainly, Hathor and other cow/sky goddesses such as Nut and Bat were involved in Horus, Re and other primeval solar myths before Isis. Both Isis and Hathor were concurrently involved in the various later versions of the Osiris/Seth/ Isis/Horus myth.

However, it was Isis who became both the eminent embodiment of feminine qualities, such as motherhood, beauty, and marital fidelity, and the personification of the king's throne. The figurine amulet associated with her from as early as about 2650 BC, the *tiet*, the knot or blood of Isis, which resembles a stylized human figure with its central point being a knot in the form of a throat, seems to have symbolized life and welfare in this life and in the next life. In her Isis-Cow form, with a solar disk and cow horns headdress, she was also mother of the Apis Bull, the animal aspect/incarnation of the god Ptah, and these mother-of-Apis cows were mummified and entombed in the *Iseum* in Memphis. She was also "the great white sow" of Heliopolis. Her main cult center was in Pi-aaleq (Philae), near the border with Nubia, but she was revered and invoked throughout Egypt. Almost as important as Isis' status as "great mother" was her status as a magician, as *weret hekau,* "great of magic," second only to Thoth. Eventually, Isis became the most "exported" Egyptian goddess.

As to Horus, in all his numerous forms and functions, enduring admiration was the norm.

The c. 1400 BC *Great Hymn to Osiris* sums up the enduring feelings for Osiris, Isis and Horus. Osiris is he "Whose name endures in peoples' mouth...That his name be foremost...Awe inspiring to all lands..." Isis "sought (Osiris) without wearying...roamed the land lamenting, Not resting till she found him...clever-tongued whose speech fails not..." Horus is "firm-hearted, justified...Sky, earth are under his command, Mankind is entrusted to him..." As to Seth, he is dismissed as the "rebel...the foe...the disturber...the offender..."[117]

MAJOR ARCHETYPES, INCLUDING THE FIRST HOLY FAMILY

Osiris, Isis and Horus provided Egypt, and then perhaps other religions, with a familial role model — a familial archetype, history's first holy family. Osiris was the perfect, good, powerful, handsome father. Isis was the epitome of the perfect, beautiful, loyal, consoling wife and mother. Horus was the epitome of the perfect, brave, intelligent, dutiful, avenging son who gloriously fulfills the promise placed in him. Osiris, Isis and Horus represented warmth and affection and the three became the most popular triad in Egypt and the symbol of the ideal family. Three thousand years before the Christian Holy Family, Jesus, Mary and Joseph, Osiris, Isis and Horus were the perfect, warm family, the familial archetype, the first "holy family" in history.

---

117. Lichtheim, Miriam, *Ancient Egyptian Literature, Volume II,* pp. 81-85.

Within this "holy family," major individual archetypes — primordial personalities — were eminently consecrated and from then on played important roles in the history of mankind.

The most important of these archetypes was Osiris as the epitome of the savior. He was probably the first personal savior god in history, the first god who could save an individual while alive from the anguish of one day being utterly extinguished. When a person was dead, he saved him from the dreadful consequences of death.

Osiris was also a victim. Like all divine sacrificial victims, he was deeply perfect, innocent and pure, at least by Egyptian standards. He had wrought only good and was treacherously murdered. He was perhaps the first archetype of this type and perhaps, until the advent of Jesus, he was the most perfect savior and sacrificial victim. And he was probably the first warm and affectionate god.

Such archetypes are so much part of conventional wisdom that it is easy to overlook the fact that they must have been invented at some point in time; and that the first written records we have of them come from Egypt.

POSSIBLE ANALOGIES BETWEEN MYTH AND REALITY

Of course, it is a normal temptation in the case of a founding myth to try to sort out possible analogies between myth and history. Despite all the contradictions, the result concerning Egypt yields some degree of plausibility.

The historical time frame of the myth seems to be a period of frequent warfare between *Ta-Shema* and *Ta-Mehu*, Upper and Lower Egypt, or some of the nomes within each region, perhaps c. 3200–3100 BC. It is a time when Egypt was supposedly still directly governed by its gods.

Historically, it is reasonable to assume that the Horus-Seth episodes in these myths partially mirrored these wars or conflicts which preceded the setting up of the unitary Egyptian state around 3100 BC and the succeeding attempts to reconcile the north and the south and the divine functions of Horus and Seth.

We know from the "Scorpion" mace-head (c. 3150 BC) and the Narmer and other palettes (c. 3100 B.C) that peoples of the north, of the Delta, had been vanquished by peoples of the south. Historically, it is reasonable to assume that a pharaoh with a Horus name, like Narmer, King of Hierakonpolis, or the king of another powerful city in Upper Egypt, like Thinis, or Aha/Menes of Thinis or

Hierakonpolis, logically became the pharaoh of all Egypt, of *Ta-Wy*, the Two Lands.

Conflict, but even more so the vital necessity of reconciliation, peace, and union between the north and the south and between the warring gods Horus and Seth, were evident. We know that legitimacy and strength were frequently drawn from both Horus and Seth.

We owe much to the Englishman William Matthew Flinders Petrie (1853–1942) for our knowledge of this early period. Together with the American G.A. Reisner (1867–1942), Petrie was the first truly scientific Egyptologist-excavator. Petrie's achievements go beyond Egyptology — with his inventions of stratigraphic excavation and sequence dating, he was in many ways the founder of modern archaeology. His seventy devoted, impassioned and eccentric years in archaeology read like a lyrical poem engraved with the exemplary love with which he carried out his work. His fabulous finds include countless early decorated pottery, statues, palaces, pyramids, seals, jewelry, amulets, clothing, labels, tools, utensils and furniture, thousands of tombs of humans and animals including some of the oldest skeletons, the ruins of the predynastic Seth Shrine in Nubt (Ombos) and the famous Merenptah Stele, which contains the first known mention of Israel. Petrie also excavated Pharaoh Akhenaten's (c. 1352–1335 BC) Atenist monotheistic city of Akhetaten (El Amarna), made the first evaluation of Akhenaten's revolutionary solar monotheism and art, carried out the first scientific study of the Giza pyramids and was the first to call for the x-raying of mummies. His humorous, wry eccentricity and his frankness apparently knew no bounds — he worked naked in the Giza Pyramids. He pronounced the prophetic words: "Well, that's going to annoy the Church," when he discovered the first mention of Israel. He decreed that at his death his head should be cut off and donated to science, which was done; but the Second World War prevented shipment of his pickled head to London and it stayed under his beloved wife Hilda's bed for four years.

Among the Petrie finds and interpretations which most advanced knowledge of early unified Egypt and its possible links to mythology occurred in 1900 and 1901 at the Abydos Necropolis at Umm el-Qa'ab. Using his invention of sequence dating based on cultural stages and pottery, Petrie re-appraised the earlier finds (1894-98) by the Frenchman Emile Amélineau (1850–1915) of Egypt's oldest royal tombs.

Petrie came up with more accurate identifications and conclusions concerning the approximately sixteen brick-encased pit tombs of all the kings of the First Dynasty, and notably those of Aha (B19/15, c. 3100 BC), Den (c. 2950 BC) and perhaps that of Narmer himself (B17/18, c. 3100 BC), and some of the Second Dynasty kings. Steles naming the pharaohs, stone vessels, furniture, 18 ebony and ivory labels and seals, some belonging to Narmer and Aha, were found at Umm el-Qa'ab.

Another great early Egyptologist/philologist, the German Kurt Sethe, drew the fabulous conclusion that the hieroglyphic Horus name inscriptions on some of the objects found at Umm el-Qa'ab matched with the birth names or some of the other royal titulary names in the *Kings Lists* by Manetho and the Turin Royal Canon Papyrus.

Although controversy exists until today whether the Abydos tombs were indeed tombs or rather cenotaphs — with the real tombs being in Memphis — it became possible to conclude that a Narmer (Menes?) or an Aha (Menes?) had indeed existed, perhaps around 3100 BC, as well as all the other early kings with Horus names, and Peribsen (c. 2700 BC) with a Seth title and Khasekhemwy (c. 2650 BC) with a double Horus and Seth title. This discovery, coupled with the discovery of The Narmer Palette, the Narmer and "Scorpion" mace-heads, the tombs and clay, stone and copper inscribed seals and the objects in Naqada and Memphis, in six short years from 1895 suddenly gave a considerable degree of reality to the entire Early Dynastic Period of Egypt and its atmosphere of conflict and reconciliation.

A link between myth and reality now became plausible, or at least possible. The patron falcon god of victorious Hierakonpolis could have been named Horus and could have been the model for the Horus in the myth. The Hierakonpolitan theologians may have decreed that Horus, the god of their city and other major cities in Upper Egypt, like Edfu, was incarnated in the first pharaoh of united Egypt. A falcon Horus, who had assimilated the Nekheny, the original falcon emblem/totemistic god of Hierakonpolis, and had become "Horus the Nekhenite," was an eminently logical choice as the royal and chief god, as the incarnation of divine kingship. Horus' roots and continued worship in Lower Egypt further facilitated this choice. Horus, the falcon king of the sky, the royal emblem/totem and the instrument of divine kingship in both Lower and Upper Egypt, was the perfect choice.

On another level, the semi-historical level, one of the oldest records of a battle between the south and the north, The Palette of Narmer, depicts a falcon, presumably Horus, in the role of handing over the conquered land of the papyrus (Lower Egypt) to Narmer, wearing the white conical *hedjet* Crown of the King of

Upper Egypt. Presumably, or at least logically (if the term *logical* has any meaning in this type of tale), this falcon was the protector god of Hierakonpolis in Upper Egypt and the heroic god in the great battle between Upper and Lower Egypt as symbolized in the Horus/Seth battle. And, presumably, this falcon became a form of Haroeris, Horus the Elder.

Equally reasonable would have been the elevation of the vulture goddess Nekhbet of Hierakonpolis' twin city Nekheb (Eileithylaspolis) as the proctectress goddess of the pharaohs of the Two Lands, alongside Wadjit, the cobra goddess of Pe-Dep, the twin cities of *Per* Wadjit, the house of Wadjit. There were so-called "Divine Souls" in both cities. These "souls" could have been emblem/totems of early kings somehow linked to Horus — the falcon-headed "Divine souls of *Pe*" and the jackal-headed "Divine Souls" of Nekhen of Horus as "The Jackal of Southern Egypt, Opener of the Ways." The goddesses Nekhbet and Wadjit became theologically linked, twinned, just as *Pe* and Nekhbet were twin cities on the theological level, and the Nekhbet vulture and the uraeus cobra were depicted on the pharaoh's *nemes* headdress. An ivory tablet belonging to King Aha, found in Naqada by Jacques de Morgan (1857–1924) in 1897, shows a vulture and a cobra, Nekhbet and Wadjit: "The Two Ladies." By Anedjib's reign, from c. 2925, "The Two Ladies" as protectresses of the Two Lands became part of the official royal titulary as the *nebti* or "Two Ladies" title.

Practically speaking, the only point which seems difficult to understand is why Menes, or whoever won the battle over Lower Egypt, would have built a temple to Ptah in Memphis — or only a temple dedicated to Ptah. Of course, it could be that Menes sought to enhance the role of Memphis and its henotheistic god, Ptah. Whether or not it was Menes who built the Ptah temple, it is an historical fact that there were no Horus temples in Memphis until the 14th century BC during the New Kingdom and that Pharaoh Khephren's Memphis/Giza Sphinx was not divinized as Horemakhet (the Horus in the Horizon form of Horus) until the New Kingdom (c. 1550 BC). Even if it were opportune to appease Ptah as the Memphis henotheistic god, one would expect that there should have been a Horus Temple as well.

And so the theological underpinnings for the union of Upper and Lower Egypt were near perfect. Moreover, almost all of this could have been carried out without any major contradiction to Upper Egyptian, and especially Hierakonpolitan, theology. Hierakonpolis could have imposed its theological views as consequences of its political and military power, while also taking into account the feelings, political power and theology of Lower Egypt and Buto.

As hazy and unprovable as all this is, it nevertheless seems to mirror the sublimation of war into a divinely ordained religious act of divine kingship and reconciliation and the mythological and religious justification of the entire process. The conquest of Lower Egypt, the Delta, or parts of it, by an Upper Egyptian King, the gradual unification and reconciliation of the two regions of Egypt, and the establishment of a capital of the united land, *Ta-Wy*, the Two Lands, at Memphis might have been the real terrain from which the Osiris/Seth/Isis/Horus myth was invented.

It is also quite possible that the main characters in the myth were first of all heroes or local kings who became primordial father images (Freud) or heroic and villainous archetypes (Jung). It may well be that Heliopolitan mythology, as expressed in the Pyramid Texts, describing a kingly rule on earth of the gods including Osiris, Seth and Horus, was a distorted reflection of a real situation. In other words, Osiris, Seth and Horus did not begin their careers as gods but as human kings (who negotiated, bargained and fought over who owned what portions of the land) and then were eventually deified in a type of ancestor worship of the dead hero or king.

We see from the 4th century BC *Book On Overthrowing Apophis* that Re and the pharaoh as a kind of god/father/hero image on earth are synonymous in the struggle against Apophis: "...O Re! Behold I have driven away thy enemy (Apophis)...burn up every enemy of the pharaoh..."[118] The magical ceremony related in the book, of burning a drawing of Apophis in green ink on papyrus and burning the names written in wax of the pharaoh's (and one's own) enemies were already carried out during the New Kingdom (from c. 1550 BC), in several daily ceremonies in the Thebes Karnak Temple.

Certainly, Jung (but also Freud) would subscribe to such an interpretation in which basic, remote events and experiences, emblem/totems and archetypal personalities were gradually organized and transformed into mythology, theology, religion and politics. In any case, there is no historical doubt that the Osiris/Seth/Isis/Horus myths gradually were used more and more for political and religious motives as a founding national unification and reconciliation myth, as an instrument to influence and reinforce the view of sacredness and union of the Two Lands, as a justification for pharaonic sovereignty and as an illustration of theology and magic.

---

118. Wilson, John in *Ancient Near Eastern Texts Relating to the Old Testament*, p. 67.

The Osiris/Seth/Isis/Horus myth was nevertheless a perfect fit for Egypt's needs over thousands of years. Succeeding superimpositions of myth fabricated by the theologians seem to have been invented to meet changing political necessities linked to the rise of dominant political regimes and clergies and their corresponding major cities. The stress was on reconciliation and sharing between the two parts of Egypt, including reconciliation and power sharing between Horus and Seth, during the Old Kingdom (2686–2181 BC). This metaphorically and lyrically mirrored the necessary religious and political ingredients, which after the war had enabled Egypt to become both history's first nation and the first sacred nation.

These same values were exalted when the 25th Dynasty (c. 747–656 BC) Kushite invader/conquerors of Egypt sought to promote peace and reconciliation. When, at times during and after the New Kingdom (c. 1550–1069 BC), Egypt felt the need for both more credible morality and a god with whom their hated Asian enemies could be identified, then the defeat of good over evil and a universal whipping boy in the form of Seth were stressed.

CHAPTER 7.
THE ARTISTIC CONTEXT

THE FRAMEWORK FOR ART & ARCHITECTURE: RELIGION, MAGIC AND DEATH.
ART AS WHAT THINGS SHOULD BE, RATHER THAN WHAT ACTUALLY IS

The central means of expression in ancient Egypt was not words, but what we today call art. Egypt expressed its outlook — its cosmogony, theology, mythology, rituals and political and social structures — primarily with images and architecture. This was clearly linked to Egypt's immanent, animistic and magical approach to existence. Within this context, words, writing — hieroglyphics — were also art. They were basically perceived in their non-abstract dimension as pictograms, images, which came from the gods — *medu netjer*, "the words of the gods."

The framework for Egyptian art and architecture was religious and magical. Figurative art had probably rarely been anything else but religious, since it was invented; but the Egyptians reached new heights in subordinating almost the entirety of their art and architecture to religion, even in the depiction of scenes of daily life. The earliest surviving examples of figurative art are by the European Cro-Magnons, from Aurignacian and then Gravettian times, beginning 32,000 years ago and the Magdalenian (Lascaux) civilization (c. 17,000 BP). But the Egyptian centrality of art, and certainly architecture, both in means of expression and in magic, seems to go beyond anything that came before. It may only have been matched afterwards by the African civilizations (c. 800 BC–1700 AD).

It is difficult to judge which society, Egypt or Sumer, had a more magical, mythological outlook in 3000 BC, but it seems certain that Egypt's religious leap ahead of Sumer was accompanied by an evident and revolutionary leap ahead in architecture and the arts. As early as the opening of the Old Kingdom (c. 2686 BC), it is already possible to speak of an Egyptian mastery of the arts and architecture linked to a religious and magical system. The far more refined, typically Egyptian forms superceded the crude but expressive forms of West Asian, and especially Sumerian, art.

For the Egyptian artist, as for society in general, the notion of art for art's sake, or art as an independent endeavor, was entirely absent. The word for art was the same as for crafts — *hemut*. Egyptian artists, architects and craftsmen were always religious civil servants linked to the clergy and to the reigning pharaoh. As *hemutiu*, artificers and craftsmen, their patron god was Ptah and at various periods they were supervised by high priests like the Memphis Temple of Ptah *Uer-kherep-hemutiu*, the Grand Commander of the Artificers or craftsmen, a pharaoh's Overseer of Works or Chief, or Overseer, Sculptor, the *Imey-er-genewtey*, or a high ranking steward.

Cyril Aldred, in *Egyptian Art*, emphasized the close connection between art, words, religion and magic. Noting that Egyptian art is almost always accompanied by a hieroglyphic inscription which is "a creative utterance," which "sets the scene" and that a statue "is not complete, and represents nobody without its inscription," he concluded that "Egyptian works of art...represent ideograms writ large — the idea of objects rather than their exact realization in a spatial context — that is because, like the 'god's words', or the writing that conditioned them, both are concerned with the practical functions of making a statement...The purpose of such statements is to cast a spell, to impose a favorable order upon the universe..."

Aldred pointed out that "The position of such a work of art...is seen in the magical ritual, the 'Opening of the Mouth,' that each statue, painting, relief or building had to undergo on its completion to ensure that it was transformed from an inanimate product of man's hands into a vibrant part of the divine order charged with numinous power."[119] Indeed, the final act in artistic creation was

---

119. Aldred, Cyril, *Egyptian Art*, p. 18.

the "Opening of the Mouth" ritual; the image was brought to life just as the son and heir of a deceased person, assisted by a priest, in funerary services touched the mouth of the mummy and his statue with a magical instrument to revive the deceased bodily functions from death to life.

The materialization in sculpture or painting of a god, a religious belief, or even an ordinary scene, magically rendered them real. This was eminently the case for the *khenty*, the *tut*, the statue, the image; a statue of a god was not just a statue, it was the god; the *ka* soul of the god lived in the statue. *Every* statue of a god or a pharaoh was the god. And paintings in a tomb were not just paintings; they were real. They were meant to magically serve the deceased by re-creating the scenes of life; paintings of food could become real food, if the correct incantation was pronounced. The material temple was not only a house for gods and their worship; it was a replica of creation and the orderly universe.

In Egypt's Early Dynastic Period (c. 3100–2686 BC), art was largely narrative art and often had to do with describing wars, but even in this period we can see the tendency to depict the ideal essence of things, what things *should be*, rather than what actually is, or actually happens.

This tendency was rapidly amplified and at least by the opening of the Old Kingdom (c. 2686 BC) was linked to one of the chief purposes of Egyptian art — the permanency of creation and its continuation in the afterlife. Much of Egyptian art was in one way or another concerned with death. Art and architecture provided the magical instruments which would ensure that the deceased would live on eternally in the afterlife, could repeat life, *wehem ankh*, and not die a second time, *temt mit em nem*, that is, be damned to a "second death" after ordinary death. This funerary art at first concerned only the pharaohs, who expended great efforts and expense in order to be *aper*, "equipped," as they said, for the afterlife. Being "equipped" meant having a solid tomb, but it also meant statues, paintings, amulets, furniture, goods and food for a prosperous afterlife.

The belief that burial in massive structures was a vehicle for afterlife, or even ensured an afterlife, led first to the building of solid mastaba tombs, from about 3100 BC, and then to the enormous solar symbol ladders to the afterlife pyramid-tombs and places of worship and offering for the deceased pharaoh. In this sense, the first pyramid ever built, around 2660 BC, the Sakkara Step Pyramid, was the first application of a new religious concept in which a material structure became a vector for the pharaohs towards the afterlife in the stars or in the "lightland" of the sky. In the New Kingdom, from the early 15th century, huge rock-cut tombs became the material vectors for the afterlife.

In this life, or rather for this life, art and architecture essentially meant the creation of images of the gods, including the pharaoh-gods, the illustration of religious beliefs, the serving of religious concepts through the building of temples for the appeasement and worship of the gods, the practice of funerary cults, and the use of amulets. The glorification of gods and pharaoh-gods was the main theme of Egyptian art, with the tasks and preoccupations of ordinary human beings — the commoners — usually playing only minor roles. Scenes devoted to all aspects of ordinary daily life were frequent, but both in funerary and "this life" art they primarily illustrated permanent reality, the way things should absolutely be in a well-ordered hierarchical society, rather than what was actually happening.

The clear, primary aim of most Egyptian art was to manipulate the gods and "equip" someone for the afterlife. This manipulation was carried out in an extraordinarily coherent manner; it faithfully illustrated and even accentuated the basically contradictory and confused nature of Egyptian religion, the afterlife and mythology. This kind of curious "coherency" was particularly evident in Egyptian art, but it was basically the vivid illustration of a twin Egyptian trait — the Egyptians were pragmatic and unimaginative; they did not let their imaginations run wild in all directions, but at the same time they displayed immense imaginative capacity within strict frameworks, such as those provided in theology and art.

Another very important aim of Egyptian art was to manipulate humans. In this sense, it was essentially a medium, a tool for information, communication and indoctrination. It delivered a politico-religious message in which the powers and the relations between the gods, the divine kings and humans and animals were clearly illustrated, just as the great powers wielded by the "perfect, good" king and the ruling elite and the status of each social class and their relations were clearly illustrated.

With the possible exception of the proto-monotheistic Pharaoh Akhenaten's (c. 1352–1336 BC) "Amarna art" (see Volume II), the Egyptian artist basically sought to permanently fix the absolute, the symbolic, the ideal, the essence of what things should be. Of course, this was the case for the gods and the divine pharaohs who were portrayed in ideal situations of stiff solemnity, power and youth. The pioneer who forged our early understanding of Egyptian art, the German Egyptologist/art historian Heinrich Schäfer (1868–1957) noted, in 1919: "the idealizing representation of kings is based on the desire to lift the "good gods" (the kings), sons and likenesses of the gods, above what is human, imperfect and subject to chance...it is impossible that the long line of Egyptians kings included only men whose bodies were perfectly healthy for all their lives. And yet apart from Amenhotep IV (Akhenaten)...there is hardly any king who shows a deviation from the body form thought to be the ideal at the time. Some kings are thin and slender, others broad and thickset, some severe and others more abundantly developed, but their bodies are almost always well formed..."[120]

Private art, the sculpture and painting depicting notables and ordinary people, followed the same basic tenets — serving the gods and proving that a person had lived in compliance with his or her hierarchical rank within the divine order. The goal was the same as for royalty — proving one's worthiness for entry into the *Duat* afterlife and being "equipped" to "repeat life" there, and the method was the same — depicting things as they should be, rather than as they were. The notable was almost always portrayed exuding success and prosperity, defiantly standing with one foot forward and carrying a staff and a scepter. Women, whatever their social rank, were almost always depicted with a young, slim allure. Commoners were almost always depicted in a simplified way.

Art and architecture, particularly in the temples, were the mirrors of creation and told the wonderful stories and especially the exploits of the gods and the pharaohs. For the pharaohs, this frequently included their military victories (or fictitious victories) and the foreign captives and booty they brought back to Egypt as well as their devotion to the gods and their ritual and daily occupations.

And yet somehow this artificial system of depicting idealized essence was not airtight. While it was followed almost absolutely for the depiction of gods and pharaohs, resulting in stereotypes, there are many examples of *Book of the Dead* vignettes of "friendlier" gods. Meaningful individual characteristics of pharaohs and notables were also frequently depicted, especially in sculpture. In some of Egyptian history, this sidebar became a tendency which soared to great artistic heights.

The American Egyptologist/art historian William Stevenson Smith (1907–1969), in *The Art and Architecture of Ancient Egypt*, noted that "Egyptian art...displays the same approach to representation which is common to all other ancient peoples before Greek times. All pre-Greek peoples give us a kind of diagram of a thing as a man knew it to be, not as it appears to the eye under transitory circumstances." But Smith added: "In spite of this attitude towards visual

---

120. Schäfer, Heinrich, *Principles of Egyptian Art*, p.16.

impressions, the Egyptian had an instinct to imitate closely what he saw about him...Thus, within certain limits of his conventions, the Egyptian approaches his subject with careful, painstaking attention to detail." Schäfer also saw true portraiture as something rare in Egyptian art, but nevertheless there: "Egyptians are probably the first to be aware of the nobility inherent in the human form and to express it in art."[121]

In short, even if reality and its "details" sometimes burst through, the main thrust of Egyptian art was to stiffly represent an idealized world and idealized people in a system which encompassed everything from the beginning — creation — to the afterlife. This was necessarily linked to absolute situations that only a magical approach could "grasp" and justify and that was dominated by death. The mystery, magic, extreme pliability and immediacy of plastic art and architecture were superior vectors for the creation of a divinely ordained ideal world based on the Egyptian divine immanence approach to the sacred. It was this concept of the sacred that the Egyptian artist basically served.

In her book *Arrest and Movement*, H.A. Groenewegen-Frankfort gives perhaps the best description of how the Egyptian artist used a code and artificially manipulated the "space-time" of immanence to produce what she called "the logical concept (of) non functionalism." This approach, exemplified by Old Kingdom art (c. 2686–2181 BC), renders objects and figures "independent[ly] of the[ir] actual appearance in space" and "therefore lacks corporeality in the functional sense of that word." It constitutes a "transcendence of actuality," "a transmutation of the ephemeral into the typical and essentially timeless"; "actuality was irrelevant in the face of death." The result of all this for Groenewegen-Frankfort was the non-depiction of "an event in space and time," "an obstinate prejudice against illusionary space [which was not] a mere aesthetic whim..." "New subjects, new mannerisms, might be introduced and copied but never those which rendered human beings functionally or which aimed at illusionary space: these were consistently — and we may believe, deliberately — rejected."[122]

In the final analysis, Egyptian art was not art as we define it.

The immense aesthetic quality of Egyptian architecture, art and artifacts, the search for the truth about a person which we often find in the sculpture and

121. Smith, W. Stevenson, *The Art and Architecture of Ancient Egypt*, pp. 1 and 3. Schäfer, Heinrich, *Principles of Egyptian Art*, pp. 171 and 16.

122. Groenewegen-Frankfort, H.A., *Arrest And Movement, Space and Time in the Representational Art of the Ancient Near East*, pp. 7, 51, 37, 97.

sometimes in the painting, and the search for the right line, the right perspective in Egypt's architecture — even if they were not primary intentions — all seem to indicate that many artists and craftsmen may have not been just religious civil servants. Much like the Magdalenian artist-magicians, it seems a foregone conclusion that the Egyptian artist was also a bit of an artist in our modern sense, somebody seeking to convey a personal aesthetic, emotional and philosophical experience even when the rules of the game largely prohibited him from doing this. Egyptian art is spontaneously and primarily seen as art and not religion by the millions of people who today flock to the museums and to Egypt. An art which in no way was meant as art for art's sake, whose historical context indicates the opposite, is somehow recognized as eminent example of just that.

Egypt's magnificent architecture and art would have been impossible without fervent religious certitude and fervent religiously motivated craftsmen and workers. The framework of the religious and magical system and the strict socio-political system seem in themselves insufficient explanations. The preparation and transport of two-ton slabs of stone for the pyramids, of obelisks weighing hundreds of tons, the construction of temples covering scores of acres, the carving and painting of fabulously detailed reliefs, the sculpting of thousands of statues and colossi, all bear witness to times of great religious certitude — or to blind faith and blind hope — in any case, to the power of religious illusion.

While the craftsmen and even the hundreds of thousands of conscripted laborers probably were consenting, for the most part, the pyramids, temples and tombs were indeed built over thousands of years with sweat and blood and a degree of constraint. The elite craftsmen worked on these projects under much better conditions, but not all the time. Strikes occurred, usually for non-payment of wages in kind or mistreatment by overseers or notables. A detailed description of one of these strikes by royal craftsmen in the Theban Deir el-Medina workers' village is contained in the Turin Strike Papyrus. It tells us how the craftsmen and artists, led by a scribe and two foremen, struck during the 29th year of Rameses III's reign (c. 1184–1153 BC) for three days because they were literally suffering from hunger: "It's because of hunger and thirst that we have come here. We have no clothing, no oil, no fish nor vegetables. Go and tell this to the pharaoh, *ankh, udja, seneb*, life, prosperity, health, our perfect Lord. And go tell it also to the vizier, our superior, so that our supplies are delivered...Tell our superiors that we will not return [to work]!"[123]

---

123. From the French text in www.cur-archamps.fr/2terres.

Yes, there was certitude and consent and devotion to the pharaoh, but these feelings may have been not as unimpaired or lofty as we generally suppose. Constraint was certainly involved in carrying out the mind-boggling, immense building projects of many of the pharaohs, just as constraint was an integral part of the Egyptian and almost all other religions ever invented. Perhaps, much of Egypt's architecture and art were accomplished with the help of both the gods and a stick.

THE STRICT DESIGN RULES OF EGYPTIAN ART AND ARCHITECTURE

Egyptian artists and craftsmen used a great variety of materials — wood, pottery, ivory, animal bone, stone of many kinds, gold, silver, gems, copper, bronze, ceramics, pigments, and two mediums that had never been used before — papyrus from about 3150 BC and cut stone for architecture from about 2660 BC.

Their plastic arts had clear religious goals, and by the same token obeyed strict, symbolic design codes and used a series of conventional physical postures and gestures. The American Egyptologist Richard H. Wilkinson, in *Reading Egyptian Art*, has emphasized the close connection between hieroglyphic signs, their forms and meanings, and the content of Egyptian art: "[I]t is probably not overstating the situation to say that hieroglyphic signs do form the very basis of Egyptian iconography, which — just like the written inscriptions — is concerned with the practical function of making a clear and often specific symbolic statement." Wilkinson made an inventory of nearly 100 glyphs that are consistently used to convey exact meaning. These range from the glyph for "call" or "summon": "the figure of a man with one arm raised, beckoning or calling...especially...where relatives are shown invoking or calling forth the spirit of the deceased," to the glyph for "rejoice": "a man with both arms raised high in jubilation," to the glyph for "embrace or hold": "two arms reaching out in an embrace," to the glyph for "mourning woman": "mourners...with one hand raised to their heads"[124]

We consistently find these conventional gestures, as well as dozens of other image-signs which had immediate meaning for the Egyptian — like

---

124. Wilkinson, Richard H., *Reading Egyptian Art, A Hieroglyphic Guide To Ancient Egyptian Painting And Sculpture*, pp. 10, 23, 28, 51, 35.

upraised arms to indicate the *ka* double soul, a seated man with bent knees to indicate a god, the Horus *wedjat* eye to indicate healing and protection, a jug to indicate the *ieb*, the heart, a lapwing *rekhyt* bird to indicate commoners or captives, a *mehyt*, papyrus, clump to indicate the land of Lower Egypt, and myriad animals which indicated specific gods and their particular functions and powers, like the falcon for Horus, divine kingship and the sun, a cow for Hathor and Isis and the celestial zone, an ibis for Thoth and writing and the transfigured spirit, and countless others.

The human body was usually not constructed according to normal perspective, but in stylized standing, sitting or kneeling positions, and obeyed precise, pre-defined artificial proportions. The size and proportions of a person also depended on his religious and political class and on sex — gods and pharaohs were biggest, nobles less big, and women, peasants and children (with a side-lock of hair), were artificially small and usually placed behind and to the left of the important figures. Clothing (or its absence, for pre-pubescent children), headdresses, ornaments, attitudes, social and class functions and situations also obeyed strict design and color rules. Kings in battle, like Sety I (c. 1294–1279 BC) and Rameses II (c. 1279–213 BC), were depicted in many temple murals as occupying more than half of the total scene, while their enemies were minute in comparison.

A grid of proportions was systematically used in a preparatory drawing on papyrus or a preparatory model in plaster or stone. By using this grid, artists were able to obtain gigantic dimensions without an appreciable loss of aesthetic quality.

For the human body, the grid had 18 rows of squares — two from the head to the bottom of the neck, 10 from the neck to the knees and six from the knees to the feet. One row of variable size was added above the head for hair and headdresses. Fourteen rows were used for seated figures. This grid was used from about 3000 BC to about 525 BC, when 21 rows went into use. A grid of squares was also used for drawing animals.

The visible result of this grid system was an accentuation in the size of the head, the chest and the stomach. This was clearly not just an aesthetic cannon; it emphasized the parts of the body which were considered religiously important. Coupled with other techniques, it also produced role models for masculinity and femininity.

In painting, faces were usually in profile and looked to the right, but like Cubism this style artificially took into account some frontal characteristics. In sculpture and painting, the eyes were accentuated and artificially slanted. For males, the shoulders were exaggerated, and for women breasts and the pubic mound were accentuated in artificially slim bodies. This technique of accentuating key features was part of a process aimed at summing up a person's character, at showing what a person really was spiritually (or should be, according to his social class). However, in sculpture, heads were often depicted with a dose of reality and sometimes this was extended to the depicting of bodies — even going as far as caricature when it came to the painting and sculpting of foreigners.

In both painting and sculpture, colors were limited to a garish spectrum without nuances or mixing, of red, yellow, white, black, blue and green. These colors seem to be part of a code, adding to the meaning of the images, but frequently their exact significance is somewhat unclear today. Generally, reddish-brown ochre was used to color the faces and bodies of Egyptian men, indicating youth and strength; yellow or white was used for women; blue, white, green and gold for divine beings, with gold indicating the eternal quality which never faded; black symbolized an association with the fertility of the Nile Valley "Black Land," *Kemet*, and also death and life in the *Duat*, the afterlife and afterlife gods; green was for fertility and vigor, as well as for resurrection and the afterlife and sometimes for the earth god Geb and for the resurrected Osiris; and red, the color of Seth, was used for pernicious forces. A color code was also used to depict foreigners, as discussed in Chapter 3.

Although not a formal rule, gigantic proportions were one of the outsanding characteristics of Egyptian sculpture — as it was in Egyptian religious architecture. The building of colossi, sphinxes and obelisks was an obligation for the pharaohs, both to glorify the gods and themselves. Extraordinary size was obviously linked to the importance of what was being depicted, especially when it came to gods and pharaohs. It was also symptomatic of hyperbolic religiosity and zoolatry.

Gigantic size is one of the most extraordinary aspects of Egyptian sculpture. Even more impressive than the technical skill was the artists' fabulous capacity to conserve deep emotional and aesthetic qualities despite the crushing, outrageous non-human and non-animal proportions employed.

Shesep ankh, "living image," was probably the original Egyptian term for what we know by the Greek term "sphinx"; it seems to indicate that the sphinx was conceived as a protective *ankh* vital life force in the form of a gigantic amulet. The sphinx represented the protective power of the gods and animals leagued together to protect the pharaoh-god and identified with his human form. The first known sphinx was built by Pharaoh Radjefra (c. 2566–2558 BC), at his pyramid complex in Abu Roash, northwest of Memphis. (A fragment is now in the Louvre Museum.). Of course, the most fabulous was the "Great Sphinx," built by Radjefra's son, Khephren (c. 2558–2532 BC), which was a mixture of sculpture and architecture and will be discussed in the next section. Pharaoh-protecting sphinxes, although never anywhere as big the Great Sphinx, depicting composites of humans, hawks, rams and lions, continued to be built throughout Egyptian history, including into the Late Period. The 8.2-foot lion sphinx, probably of Amenemhat III (c1855–1808 BC), found in Tanis (and now in the Cairo Museum), exudes such hard knife-cutting power that three later pharaohs re-named it their own names, Rameses II, Merenptah and Psusennes I. The Nubian Pharaoh Taharqa's (690–664 BC) lion sphinx in the Amun Temple in Kawa, Upper Nubia (now in the British Museum), although small, also radiates mysterious power.

The building of colossi also began during the Old Kingdom and continued throughout Egyptian history. When colossi depicted a pharaoh, they obeyed a simple rule — they were idealized representations which supposedly revealed the divine aspects of the pharaohs-gods rather than being simple likenesses. They were meant to instill awe, reverence and also frequently fear of the great power of the pharaoh. Of course, the tallest colossi ever built was by the megalomaniac Rameses II (c. 1279–1213 BC), found in the Amun Temple in Djanet (Tanis), in the Delta, by Petrie in 1884. It is 90 feet tall; one of its eyes is 16 inches; it weighs 900 tons; and was sculpted from a single piece of stone. The four seated colossi of Rameses II on the facade of the Abu Simbel Temple in Nubia are 69 feet high. The fallen colossus of Rameses II in his Ramesseum mortuary temple in Thebes was 66 feet high, had a 3 foot 6 inch ear and weighed 1000 tons. Perhaps the most impressive colossi (now accentuated by their forlorn isolation in a vast open plain, previously occupied by the enormous Malqata Palace) are the twin 49-foot statues of a seated Amenhotep III (c. 1391–1352), near Thebes, called the Colossi of Memnon (one of which used to sing on windy mornings, before Roman Emperor Septimus Severus (AD 193–211) had its cracks repaired). Akhenaten's colossi in his Karnak *Gempaaton* averaged a mere 13 feet.

Colossi of the gods, in human or animal form, also frequently succeeded in a perfect marriage of an emphasis on the religious importance and character of the god concerned, and aesthetic perfection. This was particularly true of the outsized animals, as individual sculptures or as parts of colossi, such as rams for Amun, baboons for Thoth, cows for Hathor, cats for Bastet, bulls for Ptah, Re scarabs for Khepri, hippopotami for Seth, crocodiles for Sobek and falcons for Horus, Re and Montu. The opulently magnificent Thoth/baboon colossus built by Amenhotep III (c. 1390–1352) in Hermopolis is 14 feet 9 inches high.

The opposite of the colossi — miniatures — of human and animal gods and goddesses, were often used as amulets. Many of them, too, are amazingly expressive objects, especially the animals. Despite their tiny size, hippopotami roar as if they were alive, falcons are truly mysterious, bulls are indeed massive and powerful, gazelles are graceful, lions majestic and cats really seem to meow. The crystal figurine of the childbirth goddess Taweret in the British Museum, with its satisfied hippopotamus face and convincingly sagging breasts, is only 3.7 inches. The faience winged scarab amulet in the Oxford Ashmolean Museum radiates protection, with wings just 3.4 inches wide and a scarab 1.3 inches high.

Both in colossal and miniature forms, the falcon, the *bik*, may be the most dazzling figure. It so frequently exemplifies outstanding religious and aesthetic criteria combined with majestic pride and almost human thoughtfulness — right from the limestone six-inch falcon/Horus on Pharaoh Djet's Abydos stele (c. 2980 BC and now in the Louvre Museum), to the diorite one-foot falcon/Horus perched on Pharaoh Khephren's back (and now in the Cairo Museum), to the alabaster two-inch falcon/Horus perched on Pharaoh Pepy I's (c. 2321–2287 BC) throne (now in the Brooklyn Museum), to the row of falcons at Karnak Temple and even to the colossi falcon/Horuses at Edfu Temple — the pair at the entrance and especially the stern falcon, wearing the *pschent* intertwined double crown, leading into the hypostyle hall — despite Edfu having being built and decorated under Greek and Roman rule (c. 237–57 BC).

Egyptian architecture also was subjected to strict rules, although there was scope for invention — particularly concerning size and interior design, both for pyramids and temples.

Pyramid is the English term for the Greek *pyramis*, known to Egyptians as the *mer*. After Djoser's (c. 2667–2648 BC) six-tiered "Step Pyramid" and perhaps only about 50 years of experimentation, the standard form of the *mer* was established. Snofru's "Shining Pyramid" (c. 2613–2589 BC) in Dashur is the first true pyramid. It rose to 341 feet and was inclined at 43°22'. Although evolution in pyramid building was continual, the true pyramid became a relatively standardized type of construction.

As impressive as they are, it was not Khufu's and Khrepren's "Great Pyramids" built (c. 2589–2532 BC) at Rasetau (Giza), near Memphis, but the much smaller Fifth Dynasty (c. 2494–2345 BC) true pyramids in Abusir, north of Memphis, which best exemplified the rules for pyramid construction and mural and sculpted relief decoration. Sahura's (c. 2487–2475 BC) "pyramid where the *ba* spirit rises," was a "mere" 258 feet high. Magical utterances (Pyramid Texts) to facilitate and protect the pharaohs' afterlife were carved on the walls of at least nine pyramids for pharaohs and one for a "great royal wife," from Pharaoh Unas' (c. 2375–2345 BC) "Pyramid which is beautiful of faces" to Ibi's (c. 2181–2125 BC) pyramid, the name of which is unknown.

The pyramid always had four sides of roughly equal isosceles triangles, an almost precise astronomical orientation to the four cardinal points and a culminating overlaid golden peak, the *benbenet*, the pyramidion. The pyramid's shafts were aligned to various stars and notably to the Orion Constellation, the home of Osiris, which enabled the *ba* roaming soul of the pharaoh to leave the tomb.

The focal point of the pyramid was its underground burial chamber. Djoser's measured 9 by 6 by 5 feet. The so-called "King's Chamber" in Khufu's (Cheops, c. 2589–2566 BC), "The pyramid which is the place of sunrise and sunset," was 34.4 by 17.2 by 19.1 feet, and Khafra's (Khephren, c. 2558–2532 BC) burial chamber in the "Great, or Second, Pyramid" was 46.5 by 16.5 by 22.5 feet. The three "Great Pyramids" in Giza contained two other burial chambers above ground level, in addition to the underground burial chamber.

The pyramid was the central structure of a vast complex. Small pyramids, usually for the wives of the pharaoh, were situated nearby. Pits alongside the pyramid contained *wia*, solar barques, which enabled the pharaoh to travel across the sky to join Re in "lightland." The main pyramid was linked by causeways to two temples, the valley temple and the mortuary temple. The valley temple was probably where embalmment, mummification and the "Opening of the Mouth" ceremony were carried out. The mortuary temple contained a *ka*-statue of the dead king and was where cult worship and *hetep*, offerings, took place.

The size, the height, the interior layout of burial chambers, shafts and corridors and the decoration of the pyramids and connected temples varied considerably over the more than 1000 years during which they were built, until about the end of the Middle Kingdom (c. 1650 BC).

The ideal angle of inclination of the pyramid seems to have been a steep 53°7'48," but even after this angle was discovered, the angle of inclination of the pyramids varied widely. Some, notably Khufu's "Great" or "First Pyramid," show an extraordinarily precise use of the *pi* ratio (3.141592) in the relation between the height and base. This was almost certainly achieved pragmatically, as there is no indication in any Egyptian text of a theoretical knowledge of *pi*.

Despite all the loony theories about pyramids (see Volume II), their function and symbolism were clear, at least in an overall way. The pyramid complex was the material expression of the concept of providing a solid, massive, eternal tomb for facilitating, protecting and organizing an eternal afterlife for the pharaoh. It was a place of mortuary rituals linked to sun worship, to the idea that the dead pharaoh-god used the pyramid ladder to the sky to join Re in "lightland." Its golden peak pyramidion, the *benbenet*, represented the primeval *benben* mound on which the rays of the rising sun settled. The pyramid, culminating with its *benbenet*, was a place which shines, which rises (*weben*); and many of the names of the pyramids incorporate the ideas of rising, the sun and shining. The pharaoh was resurrected on the *benben* as represented by the pyramid and rose to the sky on the sun's rays which fell on the *benbenet*. The pyramid was a pharaoh's supreme way of manifesting his connection to the sun god Re.

The rock-cut tombs, which replaced the pyramids in the New Kingdom (c. 1550–1069 BC) as the afterlife entry point for the pharaohs, also obeyed a large set of construction rules. The tombs were built according to a schema of sacred symbolism with mazes of chambers, corridors and shafts. From Horemheb's time (c. 1323 BC, KV57), they were built around straight corridors, a factor perhaps linked to Atenist solar theology. They contained fabulous mural reliefs and paintings, sculptures, funerary texts, *ushabti* statues, canopic jars, boats, jewelry, and stocks of food, clothing, furniture and weapons. They were cut deep into the mountain rock to foil grave robbers — Hatshepsut's tomb (c. 1473–1458 BC, KV20) is 700 feet from its entrance and goes down 320 feet. However, as much (and probably more) damage and pillaging was done by the New Kingdom priests who organized systematic looting of precious objects and building materials for their own profit and for reuse in other tombs. Some pharaohs were wiped out from history by wiping out their names and smashing their statues and temples; this also led to considerable loss, notably concerning Hatshepsut, who was seen as persona non grata by Thutmose III (c. 1479–1425 BC), and

Akhenaten (c. 1352–1336 BC), who was viewed as a criminal heretic by Horemheb.

From the earliest times the temples, *the hewet netjer*, the House of the god, culminating in the New Kingdom temples and continued by the temples of the Greco-Roman Period, were subject to a body of sacred architectural rules. The temple was the home of the gods and a place for the pharaoh and the priests to engage in ritual and worship. It was built on high ground, always orientated east-west, on a site that was considered to be naturally sacred and its architecture was seen as a mirror of creation and the orderly universe. Its enclosing walls were meant to keep out primordial chaos and disorder, *izfeh*.

Over thousands of years, its architecture hardly varied and consisted of a dock on the Nile for the boats used to parade the statues of the gods, a road of sphinxes, the *dromos*, leading to the opening gate pylon, the *bekhenet*, forecourts and open hypostyle halls all slanted upwards and culminating in the *ra per*, the *naos* sanctuary, where the gods of the temple lived in their statues and which was the *benben* primeval mound. The sun rose on the horizon over the *bekhenet* and penetrated into the temple up to the *naos*.

During the Fifth Dynasty (c. 2494–2345 BC), a unique form of temple — the Re sun temple — was built by all of the pharaohs except the last two. This type of construction may have been a copy of the original Heliopolis Re-Atum Sun Temple or a Re-Horakthe Sun Temple built by Pharaoh Djoser (c. 2667–2648 BC); it was later discontinued. The greatest of these Re sun temple complexes to have survived was Abu Ghurab, northwest of Memphis, built by Pharaoh Neuserre (c. 2445–2421 BC). It was built in stone and much of it was excavated between 1898 and 1901 by the German Egyptologists F. W. Von Bissing, Ludwig Borchardt and Heinrich Schäfer.

Usually, the sun temples were constructed along a similar architectural plan to the pyramid complex. The Abu Ghurab sun temple contained a roofless court with an altar and a platform topped by a shortened obelisk, with its golden *benbenet* pyramidion (although sometimes sun temple obelisks were huge). The obelisk, the *tekhen*, represented the sun, Re, and like the *benben*, symbolizing the original primeval mound, was the point where the first rays of the rising sun (Re) fell in the morning. A pit containing a *wia*, a solar barque was situated just outside the temple enclosure. A causeway connected the upper sun temple to a valley temple.

Obelisks were systematically linked to temples, but were sometimes also used in front of tombs. The forerunner of the authentic tall obelisk topped by a golden *benbenet*, prymadion, like the pyramid, was the *benben* stone in the Heliopolis sun temple (built c. 2660 BC). After the building of the first tall *tekhen* in Heliopolis and in the sun temples, they became one of the most characteristic structures of the Egyptian religious architecture. *Tekhen*, like the *benben* and the *Benu* bird, were etymologically linked to *weben*, to shine, to rise. The *tekhen* developed into a solar cult pillar containing the sun's (Re's) rays. They were usually a single piece of stone weighing hundreds of tons, often 80 feet high, and were placed in pairs. It seems that Egypt's great conqueror pharaoh, Thutmose III (c. 1479–1425 BC) attempted to build the biggest obelisk — a granite stone 137 feet high weighing 1170 tons — whose cutting was apparently abandoned in the Elephantine quarry after it developed several cracks.

A High Point in the History of Plastic Arts: The Atypical Master-pieces of the Fifth Dynasty and the Amarna Period

Few societies in history have given such immense aesthetic pleasure to succeeding generations as the ancient Egyptians (unwittingly!) did. It was not only magnificent, but in sheer volume the number of Egyptian works surpassed anything seen before, and anything that was to come, until the opening of the great period of temple building in India in about the ninth century AD and the flowering from the 11th century AD of Christian architecture and art, especially in Italy and France.

Art and architecture have provided us with an exceptionally ample description and insight into ancient Egyptian society and its inner workings, its nuts and bolts. More than any other ancient society, Egypt has displayed for us their religious beliefs, myths, rituals — even if we have great difficulties in understanding many of them — their hopes, fears, politics, economics and lifestyles. In addition to the hundreds of extraordinary sites in Egypt, the major museums of the world, and especially the Cairo Museum, the British Museum, the Louvre and the New York Metropolitan, possess hundreds of thousands of Egyptian works of art; the Cairo Museum alone possesses more than 130,000 objects.

This very great abundance has led to an insatiable thirst to know more about ancient Egypt and to an enormous number of loony theories and so-called mysteries.

Truly, never before had so many artists, craftsmen and workers been involved in the creation of art, architecture and artifacts for use in this life and especially for use in the afterlife. Tens of thousands of religiously motivated, but cloistered, artists and craftsmen, with the status of civil servants, were permanently creating art in Memphis — the city of the Ptah, the patron god of the arts and crafts — and in Heliopolis and Thebes and many other cities. Hundreds of thousands of conscripted workers were on the job (especially when there was no farm work to do during the *akhet* inundation season), quarrying, cutting, lugging, and placing stone and wood.

Although the names of many great artists and artistico-religious officials have come down to us, their numbers are small compared to the vast number of anonymous artists. Some of the greatest were the deified Imhotep, "Master of Works" for Pharaoh Djoser (c. 2667–2648 BC) and architect of the Step Pyramid; Mertesen, the Eleventh Dynasty (c. 2125–1985 BC) "Overseer of artisans, the painters and sculptor"; Inene, the painter and architect who inaugurated the move towards secret deep rock-cut tombs in western Thebes with Thutmose I's (c. 1504–1492) TT38; Senenmut, Steward of Hatshepsut (c. 1473–1458 BC) and architect of her Deir el-Bahri mortuary temple; Puymere, another of her architects who built a beautiful shrine for the mother goddess Mut; the deified architect/sculptor Amenhotep son of Hapu (Huy); Ma'nakhtuf, the architect and Men the Chief Sculptor of one of Egypt's greatest builders, Amenhotep III (c. 1390–1352 BC); Bek and Tuthmose, the Chief Sculptors of Akhenaten (c. 1352–1336 BC) and Bekenkhons, the "First Prophet and Master of Works" of Rameses II (c. 1279–1213 BC).

With its clear religious goals and its multitude of design, posture, gesture and color rules, Egyptian art was a kind of strict metric verse with guidelines for a pre-defined content of representation, imitation and illustration. The resulting easily recognizable Egyptian style and spirit basically remained the same over nearly 3000 years, with the sole exception of the monotheistic Amarna Period (c. 1352–1323 BC). Masterpieces were produced at least right to end of the Ramesside Period (c. 1069 BC). Beyond this period, decline set in in the form of blind repetition of old forms without the old inner inspiration — despite attempts at revival, for instance during the Kushite (c. 747–656 BC) and Saite (c. 664–525 BC) periods.

This art was magnificent in the true sense of this word — it magnified, it inspired awe, it was splendid in its richness and it was frequently solemn and grave. It went beyond the hurry-scurry of life in an attempt to depict what it believed to be eternal. And yet with all its magnificence, the stiff framework of Egyptian art inevitably generated serious limitations, at least in the sense of how we understand art today.

Given its theological thrust — to depict idealized people within an idealized world — images of real people with their qualities and defects, and real scenes with their unexpected beauty and imperfections, were rare. And so the key limitation of Egyptian art was that it was rarely tragic; it rarely cut through the mass of hypocrisy to the heart of the human struggle. Egyptian art was intrinsically condemned to a cut-and-dried tendency of repetitive, mechanical, stereotyped and dogmatic representation, both religiously and artistically. One of the curious results is that it is extremely difficult to establish today to what degree Egyptian pictorial art represented the authentic physical features of pharaohs, notables and commoners and to what degree they were stereotyped features.

Once one has absorbed the main thrust of Egyptian art, what becomes most appealing asre the exceptions. Especially in sculpture, the Egyptian artists often escaped from strict design codes, or they adhered to the models in original ways that allowed more truth to appear.

The very essence of geese seems to be captured in the geese depicted in Intet's Maidum mastaba (c. 2630 BC); the antelopes from Sahura's Abusir pyramid (c. 2487–2475 BC, now in the Berlin Ägyptisches Museum) may be the most graceful ever carved. There cannot have been a more *no-nonsense vizier* vizier than Ankhhaf (c. 2560 BC, in the Boston Museum of Fine Arts), nor a more forlorn foreigner than the Twelfth Dynasty (c. 1985–1795 BC) statuette of a foreign woman and her child (in the Edinburgh Royal Scottish Museum).

This type of *truth*, or realistic, art, especially in portraiture, somehow even constituted a tendency, during two periods in the history of Egyptian art, the Old Kingdom Fifth Dynasty (c. 2494–2345 BC) and the brief Amarna Period of Pharaoh Akhenaten (c. 1352–1336 BC). Many examples can be cited from these two periods, although the choice made is certainly largely subjective. The painted limestone statue of a dour, proud seated *sesh*, scribe from the Fifth Dynasty (in the Cairo Museum), the limestone statue of an introspective but slightly smiling Memy-Sabu and his wife who seems to be in a world of her own (in the New York Metropolitan), the painted statuette of a tired, hard-working brewer (in the Cairo Museum), the wood statue of the slender, worried, even fearful — but striding forward — "chief of the royal farmers" Metjety (in the Brooklyn Museum), the opulent so-called "Cheikh el Balad" (in the Cairo

Museum) are superlative, as are the series of colossi and heads of Akhenaten, all strange, tragic, but calm and self-satisfied (in Cairo, Luxor and the Louvre), and the mural painting featuring two affectionate, serious, but playful daughters of Akhenaten (in the Oxford Ashmolean Museum), from the Amarna Period. Only in the reign of the proto-monotheistic Pharaoh Akhenaten did the depiction of a relaxed, affectionate pharaoh and purely human emotional themes and everyday, secular subjects became usual: and that was a revolution in its own right.

From the point of view of the history of art, the Fifth Dynasty and Amarna must be the two finest periods in Egyptian art. It was then that the artist best managed to combine his theological obligation to depict idealized essence with his natural inclination to depict reality.

While the art of earlier and later civilizations also adhered to strict codes, the enormous system of rules in Egypt reflected an extraordinarily rigid and hierarchical society and gradually led to the blind, soulless application of these rules that left no room for exceptional achievement. The African sculpture which has come down to us from the 8th century BC also constantly operated within a symbolic religious code of meaning and strict design rules and yet it generally produced a frank, intense art, which in many cases surpasses Egyptian art; but then, that may have been the high point in the history of sculpture.

Despite this criticism that we may (somewhat unfairly) impose from a different society in a different millenium, it would seem that art had never been so vivid and meaningful since the end of Magdalenian times, more than 6000 years earlier. At their conventional best, Egyptian artists magnificently depicted the "truth" of the system they represented. At their unconventional best, despite all the rules, and in all periods, some Egyptian artists escaped formalistic conventions and attempted to depict the "truth" as we see it today.

Given the modern infatuation with Egyptian art and the frequently dithyrambic praise it receives, it is important to somewhat temper the ambient enthusiasm and to state simply that Egyptian painting and sculpture was not *the* high point in the history of plastic arts, but despite its limitations was certainly one of the high points.

A REVOLUTION IN WORLD ARCHITECTURE

For monumentality, stark aesthetics, awesomeness and technological prowess, Egyptian architecture has rarly been rivaled, much less equaled.

The invention of monumental cut stone architecture, around 2660 BC, with Pharaoh Djoser's so-called Step Pyramid at Sakkara, near Memphis, opened a new era of architectural achievement for mankind. The use of masoned stone in the building of the Step Pyramid was a considerable technological advance over the use of the mud and burnt brick in the Sumerian temples and tombs and the earlier mud-brick Egyptian mastaba tombs. However, the Egyptians did not surpass the technological feat of the use of arches and domes, which were being introduced in Sumer at about the same time as the first pyramids were being built.

The Step Pyramid rose to 204 feet and its sides at the base varied from 358 to 411 feet. This elevation was also a considerable advance over the heights Sumerian architecture had reached. Its wall-enclosed precinct, including buildings and *heb-sed* festival model structures, was 1800 by 900 feet and it had 14 entrance gates. A new era of technology was also inaugurated with the quarrying of stone in Elephantine and its hauling on barges more than 600 miles downstream to Memphis.

Never before had stone been used so massively and monumentally. Never before had such a vast space been devoted to a religious practice. Never had the aesthetics of monumental architecture been so perfected. While the Aurignacians, Gravettians and Magdalenians — Cro-Magnon man — were the authors of the revolution that was figurative art, the Egyptians were the authors of the revolution represented by monumental stone architecture. William Stevenson Smith has summed it all up: "[T]he exuberant virtuosity displayed by the buildings of the Step Pyramid...the architecture of the reign of Zoser...more than anything else, presents us with the picture of a young civilization reaching maturity...the results which they achieved seem as surprising and fresh to us now as they must have been to their admiring contemporaries...The marvelous facility with which huge stones were handled became one of the outstanding characteristics of Egyptian architecture."[125]

Stone had long been seen by man as one of the most permanent natural materials, somehow suggesting eternal values. The Gravettians and the Magdalenians had used it to carve "Venuses" 30,000 years ago. The peoples of Western Europe, from as early as 4500 BC (but mostly after 4000 BC), built huge, crude uncut stone communal graves known as megaliths. This was already an attempt to give a monumental quality to death. And recently, it has been

---

125. Smith, W. Stevenson, *The Art and Architecture of Ancient Egypt*, pp. 288, 35, 30, 2.

discovered that some cut stone was used to build 60-foot-high temples in Caral, Peru, possibly around 2627 BC, in a step-pyramid form similar to the Sakkara Step Pyramid.

But it was the Egyptians, in both architecture and sculpture, who seem to have been first to apply clearly the concept and the feeling that stone symbolized eternity, and to illustrate this in immense monumentality. Stone was the perfect material ensuring permanency, eternity. It seems that this must have been a central aspect in the thinking of Imhotep when he built the built the first pyramidal tomb, the so-called Djoser Step Pyramid. It seems that Imhotep could have been the mankind's first architect, as we understand this term today: the identifiable author of the revolution of monumental stone architecture.

Although not a true pyramid in geometric terms, the Step Pyramid represents the invention of a new architectural form which rapidly led to the true pyramid. The architectural origin of the Step Pyramid owed much to the Early Dynastic (c. 3100–2686 BC) monumental mastaba tombs: Imhotep seems to have had the idea of superimposing six mastabas to achieve greater monumentality and elevation. It seems to have also evolved from the Early Dynastic Abydos Umm el-Qa'ab royal tombs and their enclosures and funerary boat pits. Perhaps the earlier Sumerian monumental platform temples, like those in Eridu and Uruk, apparently built before c. 3400 BC on elevated mounds with superimposed forms or stories, also played a role in the conception of the pyramid. The platform temples prefigured the *ziggurat*; but the first true *ziggurat* was not built before about 2200 BC in Ur, more than 400 years after the Step Pyramid. In sheer size, the Step Pyramid by far surpassed the earlier Sumerian temples and the later ziggurats. All these elements indicate how revolutionary the pyramid was.

It is impossible to mention the Step Pyramid without mentioning the French Egyptologist Jean Philippe Lauer (1902–2001), who in the course of more than seventy years did more than anybody else to excavate, renovate and rebuild the Djoser Step Pyramid and its surroundings. Lauer brought the Step Pyramid back to life. It was even he who accidentally found what is considered by some to be Djoser's mummified foot — he tripped over it! For many years, he lived in a villa overlooking the Step Pyramid, which became a rallying point for a new generation of Egyptologists. (It is a pity that the Egyptian Government authorized the building of a modern structure so close to the pyramid, but that is another story.) Lauer's unceasing passion and eccentricity remind me of Petrie.

An artificial true pyramid was created in Maidum, 30 miles upstream from Sakkara, in about 2630 BC, when a step pyramid probably built for Pharaoh Huni (c. 2637–2613 BC) was filled in — perhaps by Pharaoh Snofru (c. 2613–2589 BC). About 20 years later, the first pyramid planned as true pyramid, "Snofru Appears in Glory," now known as "The Red Pyramid," was built for Pharaoh Snofru in Dashur, a few miles south of Sakkara. This pyramid's 43°22' angle of inclination was perhaps chosen due to fears that it would collapse if the angle was steeper, since the angle of Snofru's earlier pyramid at Dashur, "Snofru of the south appears in glory" ("The Bent Pyramid") was changed midway up from the planned 54°27'44" to 43°22'.

Pharaoh Khufu's (c. 2589–2566 BC) Giza "Pyramid which is the place of sunrise and sunset," (now known as the "Great", or "First Pyramid") was 481 feet high, had sides 755 feet long and was almost perfectly oriented true north. More than 2,300,000 stones weighing about two and a half tons on average and sometimes as heavy as 15 tons were used in its construction. The volume of all this stone has been estimated at 94 million cubic feet. Herodotus says that it took "A hundred thousand men" to build it, working in "gangs" for "three month periods" for "twenty years..." The American Egyptologist Mark Lehner, in the most recent comprehensive book on the pyramids, *The Complete Pyramids*, opts for a figure of 20,000 to 30,000, working in four annual rotations and divided into *pylai* or groups of workers.[126]

Pharaoh Khafre's (Khephren, c. 2558–2532 BC) nearby "Khafre is Great" (now known as the "the Second Pyramid") was barely less fabulous, rising to 471 feet and measuring 707 feet at the base of its sides. Pharaoh Khephren's pyramid complex included the "Great Sphinx," which was a mixture of sculpture and architecture. It is 240 feet long, 66 feet high; its paws are 50 feet long and its head 30 feet long and 14 feet wide. Perhaps it represented a composite of the pharaoh-god Khephren, the sun god Re-Atum and the ferocious powers of a lion, all leagued together to protect Khephren's tomb. It gradually came to be seen as a manifestation of Horemakhet (Horus in the Horizon), rather than of Khephren himself.

The last pyramid built at Giza, Menkaura's (c. 2532–2503 BC) "Menkaura is Divine" (now known as the "Third Pyramid"), rose to a mere 215 feet and appears to be a "midget" next to the two others.

126. Herodotus, *Books I-II*, 2.124.3-5 and Lehner, Mark, *The Complete Pyramids*, p. 224.

So far, 97 major pyramids have been found in Egypt, with 36 of them in the zone stretching more than 65 miles from Abu Roash in the north to Maidum further south. The building of the pyramids was unquestionably the greatest architectural achievement of the Old Kingdom (c. 2686–2181 BC), just as the building of the temples was the greatest architectural achievement of the New Kingdom (c. 1550–1069 BC).

The greatest of the New Kingdom temples was in Waset (Thebes). The Karnak temple complex, on the east bank of the Nile, was indeed just what the Egyptians named it: *Ipet-isut*, "the most selected of places." The Karnak Temple Complex covered at least 247 acres and perhaps as much as 300 acres. It was by far Egypt's largest temple precinct and was built, rebuilt and embellished from about 2100 to 323 BC. It attained the apex in its magnificence and size during the New Kingdom under the reign of Rameses II (c. 1279–1213 BC).

The fabulous Amun Temple, the central temple of Karnak, was 1837 feet long and covered 61 acres. The avenue of ram-headed sphinxes, the *dromos*, is more than 900 feet long and lines the majestic road leading to the temple's main entrance *bekhenet*, or pylon. This pylon was 370 feet wide. The highest *tekhen*, obelisks, in the temple enclosure, between Pylons 4 and 5, were the 97-foot, 323-ton granite pair erected by Hatshepsut (c. 1473–1458 BC), one of which is still standing. The Great Hypostyle Hall of the Amun Temple, embellished by Sety I (c. 1294–1297 BC) and Rameses II, had an area of about of 1.3 acres and 134 columns, most of them 69 feet high.

The Karnak Precinct also included great temples devoted to the war god Montu, the mother goddess Mut and Amun's and Mut's son, the young moon god Khons. For a brief period around 1353 BC, it also included a temple built by Amenhotep IV (Akhenaten), dedicated to the proto-monotheistic sun god Aten. Karnak also housed about 20 smaller kiosks or shrines for the creator and crafts god Ptah, the afterlife god Osiris, the hippopotamus mother/protectress goddess Opet, the goddess of order and truth Maat and several lesser deities and hundreds of statues of the lioness-headed war goddess Sakhmet. Karnak's sacred lake, the *Birkhet Habu*, the biggest in Egypt, had an area of more than two acres. The statues of the gods on *wia*, divine barques, notably Amun in his magnificent ram-headed *Weseghatamun* ("Mighty of Brow is Amun") with rams' heads on its prow and stern, sailed on the *Birkhet Habu*. A huge flock of geese, Amun in animal form, frolicked on the *Birkhet Habu*.

Almost two miles of human-headed sphinxes lined the *dromos* road upriver to Karnak's sister temple of Luxor (the *Ipet-resyt*, the southern select place), also dedicated to Amun, in his *kamutef* ("bull of his mother") form as the ithyphallic god of virility and fecundation, Min. Luxor was "only" 853 feet long and about 373 feet at its widest points; its two seated colossi of Rameses II were only 25 feet high and its two entrance *tekhen*, obelisks, in front of the main *bekhenet*, pylon, were only 82 feet high! Inside the temple, reliefs and hieroglyphs tell the story of Rameses II's "victory" against the Hittites at Kadesh in c. 1274 BC, reliefs which today seem to be magnificent caricatures.

Luxor was solely used for festivals, especially the annual *Opet* celebration in which the statues of the gods and goddesses led by Amun-Re arrived in procession from the Karnak Temple in one of Egypt's most magnificent, joyous and popular festivals which lasted as long as a month.

Despite being defigured and looted over more than a thousand years by successive invaders and occupiers, beginning with the Assyrians in 664 BC, the use of this sacred site as a temple for Sol Invictus during the Roman Period (after 30 BC) and the continued presence of a mosque inside the temple precinct, the stark beauty and emotional intensity of Luxor is still unforgettable today, especially at twilight.

After all these figures and descriptions, what can be said about Egypt's second biggest temple precinct, the fabulous *per* Ra, the house of the sun, in Heliopolis? Its original construction may date to Djoser's reign (c. 2667–2648 BC), and it was probably built on the site of a predynastic sun shrine. It was embellished and enlarged over more than 2000 years. Almost no remains of the early temple have been found, although the Fifth Dynasty sun temples were probably built from c. 2494 BC as replicas of Heliopolis.

Heliopolis was medium-sized, compared to Karnak. According to Herodotus and other sources, its enclosed temple precinct, administrative buildings and living quarters encompassed a space of about 3608 feet by 1558 feet, that is, 129 acres. Heliopolis was probably the biggest temple in the world, for 1000 years, until the heyday of the Karnak Amun Temple.

All that remains today of Heliopolis is a single 68-foot-high *tekhen*, or obelisk, that of Pharaoh Senwosret I (c. 1965–1920 BC), which still stands on the original site of the Sun Temple. It is the oldest surviving obelisk in Egypt. Heliopolis' treasures, including its statues, walls and even its door frames, were taken away by the Persians, Greeks, Romans, Moslems, French and British. The many Heliopolitan obelisks, linked to the sun cult, were stolen and re-erected in Greek Alexandria, Rome, London, New York and elsewhere.

The great temple complex in Djanet (Tanis) dedicated to Amun (and with smaller temples for Horus, Mut, Khons and the imported Asian goddess Astarte) has suffered a fate almost equivalent to that of Heliopolis. It is now an almost total ruin, but when it was still flourishing in Psusennes I's reign (c. 1039–991 BC), its enclosed area measured 1411 by 1214 feet. The broken columns and blocks, the sacred lake, the royal necropolis, sculptures, sphinxes, obelisks, silver coffins, funerary masks and other funerary equipment, jewelry, gold and silver bowls and vases and decorations discovered on this site indicate fabulous monumentality and splendor, but also lead to uncertainty about who built what.

By any modern standards, the two rock-cut speos temples at Abu Simbel would be considered immense. By ancient Egyptian standards, they were merely medium-sized. Abu Simbel is near today's sun-scorched desert border with Sudan, but it was in the heart of Wawet/Nubia when it was built by Rameses II in the early 13th century BC as a place of worship for Amun-Re, Re-Horakthe, Ptah and Rameses II himself.

The facade of the Abu Simbel so-called "Great Temple" is 125 feet wide and 108 feet high. It is decorated with four 69-feet-high colossi, all representing a seated Rameses II. The temple's Grand Hall is 152 feet wide and 57 feet high. Twice a year, at the solstices, the sun penetrated through the entire temple to the far-end *naos* where the statues of Re-Horakhte, Amun-Re and Ptah and the pharaoh-god Rameses were housed. The sun illuminated all the statues except that of the chthonian Ptah. The so-called "Small Temple," near the Great Temple, was built for the goddess Hathor and Rameses' "great royal wife," Nefertari, but here too Rameses II erected four 33-foot statues of himself alongside two of Nefertari.

Rameses II was a megalomaniac. He was probably Egypt's greatest builder, and one of its most fervent imperialists. He himself was six feet tall, five inches taller than the average. Above all, he was one of several pharaohs who were not content with their status as a pharaoh-god. He decided that he was as divine as a *netjer ah*, a "great god," and this was the deep *raison d'être* for the Abu Simbel Temple. It was not really fundamentally dedicated to the holy Theban organic triad of the "great gods" Amun, Re and Ptah as aspects of Amun; it was above all dedicated to Rameses II and its name was quite simply the "Temple of Rameses."

The awe-inspiring beauty and mystery of the Abu Simbel Great Temple, first rediscovered for humanity in 1813 by Jean-Louis Burckhardt, was almost lost forever when the Aswan High Dam raised the level of the Nile in the early 1960s. It was rescued by the international community (led by UNESCO and largely motivated by the American Egyptologist John A. Wilson and the French Egyptologist Christiane Desroches-Noblecourt), between 1964 and 1968, when both Abu Simbel temples were cut into thousands of blocks and almost perfectly reconstituted about 700 feet above the Nile. Our modern engineers and architects unwittingly proved the remarkable skill and accuracy of their Egyptian predecessors when they failed to perfectly calculate and re-position the entry of the solstice sun into Abu Simbel's naos.

And yet the vast, open temple spaces we see today are no doubt pale shadows of the splendor of the temples in ancient times. The temples have been emptied of most of their ritual trappings and fittings, of their golden decorations, and the colors of their reliefs have faded or disappeared. Generations of zealous rival Egyptian clergies, Copts and other Christians and foreign invaders have erased many of the hieroglyphic inscriptions and chiseled the faces off many sculptures to obliterate the existence and memory of supposedly unorthodox or heretical concepts, gods and pharaohs. Many, if not most, of the temples were also transformed into churches and mosques; and some mosques still exist within ancient temple precincts.

One of the most astonishing and original architectural and engineering achievements was the City of the Living Dead, the Theban necropolises, on the west bank of Nile and especially "the Place of Truth," *Set-Maat*, the Valley of Kings. The Valley of the Kings with 62 tombs of pharaohs, the Valley of Queens with 75 tombs of royal wives and princes, the El Tarif Eleventh-Dynasty (c. 2125–2055 BC) and the Dra' Abu el-Naga Seventeenth-Dynasty (c. 1650–1550 BC) royal tombs, the 415 tombs in the Western Valley necropolises of the notables and the Deir el-Medina craftsmen and workers necropolis cover a zone of more than three square miles.

More than 15 mortuary and cult temples for pharaohs and several palaces were situated in western Thebes. At the sacred site of Deir el-Bahri, traditionally devoted to the mother cow/afterlife cult of Hathor, numerous funerary temples and tombs were built, including the funerary temples of Pharaohs *Nebhepetre* Mentuhotep (c. 2055–2004 BC), Hatshepsut (c. 1473–1458 BC), Thutmose III (c. 1479–1425 BC) and later the fabulous *Khnemt-waset*, the Ramesseum of Rameses II (c. 1279–1213 BC) and Rameses III's (c. 1184–1153 BC) *Khnemt-neheh*, "The Mansion of Millions of Years." Perhaps, the finest, and still standing, of the New Kingdom mortuary temples is that of Hatsheput, the *Djeseru-Djeseru* ("Holy of Holies"). Its three pillared terraces, joined by two ramps, stand with stark elegance at the end of an open, sun-scorched valley at the bottom of high cliffs. Twenty-eight sculptures of Hatsheput, more than 100 sphinxes and reliefs on the walls of the temple tell the tale of Hatsheput's divine birth, her trading expedition to Punt, the Sinai and Byblos and other features of her life. A relief of Ity, the Queen of Punt, on the south wall of the Punt colonnade (now in the Cairo Museum), is surely one of the most grotesquely magnificent images ever sculpted by an Egyptian artist — her enormous size and especially huge behind and her wrinkled masculine face represented the exact opposite of the idealized slender, youthful, beautiful form of women as depicted in traditional Egyptian art.

Nature had endowed the "Place of Truth," *Set-Maat*, the Valley of Kings, with a rock pyramid-like formation on top of the hills overlooking the valley, making it a natural pyramid, a natural sun-linked afterlife structure. The Greeks, greatly impressed by these tombs, called them *hypogea*, "things under the earth." It was here that most of the New Kingdom pharaohs were buried between c. 1492 BC (Thutmose I, Tomb KV38) and c. 1069 BC (Rameses XI, KV4), as well as at least one queen-pharaoh (Hatshepsut, c. 1458 BC, KV20) and some top civil servants.

Sety I's tomb (c. 1279 BC, KV17) was rediscovered by the Italian adventurer, circus strongman and mercantilist, amateur archeologist Giovanni Battista Belzoni, in 1817. (In the same year, he became the first modern European to explore the sand-covered Abu Simbel Temple!). It is the most intricate, the biggest, and to my mind, the most beautiful of all the tombs in the Valley of Kings. It has ten major chambers joined by six straight, descending corridors over a distance of perhaps more than 750 feet. It is decorated with finely executed paintings illustrating worship of Re in the *Litany of Re*, the worship of Sety himself as Osiris upon death, *djed* pillars and some of the most complete texts and scenes from various funerary texts like the *Book of the Dead*, the *Book of Gates* and the *Book of Amduat*. The complete text of *The Book of the Divine Cow* and its tale of how Re was tempted to destroy rebellious mankind and then saved it from destruction and retired from governing mankind is also inscribed on its walls. Its funerary chamber, or Hall of Gold, with its six pillars and vaulted ceiling of astronomical themes is breathtaking. Researchers continue to excavate the totality of this tomb — and the fourth generation of the Abd el-Rassul family of tomb robbers (since the 1881 find in Inhapy's Deir el-Bahri cache), continue to claim that there is much more to be found in Sety's tomb.

The world was amazed by the treasures and beauty discovered in 1922 by Howard Carter (1874–1939), in Pharaoh Tutankhamun's (c. 1333–1326) KV62 tomb. That is the only tomb of a pharaoh ever found which had not been looted, but it is one of the smaller tombs in the Valley of Kings. The Cairo Museum exhibits an astounding collection of some of the 5000 objects found in KV62. It includes a finely carved golden mummy mask of Tutankhamun, idealized so that his *ba* and *ka* souls could recognize him in the afterlife; 143 amulets, bracelets and jewels in his mummy wrappings; a gold *nemes* headdresses with their Wadjit uraeus snake and Nekhbet vulture; a magnificent scarab resurrection pectoral; *was*-scepter divine dominion fetishes, gold and lapis lazuli crooks, flails and daggers, golden finger and toe stalls and sandals, intricately decorated canopic jars with Tutankhamun's innards, vases, lamps, weapons and shields, musical instruments, boat shrines, chairs, headrests and beds, chests of linen clothing and food and even chariots for his horses and of course a full set of 365 *ushabti* statuettes and their 36 overseers to do the menial work for Tutankhamun in the *Aaru* Field of the Reeds in the afterlife. Tutankhamun's mummy was placed within four successive shrines which contained a stone sarcophagus which in turn enclosed three anthropoid hieroglyphically inscribed coffins, the last one made of 242 pounds of gold.

As stated earlier, Egypt functioned on the basis of two economies — one for the living and the other mobilizing thousands of craftsmen, artists and laborers, entirely and extravagantly devoted to preparing for the needs of the dead. If ever any proof of that was needed, it can be found not only in the small tomb of the minor pharaoh Tutankhamun, but in the consequential question that it raises.

What magnificence could have been discovered in the tomb of Egypt's greatest builder, Rameses II (c. 1279–1213 BC, KV7), one of the biggest tombs in the Valley of Kings (8,823 square feet with a burial chamber of 1948 square feet)? It has been flooded, looted and also partially dismantled by priests, foremen and workers, as the Turin "Strike" Papyrus tells us. And what magnificence would have been found in the more than 110 corridors and rooms of KV5, the immense tomb Rameses II built for 52 of his sons, had it too not been repeatedly flooded, robbed and dismantled by priests? KV5 was rediscovered in 1987 by the University of California/Berkeley Theban Mapping Project and has almost definitively been identified as the tomb of many of Rameses II's sons.

Fear of looting, or the rapacious attitude of the 21st Dynasty (c. 1069–747 BC) priests paradoxically also led to several extraordinary discoveries in the

Theban Necropolises. In 1881, Emil Brugsch (1842–1930), excavated a cache in Inhapy's Deir el-Bahri tomb (TT320) in a deep and elaborately built secret shaft; it contained 40 reburied royal mummies including some of Egypt's greatest pharaohs like Rameses II, Sety I, Thutmose III (1479–1425) and Ahmose (1550–1525) and the mummy of Maatkara (fl.c. 1000 BC), both "the god's wife" of Amun and the chief priestess, *dwat netjer*, "Divine Adoratrice," of Karnak and coffins, canopic jars, statuettes and numerous other objects. In 1891, Georges Daressy (1864–1938) found a 508-foot long cache in Deir el-Bahri II (Bab el-Gasus); it contained 153 mummies and 200 sculptures of priests. In 1898, Victor Loret (1859–1946) found Amenhotep II's tomb (KV35) in the Valley of Kings; in addition to Amenhotep II, it contained a cache of 14 royal mummies, including Amenhotep III (c. 1390–1352 BC) and Merenptah (c. 1213–1203 BC) and one of the biggest collections of royal funerary objects. In all, Loret found 16 tombs in Thebes.

The private tombs of the notables in western Thebes were also impressive and magnificently decorated structures. Senemut, Hatsheput's royal steward, the architect of her mortuary temple and perhaps her lover, built two fabulous tombs for himself — TT71, with one of the first pillared porches and chapels decorated with paintings and a curious frieze of Hathor heads, and TT353, which contained the first known ceiling decorated with astronomical themes. The reliefs and inscriptions in Rekmira's (Thuthmose III's, c. 1479–1425 BC, fiercely loyal vizier) TT100 provide us with a huge amount of information on a vizier's duties, on the crafts, agriculture and trade. It contains reliefs of tribute brought to Egypt by Nubians, Syrians and Cretans, illustrating their ethnic characteristics and an array of typical African animals. The carved reliefs in Ramose's TT55, a vizier under both Amenhotep III and Akhenaten (c. 1390–1336 BC) were among the finest produced during his time, especially those of Akhenaten and Nefertiti. Ipy's TT217, a sculptor in Rameses II's era (c. 1279–1213 BC) is small, but full of extraordinary paintings, including many everyday, garden and agricultural scenes and one with a *shaduf* (an irrigation water wheel) being used.

The nearby craftsmen's family tombs in Deir el-Medina are touching — for their simple belief in the afterlife, their less rigid artistic style and their relatively simple construction. Many were topped with small brick imitation pyramids, which was a clear indication that the use of this pharaonic symbol had now spread to all classes of society. Some of these tombs were magnificently decorated, like that of Sennedjem's (a royal official, c. 1270 BC) TT1. This tomb was not looted and has a beautiful vaulted funerary chamber entirely decorated with magical reliefs, scenes of his wife and him revering the gods, an expressive scene of Re as a cat and the serpent Apophis, a scene of Sennedjem playing the *senet* board game and a mural of the Field of Reeds in the afterlife with the deceased farming and reaping and fabulous plants and fruit trees. TT3 of the craftsman/foreman Pashedu (fl. 1294–1279 BC) has a Horus falcon and a curious *wedjat* Horus eye with an arm extending an offering to Osiris and paintings of Anubis crouched on sarcophagi.

With the adventure begun by Imhotep and the building of the Step Pyramid in c. 2660 BC, Egyptian architecture became the high point of world architecture and maintained this position for more than 2000 years. Over that period and longer, hundreds of pyramids and temples and thousands of massive tombs and tall obelisks were built in Egypt.

EGYPTIAN MONUMENTAL ARCHITECTURE IN THE HISTORY OF BUILDING

The comparison between ancient Egyptian monumental architecture and other magnificent structures in the history of mankind is startling. In their day (c. 2589–2532 BC), Khufu's and Khepren's Giza pyramids were the largest and tallest structures ever built and it was almost 4500 years before a taller structure was completed: Cologne's Kölner Dom Cathedral (1880). No larger structure than the Karnak Temple Precinct was built before the 20th century and it still remains the largest space ever built for a religious purpose. No bigger or more extravagant tomb complex than the Valley of the Kings has ever been built. Of course, all of mankind's great structures —Egyptian or otherwise — shared a common denominator of great beauty, but for thousands of years the Egyptians had the corner on massive scale and (for the most part) technological superiority.

The Sumerian *ziggurat* temples, built from about 2200 BC, were usually about 125 feet by 170 feet at their base and averaged 40 to 80 feet in height. The Babylon Marduk Ziggurat (probably the Tower of Babel in the Bible), when it was restored by King Nebuchadnezzar at the late date of c. 605-561 BC, managed to rise to 325 feet.

Beyond the interminable arguments about the exact size and site of Solomon's Temple Precinct in Jerusalem, the *Har Habbayit Yhwh*, the Temple Mount (finished c. 958 BC, perhaps partially rebuilt by Hezekiah, c. 715 BC and then by Zerubbabel, c. 520 BC), including porches, courts and chambers, perhaps had a perimeter of about 2000 cubits (3444 feet) and covered about 17 acres. The temple itself, without its side buildings, was probably a mere 180 by 90 feet and 50 feet high. According to Josephus in *Antiquities of the Jews* and *The Jewish Wars*, Herod's Temple Mount (built from c. 20 BC), began with an area of four stades, that is, only about 8.4 acres, before being enlarged to six stades, about 22.5 acres. The present Moslem *Al-Haram al-Sharif*, presumably on the site of the Temple Mount, with the *Dome of The Rock* and *Al Aqsa* Mosques, covers about 37 acres.

The Greek Temple of Artemis in Ephesus, Asia Minor (550 BC, rebuilt 356 BC), covered 1.5 acres. The Parthenon Temple to Athena on the Acropolis (450–330 BC), was 0.53 acres.

The great Christian cathedral builders raised more but not larger structures than the ancient Egyptians. The 107-foot wide central dome of the Hagia Sophia Church in Constantinople, finished in AD 537, was probably the most magnificent built to that date. Notre Dame Cathedral in Paris, one of the first truly monumental Christian churches, built between 1160 and 1350, is 427 feet by 157 feet inside its walls and its two towers rise to 223 feet. The Kölner Dom Cathedral, built from 1248 to 1880, has twin bell towers rising to 515 feet. St. Peter's Basilica in Rome (1626) is 452 feet tall and the total area of the Vatican covers 109 acres.

The Karnak Temple Precinct or the pyramids were bigger than several of any of the biggest Christian cathedrals combined.

The largest mosque ever built, the Shi'ite Great Friday Mosque (9th century AD) in Samarra, Iraq, covered 9.2 acres; it is now in ruins. The 10th-century Cordoba Mosque was 5.8 acres and the Damascus Umayyad Mosque (AD 715) covers 3.9 acres. The Sultan Ahmet "Blue Mosque" in Istanbul (1616) covers 1.14 acres, has six minarets, 260 windows and 30 cupolas. The *Al-Haram* Mosque in Mecca, including its vast courtyard arround the *Ka'ba*, now covers about 39 acres. The largest modern mosque, the Hassan II Mosque (1993) in Casablanca, has an area of 4.94 acres and a minaret which rises to 656 feet.

The great Indian temple builders eventually built more temples than ancient Egypt, but never built bigger temples — the Vishnu-Shiva Ranganathar Temple in Srirangam, Tamil Nadu, (c. 1335–1565 AD) was within a temple-city enclosure of consecrated and ordinary living sites of about 156 acres, the Krishna-Jagannatha Temple in Puri (c. AD 1198) rises to 200 feet and its perimeter is about 2625 feet and the Lingaraja Shiva Temple in Bhubaneshwar

(c. AD 1000) is 157 feet high and it sides are 492 feet. Benares, Hardwar and other Indian holy cities contained hundreds of impressive temples, but none came close to the dimensions of Egyptian temples.

It took almost 4500 years to build anything taller than the Khufu and Khephren pyramids and anything bigger than Karnak. It was only in 1943, with the completion of the Pentagon in Washington, with 6.5-million square feet of floor space, that the dimensions of Karnak were approached. Karnak was the epitome of ancient temple architecture.

Chapter 8.
The Social Context of the Egyptian Politico-Religious System

Revered Elite Rulers and The Ruled. The Pharaoh and His Subjects — A Sanctified Order

As a direct consequence of Egypt's approach to the sacred, its cosmogony, its mythology and its theocratic religion, the society was a sanctified hierarchical order. The gods ruled in all the elements of nature in the *pet*, the sky, and in the *Duat* underworld afterlife and the pharaoh-god ruled several broad classes of society with several sub-categories within these classes. This constituted a system of *imakhu*, a relationship between the pharaoh and all his subjects of the pharaoh. In practice, *imakhu* was only thoroughly applied to the enlarged family and entourage of the pharaoh who were linked to him by ties of blood, common upbringing and education, mutual economic interests and of course the divine will of the pharaoh.

The first, and at least physically closest, circle to the pharaoh was the group called the *henmemet*, the solar retinue, the sun folk. The *henmemet* were the bodyguards and personal attendants of the pharaoh. These roles even extended into the afterlife resurrection process in the sky of the pharaoh and the *henmemet* may have also been linked to the *Shemsu-Hor*, "the followers of Horus," giving them a mysterious and quasi semi-divine status.

The *pat*, the noblemen, or notables, were the second circle. This group of close associates of the pharaoh were all members of his enlarged family, until about 2500 BC.

The rest of Egyptian society were the commoners, the *rekhyt*, literally, lapwing birds. This term was used from about the beginning of the Old Kingdom (c. 2686–2181 BC) to designate the pharaoh's commoner subjects, including peasants and craftsmen; earlier, it designated only captives. Commoners, nobles and sun folk were categories that described not only the population of Egypt, but all of mankind.

This system of a small circle of "revered" rulers and a huge group of commoners probably emerged in the Old Kingdom and in the late part of that period was stabilized and then changed very little throughout Egyptian history. High appointments, including high priests, senior civil servants and high ranking military officers, were systematically made from the ranks of the elite *pat*, whose male members received an education from the scribes in all available fields of knowledge, presumably including administration techniques. Members of the *rekhyt* never received a formal education; pragmatically, boys generally leared the trade of their fathers and girls learned domestic skills.

This tight class system was similar to other societies of the time, and it would be unfair to judge it by modern standards. However, if we used modern terms wewould have to say that it was a totalitarian system which used all available means, beginning with societal and property structures, religion, and art, to perpetuate the wealth and privileges of the pharaoh and his ruling class. This fundamental inequality between the pharaoh and his (usually subservient and small) ruling class and all others was a primary cause for the strong tendency to maintain the status quo, once the ruling class had won, or to promulgate only gradual or merely theoretical reforms, such as the right to an afterlife for everyone. However, in some respects — women's rights and slavery — Egypt was an unusually mild society for its time.

THE *NETJER NEFER*, THE PHARAOH-GOD

"Pharaoh," the conventional term for the designation of the Egyptian king, seems to have been a Hebrew or Greek word, and came into use around 1000 BC. It was probably a deformation of the Egyptian term *per-aa*, the grand house, that is, the palace. Starting in about the New Kingdom (c. 1550 BC), the term *per-aa* was used by the Egyptians to designate both the palace and the ruler. Ancient terms for the king, the exact meaning of which remains unknown, continued to be used: *nisut* for divine king and *bity* for reigning king, but also indicating "he [the ruler] of the sedge and the bee," the south and the north.

Countless texts and images show that the pharaoh was unquestionably a god, a *ntr.nfr*, *netjer nefer*, a "perfect god." We have seen in Chapter 5 that the pharaoh was believed to have been the divine King of Egypt perhaps even before the earth and the gods existed and certainly the reverence was reinforced by everything from the signs at his birth, to his designation as "Horus in the nest," as future pharaoh, to his *kha*, coronation, to his link with Isis and her pedestal or throne headdress as the personification of the king's throne and as the mother of the god/king, and to the periodic regeneration in the *heb-sed* jubilees which magically assured that his powers could not wane. Roughly from the time of the unification, around 3100 BC, the pharaoh was seen as the incarnation of Horus; from about the middle of the Fourth Dynasty (c. 2566 BC, with the Pharaoh Radjedef), his godliness also derived from being the son of Re; and then from about Pharaoh Amenemhat I's time (c. 1985–1955 BC), he was a god because he was the son of Amun-Re.

The same 14 *ka* — double guardian souls and life principles — which flowed through Horus' or Re's veins also flowed through the veins of the pharaoh. He also alone possessed the *ba*, the roaming soul, before ceding soul and afterlife privileges to all Egyptians at the end of the Old Kingdom (c. 2181 BC).

However, as divine as all this made him, the "perfect god"/pharaoh was not as divine as a "great god," a *ntr.aA* or a *wr*, a *wer*. If any clearer definition of the pharaoh's divineness is possible, it would seem that he was among the "small gods," the *ndsw*, *nedsew*, the "small ones." However, the pharaoh was the only divine/human junction between the various forms of divinity.

This pharaoh-god was the divine head of a vast theocratic system, the pivot of all Egyptian religious, magical, political and economic life; and he was not only the divine King of Egypt, he was the divine King of the Universe, just as the gods Re, Geb, Osiris and Horus had ruled the universe before him.

The pharaoh was the high priest, over every single god in the pantheon. He delegated these duties to priests, but in art, it was usually the pharaoh who was depicted as carrying out temple rituals. The pharaoh, according to his sovereign desires, provided both vital, creative energy in the form of the *ka* and material subsistence to his people.

The pharaoh was a magician, a sorcerer. He had a team of magicians led by a chief sorcerer; Imhotep (fl.c. 2650 BC) and Hetepi (fl.c. 2063 BC) were two of the best known of these "chiefs of *heka*." But it was the pharaoh himself who possessed the greatest *heka*. He wore the all-powerful *uraeus* emblem/amulet on his *nemes* royal headdress, which was *weret-hekau*, "great of magic."

Because of his immense *heka*, the pharaoh magically kept things going right. The pharaoh-god was believed to be the omnipotent provider of all good things, of *ankh, udja, seneb*, life, prosperity, health, of everything that made life possible. He was "the good god" and "lived by *maat*," *ankh-em-maat*; he supervised the application of the *maat* principle, which in its primary form meant maintaining the primeval, natural order and harmony of the universe and protecting Egypt from disorder, *izfeh*, but it also meant maintaining naturally "true" and harmonious daily life in Egypt. The pharaoh was governor of the *maat*. He guaranteed the fertility of the land and cattle and the annual Nile fertilizing flood waters. He guaranteed the correct functioning of a system of courts of justice that any Egyptian could petition. He alone was responsible for vanquishing the evil enemies of Egypt. One of the most traditional depictions of the pharaoh is him holding a foreign prisoner by the hair and smiting him with a mace. The pharaoh, as the god-leader of the gods' people, was obviously supposed to win all the battles he engaged against other peoples — who were obviously villains — a responsibility which, of course, was not easy to fulfill and sometimes was not fulfilled even when victory was proclaimed.

Much like shamanistic sorcerers, the pharaoh was bedecked with amulets to protect him and with insignia indicating his divinity. These included the all-powerful *uraeus* cobra of the protectress of Lower Egypt, Wadjit, and the vulture of the protectress of Upper Egypt, Nekhbet, on his *nemes* royal headdress; the holy false beard; the divine bull's tail tied to his belt, the *was* scepter of divine dominion; and the royal *hekat* and *nekhakha*, the crook which symbolized his role as the guardian shepherd of the people and flail which symbolized majesty and dominion. In addition to the *hedjet* and *deshret* crowns of Upper and Lower Egypt, the pharaoh wore the *pschent* double intertwined crown of the Two Lands and the ritual *atef* crown, linked to Osiris and composed of the *hedjet*, two plumes and a disk. From the New Kingdom (c. 1550 BC), he also wore the *khepresh*, a blue helmet made of electrum, sometimes called the military crown.

Of all the pharaoh's amulets and insignia, none proved both his godliness and his supreme power in the world and protected him more than the *shenu*. The *shenu*, which might even be transformed into a huge sarcophagus for the dead pharaoh, was the supreme amulet. The *shenu* has come to be known as the "cartouche" — it was so named after a rifle cartridge, whose shape it resembled, by the French scientific team that accompanied Napoleon's occupying force in Egypt between 1798 and 1801.

The *shenu*-cartouche seems to have originated with the *shen* ring, a looped rope without beginning or end, symbolizing eternity and protection. The *shenu* was an elongated oval enclosed by a rope knotted at the bottom; it symbolized what the sun enclosed, that is, the entire universe. *Shenu* as a word meant endless, encircling eternity. From the Fourth Dynasty (c. 2613–2494 BC), the *shenu* as a royal cartouche was used to contain the hieroglyphs of the pharaoh's *nisut-bity* name, or praenomen throne name, linked to his sacred role as divine (*nisut*) and reigning (*bity*) ruler of the united lands. In the Fifth Dynasty (c. 2494–2345 BC), a second cartouche was added containing the pharaoh's nomen, or birth name, introduced by the title "Son of Re." By the Middle Kingdom (c. 20551–650BC), the pharaoh's royal titulary had five names, three proving his divinity and two linked to his role as leader of the Two Lands. The three other royal titles, in addition to the praenomen and nomen, were the Horus Name — which designated the pharaoh as the god Horus on earth — the *nebti* or "The Two Ladies," indicating the pharaoh's rule over the two regions — and the Golden Horus Name — linking the pharaoh to the sun, divinity, eternity, earthly gold and perhaps to Horus' victory over Seth. The four titles, in addition to the nomen birth name, were chosen at the pharaoh's coronation.

In the Early Dynastic Period (from c. 3100 BC), before the formal advent of the cartouche, the pharaohs' names were already magically protected in elaborately hieroglyphically designed arrangements resembling the cartouche. Several of these emblems, *serekh*, or "pre-cartouches," including those of Narmer, Aha and Den, engraved on clay seals have been identified. They depict a facade, the pharaoh's Horus name, and a falcon on top. In one case (Peribsen, c. 2700 BC), the *serekh* is topped by a Seth animal and in a few cases, by a Seth animal and a Horus falcon facing each other. Huni (c. 2637–2613 BC) was the first pharaoh to use the *shenu*/cartouche rather than the *serekh* to enclose his *nisut-bity*. Nyuserra (c. 2445–2421BC) in the Fifth Dynasty, added a second cartouche, enclosing his nomen. Gradually, the two-cartouche name, as the materialization of the pharaoh's divinely empowered names, became the norm.

The pharaoh's names, like every other Egyptian's, constituted a soul, the *ren* soul name, but they were also supreme names, they were god-given within the cartouches, magically protected him against enemy spells and protected his eternal existence, in this life and in the afterlife. Above all, the *shenu* protected the pharaoh against the lost of his *ren* name soul. Nevertheless, this great protection sometimes turned out to be inefficient. The obliteration, the hammering out of a pharaoh's *shenu*, his names — and thus his second death and eternal elimination — was the terrible posthumous punishment meted out to Pharaoh Akhenaten, in the 14th century BC, and others.

More prosaically, the pharaoh's names were often an indication of what they thought of themselves, what were their theological preferences and what were their policy priorities. They sometimes even changed their titularies to reflect changed events in their reigns.

The *serekh* Horus name of Aha (c. 3100 BC), perhaps the conqueror of Lower Egypt and the founder of unified Egypt, was "the fighter," the "Horus who fights." Khasekhemwy's (c. 2686 BC) *serekh* name means "The Two Powers are Crowned," a reference to peace between the rival gods Horus and Seth, following Peribsen's rejection of Horus in favor of Seth as royal protector god.

The Golden Horus name of Userkaf's (c. 2494–2487 BC) was "He who puts Maat into practice," meaning that it was he alone who maintained the natural order of the universe — and this at a time of rising priestly power. The Golden Horus name of Thutmose III (c. 1479–1425 BC), Egypt's greatest empire builder, was "Powerful of strength, Holy of Appearance," Thutmose IV's (c. 1400–1390 BC), was "Strong of arm, oppressor of the Nine Bows," but in fact, he sought peace with West Asian rivals.

Khufu's (Cheops, c. 2589–2566 BC) nomen was "Khnum protects me." The nomen of Amenemhat I (c. 1985–1955 BC), who promoted Amun to chief god status, was "Amun is at the head." Rameses I's (c. 1295–1294 BC) nomen was "Re created him." When he became the Atenist monotheistic Akhenaten, Amenhotep IV (c. 1352–1336 BC) changed his nomen from "Amun is satisfied, the god ruler of Thebes" to "One who is useful to Aten."

Horemheb's (c. 1323–1295 BC) praenomen was "He whom Re has chosen, the Son of Re," reflecting worries about his legitimacy, while the powerful Rameses II (c. 1279–1213 BC), who had no such qualms, chose the praenomen "Strong in right is Re."

The full titulary of Rameses II was: "Horus, Strong Bull, beloved by Maat. The Two Ladies, the Protector of Egypt, he who strikes the foreign countries. The King of Upper Egypt and Lower Egypt. Usermaatra-Setepenra (Strong in right is Re). The Son of Re, Rameses, (Re created him), meryamun (beloved of Amun), given life eternally like his father Re."

Of course, as a god, the pharaoh was not subject to death. That had been so even before the rise of Osirisian afterlife concepts around 2375 BC. Before and after Osiris, the pharaoh's correct application of the *maat* system was the main criteria for his afterlife and it was always taken for granted that he did apply it fully. But several Pyramid Texts utterances show that a judgment took place, even if it was quasi-automatic and devoid of moral implications. Nevertheless, pharaohs like Pepy I seemed to want nothing to do with judges: "I...shall not be arrested...nor cited to the magistrates...neither executed, nor found guilty." And as we see in numerous utterances, all the pharaohs proclaimed themselves "righteous" and feared, and were ready to cajole or bribe the ferryman Mahaf, "Face Behind," whose job was to boat them over to the Field of Rushes in the sky. Mahaf seems to have been delegated by Re to act reluctantly and to submit the pharaohs to some kind of a test (much like the ferryman Urshanabi on the "waters of Death" in the Sumerian Gilgamesh tale).[127]

The dead pharaoh's divine afterlife rights were immense. The pharaoh went into "lightland" in the sky, where he enjoyed an eternal afterlife, with Re and the other gods and goddesses becoming his brothers and sisters in the solar boat, "the barque of millions of years," from where they governed the universe. Utterance 571 claims that "...the King will not die...for the King is an Imperishable Star..."

Utterance 263, in Pharaoh Unas' (Wenis, c. 2375-2345 BC) pyramid tells us: "The sky's reed-floats are launched for Unas, That he may cross on them to lightland, to Re..." Utterance 467 in Pepy I's (c. 2321-2287 BC) pyramid notes: "I am not for the earth, I am for the sky." Utterance 306 exalts: " 'How lovely to see! How pleasing to behold!' say they, namely the gods, when this god, when you [the king, Pepy] ascend to the sky." In Utterance 486, Pepy I even identifies himself with the primordial situation before creation and is certain of the aid of Re and the other gods: "Pepy was born in *Nun* [primordial chaos], Before there was sky, Before there was earth...The Enneads will support him, Re will take Pepy by the hand, To where a a god may be..."

Utterance 373 in Teti's pyramid says: "...The gatekeeper comes out to you...Takes you into heaven, to your father Geb, He rejoices at your coming...Kisses you, caresses you...The hidden ones worship you..." Utterance 407 states: "Teti will take his pure seat in the bow of Re's bark: The sailors who

---

127. Faulkner, R.O., *The Ancient Egyptian Pyramid Texts*, Ut. 486, p. 173 and ferryman judgement Utterances 516 to 522, pp. 190-195.

row Re, they shall row Teti! The sailors who convey Re about lightland, They shall convey Teti about lightland!...Teti will command one greater than he!"

Pharaoh Unas in Pyramid Text Utterances 273-274 made the most extravagant claims of all. Unas even believed that his afterlife rights included the right to eat other gods in the sky in order to appropriate their powers: "...At seeing Unas rise as power, A god who lives on his fathers, Who feeds on his mothers!... Unas is the bull of heaven...Who lives on the being of every god, Who eats their entrails...Unas is he who eats men, feeds on the gods...Cooks meals of them...in his dinner pots...eats their magic, swallows their spirits: Their big ones are for his morning meal, Their middle ones for his evening meal, Their little ones for his night meal...And the pots are scraped for him with their women's legs." Of course, Unas also saw himself as wielding immense power in the afterlife, as being "crowned as lord of lightland."

In Utterance 218, Unas and some others pharaohs who used this spell, literally proclaimed that they were appropriating Osiris' role as King of the Dead: "O Osiris...This King comes indeed, importuning [?] the Nine [the gods and goddesses of the Heliopolitan Ennead], an imperishable spirit, who surpasses you, who is like you, who is more weary than you, who is greater than you, who is more hale than you, who shouts more loudly than you, and your time yonder is no more."[128]

The vast and intricate system which empowered the pharaoh as a god, as the creator of everything and as the provider of everything necessary for life is well illustrated by the words of Sehetep-ieb-Re, Amenemhat III (c. 1855–1808 BC) Chief Treasurer. The inscription on his Abydos stele (now in the Cairo Museum) states: "I cause that ye know a counsel of eternity...Worship King Ni-maat-Re (Amenehat III), living forever...He is Re...He is one who illuminates the Two Lands more than the sun disc. He is one who makes the land greener than [does] a high Nile...He supplies them who tread his path. The king is a *Ka*...the Khnum of all bodies. The begetter who creates the people...the Bastet who protects the Two Lands...there is no tomb [no afterlife] for a rebel against his majesty..."[129]

Of course, this text is not an isolated declaration — over more than 2500 years, the dithyrambic glorification of the pharaoh-god and absolute

---

128. *Ibid.*, Utterances 571, 467, 306, 486 and 218, pp. 226, 156, 94, 47, 45 and 46. Lichtheim, Miriam, *Ancient Egyptian Literature, Volume I*, Utterances 263, 373, 407 and 273-274, pp. 34, 41-42, 43-44 and 36-37.

129. Wilson, John in *Ancient Near Eastern Texts Relating to the Old Testament*, p. 431.

subservience to him were among the central themes of Egyptian religion, literature and the autobiographical declarations on steles and in tombs. Everywhere in relation to the pharaoh, we find one of Egypt's most fundamental and ringing declarations of good wishes and praise — *ankh udja seneb*, life, prosperity, health!

Weni, a high official under Pharaohs Teti, Pepy I and Mernere (c. 2345–2278 BC) in the Old Kingdom goes to great pains to prove that he was loved and appreciated by these pharaohs. He noted in his Abydos tomb-chapel autobiography (now in the Cairo Museum): "As King Mernere who lives forever is august, exalted, and mighty more than any god, so everything came about with the ordinance commanded by his *ka*."

Ikhernofret, a high official under Senwosret III (c. 1874–1855 BC) in the Middle Kingdom who was in charge of the annual Abydos Osiris festival (the so-called mysteries of Osiris' death and resurrection) proudly stated on his Abydos funerary stele (now in the British Museum): "...my majesty...relying on your doing everything to the heart's content of my majesty...I did all that his majesty commanded in executing my lord's command for his father Osiris..."

The mindset that the pharaoh was divine was such that in one of Egypt's most popular tales, the Twelfth Dynasty (c. 1985-1795 BC) *Tale of Sinuhe*, a court official, Sinuhe, on the run in the West Asian *Retjenu* and fearing for his life due to the "turmoil" caused by the apparent murder of Amenemhat I (c. 1985–1955 BC), describes Senwosret I (c. 1965–1920 BC) before he had even officially become pharaoh as "...a god without peer, No other comes before him; He is lord of knowledge, wise planner, skilled leader, One goes and comes by his will."[130]

This absolute reverence for the pharaoh was not limited to the notables; even the striking, angry, starving craftsmen at Deir el-Medina during Rameses III's reign (c. 1184–1153 BC), who stated their demands in no uncertain terms, blamed the problems on the Overseer and lauded the pharaoh, certain that as soon as he was informed, the situation would be corrected.

The attitude of the Deir el-Medina craftsmen to the pharaoh may not have been hypocrisy and kow-towing, or at least not exclusively that. Numerous tales and texts attest to the fact that pharaohs did indeed insist that justice should be correctly dispensed, even to the poor. The Middle Kingdom (c. 2055-1650 BC) tale of *The Protests Of The Eloquent Peasant* movingly relates how the peasant Knup-

---

130. Lichtheim, Miriam, *Ancient Egyptian Literature, Volume I*: Weni, p. 22, Ikhernofret, p. 124, Sinuhe, p. 225.

Anup, robbed of his meager goods by a person of higher standing, finally wins justice in the courts at the prompting of the pharaoh; the peasant's words were "more pleasing [to his Majesty's] heart than anything in this entire land." Thutmose III told Vizier Rekhmire: "See to it that all is done according to the law, That all is done exactly right...Do not judge unfairly...Regard one you know like one you do not know..."[131]

Of course, the pharaoh was also the greatest warrior who won all the battles almost single-handedly, even when in fact historical documents prove that he did not win. Rameses II (c. 1279–1213 BC) did not manage more than a stalemate against the Hittites at Kadesh in c. 1274, but the *Bulletin*, carved on the walls of many temples, notably Karnak, Luxor and Abu Simbel, noted that "The strong-Bull-beloved-of-Maat, the King of Upper and Lower Egypt...mounted 'Victory-in-Thebes', his great horse, and started out quickly alone by himself...His Majesty slew the entire force of the Foe from Khatti...and His Majesty was alone, none other with him."[132]

Of course, the pharaoh was also the greatest sportsman: "If he [Thutmose III, c. 1479–1425 BC[spent a moment of recreation by hunting in any foreign country, the number of that which he carried off is greater than the bag of the entire army." As to Amenhotep II (c. 1427–1400 BC), "...he rowed at the stern of his falcon-boat as the *stroke* for two hundred men...He drew three hundred stiff bows...He trained horses without their equal: they would not grow tired when he took the reins, nor would they sweat (even) at a high gallop."[133]

Even in the Late Period, with Egypt suffering from a dislocation of the very foundations of its religion and society, we find the same glorification of the pharaoh. Even the next to last indigenous pharaoh of Egypt, Nectanebo I (c. 380–362 BC) was described this way: "She [the goddess Neith] raised his majesty above millions...She enslaved for him the people's hearts, And destroyed all his enemies..."[134]

Despite the pharaoh's seemingly airtight system of divine titles, magical powers and potent amulets, his unlimited glorification and the dependence of everybody on his good will, the pharaohs did not always succeed in convincing

---

131. Wilson, John in *Ancient Near Eastern Texts Relating to the Old Testament*, p. 410 and Lichtheim, Miriam, *Ancient Egyptian Literature, Volume II*: pp. 22-23.

132. Lichtheim, Miriam, *Ancient Egyptian Literature, Volume II*: pp. 60-62.

133. Wilson, John in *Ancient Near Eastern Texts Relating to the Old Testament*, pp. 243 and 244.

134. Lichtheim, Miriam, *Ancient Egyptian Literature, Volume III*, p. 87.

people (or themselves) that they were real, omnipotent gods. Opposing the divine pharaoh supposedly was always doomed to failure, but plots and revolts by members of the royal family, the *harem*, high priests, notables, nomarchs and generals were frequent, and such events could not have occurred had the pharaoh been truly and roundly perceived as a god. Amenemhat I (c. 1985–1955 BC), who was not a member of the royal family — his father was the priest, Sesostris, and his mother, a Nubian, Nofret — and who fought his way to the throne, seems to have survived an assassination attempt, taken extreme measures to prevent further attempts, and may have nevertheless been murdered. Rameses III (c. 1184–1153 BC) may have been murdered as a result of a plot by one of his minor wives; that incident led to the execution of numerous officials and their wives. The x-ray examination of the "boy-king" Tutankhamun's (c. 1336–1327 BC) skull has revealed traces of a hemorrhage, which makes the circumstances of his death mysterious.

A major decline in the pharaohs' authority clearly took place during the First Intermediate Period (c. 2181-2055 BC) when many local rulers vied for power after a general economic collapse had occurred. Several other periods of decline in the pharaoh's powers or a succession of weak pharaohs occurred in Egyptian history. These declines usually occurred because the administrative and religious elite, headed by the high priests and nomarchs, temporarily confiscated much of the pharaohs' politico-religious-economic power. Volume II will discuss the case from the time of Rameses IV (c. 1153-1147 BC) and into the Third Intermediate Period (c. 1069–747 BC) and beyond, when Egypt sunk into a long and generalized decline. Foreigners who had settled in Egypt sometimes seized power and created their own pharaonic dynasties, as in the 22nd and 23rd Libyan Dynasties (c. 945–715 BC), or when a dislocated, divided Egypt fell to the former Nubian vassals who created the 25th Kushite Dynasty (c. 747–656 BC); this further decreased respect for the pharaoh. During times when Egypt was being conquered by other world powers like Assyria (669 BC), Persia (525 and 343 BC), Greece (332 BC) and Rome (30 BC), it seems highly doubtful that the the pharaoh was confidently considered omnipotent.

However, whatever the period — prosperous or decadent — many pharaohs clearly sensed some skepticism concerning their divinity or at least their "small" divine status and found it prudent to go a step further by decreeing themselves as fully divine as the greatest of the gods. This tendency seems to have existed as early as Pharaoh Djoser (c. 2667–2648 BC). Amenhotep III (c. 1391–1352 BC) and Rameses II (c. 1279–1213 BC) built great temples for their personal worship while they were still alive, although generally, cults to the pharaoh were not systematic, except in their mortuary temples after death. Hatshepsut (c. 1473–1458 BC), although she had usurped the throne, not only made the usual claims to the "perfect god" title of a pharaoh and to being born of Amun and her mother (Queen Ahmose), but particularly insisted on her "divineness." The inventor of proto-monotheism, Amenhotep IV (Akhenaten), not only accentuated the usual divineness of the pharaoh, but decreed that only he knew the sole god Aten and access to Aten could only be obtained through him.

Perhaps Rameses II went furthest down this road of extravagant deification by putting himself on a par, or even higher, at the Abu Simbel Temple, with "the great gods" Re-Horakhte, Amun-Re and Ptah. But Amenhotep III, Horemheb (c. 1323–1295 BC), Mentuhotpe II (c. 2055–2004 BC) and several other pharaohs took variants of the same path.

In Amenhotep III's case, a truly surrealistic relief illustrating his full-fledged divinity has survived in the Soleb Temple near Wawa and the third cataract of the Nile in Nubia, where both Amun-Re and Amenhotep III were the revered gods. It shows Amenhotep III as pharaoh making an offering to himself as *Nebma'atre* (his praenomen throne name, "Re is the Lord of Maat — of order, of truth") in the combined forms of a moon god and a pharaoh.

Even if he was not as divine as the other gods, the key to and the justification of the pharaoh's power always remained his status as a god. This was the case right to the very last indigenous Egyptian pharaoh (Nectanebo II, c. 360–343 BC).

Of course, it was in the obvious interest of the pharaoh to maintain the concept of his divinity, but most of the time it was also in the interest of the ruling class, who could legitimately fear that without a divine pharaoh the entire pyramid of the Egyptian class system and values might collapse, putting an end to their own power and privileges. The elite also depended on the pharaoh's generosity for the afterlife — it was the pharaoh who provided them with a plot of land for their tomb and with several of the key elements which constituted this tomb, like the sarcophagus, the offering table and the false door. It was the pharaoh who granted permission and was the intercessor for making the vital offerings, *hetep*, to the dead — *hetep di nesu*, "an offering which the king gives," was inscribed on the tomb false doors and offering tables.

During the Early Dynastic Period and the early part of the Old Kingdom, the pharaoh was the divine owner of the bulk of Egypt's agricultural land and all its resources, in particular its gold stocks. He allocated some of this land to his family, the high priests, the nomarchs and members of his small standing army and reserved vast domains to provide resources for the building and upkeep of his pyramids, temples, and palaces. The vast *hetep*, system of funerary and afterlife offerings for his tomb, sometimes called *aut*, mobilized incredibly huge resources.

From about the Sixth Dynasty (from c. 2345 BC), the peasants and craftsmen were theoretically free and could own property, but this probably only concerned a small middle class. Moreover, given the system of heavy taxation and severe punishments for default, indirect ownership by the pharaoh and his entourage remained the dominant reality. At least from the late New Kingdom, in Rameses III's time (c. 1184–1153 BC), the temple clergies, and especially the Theban Amun-Re the pharaoh in their ownership of farmland, serfs, servants and slaves.

Royal polygamy as such is only clearly attested from the Thirteenth Dynasty (c. 1795–1650 BC), but it seems that in addition to his chief wife, the *hemet nisut weret*, "the great royal wife," the pharaoh always had at least several other wives, favorites — *hib-ieb*, one who is in the heart — and tens and sometimes hundreds of concubines. He frequently married his sisters and sometimes his daughters, despite the fact that exogamous and monogamous relations were the general rule for most Egyptians. He had tens and sometimes hundreds of children, who also frequently intermarried. Perhaps the record for the hypersexual activity, or hyper paternity, of a pharaoh was attained by Rameses II (c. 1279–1213 BC), reputed to have had as many as 200 wives (some of them near relatives) and concubines and perhaps as many as 111 sons and 51 daughters.

The pharaoh was served by thousands of servants and slaves. He conscripted hundreds of thousands of people to build canals, roads, pyramids, tombs, temples and palaces, either for his own personal benefit or for what he decided was in the divine and national interest. He amassed vast surplus wealth in this manner at hardly any cost except for the housing and feeding of the conscripts. Even this vast wealth sometimes proved to be insufficient to maintain the incredibly onerous afterlife system of mummification, tombs, afterlife furnishings and art and offerings (see Volume II, Chapter 1).

Egypt never developed an authentic monetary economy, even after coins were invented in the 7th century BC (apparently by the Anatolian Lydians). From the pharaoh down to the poorest peasant, wealth and remuneration were measured by property, gold, silver and other metals, cattle, agricultural produce, and crafted goods. Taxes for political and religious purposes were paid in labor, land, goods and agricultural produce. During the New Kingdom (c. 1550 BC), various metals, such as silver, gold and copper, were used as standards of value, as *hedj*, as a kind of money. Some of these standards bore the seal of temple treasuries. The curious effect of all this is that while coins, and especially Lydian coins, never contained their announced value in gold, silver or electrum, the Egyptian non-monetary standards constituted exact values.

RICH AND PRIVILEGED: THE ROYAL FAMILY, TOP ADMINISTRATORS AND GENERALS

The pharaoh's enlarged family was the backbone of his political, economic, military and religious administration in the first centuries of pharaonic rule, and throughout Egypt's history members of the pharaoh's family held key posts. The royal family frequently included hundreds, and sometimes thousands, of people. The second circle — the *pat* associates, notables — linked to the pharaoh in the *imakhu* system, were members of the pharaoh's enlarged family, at least until about 2500 BC. These people enjoyed immeasurable wealth, and extraordinary privileges. Upon death, they were lavishly mummified and buried in fabulous tombs.

The *pat* — high priests, senior civil servants, the nomarch-governors of the *sepat*/nome provinces and top generals — enjoyed privileges in life and death which today would only be possible for billionaires. The political leaders lived in luxurious properties along the Nile and "employed" hundreds of servants and slaves. Their properties were usually totally self-sufficient in terms of emmer wheat, barley, vegetables, fowl, fish, fruit and wine and sometimes for crafted goods.

The top position among the notables, at least from about the Second Dynasty (c. 2890–2686 BC), was probably the *tjaty*, a kind of prime minister, whom we now usually refer to as the vizier. The *tjaty* was the chief administrator of Egypt. He was often simultaneously the *imn-r-kat nesw*, the Overseer of Royal Works, who managed the entirety of the pharaoh's properties. The vizier was also in charge of justice and as such held the title of priest of Maat; in this role, he was assisted by an assembly of advisers, the *kenbet*. He supervised the Overseer of the Seal, the head of the treasury, with its vast stocks of gold and other precious minerals, mostly garnered from foreign looting campaigns and tribute levied from vassal states. Two generals, the chiefs of soldiers and military supplies; a director of the pharaoh's construction projects; and a chief steward of agriculture and royal estates also served under him. From Pepy II's time (c. 2278–2184 BC), there were two viziers, one for the north and one for the south.

The *hery-tep a'a*, ("great overlord") nome nomarch, was usually a son or a grandson of the pharaoh, a *sa-nisut*, a prince, who carried the titles "First Under the King" and "Companion of the King (*reht-nisut*)." He was in charge of maintaining the nome irrigation, canals and roads, managing the local police and militia forces, and overseeing the rendering of local justice. He supervised the work of the peasants and craftsmen and remunerated them in kind. He also was often the mayor of his nome capital and oversaw the work of the other mayors (*hery-tep* or *haty*).

There was considerable interpenetrating between the highest classes. Major functions could be held consecutively or concurrently and it was not unusual for a high ranking soldier or a nomarch to also be a high-ranking priest.

As members of the pharaoh's enlarged family, the top administrators, priests and soldiers probably numbered no more than about 5000 people until about 2500 BC. After 2500 BC, top administrators and priests were more and more numerous and so, frequently, positions had to be filled by non-family members. They too perpetuated the unequal class system by continuing to monopolize most of the surplus wealth. The office of the nomarch gradually became a largely hereditary function. In addition to their privileged religious rights and due to the delegation they received from the pharaoh, the nomarchs controlled most of Egypt's surplus production.

THE CLERGY GAINS WIDESPREAD POWERS

Given Egypt's theocratic organization, it is almost redundant to say that the priestly class played a central role in society, in matters of religion, politics, economics, art, education, medicine, sorcery, secret teachings and popular amusements organized alongside religious festivals. This power sometimes slid into almost absolute political and economic power. The question can nevertheless be asked whether it was not above all their immense wealth which was the key lever of their power.

In Egypt's first economy, the economy of this life, the priests were landlords, producers, controllers, tax agents and receivers and traders of goods in addition to their priestly tasks. In the economy of the afterlife, the net value of what the priests controlled was perhaps even greater than that of the first economy — mummification, funerary rituals, tombs, art work, furnishings, funerary texts, amulets and perpetual offerings and prayers. The high priests were the equivalent of today's Chief Executive Officers at the head of multinational conglomerates in a global economy.

Major temple complexes were staffed by tens of thousands of priests, laymen and workers and tens of thousands of slaves. They included extensive plots of land, granaries, workshops, gardens and huge herds of animals. From the late New Kingdom (c. 1099 BC, Rameses XI's reign), with the rise of religious fundamentalism and totalitarianism, the economic power of the temples and especially of the Great Amun-Re Karnak Temple rivaled, and perhaps sometimes even surpassed, that of the pharaoh. By Rameses III's time (c. 1184–1153 BC), temple wealth was fabulous, as the Great Harris Papyrus from the end of his reign tells us. The staff of the Amun-Re Karnak Temple numbered 81,322, there were 421,362 heads of cattle, 620 square miles of farmed land and 83 boats. The Re Heliopolis Temple had a staff of 12,963 and 114 square miles of arable land; the Ptah Memphis Temple had a staff of 3,079 and 10,047 heads of cattle. Of course, the figures for staff excluded slaves, who were frequently numbered in tens of thousands. It has been estimated that by the end of Rameses III's reign, the temples owned about 30% of Egypt's farmlands and 20% of the population as serfs.[135]

An additional and considerable source of wealth for the priests, in all periods, was their right to deduct a portion of the offerings made for the upkeep of the temple, the servicing of tombs and the *hetep*, offerings, for the dead in the afterlife. These deductions were in addition to a free and abundant supply of the best food and drink which the people provided for the temple priests.

Egypt's clergy did not begin as a caste, but at various periods it became a virtual hereditary caste and eclipsed the power of the pharaohs. At other periods, it organized local theocracies holding power over several nomes. From about the Twentieth Dynasty (c. 1186–1069 BC), the Theban clergy's immense power

---

135. Breasted, James Henry, *Ancient Records of Egypt*, Vol. 4, pp. 92-107, Sauneron, Serge, *Les Prêtres de l'ancienne Egypte*, Editions du Seuil, Paris 1998, p.65 (American translation published by Cornell University Press, Ithaca, N.Y., 2000 and Wilson, John in *Ancient Near Eastern Texts Relating to the Old Testament*, p. 260.

enabled it to control the pharaoh's political and religious policies. This was done by the Amun-Re clergy, who disguised their decisions through an even greater than traditional use of oracles, who supposedly spoke and imposed the will of Amun. In this fundamentalist manner, the Theban clergy thoroughly subjected the reigning pharaoh to Amun, but of course in fact ruled with very little effective interference from the pharaohs and the nomarchs. The apex of Theban clerical fundamentalism came with the 21st Dynasty (c. 1069–945 BC). The Thebes/Amun clergy, backed by Libyan generals, then constituted a theocracy holding sway over all of Upper Egypt and Nubia and paying little or no attention to the pharaohs ruling from Tanis.

The *hem-netjer-tepey*, the high priests or prophets of the greatest temples, such as the *Uer-maa* (Great Seer) of the Re Temple in Heliopolis, the *Uer-kherep-hemutiu* (Grand Commander of the Artificers or craftsmen) in the Ptah Temple in Memphis or the First Prophet of Amun in the Amun Temple in Karnak/Thebes, led the performances of magical rituals and were believed to speak the words of the gods.

The main duty of the officiating high priest and his assistants was to serve the god-statues in the *ra per*, the *naos* inner temple sanctuaries: they would awaken them, wash, anoint, dress, feed with offerings three times a day, worship them and put them to sleep. Most temples had tens of ceremonies which were performed daily by the priests; in the Karnak Amun-Re Temple, there were 60 daily ceremonies.

The officiant (and many other categories of priests) was obliged to ritually wash four times in 24 hours, respect the alimentary taboos of his nome (and, especially, not eat fish), not wear woolen garments and be totally shaven of all bodily hair including his head), get circumcised and be sexually abstinent. The priests usually wore the popular Egyptian kilt, the *shendyt*, but added animal skins, sashes and pectorals.

During the Old and Middle Kingdoms (c. 2686–1650 BC), the great majority were not full-time or career priests, never went near the statues of the gods, and often did not have much religious knowledge. However, the material benefits which could accrue gradually led to a market in priestly positions, and some inheritance, despite the pharaohs' attempts to personally control the appointment of the main priests. By the Late Period (c. 747–332 BC), the priesthood was a hereditary caste, jealously guarding its privileges.

There was considerable specialization among the priests. There were *uab* (pure) ritual and purifier priests, *hem-netjer* (god's servant) temple assistants, lector priests (*hery heb*) who recited incantations in the temples and at funerals and joined the fighter priests (*ahawa*) for the practice of magical execration curses and healing incantations, *sem* and *hem-ka* priests who officiated at funerals, practitioners of mummification led by the *hery seshta*, "the overseer of mysteries" and caretakers of the dead, keepers-of-time or "hour priests" who observed the nightly movement of the stars and calculated the hours, days and months in the calendar, dream interpreters, purveyors of amulets and *heka*/spells and curses, musicians, *sewnew* healer-medical doctors, craftsmen-artists who established the plans for temple and tomb murals, and so on.

The *sesh* priests, scribes, were a particularly important category in the clergy and were highly respected. Thoth, the god of wisdom and writing, was the god of their corporation. They were employed for the writing of pharaonic decrees, administrative records, magical incantations and temple and funerary texts. Together with the notables, they represented the tiny literate elite and, as such, were the executing agents of a system which could not function without them. Their power and prestige were such that they frequently rose high in the political and religious hierarchy. More than most of the other categories of priests, they tended to transmit their title and knowledge to their sons.

Most of the lower-ranking priests, the *uab* and the *hem-netjer*, carried out practical duties related to the upkeep of the temples, the service of the pharaohs and the care of the dead in the afterlife. For most of these, duties were rotated and periods of service as priests were interspersed by longer periods of ordinary life within society.

There was also a category of priestesses, the *uabet*, including *hemet-netjer*. They were generally subordinate to the male priests, but sometimes reached positions of high religious authority, notably in the service of the mother and female principle goddess Hathor. From Hatshepsut's reign (c. 1473–1458 BC), the daughter of the First Prophet of Amun was known as *dwat netjer*, "divine adoratrice," a position which eventually evolved into being Chief Priestess of the Karnak Temple. Women also served as *heset-netjer* and *shem'a*, singers, and *habew*, dancers. The priestesses were usually tattooed, wore an abundance of necklaces and bracelets, and usually the same tight-fitting dress as other women. However, many images show that the *shem'a* and *habew* often performed naked. Apparently, the gods loved to listen to music and religious festivals featured female musicians. The Greek historian Diodorus Siculus, who wrote in the first century BC that most Egyptians considered it "undignified" to play music, was probably wrong. Unfortunately, we do not know what Egyptian music sounded like because they had no system of musical notation.

Another important task of the priests and priestesses was the organization of the *heb*, religious festivals. From the earliest times, these festivals were frequent both in the great temples and the minor, local ones. By Rameses II's time (c. 1279–1213 BC), there were 60 annual festivals. They usually featured the procession of statues of the gods, which were used as oracles by the people, animal sacrifices, the distribution of free food and drink, music, singing and dancing. There were also secret ceremonies linked to divine marriages and sexual intercourse among the gods and the goddesses, as well as secret ceremonies linked to Osiris' resurrection and the pharaoh and his divinity. Some of the key festivals were the New Year "Emergence of Sopdet" Festival, which opened the *akhet* inundation season, the Festival of the Nile, the Night of Tears, the Festival of the Raising of the Sky. From the New Kingdom (beginning c. 1550 BC), the *Opet* Festival, in which the statues of the gods were taken from the Karnak to Luxor Temples, and the Beautiful Festival of the Valley, in which the statues of Amun, Mut and Khons were taken in a maritime procession in golden shrines from the Karnak Temple to the sacred temple and mortuary Hathor site of Deir el-Bahri across the Nile, were key events. But it was of course, the *heb-sed*, the royal jubilee, in which the pharaoh's divinity and power were re-affirmed and which was theoretically held only once every 30 years, which was the supreme moment not only for the pharaoh, but also for the priests.

THE TEMPLE HOUSE OF LIFE: SCRIBES, HEALERS AND DREAMWEAVERS

Many categories of priests, especially starting in the New Kingdom (from c. 1550 BC), served in a unique Egyptian institution, the *per-ankh*, the "House of Life," which seems to have been an annex to all the major temples. We know of such Houses of Life in the Memphis-Ptah Temple, the Gebtu (Koptos)-Min Temple, the Abydos-Osiris Temple, the Esna-Khnum Temple, the Amarna-Aten Temple and Edfu-Horus Temple. People came there to learn, to be healed, to buy amulets and funerary texts and to participate in controlled dreaming. *Sesh-per-ankh*, scribes of the House of Life, *pa-hery-tep*, dream interpreters, doctor-healers, teachers, sorcerers and makers and sellers of amulets staffed the Houses of Life.

Religious texts were copied for temple and individual use; this was a major activity of the Houses of Life. From the New Kingdom, many priests were employed in preparing and selling copies of *The Book of the Dead* and other collections of funerary texts and spells inscribed with an individual's name and containing numerous paintings (known as vignettes). These books probably constituted a major source of income for the scribe priests.

Libraries, known as *per medjat* ("house of papyrus rolls"), were linked to the Houses of Life. They apparently contained a wide variety of papyri of incantations and magic ranging from how to kill demons, how to repel crocodiles, and how to protect oneself against the evil eye, to how to protect houses and cities. There were papyri on how to interpret dreams, papyri on pharaonic protocol ranging from the organization of pharaonic processions, protecting the pharaoh in his palace, worship and festival procedures, the processions of gods and temple life, military techniques and the capture of prisoners, and papyri on hunting, medicine, cosmology, myths and tales, mural painting and sculpting, etc. In other words, the *per medjat* contained all available information and knowledge of the time.

Medicine, intimately linked to incantations and amulets, to a medical *heka*, medical magic, was a major occupation of specialized priests, the *sewnew* doctors, in the Houses of Life. For the *sewnew*, there was no separation between their role as doctors and their role as priests of *heka*. For the Egyptians, like the Sumerians, illness, disease and accidents were caused by the gods and therefore had to be fundamentally treated by religious magic. However, this did not stop the pragmatic priests from inventing an elaborate, practical medical system, even if today this system sometimes seems comical and fantastic. The Egyptian medical system was considerably more advanced than those of its neighbors, for thousands of years. It included elements of what can be qualified as experimental scientific medicine, but unlike the Greeks and of course, Hippocrates (c. 460–377 BC), it was utterly incongruous for an Egyptian priest/doctor to search for purely mechanical physical causes for illness and disease and act accordingly.

The Egyptian *sewnew* priest-doctors dealt with a wide range of ailments, burns, injuries, bone fractures, dental problems, pain relief, female contraception and fertility, pregnancy testing and deformities like dwarfism. Egyptian medical texts give detailed anatomical descriptions and studies of the dental, circulatory, muscular and urinary systems. An impressive array of surgical instruments was used, including knives, hooks, drills, forceps, saws and shears. The medical treatments, called *seshau*, included numerous concoctions, techniques and surgery, but indispensable *ru* — incantations, spells and amulets, always accompanied them.

The Ebers Medical Papyrus (c. 1555 BC, but perhaps partially going as far back as 3000 BC), the Edwin Smith Medical Papyrus (c. 1600 BC, but probably partially dating from the Old Kingdom, c. 2686–2181 BC), the Kahun Medical Papyrus (c. 2100–1900 BC) and other papyri list more than a thousand cures. Some of these were allegedly invented and used by the gods.

Remedies included "water of pig's eyes mixed with honey," crushed pig's teeth, turtle's brains, ram's hair, excrement of various animals, the milk of women who had had a male child, extracts of papyrus and lotus flowers, plants and herbs from acacia to thyme — and *degem*, that is, plain old castor oil. Headaches, toothaches, hangovers, indigestion, food caught in the throat from poor swallowing, diseases of the eyes, ears, nose, throat, tongue, skin, stomach, hair, genitals and anus are listed, as well as some illnesses which cannot be identified — *wekhedu*, *genew* or *aaa*. And of course, there was a mysterious disease caused by foreigners — "the Asiatic disease" — which was conjured by repeating a spell four times to Re and Seth "over fresh moringa oil and residue of a cooking vessel [and] tortoise shell."[136]

No great criticism can be made of the description in the Ebers Papyrus of how Isis treated Re's headache — a mixture of coriander, poppy, juniper and wormwood mixed with *bit*, honey, and smeared over his head; but what are we to make of the Kahun Papyrus' recipe for contraception which includes eating crocodile dung, honey and sour milk? The systems recommended for verifying pregnancy were also astounding — sticking a few *hedjew*, onions, into the vagina and then deciding by the odor or by urinating on emmer and barley, with a sprout on emmer indicating a baby girl and on barley a baby boy. Fertility was ascertained by placing garlic in the vagina overnight; if the woman felt a taste of garlic in her mouth in the morning, it meant she was fertile.

The Houses of Life had many other functions. It was perhaps in the Memphis House of Life that the astute 12-month solar calendar of twenty-four hour days, plus five additional "epagomenal days" (named for the birthdays of Osiris, Isis, Horus, Seth and Nephthys) and together making 365 days, was invented around 2800 BC. This system was eventually corrected for leap years and major time rectifications every 1400 years.

---

136. Borghouts, J. F., *Ancient Egyptian Magical Texts*, p. 37.

It was probably in the Houses of Life that Egyptian mathematics, geometry and the art of writing were developed and perfected. It was also in the House of Life that the priests took charge of educating the young sons of the pharaoh's entourage and the notables. *Sebi*, the circumcision ceremony, was also practiced here. This practice was seemingly associated both with ritual requirements and a concept of cleanliness. It was usually reserved for pubescent male members of the pharaoh's entourage, the notables and the priests, although the sons of wealthy commoners were also sometimes circumcised, as reported on the First Intermediate Period (c. 2181-2055 BC) Naga-ed-Der Stele (now in the Oriental Institute of the University of Chicago). [137]

The interpretation of dreams seems to have been one of the most popular functions of priests connected to the Houses of Life. Dreaming was of course of great religious importance, well before (and after) ancient Egypt, but the Egyptians developed one of the most elaborate systems of controlled dreaming and dream interpretation in history. Provoked dreaming and dream interpretation became key elements in Egypt's *heka*, magic, system.

The Egyptians believed that the *reswet*, the dream, had its source in the realm of the divine, in the portion of the divine that every man carried within himself, that is the *ka*. For the Egyptians, the dream state was in a realm close to death, the realm where a man met his *ka* and where he was close to the gods and able to see and live experiences inaccessible in ordinary life. An individual dreamt with his *ka*, his double, his other, truer and more perfect self, and was plunged into a world of temporary death and into original chaos. In this state, he had access to the gods, to the demons and to the souls living in the *Duat* nether world. This enabled a person to be healed of illness in a dream, receive answers to questions and advice and orders from the gods, foretell events and act accordingly, either to obtain success or prevent disaster.

Such beliefs apparently led the Egyptians to adopt methods of provoked and controlled dreaming similar to those which are described in Shamanistic and other systems (most recently in Carlos Castaneda's books on the Mexican Yaqui esoteric system).

Of course, the sons of the gods, the pharaohs, were the privileged dreamers, the privileged receivers of messages from the gods; but it was usually the priests who interpreted these dreams, as they did all others. One of the most famous dreams by a pharaoh, that of the future Thutmose IV (c. 1400–1390), was

---

137. Wilson, John in *Ancient Near Eastern Texts Relating to the Old Testament*, p. 326.

inscribed on the stele between the paws of the *shesep ankh*, the "living image" the Great Sphinx of Giza. At that time, Horemakhet, "Horus in the Horizon," was believed to be the god incarnated in the Great Sphinx. "Horus in the Horizon-Khepri-Re-Atum — appeared in a dream to the young Thutmose, telling him he would one day become the Pharaoh of *Ta-Wy*, the Two Lands, and asking him to remove the sand around the sphinx which was suffocating him. Of course, Thutmose cleared away the sand and despite the fact that he was not the eldest son of the reigning pharaoh, Amenhotep II (c. 1427–1400), he became pharaoh some thirty years later. Amenhotep II, Sety I (c. 1294–1279 BC), Merenptah (c. 1213–1203 BC), Tanutamani (c. 664-656) and many other pharaohs all had dreams in which the gods foretold that they would win key battles.

The so-called "Dream Book" in the Chester Beatty III Papyrus (dated to the beginning of the Nineteenth Dynasty, about 1295 BC and now in the British Museum, but whose contents probably originated in the Middle Kingdom, c. 2055-1650 BC), as well as papyri dating from the period of Roman occupation (30 BC–395 AD), provide us with the grids of dream interpretation used by the priests. These grids might appear comical to us today because we no longer possess the context to understand why symbolic meaning was attributed to certain situations and objects. However, Freud's dream code sprang from the same belief as the Egyptians, and religions in general: that dreams have coded meaning (see Volume II, Chapter 6, on Egypt's role as a hinge society).

The Egyptian dream grid said that if a man saw himself in a dream "sitting in a tree," it was a good sign indicating "the destruction of his enemies." If he saw himself "gaping into a deep well," it was a bad sign indicating that he would "go to prison." "Seeing a dwarf" meant that he would "lose half of his life." Seeing somebody "wearing Asian clothes" meant that he would "lose his job." Seeing himself "eating a cucumber" was an ill omen meaning that "trouble was on the way." Seeing himself "visiting Busiris" was good; it meant that he would "live to an old age." Seeing "a snake" was good — "provisions" would be forthcoming. A woman who dreamt that she gave birth to a cat meant that she would have "many children," but "giving birth to a donkey" meant that she would have "an idiotic child."

Sex was seemingly omnipresent in Egyptian dreams and gave rise to what now seem to be some extraordinary interpretations. Seeing oneself in a dream "making love to a woman" was a bad sign meaning "mourning"; seeing "the vagina of a woman" was also bad and meant "great misfortunes." On the other hand, making love to one's mother, sister or a cow were good omens for a male dreamer, while making love to a jerboa meant that "a legal trial" was upcoming. It was a good sign if a woman saw herself making love to a ram, as "the pharaoh would be generous with her," but making love with a horse was a bad because she would be "violent with her husband."[138]

We know for certain that during the Greek Ptolemaic Period (c. 332–32 BC) and afterwards, provoked and controlled dreaming was a standard practice in the temples of the Greco-Egyptian god Serapis, especially in Alexandria and Memphis. Spending a night of provoked and controlled dreaming in a temple-linked dormitory, under the guidance of a priest, whom the Greeks called an *Oneirocrite*, was a popular practice. Some Egyptologists believe that it was the Greeks who introduced controlled dreaming into Egypt. However, from the context of texts like the Chester Beatty III Papyrus, it seems almost self-evident that such practices existed much earlier in the Egyptian temples and/or Houses of Life among the pharaoh's entourage and notables, before gradually spreading to commoners. Moreover, the *Oneirocrite* seems to be the Greek version of the *pa-hery-tep*.

During the Greek Period, the god Bes, officiating from the ruined Osiris Temple in Abydos, was a noted dream oracle. As a *panthee*, a god with a specific *heka*, magic, protective role, Bes was considered by both the Egyptians and the Greeks to be especially powerful in warding off the dangers inherent in the dream state.

The *pa-hery-tep*, or *Oneirocrite*, dream interpreter assured that the goddess Neith or the god Bes would protect the dreamer, interpreted the dream, and called upon Isis to prevent bad dreams (presumably nightmares), and to console and heal if the dreamer came out of his session in a disturbed state. If a bad dream occurred, Isis was invoked in a spell — "Come to me, my mother Isis! Look, I see something which is far from me, in my own city! — and "fresh herbs soaked in beer and myrrh" were rubbed on the dreamer's face.[139] Isis, linked to consoling and healing, was also a frequent apparition in dreams and visions (like the Christian Mary).

---

138. Sauneron, Serge in *Les Songes Et Leur Interprétation*, Editions du Seuil, Paris, 1959, pp. 33-37, Sauneron, Serge, *Les Prêtres de l'ancienne Egypte*, pp. 183-185 and Wilson, John in *Ancient Near Eastern Texts Relating to the Old Testament*, p. 495.

139. Sauneron, Serge in *Les Songes Et Leur Interprétation*, Editions du Seuil, Paris, 1959, pp. 33-37, Sauneron, Serge, *Les Prêtres de l'ancienne Egypte*, pp. 183-185 and Wilson, John in *Ancient Near Eastern Texts Relating to the Old Testament*, p. 495.

According to *The Magical Papyrus of London and Leiden*, written questions were addressed to Bes and replies were given to the questioners who spent the night in a dormitory-dream room linked to the temple precinct. This text notes the various stages in provoked and controlled dreaming, including purification with a solution of water and natron, the application of a specially concocted ointment over the eyes, spells and incantations and staring at a magically inscribed lamp until Bes appeared, and then going to sleep.

THE SMALL CLASS OF PROFESSIONAL SOLDIERS

During Egypt's early history, and particularly during the Old Kingdom, there was apparently no need for a standing army of any importance. There were many battles but few large-scale wars. *Wa'ew*, soldiers, in this period went barefoot, were dressed in *shendyt*, kilts, or were naked, carried nome totem banners and were armed with maces, spears, bows and arrows and shields. They constituted the royal guard and small militias in each nome capital controlled by the nomarchs, with supplementary soldiers being conscripted according to need. Their main tasks were maintaining order at the site of major construction projects such as pyramids and temples, for which peasants and craftsmen had been conscripted. The soldiers also accompanied trading and plundering missions. The militias and conscripted soldiers were rarely sent into war abroad in great numbers. However, this apparently sometimes occurred, under Pharaoh Pepy I (c. 2321–2287 BC) or Pharaoh Merenra (c. 2287–2278 BC) to name just two, when the militias assisted by great numbers of conscripts from throughout Egypt and Nubia invaded the West Asian *Retjenu* to put down the "sand-dwellers" (the *Shasu*).

Professional soldiers constituted a small class. They were given a plot of land and abundant supplies of food and wine. The pharaoh was always the commander-in-chief of this corps. The practical duties of defending the borders, and staging campaigns for loot or invading other lands, were usually planned and carried out by this small standing group of generals and soldiers.

Except for the "natural right" Egypt believed it had to annex Nubia, it had no need of colonies and only occasional need of the wealth of other lands. Its agricultural and economic power were such that it usually had no intrinsic need to make war against other peoples, except occasionally for gold, granite, timber, spices, rare animals, precious stones and slaves. This self-sufficiency was coupled with religious and cultural self-assurance and a refined life. On a relative basis, even the peasants had a good life compared to peasants in neighboring countries. Moreover, Egypt was protected from invasion on all its borders by the natural barriers constituted by deserts and the sea.

Compared to Sumer, during the Third Millennium Egypt was a paragon of virtue. War was a daily preoccupation of the Sumerians and an intimate part of their culture. The fact that Sumer was situated in an open area with no natural barriers against invasion certainly forced the Sumerians to adopt a tough military stance, but it also seems clear that they enjoyed making war.

Foreign mercenaries were used throughout Egyptian history — Nubians and Libyans in the Old Kingdom, Medjay Nubian desert nomads in the First Intermediate Period (c. 2181–2055 BC) Africans, Syrians and "Sea Peoples" in the New Kingdom (c. 1550–1069 BC) and Greeks, Lydians and Hebrews in the Late Period (c. 747–332 BC).

Only by the First Intermediate Period (c. 2181–2055 BC), a time of political instability and the breakup of the country into many rival states and economic collapse, is it possible to speak about professional armies of significant size in Egypt.

And it was not until the New Kingdom that a big and permanent army — the *mesha* — was organized. The officers of this huge army were Egyptians, but once again most of the *wa'ew*, the soldiers, were mercenaries. This great fighting force reflected Egypt's imperial thirst for the control of foreign lands, their peoples and their resources. This was especially so from c. 1458 BC, when Thutmose III embarked on his vast military campaigns in West Asia *Retjenu* and deep into Nubia.

However, the need for a powerful army was not only linked to the constraints of Egypt's rise to the status of the world's greatest imperialist and colonial power, but also to the great power rivalry in the turbulent West Asian continuum of that time. Egypt had no choice but to fit into a pattern of generalized wars of conquest.

Probably Egypt also had to control the buffer zone constituted by Palestine, Syria and the Levant and its main trade routes in order to keep from being vassalized itself by Babylonia, Assyria, the Hurrians, the Hittites and Mitanni.

Until the New Kingdom, Egypt was one of the least aggressive countries of antiquity and did not seem to have a natural love of war. Indeed, Strabo (c. 60 BC–AD 38), in his *Geography*, noted that in the first century AD Egypt was "self-sufficient" and "not very inclined towards warfare," something which amazed the warlike Romans. Adolf Erman also believed that the Egyptians had always been basically "peaceful," but also that "they lack the taste for struggle and heroism."[140] Erman was quite simply wrong in making such an across-the-board evaluation and it seems that Strabo did not take into account the temporal context of the Egyptian attitude. The Egyptian non-inclination to war during the time of the Roman occupation probably had more to do with their state of general decline and subservience to their colonial masters than to a natural distaste for war. During the New Kingdom and to some extent even during the Middle Kingdom (c. 2055–1650 BC), the Egyptians had amply demonstrated that they had evolved into one of the most imperialistic countries in the world.

CRAFTSMEN AND PEASANTS: VIRTUALLY SERFS

When it comes to the religious practices and societal rights of the so-called *rekyht*, commoners — peasants, craftsmen/artists, tradesmen and laborers — we don't know much. Most of the information unearthed to date relates to Egypt's royal religions and the rights of the pharaohs and notables. Very few commoners could afford sturdy tombs or elaborate mummification (and if they could, they might have tended toward the beliefs of the elite, anyway). Moreover, they were usually unable to leave autobiographical records, even on *ostraca*, or potsherds, because they were almost all illiterate. A few commoners did rise to high rank, but they were indeed exceptions.

Religion was strictly a matter between the pharaoh, the priests and the gods. The commoners had no significant role. They were obliged to be satisfied with their social rank and what the pharaoh-god magically accomplished with the gods to maintain the universal, national, and natural order and harmony. They could not participate in temple life beyond the entrance courtyard, where they grouped themselves at the first *bekhenet*, gateway-pylon, gaping for a glimpse of the ceremonies taking place in the far off *naos* sanctuary where the statues of the gods were housed.

Rituals and prayers in the home and in local shrines dedicated to minor gods were apparently widespread, but it seems that magic, in the forms of

---

140. Strabo, *The Geography of Strabo*, 17.1.53 and Erman, Adolf, *La Religion des Egyptiens*, pp. 189-190.

amulets, spells and curses, was the most extensive daily religious experience of the commoners. For them, the most important religious periods were the numerous religious festivals when the statues of the gods, concealed in portable shrines, were paraded in procession. On these occasions, the people assailed the gods in their function as oracles with questions. The gods graciously replied with a yes or a no, concretized by a forwards or backwards movement by the priests carrying the god in his shrine.

Once all the people had been granted a right to an afterlife, at least from the beginning of the First Intermediate Period (c. 2181 BC), the most important religious event — at least for richer commoners — must have been the elaborate ceremonies and rituals surrounding death, mummification, the funeral and burial in a tomb with magical funerary texts, provisions, furniture and art work. However, the cost of fulfilling all of these duties was so high that most ordinary people went through a bare minimum of them. Quality and cheaper forms of mummification and sturdier tombs for commoners did not become frequent until the Late Period (beginning c. 747 BC). During the Late Period, commoners also seem to be more frequent visitors to the "Houses of Life."

As we have seen, until about the Sixth Dynasty (from c. 2345 BC), the agricultural and crafted products of the peasants, tradespeople and craftsmen belonged to the pharaoh, who left them a portion for their subsistence. After this date, peasants, tradespeope and craftsmen were theoretically free and could own property. A small middle class emerged as a result, but we still know very little about them. Most commoners remained directly attached to the pharaoh's, notables' or temple estates and were considered to be *semedet* or *meret*, servants, serfs. The huge Cairo Museum collection of "installations" — scale models — of commoners baking, brewing, working in granaries, farming and fishing, provide some information concerning the daily life of ordinary people.

The peasants — the *sekhty*, field workers — worked hard and long hours, whether they were male or female. This was especially the case from the end of the *akhet* inundation season to the end of the *shemu* harvest season eight months later. During *akhet*, they were also subjected to conscription for construction tasks and for army service, for which they were meagerly paid in kind.

The peasants were under tight surveillance by scribe/tax collectors and subjected to heavy taxes and beatings, severe penalties and punishments for default. Taxes were usually about 60% of their harvest and the land they worked was usually rented for about three bushels of produce per acre. Finished products such as bread, mats and linen, were also used as tax payments.

The workload of the craftsmen and artists, *hemutiu*, who were considered to be a single profession, must have also been immense. They produced buildings, temples, tombs, art, amulets, artifacts, canals, boats, chariots, weapons and the goods of daily life ranging from papyrus, jewelry, fine linen and cosmetics to tools and furniture. Their production for Egypt's second and parallel economy, for the afterlife, was probably even greater.

The sculptors (*genewtey*) and craftsmen of the big temple cities like Memphis, Heliopolis and Thebes constituted an elite, privileged caste. They were organized into virtual religious brotherhoods. They usually took great pride in their work and were not harassed to produce quickly. They were housed, fed and paid in kind, but were practically cloistered, although some outside contacts clearly existed. It seems certain that the craftsmen were much better treated than the peasants; at the least, they were not in the same category of *semedet*, servants.

At the peasant level, little is known about the daily life of the craftsmen. However, the more than 30,000 ostraca (found in a well), 200 hieratic papyri, many steles and many tombs found in the ruins of the New Kingdom (c. 1550–1069 BC) Deir el-Medina workers' and craftsmen village, on the west bank across from Luxor, provide us with a unique, if incomplete, reflection of the daily life of commoner craftsmen in Egypt. The beliefs, politico-religious, economic, legal, social and family concerns and disputes, crimes, reasons for skipping work days, realistic drawings including sexually explicit scenes and trivia are recorded on these documents.

These Deir el-Medina craftsmen built and decorated the royal tombs in the Theban Valley of Kings, apparently working eight hours a day in two four-hour shifts and like all other workers were paid in kind. Their village had an area of no more than 1.6 acres, consisting of about 70 mud-brick, stone foundation, one-story, three-room houses with roof terraces, an underground storeroom and a kitchen at the back of the house. At most, the number of craftsmen was probably around 130 and the total population including women and children was no more than 1000 people. Deir el-Medina had its own courthouse, temple and necropolis.

We know for certain that these workers especially revered the mother goddess Hathor in her Theban afterlife function, the god of crafts, Ptah, and of course, Osiris, the King of the Underworld and resurrection. We know too, from the so-called "penitential hymns" found on numerous steles in Deir el-Medina, that these workers had feelings of "humility...crime and punishment, contrition and forgiveness" which seem to have contrasted sharply with the usual arrogance of the notables. Miriam Lichtheim suggests that the "penitential hymns" partially constituted a new type of "personal piety" (as J. H. Breasted believed) and a "religion of the poor" (as B. Gunn believed), but Lichtheim emphasizes that "What comes to fruition in the New Kingdom is the self-awareness of the individual person" which was "the end product of a long evolution." Indeed, statements like "Amen-Re...who comes at the voice of the poor in distress," "[I was] an ignorant man and foolish/Who knew not good from evil...The Peak [the Theban Necropolis goddess Mertseger] strikes with the stroke of a savage lion/She is after him who offends her!" or "And that my eyes may see Amun every day/As is done for the righteous man"[141] illustrate feelings which were already on the rise in the justice-hungry Middle Kingdom (c. 2055–1650 BC).

As we have seen, strikes sometimes occurred at Deir el-Medina for nonpayment of wages and mistreatment, but these occasional protests against injustice never seem to have affected the workers' deep devotion to the pharaoh-god and to the notables, and their deep religious motivations. The very title of the Deir el-Medina craftsmen, "Servants of the Place of Truth," of *Set-Maat*, of the Valley of Kings, would seem to indicate that they constituted an elite. The Deir el-Medina community cannot be seen as representative of the condition of most ordinary Egyptians. It was a closed, privileged society and many of its members clearly knew how to write, placing them in a minority of perhaps less than one per cent of the entire Egyptian population at that time during the during the New Kingdom. Some of the tombs in Deir el-Medina indicate that their owners had considerable economic resources. Some of the craftsmen were even apparently rich enough to possess several slaves, like the tomb of the craftsman Ken (TT4) indicates.

Since 1991, more than 600 tombs, containing skeletons of apparently conscripted but consenting workers and foremen — called "Friends of Khufu" and "Drunkards of Menkaure" — have also been found at the Giza pyramid site, near Nazlet-el Samman, by the Egyptian Egyptologist Zahi Hawass (b. 1947). The contents of the graves, including steles, reliefs and inscriptions, indicate elaborate religious beliefs and magical practices, including curses and lists of food offerings to the dead (cakes, onions, beef, figs, beer and wine, and more). There was a firm hope in the afterlife despite the fact that none of these bodies

---

141. Lichtheim, Miriam, *Ancient Egyptian Literature, Volume II*: pp. 104-110.

was mummified, indicating that at the time (c. 2589–2503 BC) being properly "equipped" for the afterlife was not within the reach of commoners. Dr. Hawass notes that these workers "liked beer...ate lots of bread...were generally well cared for by pharaohs [and had] an emergency medical service." Dr. Hawass notes heights of five to six feet, a low life expectancy of 30 to 35, and poor health, presumably caused by hard work. Hawass postulates that the Giza workers' village was an Old Kingdom version of the Deir el-Medina workers' village.[142]

Although, after visiting Egypt around 440 BC, Herodotus (c. 484–420 BC) reported in *Histories* that the Egyptians "are the healthiest of all men, next to the Libyans," it seems that in all periods the average Egyptian was not in very good health and was riddled with diseases and with malformations caused by hard labor. X-rays of mummies in European museums, begun by P.H.K. Gray in the 1960s, as well as various studies of mummies, skeletons and remains, frequently reveal stunted growth, arteriosclerosis, osteoarthritis, poor dentition and diseases like tuberculosis, heart ailments, leprosy and various parasitic diseases. Infantile mortality was high. After a study of 200 first century BC to fifth century AD mummies in the Duch/Kharga Oasis in the desert 75 miles west of Thebes — "a particularly poor area" — Françoise Dunand and Roger Lichtenberg, in *Mummies, A Voyage Through Eternity*, concluded that "almost everyone" among these people "of slim build and average height (men 1.65 m [5'4"], women 1.55 m [5'1"])"...suffered "from some medical complaint" and "practically everyone was in poor health."[143]

Dress, for both notables and commoners, was usually the simple kilt, the *shendyt*, with of course those of the notables being far finer. The *shendyt*, in various forms, always remained the most popular male garment, but starting in the New Kingdom (c. 1550 BC), elaborately designed shirts, caps and helmets were added. Sandals were rarely worn, and never when a notable or a royal personage was present. Wigs, made of natural hair, wool and other fibers, were a key part of male dressing customs for all who could afford them. At least from the First Dynasty (c. 3100–2890 BC), men shaved, but judging from the early palettes (c. 3100), this was not the case earlier. The palettes also show that the early Egyptians frequently wore penis holders.

---

142. Zahi Hawass in www.guardians.net/hawass/buildtomb.htm and www.guardians.net/spotlite/spotlite-hawass-2001.htm.

143. Herodotus, *Books I-II*, 2.77.3 and Dunand, Françoise and Lichtenberg, Roger, *Mummies, A Voyage Through Eternity*, pp. 92, 93, 118.

Institutionalized Male Domination Plus Unprecedented Women's Rights

Special mention has to be made concerning the status of Egyptian women. They had extensive rights and were considerably freer than those in any of the neighboring countries. Nevertheless, the central role of a woman, *set*, was to be a *hemet* and a *mewet*, a wife and a mother, and her status was determined in relation to the *hem*, the man, who became her *hi*, her husband. Marriage does not seem to have been the object of a religious ceremony. Women were usually married by 14 years old and were considered to be dependent on men, passive, and submitted. In paintings and sculptures, they were generally depicted smaller and behind their husbands. However, they had property rights, could exercise some professions, could bring cases to court, were not under the legal tutorship of men, could inherit and designate their heirs in testaments, and sue for divorce. As elsewhere, peasant women joined their husbands in agricultural tasks.

Until the New Kingdom (c. 1550 BC), it seems that dress for women was similar to the male kilt-like skirt, the *shendyt*. Women also wore long, tight-fitting, woven, transparent cotton or linen gowns (usually white and sometimes yellow or red), stretching from under their naked breasts to the ankles, and virtually revealing all their charms. Children before puberty, *mesu* or *hewew*, did not wear clothing at all and grew a lock of hair pushed to one side. Servant women, *baket*, wore the same basic female dress but were sometimes naked except for leather bands covering their breasts and groin. Wigs were important items of dress, as were necklaces and bracelets. Perfumes, oil and makeup were widely used. From the New Kingdom, these usual forms of dress for Egyptian women expanded, especially for the wives of notables, into the use of more elaborate and embroidered and beaded gowns and the use of girdles (*shesmet*) under the gowns. A coat was sometimes worn over the dress, but it too was in linen so fine that it was virtually transparent.

Women of all classes, like men, eventually won the right to an afterlife, but specific tombs for women other than the wives of notables were rare unless they themselves had achieved special status. From about 2650 BC in the Old Kingdom to the end of the Middle Kingdoms (c. 1650 BC), the pharaohs' wives were buried in small pyramids adjoining the main pyramid and from about 1500 BC in the New Kingdom in the rock-cut tombs of their husbands or in separate tombs. Most frequently, common women shared their husbands' tombs. Women were always active participants in the funerary rites for their husbands.

The first women in recorded history to become supreme rulers were Egyptians. Several became pharaohs. The first was Merneith (c. 2950 BC), who was probably a regent preceding or following the reign of Den. Other early female pharaohs were Nitiqret (Nitocris in Greek, c. 2184–2181 BC) and Sobekneferu (c. 1799–1795 BC). But of course, the most famous was Hatshepsut (c. 1473–1458 BC). "She who embraces Amun, the foremost of women," Hatshepsut was really a woman who was a *nisut*, a king, rather than a woman who was queen, and she was usually depicted with the clothing and attributes of a male pharaoh, including a false beard.

In fact, the term "queen" was never used but rather the title *hemet nisut weret*, the "great royal wife." Royal power was a male prerogative. The ambiguity of Merneith's and Nitiqret's reigns lies here. From Radjedef's reign (c. 2566–2558 BC), the Pharaoh was engendered by Re through one of his wives as Re's son. Some Egyptologists have concluded that the female pharaohs — except Sobekneferu and Hatshepsut — were regents rather than pharaohs. However, in Hatsheput's case, there is no doubt: not only was she pharaoh, but she was a powerful and authoritative ruler, despite the fact that she began as a regent for the child Thutmose III (c. 1479–1425 BC) before literally usurping his title and having herself crowned as pharaoh.

Nevertheless, the pharaoh's closest female associates received major titles and wielded considerable political and religious power. This was especially the case for the *hemet nisut weret*, the "great royal wife," the pharaoh's chief wife, and for his mother, the *mewet nisut*, the "king's mother," and for his other wives, the *hemewet nisut*, the "king's wives." While not entirely systematic, part of the pharaoh's legitimacy was frequently marriage to the "royal heiress," that is to his sister or a half-sister, a daughter of one of his father's wives.

From the Eighteenth Dynasty (c. 1550-1295 BC), one of the king's wives or daughters was the *hemet netjer nt Imen*, "god's wife of Amun," who made love with the god Amun and gave birth to the future pharaoh.

The extraordinary specificity of Egypt, including the rare possibility of a woman becoming supreme ruler, was a considerable attenuation of the restrictive customs concerning women inherited from the Neolithic agro-sedentary societies with strict patriarchal values. This easing of attitudes and religious regulations concerning women was in stark contrast to its neighbors; advanced agricultural societies in general maintained far stricter rules.

A good illustration — and far from an isolated one — is the Eighteenth Dynasty (c. 1550–1295) "wisdom text," *The Instruction of Any* (now in the Cairo

Museum) which states: "Do not control your wife in her house...Do not say to her: 'Where is it? Get it!'...It is a joy when your hand is with her..." This attitude should be compared to the far later *Instruction of the Papyrus Insinger* (in the Leiden Rijksmuseum), from the first century AD but perhaps composed at the end of the Ptolemaic Period (first century BC?). It shows to what extent Greek misogyny, so out of character with ancient Egyptian attitudes, had infiltrated traditional Egyptian religious and social values: "He who is insolent among men becomes the first among women," and "One does not ever discover the heart of a woman anymore than [one knows] the sky."[144]

Herodotus was amazed at how different Egypt was from any other country he knew and how different were Egyptian customs — "...they [have] instituted customs and laws contrary for the most part to those of the rest of mankind." He was particularly struck by the independent status of Egyptian women, who "buy and sell [while] the men stay at home and weave...men carry burdens on their heads, women on their shoulders...Women pass water standing, men sitting...No woman is dedicated to the service of any god or goddess [of course, here Herodotus is mistaken]...Sons are not compelled against their will to support their parents, but daughters must do so..." As with many of Herodotus' observations, these are a mixture of accurate observations, mistakes, and over-generalizations, but he was bearing witness to the fact that women were freer in Egypt than in any other country during that time.

The Greeks were awed by rights Egyptian women enjoyed. Perhaps as a result of this awe and incomprehension, the Greeks and the Romans gave Egyptian women the reputation of being sexually uninhibited or loose and rowdy. Herodotus, describing the pilgrimage to the cat goddess Bastet's temple in Bubastis, noted: "As they travel by river to Bubastis, whenever they come near any other town they bring their boat near the bank; then some of the women...shout mockery of the women of the town, others dance, and others stand up and lift their skirts...when they have reached Bubastis, they make a festival with great sacrifices, and more wine is drunk at this feast than in the whole year besides."[145]

Herodotus may be correct in this description of a festive atmosphere in which many women "*let their hair down*." However, in a general way, it would seem

---

144. Lichtheim, Miriam, *Ancient Egyptian Literature, Volume II*, p. 143 and Lichtheim, Miriam, *Ancient Egyptian Literature, Volume III*, pp. 190 and 195.

145. Herodotus, *Books I-II*, 2.35.2-4 and 2.60.

that Egyptian society was prudish and that monogamous marriage, family life, children and sexual fidelity were central pillars of the women's mindset. From the Middle Kingdom (beginning c. 2055 BC), the usual title for married women was *nebet per*, "Mistress of the House."

However, even if it was generally restricted to the royal family, polygamy existed. We know that the word *hebswet* designated a second or third wife or a concubine. Polygamy, harems and concubines for royalty, and the wealthy and powerful were widespread as they were throughout West Asia. Prostitution was also frequent, especially among travelling dancing and singing groups devoted to the goddess Hathor and the god Bes. These women were tattooed, wore heavy make-up and sometimes strutted about naked. One imagines that they were paid for their services, but there is no known record of this.

Of course, eroticism was not absent. Many sexually explicit sculptures, paintings, ostraca, objects and erotic love poems have been found. Egyptian texts provide numerous allusions to methods of sexual arousal (notably the use of wigs and — onions!), and dream interpretation codes for men and women use many sexual analogies. The Nineteenth Dynasty (c. 1295–1186 BC) Turin Erotic Papyrus (now in the Turin Museo Egizio) is illustrated by a variety of sexual positions and especially huge penises being thoroughly enjoyed by women.

SOFT SLAVERY

Although slavery was not officially instituted until the New Kingdom, apparently even during the Old Kingdom there was a small number of slaves — known as *hemew* or *bakew*. Most slaves served the pharaoh and his family and the top administrators, priests, and generals in tasks ranging from domestic service (*bak*), to temple, agricultural, quarrying and other duties. After the New Kingdom, slavery was very widespread. A striking illustration of this is given in the Great Harris Papyrus which notes that Rameses III (c. 1184–1153 BC) donated 113,433 slaves to the temples, with 86,486 of them going to the Amun Temple in Karnak.[146]

The vast majority of slaves were prisoners of war, refugees, and immigrants. However, some Egyptian peasants sold themselves into slavery. It was also

---

146. Erman, Adolf, *Life in Ancient Egypt*, p. 300 and 302 and Breasted, James Henry, *Ancient Records of Egypt*, Vol. 4, pp. 92-107.

possible for a peasant to buy himself out of slavery, and some middle class peasants, craftsmen, and tradespeople, even had their own slaves. Of course, slaves did not have property or inheritance rights. In some cases, they could marry free peasant women without their slave status being changed, but their children were theoretically considered to be part of the peasant class.

Compared to its neighbors, including Israel, which also practiced a relatively mild slave system, the Egyptian slave system constituted what can be euphemistically called soft slavery.

CLOSING

The preceding chapters survey the contexts that gave rise to the legendary Egypt that left such enigmatic monuments to tantalize future generations — Egypt, the trunk of the tree from which sprouted so many aspects of modern civilization.

In Volume II (Fall 2003), we will examine how these early contexts led to specific consequences, with the Egyptians creating original solutions to political, societal, religious, existential and metaphysical problems. The following are the main issues and topics examined in *Part II, The Consequences: How Egypt Became the Trunk of the Tree*:

- The search for an answer to the problem (the scandal!) of death
- Monumental tombs and mummification
- Osiris, history's first savior god
- Religion flirting with ethics
- A convoluted system of several souls and their survival after death.
- Polytheism, theocracy and monotheism
- The unbridgeable gap between the theology, the ethics and the eschatology of full-blown monotheism
- Akhenaten's invention of the first monotheism, a key step in the history of mankind
- The rapid collapse of solar monotheism and the return to Amun-Re polytheism
- The Amarna art revolution
- Egypto-Hebrew relations supposed and proven, and their central issue, the origins of monotheism
- The apex of Egyptian power in all domains: political, economic, military, religious and artistic
- Persian rule (c. 525–404 BC) and the beginning of the end of Egypt at its grandest

- Greek rule (332–32 BC)
- The rise of Christian monotheism from the Second Century AD
- The Moslem conquest (AD 642)
- Egyptian religious views compared with those of the Sumerians, Hebrews, Hindus, Zoroastrians, Greeks, early Christians and Moslems
- Egypt, an authentic and an imaginary hinge society concerning Africa, Israel, Greece, the Christian world, European esotericism and science, and loony Egyptian influences right into our time
- The rediscovery of Egypt as the trunk of the tree

SELECTED BIBLIOGRAPHY

Wherever possible, the most available editions in non-revised form are listed.

PRIMARY TEXTS

Borghouts, J.F., *Ancient Egyptian Magical Texts*, E.J. Brill, Leiden, 1978.

Breasted, James, Henry, *Ancient Records of Egypt*, Five Volumes: *The First to the Seventeenth Dynasties, The Eighteenth Dynasty, The Nineteenth Dynasty, The Twentieth to the Twenty-Sixth Dynasties* and *Indices*, Histories & Mysteries of Man Ltd., London, 1988. (Re-printed by the University of Illinois, Urbana and Chicago, 2001. First published 1906, 1907).

Breasted, James, Henry, *The Edwin Smith Surgical Papyrus*, Two Volumes, University of Chicago Press, Chicago, 1930.

Budge, E.A. Wallis, *The Egyptian Book Of The Dead*, Dover Publications Inc., Mineola, New York, 1967. (First published 1895).

Faulkner, R.O., *The Ancient Egyptian Book of the Dead*, (Editor Carol Andrews), University of Texas Press, Austin, 1997.

Faulkner, R.O., *The Ancient Egyptian Pyramid Texts*, Oxford University Press, Oxford, 1998.

Faulkner, R.O., *The Ancient Egyptian Coffin Texts*, Three Volumes: *Spells 1-354, Spells 355-787, Spells 788-1185 and Index*, Aris & Philips, Warminister, 1973, 1977, 1978.

Lichtheim, Miriam, *Ancient Egyptian Literature*, Three Volumes: *The Old And Middle Kingdoms, The New Kingdom* and *The Late Period*, University of California Press, Berkeley, 1975, 1976, 1980.

Lalouette, Claire *Textes Sacrés et Textes Profanes de l'Ancienne Egypte*, Two Volumes: *Des Pharaons et des hommes* and *Mythes, Contes et Poèsie*, Gallimard, Paris, 1987.

Moran, William L., *The Amarna Letters*, Johns Hopkins University Press, Baltimore, 1992.

Pritchard, J.B. (editor), *Ancient Near Eastern Texts relating to the Old Testament*, (Egyptian sections by John A. Wilson), Princeton University Press, Princeton, N.J., 1969.

RELIGION, MYTHOLOGY, SOCIETY

Aldred Cyril, *Akhenaten, King of Egypt*, Thames and Hudson, London, 1991.

Aldred, Cyril, *Akhenaten, Pharaoh of Egypt—a new study*, Abacus, Sphere Books, London, 1972. (First edition 1968).

Andrews, Carol, *Egyptian Mummies*, British Museum Publications, London, 1998.

Andrews, Carol, *Amulets of Ancient Egypt*, University of Texas Press, Austin, 1994.

Assmann, Jan, *Moses The Egyptian, The Memory of Egypt in Western Monotheism*, Harvard University Press, Cambridge, Mass., 1999.

Assmann, Jan, *Egyptian Solar Religion in the New Kingdom, Re, Amun and the Crisis Of Polytheism* (translated by Anthony Alcock), Kegan Paul International, London and New York, 1995.

Breasted, James Henry, *Development of Religion and Thought in Ancient Egypt*, 1972, University of Pennsylvania Press, Philadelphia (First published 1912).

Budge, E.A. Wallis, *Osiris & The Egyptian Resurrection*, Two Volumes, Dover Publications Inc., New York, 1973. (First published 1911).

Dunand, Françoise and Lichtenberg, Roger, Mummies, A Voyage Through Eternity (translated by Ruth Sharman), Harry N. Abrams, New York and Thames and Hudson, London, 1994.

Dunand, Françoise and Lichtenberg, Roger, *Les Momies et la Mort en Egypte*, Errance, Paris, 1988.

Erman, Adolf, *Die ägyptische Religion*, 1904 (translated as *A Handbook of Egyptian Religion* by A.S. Griffith in 1907 and in the fuller and revised 1934 *Die Religion der Ägypter* edition as *La Religion Des Egyptiens* in 1952 by Henri Wild, Payot, Paris).

Erman, Adolf, *Life In Ancient Egypt*, translated by H.M.Tirard, Dover, New York, 1971. (Original German edition 1886).

Frankfort, Henri, *Ancient Egyptian Religion, An Interpretation*, Dover Publications Inc., Mineola, New York, 2000. (First published 1948).

Freud, Sigmund, *The Standard Edition of the Complete Psychological Works of Sigmund Freud* (translated by James Strachey in collaboration with Anna Freud), Volume XXIII, *Moses And Monotheism*, The Hogarth Press and the Institute of Psycho-analysis, London, 1991. Also *Moses And Monotheism* (Katherine Jones, Editor), Random House, New York, 1987. (First Published 1939).

Hornung, Erik, *Conceptions of God in Ancient Egypt: The One and the Many* (translated by John Baines), Cornell University Press, Ithaca, N.Y., 1982. (Original German edition, 1971).

Hornung, Erik, *Idea Into Image: Essays On Ancient Egyptian Thought* (translated by Elizabeth Bredeck), Timken, New York, 1992.

Kemp, Barry J., *Ancient Egypt, Anatomy of a Civilization*, Routledge, London, 2000.

Morenz, Siegfried, *Egyptian Religion* (translated by Ann E. Keep), Cornell University Press, Ithaca, N.Y., 1992.

Plutarch, *Moralia*, Volume V (with *Isis and Osiris*), (translated by Frank Cole Babbitt), Loeb Classical Library, Harvard University Press, Cambridge, Mass., 1936. Reprinted 1999.

Redford, Donald B., *Akhenaten, The Heretic King*, Princeton University Press, Princeton, N.J., 1984.

Sauneron, Serge, *The Priests of Ancient Egypt* (translated by David Lorton), Cornell University Press, Ithaca, N.Y., 2000.

Wilson, John A., *The Burden Of Egypt, An Interpretation of Ancient Egyptian Culture*, The University of Chicago Press, Chicago and London, 1965. (Re-published as *The Culture of Egypt*.)

Wilson, John A., *Egypt* (pp. 31-122), in *The Intellectual Adventure of Ancient Man* (also by Henri and H.A Frankfort, Thorkild Jacobsen and William A. Irwin), The University of Chicago Press, Chicago, 1977.

ART AND ARCHITECTURE

Aldred, Cyril, *Egyptian Art*, Thames And Hudson Ltd., London, 1996.

Andreu,Guillemette, Rutschowscaya, Marie-Hélène and Ziegler, Christiane, *Ancient Egypt at the* Louvre (translated by Lisa Davidson), Hachette Littératures, Paris, 1997.

Edwards, Iorweth E.S., *The Pyramids of Egypt*, Penguin, Harmondsworth, U.K., 1972.

Groenewegen-Frankfort, H.A., *Arrest And Movement, Space and Time in the Representational Art of the Ancient Near East (Book One. Egyptian Art*, pages 15—141), Harvard University Press, Cambridge, Mass., 1987. (First published 1951).

Lehner, Mark, *The Complete Pyramids*, Thames and Hudson, London, 1997.

Malek, Jaromir, *Egyptian Art*, Phaidon Press, London, 1999.

Michalowski, Kazimierz, The Art of Ancient Egypt, Harry N. Abrams, New York, 1968, Thames and Hudson, London, 1969.

Petrie, W.M.F., *Tell el Amarna*, Methuen & Co., London, 1894.

Robbins, Gay, *The Art of Ancient Egypt*, Harvard University Press, Cambridge, Mass., British Museum Press, 1997.

Schäfer, Heinrich, *Principles of Egyptian Art* (Emma Brunner-Traut, Editor, translated and edited by John Baines), Griffith Institute, Oxford, 1986 (Original German edition, 1919).

Smith, W., Stevenson, *The Art and Architecture of Ancient Egypt*, Penguin, London, 1965. Revised edition by William Kelly Simpson, Yale University Press, 1999.

Tiradritti, Francesco, Al-Misri, Mathat, de Luca, Araldo and Mubarak, Suzanne, *Egyptian Treasures from the Egyptian Museum in Cairo*, Harry N. Abrams, New York, 1999.

Wilkinson, Richard H., *Reading Egyptian Art, A Hieroglyphic Guide To Ancient Egyptian Painting And Sculpture*, Thames and Hudson, London, 1994.

Wilkinson, Richard H., *The Complete Temples of Ancient Egypt*, Thames and Hudson, London, 2000.

HISTORY

Aldred, Cyril, *The Egyptians*, Thames and Hudson, London, 1984.

Bernal, Martin, *Black Athena. The Afroasiatic Roots of Classical Civilization*, Volume I, *The Fabrication of Ancient Greece, 1785—1985*, Volume II, *The Archaeological and Documentary Evidence*, Rutgers University Press, New Brunswick, N.J., U.S.A., 1988 and 1991.

Diodorus, Siculus, *The Antiquities of Egypt*: a translation of *Book I* of the *Library of History* by Edwin Murphy, Transaction Publishers, New Brunswick, N.J., U.S.A., 1990.

Diop, Cheikh Anta, *The African Origin Of Civilization, Myth Or Reality* (edited and translated by Mercer Cook), Lawrence Hill Books, Chicago, 1974.

Breasted, James Henry, *A History Of Egypt, From The Earliest Times To The Persian Conquest*, Bantam Classic Edition, New York 1964. (Also: Simon Publications, 2001,Two Volumes). (First edition, 1905).

Gardiner, Alan, *Egypt of the Pharaohs*, Oxford University Press, Oxford, 1961.

Grimal, Nicholas, *A History of Ancient Egypt* (translated by Ian Shaw), Blackwell Publishers Ltd, Oxford, 1994.

Herodotus, *The Persian Wars, Books I-II* (translated by A.D. Godley), Loeb Classical Library, Harvard University Press, Cambridge, Mass., 1986.

Josephus, Flavius, *The Works of Josephus*, William Whiston, translator, (Including *The Antiquities of the Jews* and *Against Apion*, Hendrickson Publishers, Peabody, Mass., U.S.A., 1988.

Redford, Donald B., *Egypt, Canaan and Israel in Ancient Times*, Princeton University Press, Princeton, N.J., 1992.

Shaw, Ian (Editor), The Oxford History of Ancient Egypt, Oxford University Press, 2000.

Strabo, *The Geography of Strabo, Vol. 8, Book 17* (translated by Horace Leonard Jones), Loeb Classical Library, Harvard University Press, Cambridge, U.S.A. and London, 1932, revised 1935. Reprinted 1967.

DICTIONARIES, ENCYCLOPEDIAS, GRAMMARS AND HISTORICAL ATLASES

Baines, John and Malek, Jaromir, *Atlas of Ancient Egypt*, LDF, Cairo, 1995 and Ed Gramham Speake, NewYork, Andromeda, Oxford, 1980. Revised and reprinted as the *Cultural Atlas of Ancient Egypt*, Checkmark Books, New York, 2000.

Bunson, Margaret, *A Dictionary of Ancient Egypt*, Oxford University Press, Oxford, 1995.

Davies, W.V., *Egyptian Hieroglyphs*, British Museum Publications, London, 1987.

Gardiner, Alan, *Egyptian Grammar*, 3rd ed., Oxford University Press, Oxford, 1982.

Hagen, Rose Marie and Rainer, *Egypt, People, Gods, Pharaohs* (translated by Penelope Hesleden), Bennedikt Taschen Verlag, Koln, Germany.

Hornung, Erik, *La Grande Histoire de l'Egyptologie*, (traduit par Michelle Lecoeur), Editions du Rocher, Paris, 1998) (Revised German edition, *Einführung in die Ägyptologie*, 1993).

Manley, Bill, *The Penguin Historical Atlas of Ancient Egypt*, Penguin, London, New York, 1996.

Posener, Georges, with the assistance of Sauneron, Serge and Yoyotte, Jean, *Dictionary of Egyptian Civilization*, Tudor Publishing Co., New York, Methuen, London, 1962.

Quirke, S. and Spencer, J., *The British Museum Book of Ancient Egypt*, Thames And Hudson, London, 1992.

Rice, Michael, *Who's Who in Ancient Egypt*, Routledge, London, 2001.

Shaw, Ian and Nicholson, Paul, *The Dictionary Of Ancient Egypt*, London, British Museum Press, New York, Harry N. Abrams, Inc., 1995.

Vernus, Pascal and Yoyotte, Jean, *Dictionnaire des Pharaons*, Editions Noêsis, Paris, 1996.

SELECTED INTERNET SITES

TRANSLATIONS OF EGYPTIAN TEXTS

www.fordham.edu/halsall//ancient/asbook04.html

www-01.uchicago.edu/01/DEPT/RA/ABZU_REGINDX_EGYPT_PHILOL.HTML

www.enteract.com

www.geocities.com/Athens/Pantheon/5061/submenu.html

TRANSLATIONS OF WRITINGS IN GREEK RELATED TO EGYPT

www.perseus.tufts.edu/

ART, ARCHITECTURE AND ARCHAEOLOGY ONLINE

www.britishmuseum.ac.uk/egyptian/ea/gallery.html

www.metmuseum.org/collections/department.asp?dep=10

www.members.tripod.com/~ib205/VK.html

www.tourism.egnet/AttractionsDetail.asp?code=6 and egnet.net/culture/images/

www.louvre.fr/louvrea.htm

www-01.uchicago.edu/01/01/MUS/HIGH/01_MUSEUM_EGYPT.html

www.brooklynart.org/collection/ancient.html

www.eawc.evansville.edu/pictures/egpages.htm

www.smb.spk-berlin.de/amp/s.html

www.2rom.on.ca/egypt/case

www.ancientneareast.net/egypt.htm

www.friesian.com/tombs.htm

www.kv5.com/html/index_new.htm/

www.pbs.org/wgbh/nova/pyramid/

DATABASES, SEARCHES, GENERAL, HISTORY, RELIGION, SOCIETY

www.thebritishmuseum.ac.uk/compass/
http://argos.evansville.edu
www.oi.uchicago.edu/OI/defaut.html
www.newton.cam.ac.uk/egypt/index.html
www.cur-archamps.fr/2terres
www.guardians.net/egypt/htm
www.ancientegypt.co.uk/menu.html
www.aelives.com/ae/htm
www.touregypt.net/Antiq.htm
www.touregypt.net/ehistory.htm
www.members.aol.com/egyptart/battle.html
www.si.umich.edu/CHICO/mummy/kings.html
www.egyptologyonline.com
www.crystalinks.com/egyptgods2.htm/

BIBLIOGRAPHIES

www.us.edu/dept/LAS/religion/rel394/KMTbibliog.htm
www.cofc.edu/-piccione/hist370biblio.html
www.thebritishmuseum.ac.uk/egyptian/ea/further/reading.html
www.brown.edu/Departments/Egyptology/biblio.html
http://guardians.net/egypt/bazaar/books/index.html
www.servtech.com/-greenman/pageMythEgyptian.html

GLOSSARY/INDEX

291

Printed in the United States
1149000002B/22-23